America and a Changed World

CHATHAM HOUSE PAPERS

Chatham House (the Royal Institute of International Affairs) in London has provided an impartial forum for discussion and debate on current international issues for nearly ninety years. Its resident research fellows, specialized information resources and range of publications, conferences and meetings span the fields of international politics, economics and security. Chatham House is independent of government and other vested interests.

Chatham House Papers address contemporary issues of intellectual importance in a scholarly yet accessible way. The Royal Institute of International Affairs is precluded by its Charter from having an institutional view, and the opinions expressed in this publication are the responsibility of the authors.

Already published

Vladimir Putin and the Evolution of Russian Foreign Policy
Bobo Lo

Through the Paper Curtain: Insiders and Outsiders in the New Europe
Julie Smith and Charles Jenkins (eds)

European Migration Policies in Flux: Changing Patterns of Inclusion and Exclusion
Christina Boswell

World Trade Governance and Developing Countries: The GATT/WTO Code Committee System
Kofi Oteng Kufuor

Exit the Dragon? Privatization and State Control in China
Stephen Green and Guy S. Liu (eds)

Divided West: European Security and the Transatlantic Relationship
Tuomas Forsberg and Graeme P. Herd

Putin's Russia and the Enlarged Europe
Roy Allison, Margot Light and Stephen White

The New Atlanticist: Poland's Foreign and Security Policy Priorities
Kerry Longhurst and Marcin Zaborowksi

Britain and the Middle East in the 9/11 Era
Rosemary Hollis

America and a Changed World: A Question of Leadership
Robin Niblett (ed.)

Forthcoming

Lands of Discord: Central Asia and the Caspian between Russia, China and the West
Yury Fedorov

Pax Bruxellana: EU Global Power and Influence
Richard Whitman

Islamism Revisited
Maha Azzam

America and
a Changed World
A Question of Leadership

Edited by Robin Niblett

WILEY-BLACKWELL
A John Wiley & Sons, Ltd., Publication

CHATHAM HOUSE

This edition first published 2010
© The Royal Institute of International Affairs, 2010

The Royal Institute of International Affairs
Chatham House
10 St James's Square
London SW1Y 4LE
www.chathamhouse.org.uk
(Charity Registration No.: 208223)

Blackwell Publishing was acquired by John Wiley & Sons in February 2007. Blackwell's publishing program has been merged with Wiley's global Scientific, Technical, and Medical business to form Wiley-Blackwell.

Registered Office
John Wiley & Sons Ltd, The Atrium, Southern Gate, Chichester, West Sussex, PO19 8SQ, United Kingdom

Editorial Offices
350 Main Street, Malden, MA 02148-5020, USA
9600 Garsington Road, Oxford, OX4 2DQ, UK
The Atrium, Southern Gate, Chichester, West Sussex, PO19 8SQ, UK

For details of our global editorial offices, for customer services, and for information about how to apply for permission to reuse the copyright material in this book please see our website at www.wiley.com/wiley-blackwell.

The right of Robin Niblett to be identified as the author of the editorial material in this work has been asserted in accordance with the UK Copyright, Designs and Patents Act 1988.

Wiley also publishes its books in a variety of electronic formats. Some content that appears in print may not be available in electronic books.

Designations used by companies to distinguish their products are often claimed as trademarks. All brand names and product names used in this book are trade names, service marks, trademarks or registered trademarks of their respective owners. The publisher is not associated with any product or vendor mentioned in this book. This publication is designed to provide accurate and authoritative information in regard to the subject matter covered. It is sold on the understanding that the publisher is not engaged in rendering professional services. If professional advice or other expert assistance is required, the services of a competent professional should be sought.

Library of Congress Cataloging-in-Publication data is available for this book.

9781405198448 (hardback)
9781405198455 (paperback)

A catalogue record for this book is available from the British Library.

Set in 10.5 on 13 Adobe Caslon by Koinonia
Printed and bound in Singapore by Fabulous Printers Pte Ltd
01   2010

Contents

Contents

Preface and acknowledgments

The idea for this book arose from the desire to offer a non-American perspective on the United States' current and future role in the world at the outset of President Barack Obama's presidency – at a period of considerable turmoil for US international relations with allies and adversaries alike. The objective has been to feed back to American audiences, as well as to the many people beyond US shores who are interested in US foreign policy, a sense of how America's power and policies resonate in what Barack Obama called 'a changed world' in his inauguration address. For this reason the contributors to this book do not recap the main international milestones of the Obama administration's first year. Instead, they seek to present a dynamic picture of the international context within which those policies are playing out and to offer ideas on how US actions might be adjusted for the new context. The underlying question each seeks to answer is whether the United States will be able to reassert aspects of its past global leadership at a time when antibodies to this leadership have strengthened across the world.

This and other questions were initially addressed in the Chatham House report *Ready to Lead? Rethinking America's Role in a Changed World*, published shortly after President Obama took office. The report drew on a series of analyses prepared by Chatham House Programme Heads, Senior Fellows and Associate Fellows that assessed the world confronting America in early 2009. A central theme of the report was the extent to which the United States needed to adapt its policies and its leadership style to a world undergoing profound structural change in terms of its balance of political and economic power. In this book, the same Chatham House analysts assess in more detail the international response to President Obama's strategy of international engagement. They seek to highlight the mindset of the different publics and policy-makers that are the targets of US policy. They also point to policy adjustments that might offer the United States the best chance to play a positive role in priority areas for its current administration.

I must offer my thanks first, therefore, to my Chatham House colleagues for persevering with this project over the past eighteen months and for revising, adapting and redrafting their contributions as the first dramatic year of the Obama presidency unfolded. Placing the impact of US policy at the heart of their regional or thematic areas of expertise has been a valuable intellectual and institutional exercise, and we all hope we have offered in return one or two valuable insights to the US policy-makers who must carry the burden of America's international responsibilities.

Second, I would like to thank the two people who have done most to pull together the chapters of this book and increase their level of substantive coherence and stylistic consistency. Margaret May works tirelessly to keep the published output from Chatham House on track and to their deadlines, and played a central role in the completion of this book, as she does for all of the Institute's major publications. Nicolas Bouchet offered invaluable support at a critical moment in the book's production, drawing together the disparate chapters, providing commentary on early drafts and helping to bring the publication to fruition.

I must also recognize the great support of Anna Dorant-Hayes, my Executive Assistant, whose managerial skills ensured that I found the time to focus on the book at the necessary moments. She also provided important research assistance for earlier drafts of my own chapter, along with Mark Leventhal, who interned in my office in the second half of 2009.

Finally, this book would not have made it from concept to publication without the forbearance and encouragement of Trisha, Marina and Saskia, with whom I am fortunate to share my life.

Robin Niblett
Director,
Chatham House

Notes on contributors

Annette Bohr is an Associate Fellow of the Russia and Eurasia Programme at Chatham House. She is the author or co-author of two monographs and numerous articles and book chapters on Central Asian domestic and international politics, contemporary history, and ethnic and language policies. She has worked as a Fellow of Sidney Sussex College at the University of Cambridge, and as a research analyst on Central Asian affairs at the University of Manchester and at Radio Free Europe/Radio Liberty in Munich.

Kerry Brown is Senior Fellow on the Asia Programme at Chatham House. He served as First Secretary at the British embassy in Beijing from 2000 to 2003. He is a research associate of the Centre for International Studies and Diplomacy at SOAS, University of London, and author of *Struggling Giant: China in the 21st Century* (2007) and *Friends and Enemies: The Past, Present and Future of the Communist Party of China* (2009).

Victor Bulmer-Thomas CMG, OBE is Visiting Professor at Florida International University. He is also an Associate Fellow of Chatham House, where he was Director from 2001 to 2006, and a Senior Distinguished Fellow of the School of Advanced Study, University of London. From 1992 to 1998 he was Director of the University's Institute of Latin American Studies and Editor of the *Journal of Latin American Studies* from 1986 to 1997. The author or editor of 20 books on Latin America, he is currently researching an economic history of the Caribbean since the Napoleonic Wars.

Tom Cargill is Assistant Head of the Africa Programme at Chatham House. His expertise covers aspects of the role of African states in international relations, particularly in UK and US policy. He has co-authored several chapters and journal articles with Alex Vines, including on UK policy to Africa under Labour, and the role of sanctions in Sierra Leone. He formerly worked as a freelance writer in East Africa.

Notes on contributors

Paul Cornish is Carrington Professor of International Security and Head of the International Security Programme at Chatham House. He was educated at the University of St Andrews, the London School of Economics and the University of Cambridge. He has served in the British Army and the Foreign and Commonwealth Office, has taught at the UK Joint Staff College and at the University of Cambridge, and was previously Director of the Centre for Defence Studies at King's College London. His research interests include the politics of the use of armed force, domestic security, counterterrorism and resilience, cybersecurity, arms control and non-proliferation, and European security and defence policies.

Michael Grubb is Chair of the international research organization Climate Strategies, headquartered at Cambridge University, where he is also a Senior Research Associate at the Faculty of Economics. He is currently writing a book integrating the lessons from 20 years of experience with climate change policy. His former positions include Chief Economist at the Carbon Trust, Professor of Climate Change and Energy Policy at Imperial College London, and Head of the Energy and Environment Programme at Chatham House, and he continues to be associated with these institutions. He has held numerous advisory positions with governments, companies and international studies on climate change and energy policy, and has published widely, including as a lead author on mitigation for several major IPCC reports.

Devika Hovell is an Associate Fellow in International Law at Chatham House. She has worked previously as a Lecturer in International Law and Director of the International Law Project at the Faculty of Law, University of New South Wales (2002–06), and as a judicial clerk to judges on the International Court of Justice (2001–02) and the High Court of Australia (1999–2000). She is currently completing a doctorate at the University of Oxford on Security Council sanctions and due process.

Bernice Lee is Research Director for Energy, Environment and Resource Governance at Chatham House and oversees all of Chatham House's work in the area of energy, climate and resource security. She has led innovative initiatives on piloting low carbon transition in China and speeding up technological diffusion of climate-friendly technologies. She has previously worked at the Aga Khan Foundation, the International Centre for Trade and Sustainable Development, the Rockefeller Foundation, the International Institute for Strategic Studies and the Strategic Planning Unit of the United Nations Secretary-General's office. She holds degrees from the London School of Economics and Oxford University.

Robin Niblett has been Director of Chatham House since January 2007. His principal substantive interests are European integration and transatlantic relations, and he is currently leading a Chatham House project on *Rethinking the UK's International Ambitions and Choices*. He was previously the Executive Vice President and Chief Operating Officer of the Washington-based Center for Strategic and International Studies, where he also served as Director of the Europe Program and its Initiative for a Renewed Transatlantic Partnership. A frequent panellist at conferences on transatlantic relations, he has testified on a number of occasions to US Senate and House Committees on European Affairs and has given evidence to the UK Commons Select Committee on Defence. He regularly provides commentary to the media in the UK, US and internationally. His publications include the Chatham House Report *Ready to Lead? Rethinking America's Role in a Changed World* (2009) and (as co-editor with William Wallace) *Rethinking European Order: West European Responses 1989–97* (Palgrave Macmillan, 2001). Dr Niblett has degrees from Oxford University.

James Nixey is Programme Manager and Research Analyst on the Russia and Eurasia Programme at Chatham House. His principal expertise concerns the domestic and international politics of the post-Soviet South Caucasus and Central Asia and he has published papers and articles in journals, and commented extensively in the national and international media. He holds degrees in modern languages and international relations and has experience working in journalism (as a reporter in Moscow in the late 1990s) and the banking sector.

Felix Preston joined Chatham House as a Research Fellow in July 2008, initially focusing on two major projects in China – one developing a roadmap for low carbon development in Jilin City, the country's first official 'pilot research area' in this field, and the other supporting the Low Carbon Economy Task Force of the China Council for International Cooperation on Environment and Development. Previously, he was a senior consultant at the environmental and energy consultancy AEA Technology, where he worked in the policy and international team. He has an MSc in Environmental Technology.

Gareth Price is Head of the Asia Programme at Chatham House. He gained his PhD, examining ethnic conflict in northeast India, from the University of Bristol. He subsequently worked for a political risk consultancy, Control Risks Group, for the Economist Intelligence Unit and as a consultant for the Foreign and Commonwealth Office. His research interests include the political economy of South Asia, the emerging global role of India and militancy in Pakistan and Afghanistan.

James Sherr is Head of the Russia and Eurasia Programme at Chatham House. Between 1986 and 2008 he was a Fellow of the Advanced Research Assessment Group of the UK Defence Academy and Lecturer in International Relations at Lincoln College, Oxford. He has previously served as a Specialist Adviser to the House of Commons Defence Committee and as a consultant to NATO and other official bodies on Russia and Ukraine.

Claire Spencer is Head of the Middle East and North Africa Programme at Chatham House, and has written and commented widely on US and EU policy towards Iran, Israel–Palestine and the broader Middle East, in addition to her core research interest, North African and Mediterranean issues, with particular emphasis on the Euro-Mediterranean Partnership and the security dimensions of the EU's relations with North Africa and the Middle East. She was previously Deputy Director of the Centre for Defence Studies, King's College London (1995–2001), Head of Policy for the Middle East and Central Asia for the development agency Christian Aid, and Senior Research Fellow at the International Institute for Strategic Studies in London. She has a BSc in Politics from the University of Bristol and a PhD in Political Science from the School of Oriental and African Studies, University of London.

Paola Subacchi is Director of International Economics Research at Chatham House. Her main research interest is in the functioning and governance of the international financial and monetary system, with a particular focus on post-crisis policy and institutional change. She is a frequent contributor to peer-reviewed journals and current affairs publications and a regular commentator for the major UK, US and other international media. Her recent (co-edited) publications from Chatham House include *New Ideas for the London Summit: Recommendations to the G20 Leaders* (2009) and *The Gulf Region: A New Hub of Global Financial Power* (2008). An Italian national, Dr Subacchi studied at Bocconi University in Milan and at the University of Oxford.

John Swenson-Wright is the Fuji Bank Senior University Lecturer in Modern Japanese Studies and a Fellow of Darwin College, Cambridge, and an Associate Fellow with the Asia Programme at Chatham House. He writes and comments regularly on the international relations of East Asia. His current interest focuses on contemporary political and security interests in Northeast Asia, with particular reference to Japan and the Korean peninsula, as well as a longer collaborative project exploring the Cold War in East Asia. A graduate of Oxford University and the Nitze School of Advanced International Studies (SAIS), Johns Hopkins University, he has a DPhil in International Relations from St Antony's College, Oxford.

Alex Vines OBE is Director of Regional and Security Studies and Head of the Africa Programme at Chatham House. His expertise is in the politics and foreign policies of sub-Saharan Africa, light weapons proliferation, sanctions and extractive industries in Africa, as well as many aspects of the relations of various countries with Africa, including China, India and the UK. He has lived and worked in a number of different African countries, including as a member and a chair of several UN Panels of Experts. He serves on a number of editorial boards, is a part-time lecturer at the Department of International Studies and Social Science at Coventry University and previously worked as a senior researcher for Human Rights Watch and Africa Analyst for Control Risks.

Benjamin Zala is Programme Manager of the Sustainable Security Programme at the Oxford Research Group and a PhD candidate at the University of Birmingham. He has previously worked with the Energy, Environment and Development Programme at Chatham House and has published on nuclear proliferation, multilateralism and International Relations theory.

Introduction

Robin Niblett

A TRANSITION IN US GLOBAL LEADERSHIP

The election of Barack Obama as the 44th president of the United States on 4 November 2008 constituted an important hinge point in the history of America's relations with the rest of the world. It closed a tumultuous chapter during which the administration of President George W. Bush had initially set the United States on a confrontational course in its international relations with both allies and opponents. While periods of heightened tension in these relations had occurred during the Cold War, the geopolitical framework of that period imposed constraints on the likely outcomes – the United States needed its allies and they in turn could not separate themselves from the guarantor of their ultimate security. Meanwhile, powers such as China or India manoeuvred and aligned themselves according to the prevailing balance in the bipolar competition between the United States and the Soviet Union. What was shocking to many US allies during the first term of the Bush administration was the sense that the United States felt it could operate without international constraints, whether posed by countervailing powers or by its commitment to the very institutions that it had created and championed during the Cold War.

That the Bush administration recognized the constraints on its margin for manoeuvre during its second term did not do much to alter the impressions caused by its first. It was only with a change in administration that change in America's foreign policies, as much as in its domestic policies, could really be possible. President Obama offered the prospect of opening a new and distinct chapter in America's international relations, one seemingly better suited to a post-Cold War world. His speeches during the presidential campaign of 2008 and immediately following his election victory acknowledged America's fundamental interdependence with the rest of the world. He spoke of strengthening alliances and international institutions, tackling common global challenges – from climate change to nuclear proliferation – on a multilateral basis within existing institutions, engaging America's opponents where possible, and tightening the bond between the United States' internal values and its external policies. These commitments signalled a United States that was willing to adapt the style and

1

the substance of its foreign policy to the emergence of a more interconnected and more multipolar world.

But even before Obama's inauguration on 20 January 2009, contradictions were apparent between the notion of a more multilaterally-minded United States and one whose leaders believed their country remained predestined to lead the world. The President's own inaugural address reminded his audience at home and abroad that 'we are ready to lead once more',[1] and Hillary Clinton, in her confirmation hearing as Secretary of State a week earlier, on 13 January, stated that 'we must strengthen America's position of global leadership' in order to ensure the United States remains 'a positive force in the world'.[2] This belief in the continuing need for American global leadership was echoed in a raft of reports and books by leading US academics and analysts in the lead-up to the presidential transition (many of their authors were former Democratic administration officials, including some who subsequently took up positions in the Obama administration).[3] President Obama entered the White House, therefore, with the desire to adapt the style and substance of America's external relations in ways that better reflected the fact that 'the world has changed', but also with the intention 'to renew American leadership in the world' in ways that implied it had not.

This book delves into the seeming contradiction between these two impulses. It examines America's engagement with a broad range of countries, regions and global issues over President Obama's first year in office in order to explore the following essential question: has the arrival of his administration and the policies it has launched enabled the United States to reclaim a position of global leadership; or has the world, at the end of the first decade of the twenty-first century, indeed changed in such a way that, despite their best efforts, President Obama and his administration must accommodate themselves to a continued waning of US international power and influence that is driven by structural factors beyond their control?

This overarching question gives rise to a number of subsidiary questions that inform each of the book's chapters. What was the legacy that President Obama and his administration inherited at the start of 2009 in terms of America's influence and leverage across countries, regions and issues in a rapidly changing world? What efforts did they undertake to adapt US policies to take account of the changed environment? How have governments and peoples around the world reacted to President Obama's international initiatives? Did these initiatives and the response to them demonstrate that the United States had retained much of its influence and underlying capacity for leadership, or that these had been eroded? Are new patterns and habits of international coordination emerging in place of deference to US leadership? And, given the experience of this past year, what steps could President Obama and his team take to pursue their goals as well as to strengthen US influence and its capacity for international leadership?

A second aim of the book is to examine how the quest to sustain US leadership appears from an external, non-US perspective. The chapters in Part I explore these questions principally from the perspective of countries within the regions of the world that form a central focus of the Obama administration's foreign policies. The chapters in Part II take a similar approach to US relations with three of the principal actors on the world stage – China, Russia and the EU – whose support or opposition will have a central bearing on the success of the Obama administration's international priorities. Part III assesses the administration's engagement with four of the world's principal global challenges – the UN and the international legal system, non-proliferation, climate change and the management of the global economy – and considers whether the United States is proving capable of adapting its style of leadership to help not only itself but also other countries and societies to deal with these challenges in a more effective manner.

Three sets of conclusions can be drawn from the chapters that follow. The first concerns the structural nature of some of the important obstacles that the Obama administration would need to overcome in order to renew America's global leadership role. The second concerns the growing limits of US influence over the decisions taken not only by the world's new emerging powers but also, increasingly, by smaller actors operating within deepening patterns of regional political and economic coordination that exclude the United States. The third conclusion, which compensates somewhat for the first two, concerns the pivotal and leading role that the United States will play in the development of effective common solutions to transnational challenges.

OBAMA'S INTERNATIONAL INHERITANCE

Far from ushering in an era of renewed US global leadership, the first year of the Obama administration appears to have confirmed many of its limits. This is not for lack of effort on the part of the President and his team, as all the chapters of this book make clear. In just its first six months President Obama announced his intention to close the Guantánamo Bay detention facility and approved the US joining the UN's Human Rights Council; he travelled to Cairo and Ankara to open a fresh US dialogue with the Muslim world; he reached out to the people of Iran in a personal televised message and to their government bilaterally through diplomatic channels; he appointed Senator George Mitchell as his Special Envoy for Middle East Peace, sending him on a series of missions to that region; he announced a firm date for the withdrawal of all US combat troops from Iraq, the end of 2011, and a thorough revision of the US strategy for Afghanistan; and he committed his administration to a 'reset' of America's relations with Russia and to a series of strategic arms reduction negotiations with its government. In his first year, President Obama also travelled to Latin America and to Africa to meet leaders there; he underscored to European governments the importance of the Atlantic Alliance at NATO's 60th anniversary summit in Strasbourg and in a series of bilateral meetings; he sent Secretary of State Hillary Clinton on a first visit to Southeast Asia and China, and followed this up in November 2009 with his own trip to four Asian countries, including China where he played down areas of bilateral disagreement and focused on the two countries' shared commitments to international economic stability and regional security; he welcomed the Indian Prime Minister to Washington and pledged to implement the various provisions of the US–Indian deal on civilian nuclear cooperation; he engaged the United States actively in the G20 summit meeting convened in London to confront the global financial crisis and, having pressed for a US cap-and-trade bill to control US carbon emissions ahead of the Copenhagen climate change summit in December 2009, passed an executive order making carbon dioxide emissions a polluting substance, thereby allowing it to be regulated directly by the US Environmental Protection Agency.

Nevertheless, as the contributors to this volume also note, the results of this blitzkrieg of diplomatic engagement have been disappointing. The Israeli–Palestinian negotiations remain in deadlock; the Iranian government has rejected a series of compromises on its nuclear enrichment programme; the situation in Afghanistan has yet to improve; Russia–US relations remain ambiguous; neither China nor India has been particularly supportive of US international priorities; improved transatlantic relations at a leadership level have not borne fruit in terms of joint actions; and the Copenhagen summit ended with a disappointing declaration, partly as a result of a disagreement between China and the United States. As individual chapters indicate, there were multiple specific political reasons for the lack of major breakthroughs in President Obama's first year. In the Middle East, for example, these included Binyamin Netanyahu's electoral victory in Israel, the continuing weakness of the Palestinian Authority and the crack-down following Iran's own presidential election. Moreover, a policy of engagement is by its very nature likely to take time to bear its fruits. In cases where this does not happen, it can still change the diplomatic and political context for future action, making a subsequent policy revision to a more confrontational approach that much easier.

Drawing longer-term insights for US global leadership from the Obama administration's first year, therefore, is a difficult process. But the chapters in this book demonstrate that this first year has confirmed certain patterns about US international influence that preceded his arrival in the White House and that are likely to continue at least throughout his term in office. Three of these lie beyond President Obama's near-term control; they are structural and constitute part of his international inheritance.

First, leaders in many countries around the world see the United States as being one of the principal sources of the problems they must deal with. Rather than reacting to new US diplomatic pressure and initiatives by changing their policy course, therefore, they are waiting for the United States to change course first. Nowhere has this been more apparent than in Europe, where US frustration with the lack of European movement on some of the Obama administration's main policy priorities (for example, committing new resources to Afghanistan; helping to house former Guantánamo Bay inmates; or being more aggressive in stimulating domestic economic demand to counter the effects of the global financial crisis) has grown over the past year. For their part, European leaders have rejected the argument that they need to adapt their policies until they are confident that the United States has successfully tackled its own problems in these areas.

This sense of the United States now being 'the source of the problem' rather than of its solution permeates a number of other chapters – whether it be those concerning US relations with China and East Asia, where US global and regional economic leadership is now being called into question, or with the Middle East, where the US invasion of Iraq has undercut US strategic credibility by replacing one source of instability (Saddam Hussein) with another (a more strategically secure Iran and a strengthened Shia presence north of the Gulf); or with countries in South Asia, which are sceptical of the Obama administration's new policies largely out of frustration with the failures of past US efforts. Overall, the result of earlier US policy failures is that international leaders are now unwilling to give the Obama administration the benefit of the doubt as it markets its new initiatives. US credibility first needs to be rebuilt – a process that is likely to take longer than President Obama's four-year presidential term.

Second, several of the chapters point to the increasingly complex political environment within which the Obama administration's international counterparts must now operate when dealing or negotiating with the United States. Both Claire Spencer's chapter on the Middle East and Kerry Brown's chapter on China highlight the rapid and massive growth of communications technologies in recent years, whether these are the satellite and cable TV channels that now span the Middle East and North Africa or the online blogging sites that have proliferated in China. Both chapters note how these technologies are increasing the internal political pressures on domestic leaders who operate in authoritarian political systems.

The trend towards more open popular means of communication and political debate could be seen as a positive development from the US perspective in terms of helping promote over time more representative forms of governance. However, what has been termed the new 'global political awakening' is also constraining the room for manoeuvre of authoritarian leaders in their dealings with the United States.[4] Much of the pressure on the Chinese government to cut back its support for America's indebted economy is coming from the 'blogosphere', which would react furiously should the Chinese leadership cave in to US pressure to revalue its currency as a way of trying to reduce the bilateral trade deficit. Similarly, authoritarian governments across the Middle East would see their already fragile credibility further eroded by a new media onslaught should they succumb to US pressure to improve their relations with Israel. The ability of the United States, under the Obama administration or any future US administration, to strike pragmatic 'Kissinger-style' back-room deals with their counterparts is now severely constrained. The United States must factor into its negotiations with almost all world leaders the sorts of multiplicity of active views and interests – linked by instantaneous communications – that are already the hallmark of politics in the United States and other Western countries.

Several of the chapters note a third and related structural constraint on America's future international influence and leverage – the growing internal and external pressure for it to shift from its recent emphasis on supporting individual, 'pro-US' leaders in strategically pivotal countries, such as Mikheil Saakashvili in Georgia, Hosni Mubarak in Egypt or Pervez Musharraf in Pakistan, to supporting the development of the political institutions and legal norms which will offer each country greater long-term political stability. The conclusion of many of these chapters is that the Obama administration will need to change its style of leadership to one that supports and enables local actors and institutions to bring about political and economic change rather seeing its role as being a leading instigator of that change. But, as Gareth Price notes in his chapter on South Asia, with regard to Pakistan and Afghanistan, US support for the rule of law, a free press, parliamentary accountability and other institutional reforms that combine to bring about 'good governance' can have the unintended effect of reducing US political influence in the country concerned. A similar potential trade-off between US influence and improving levels of local governance is highlighted by Claire Spencer, who notes that, in the Middle East, democracy and security are widely seen to be 'separate and largely contradictory objectives'.

A MORE COMPETITIVE INTERNATIONAL ENVIRONMENT

The contributors to the book also make clear that the Obama administration inherited a world in which US power had been in relative decline for a number of years, with the inevitable effect of America's diminishing influence and capacity to lead. The decline is relative because in 2009 the United States remained the most powerful nation in the world – and it will remain so for at least the next decade. This is confirmed by the fact it was a key player in political developments within each of the regions covered in Part I, the principal external interlocutor for the three actors covered in Part II, and a central protagonist in attempts to confront the four global challenges addressed in Part III. But being a central protagonist is not the same as being able to lead or to wield sufficient influence to determine outcomes.

The chapters by James Sherr on Russia, Kerry Brown on China, Gareth Price on South Asia and Victor Bulmer-Thomas on Latin America, where Brazil is playing not only a regionally but more globally assertive role, all highlight the increased confidence that above-average economic growth over the past decade has given to these countries and to their strategic ambitions. None of them – not even India or Brazil, two of the world's largest democracies – has appeared interested in supporting a Western, US-led international agenda, whether on controlling the proliferation of nuclear technology or making a meaningful contribution to an international agreement to reduce carbon emissions. They have continued through 2009 to consolidate their positions as the most influential actors in their respective regions, without overtly seeking to acquire the sort of global strategic reach that only the United States currently possesses. Instead, they have deepened forms of institutional coordination that exclude the United States – such as the annual BRICs summit and the Shanghai Cooperation Organization – while securing the elevation of the G20 summit meetings to become the world's 'premier forum for [...] international economic cooperation' in place of the US-dominated G8.[5]

US global leadership also faces increased competition from a deepening of cooperation between states in most regions of the world that necessarily reduces the scope for US bilateral leverage. In the case of Europe, this process has been ongoing for over 50 years; it is driven at least in part by a belief that European nations can better protect their collective economic and political interests by pooling aspects of their sovereignty within the European Union than they can simply by relying upon being close allies of the United States. But the process of regional cooperation intensified immediately before and during President Obama's first year in office in a number of other areas, including Latin America (as noted by Victor Bulmer-Thomas), the Caucasus (as discussed by James Nixey), sub-Saharan Africa (as noted by Alex Vines and Tom Cargill), East Asia (as noted by John Swenson-Wright) and even the Middle East (as Claire Spencer makes clear).

In many of these cases, the desire to play off the attention of the world's new rising powers against longer-standing US interests ('multi-vectoring', as Annette Bohr describes it in her chapter on Central Asia) has served as a further catalyst to the process of growing regional consultation and cooperation. The effect is that there has been little if any increase in US leverage or influence in key regions of the world even following the arrival of the Obama administration with its more proactive and engaged approach to its allies as well as to its opponents. Instead, allies and non-allies alike, from Latin America and sub-Saharan Africa to Central Asia and East Asia, have taken advantage of the growing competition between the United States and the world's rising powers for access to their resources and markets to strike a more independent strategic stance than in the past.

Drawing on many of the insights from the regional and country-specific chapters of this book, it is possible to make a negative prognosis for the reassertion of US global leadership in the world. The narrowing of the relative levels of economic and political power between the United States and its rivals for international influence have created a more level playing field for America's competitors. And, even setting aside the impact of the world's rising powers, there are fewer avenues for the exercise of US power and influence as a result of the deepening of regional cooperation, the spread of international communications and media and the greater dispersion and institutionalization of power even in authoritarian states.

But it is also clear from these chapters that the United States remains indispensable for many countries as a regional balancer and protector during a period of rapid and unsettling change in the global distribution of power. This is as true for traditional US allies such as Japan and South Korea, facing the rise of China, as it is for Ukraine, Kazakhstan or Uzbekistan, looking to manage Russian influence. As James Sherr notes, America's allies might wish that the United States were sometimes wiser but, especially today, they have rarely wished that it be weaker.

Moreover, in an echo of the vital role that the United States played in enabling European integration to take root in the second half of the twentieth century, several of the contributors observe that the Obama administration now has the opportunity to serve as an enabler of the process of deeper cooperation in a number of other parts of the world where the process is still in its infancy, from Southeast Asia to Latin America. Although such cooperation can restrict the number of direct avenues for US influence and global leadership, it opens up, in their place, a promising channel for the countries concerned to pursue their further economic and political development in a sustainable manner.

TACKLING GLOBAL CHALLENGES

Whatever the limits of US power and influence in a world of new rising powers, emerging regionalization and growing ambivalence about the value of US intervention in promoting political and economic reform, it appears from Part III that there is one broad area of international affairs where the United States will continue to play a leading role. Its active involvement and leadership will be indispensable if the world is to tackle successfully some of the major global challenges to international prosperity and security, especially in the areas of nuclear proliferation, climate change and financial stability.

Paul Cornish notes in his chapter on arms control that the United States remains the world's pre-eminent military power at both the conventional and strategic levels. However, the increasing availability of the materials, technology and expertise needed to make nuclear weapons is leading inexorably to a world of weapons proliferation, arms races and, very possibly, nuclear use. Given America's pre-eminent military position, the Obama administration will need to use all its diplomatic and intellectual resources not only to meet the immediate arms control and proliferation challenges of today but also to breathe life back into the idea that 'multilateral arms control, non-proliferation and disarmament … are all essential pillars of the global order' (p. 235). Under any circumstances, therefore, the United States will find itself at the very centre of the international debate on how to square the circle of nuclear deterrence and disarmament over the coming years – a conclusion which the Obama administration appears to have reached from the outset.

In the case of this and other, newer global challenges, however, the Obama administration will again have to recalibrate its style of leadership, serving more as a key enabler of coordinated international policies than as their initiator. Being an enabler of change in the way that the world confronts global challenges will also require the United States to lead as much through the force of its own example as by diplomatic skill or the application of its power.

As Bernice Lee and Michael Grubb observe in their chapter on the challenge of climate change, US leadership would be immensely powerful if correctly applied to tackling this new type of global challenge which cuts across sovereign borders and departmental policy jurisdictions and involves a multiplicity of public and private stakeholders. Given the size of its economy and the extent of its past and continuing contribution to greenhouse gas emissions, the United States will need to be at the centre of any global climate change agreement. However, in a world of more dispersed political power than in the mid-1990s, when the Kyoto Protocol was formulated (largely, it should be noted, to US design, even if the US Senate then refused to ratify it), the United States cannot hope to design unilaterally global treaty blueprints that other countries will simply accept, as was made abundantly clear at the Copenhagen climate summit. Nevertheless, the Obama administration could make the transition to being an enabler of an effective global response. As the authors of this chapter argue, perhaps the most promising avenue for US leadership in this context will be at the domestic level. The administration's ability to marry the power and imagination of US inventors and entrepreneurs with an effective domestic legislative, funding and regulatory environment could then drive the global effort to the next stage through the power of competition.

In her chapter on the global economy, Paola Subacchi points to a similar tension between the limits and potential of US leadership in addressing global challenges, in this case on effective global financial management. The global economic crisis of 2008–09 has undercut the potential for the United States to provide moral and political leadership in this domain for the near term at least, and the elevation of the G20 over the G8 stands as confirmation of this fact. For much of the twentieth century, the United States served as the principal designer and leader of the Bretton Woods institutions and as the dominant player in the G7. In the second decade of the twenty-first century, the United States will have to prove that it is prepared to help manage international economic affairs 'from a position of equality, as *primus inter pares* – rather than that of a hegemon'. In other words, given the still enormous size and wealth of the US economy, aspects of past US global economic leadership might yet be regained if the Obama administration could lead by its domestic example. This would require demonstrating the ability to deal with the United States' very significant domestic economic weaknesses (from its growing indebtedness to its near-bankrupt social security system) while still retaining its commitment to a liberal and open international economic outlook. Given the United States' unique economic attributes – including its large, open, financially liquid domestic markets, openness to immigration and top-class institutions of further education that drive technological innovation – the US economy is still well poised structurally to emerge strong from the current economic crisis and, as a result, to continue to underpin America's long-term potential for global financial leadership.

TOWARDS A NEW STYLE OF US LEADERSHIP

James Sherr suggests that US policy still needs to take greater account of the changed political environment in and around Russia. In fact, this observation could be applied to most dimensions of the United States' current international relations. US influence and leverage upon the world's rising powers and within its most important regions have continued to decline, despite the many policy adjustments and new initiatives undertaken in the Obama administration's very busy first year in office. The United States must now find new ways to interact with allies and other countries that are experimenting with forms of cooperation that do not include it as a founder or as a member. It is also being forced to respond to or even to join international structures and initiatives designed by others. America will need to accept that it will not always be at the heart of new regional arrangements, even if these are in regions of strategic interest, such as Latin America or East Asia, nor will it necessarily be the leading protagonist in the evolution of new international institutional developments (such as the G20). Yet each of these initiatives may have a systemically beneficial effect over the long term and would benefit greatly from US support.

US leadership in the future, therefore, will need to be exercised more in partnership with other countries than through autonomous design and political willpower. And yet credible partners are also likely to be hard to work with. Certainly, the rising powers, whether democratic or authoritarian, are likely to continue to be cautious about tying themselves to a US-conceived global agenda at the same time as they are trying to draw closer or even level with the United States in terms of political and economic power. Managing complex bilateral relations with these countries rather than trying to draw them into systems of cooperative global leadership could consume the bulk of US policy attention. And US allies that find themselves in the orbit of these rising powers – Turkey, Japan, South Korea, even EU members, for example – are likely to take a more self-interested approach when deciding whether to follow the US lead on a policy question that touches directly on their bilateral relations with China, Russia or India.

Nonetheless, a recurring theme in the book is that the United States should not hold back from trying to recruit partners in the pursuit of its international interests, even if the necessary alliances have to be constructed and reconstructed on an individual basis. The United States remains the only country capable of and interested in counterbalancing the rise of new powers across the world. And, although it will not be able to reassert at a global level the sort of leadership associated with its role in the Western alliance during the Cold War, it remains the 'indispensable nation', as former US Secretary of State Madeleine Albright liked to proclaim, without which effective international agreements and solutions to global problems will not be possible. As noted in the chapter on EU–US relations, European governments are well aware of the risks that they would face should the United States retreat into being a free agent on the world scene rather than a committed member of the Western team. There are good prospects for building common approaches across the Atlantic to global problems, whatever the likely differences in perspective the two sides may bring towards their nearer-term security concerns.

Ultimately, therefore, setting aside those specific areas where the United States brings unique forms of leverage (over the Israeli–Palestinian conflict, Iran's quest for a nuclear capability, or strategic arms control, for example), the emerging challenge for the Obama administration and future US leaders will be to learn how to share global leadership rather than renew it in US hands. As Kerry Brown states in his chapter, if China is to accept US demands that it become a responsible global stakeholder, then the United States will have to share global leadership with it in those areas that matter to China. The same applies to most other countries and challenges that now preoccupy the Obama administration. Although no other individual country matches the US desire to lead globally or possesses its leadership resources, the fact is that few now want to be led, except when facing the most serious of threats to their security.

It is for this reason that the future willingness of the United States to invest in and show its respect for the international rule of law may prove to be a supreme act of self-interest. As Devika Hovell argues in her chapter on America's new approach to international law and the United Nations, 'the legitimacy and predictability that broad adherence to international law can provide helps sustain a more secure world for the pursuit of US international political and economic interests'. Judging by the changes made in the US approach not only to the UN but also to the country's international relations as a whole in his first year, it would appear that President Obama is indeed attempting to adapt the focus and style of US global leadership. His administration is becoming more selective in its focus and inclusive in its style. He is attempting to rein in the exceptionalism that characterized much of the historical US approach to international affairs, an exceptionalism that was often justified when the United States was the main protector of global order in the twentieth century, but that is increasingly unproductive in the twenty-first. This more selective and inclusive style of US leadership may prove to be better suited, as well as more affordable, in the context of a profoundly changing world.

NOTES

1 Barack Obama, Inaugural Address, 20 January 2009, http://www.whitehouse.gov/blog/inaugural-address/.
2 Statement of Senator Hillary Rodham Clinton, Nominee for Secretary of State, Senate Foreign Relations Committee, 13 January 2009, at http://foreign.senate.gov/testimony/2009/ClintonTestimony090113a.pdf.
3 See, for example, Richard L. Armitage and Joseph S. Nye Jr, *A Smarter, More Secure America: Report of the CSIS Commission on Smart Power* (Washington, DC: Center for Strategic and International Studies); Managing Global Insecurity (MGI) Project, *A New Era of International Cooperation for a Changed World: 2009, 2010, and Beyond* (Washington, DC: Brookings Institution, Center for International Cooperation, Center for International Security and Cooperation, 2008); and Melvyn Leffler and Jeffrey Legro, *To Lead the World: American Strategy after the Bush Doctrine* (Oxford University Press, 2008).
4 Zbigniew Brzezinski, 'From Hope to Audacity: Appraising Obama's Foreign Policy', *Foreign Affairs* 88(1) (January/February 2010).
5 G20 Communiqué, Pittsburgh, September 2009, http://www.pittsburghsummit.gov/mediacenter/129639.htm.

PART I

Deepening Regionalism and the US Response

1

Latin America: forging partnerships in a transformed region

Victor Bulmer-Thomas

US POLICY TOWARDS LATIN AMERICA

If there is any region in the world where the United States might expect to be hegemonic it is Latin America and the Caribbean. However, the classic period of US hegemony was limited to the Caribbean Basin – the islands and the smaller countries on the Caribbean littoral – for a 60-year period that ran from the end of the Spanish–American War in 1898[1] to the downfall of President Fulgencio Batista in Cuba at the end of 1958.[2] In that sub-region and during those years, the United States did exercise huge influence and intervened frequently to impose its will. The overthrow through proxies of President Jacobo Arbenz in Guatemala in 1954 was perhaps the most egregious example.[3]

In the rest of Latin America, US influence was always much more limited. For example, the United States could not stop the nationalization – some would say expropriation – of Mexican oil in 1938. It was unable to persuade Argentina to declare war on the Axis powers in the Second World War.[4] It had no influence on the state-led import-substituting policies that undermined US exports to many parts of South America in the 1960s and 1970s. Last but not least, it could not stop the formation of the drugs cartels in response to the growth of demand in the United States itself.

The United States did intervene from time to time, as in the support it gave for the military coup against President Salvador Allende in Chile in 1973 or through the invasions of Grenada and Panama in 1983 and 1989 respectively, but the survival of Fidel Castro in Cuba and the anti-Americanism of successive Mexican governments until the 1980s were reminders of how limited US power could be even in its own 'backyard'. Nor was the United States able to broker a face-saving deal for the Argentine military regime (many of whose officers were US-trained) following the invasion of the Falkland Islands in 1982. Cuba, it could be argued, was saved from US intervention by its alliance with the Soviet Union.[5] Yet the end of the Cold War did not signal a US re-engagement with the region, but rather a decline in interest. The conclusion of the North American Free Tree Agreement (NAFTA)[6] and the UN-supported invasion of Haiti in 1994[7] marked the high point of engagement under President Bill

Clinton. Thereafter, the United States focused on other parts of the world. Even the financial crisis in Latin America at the end of the 1990s generated little interest despite the fact that it ushered in five years of stagnation (1998–2003) and rising poverty rates.

This was the background to the election of George W. Bush in November 2000. Yet, as so often in the political cycle, neglect under one president (Clinton) offered the next one (Bush) an excellent opportunity to improve relations with Latin America. Furthermore, the early signs were encouraging. Bush emphasized his former role as governor of Texas, a border state with a large Latino population,[8] to stress the need for closer relations with the region. Indeed, on 6 September 2001 – five days before 9/11 – the President declared that the United States had no more important bilateral relationship than the one with Mexico.[9]

The focus on Latin America proved to be short-lived, as US interests after 9/11 quickly swung towards counter-terrorism, weapons of mass destruction and preparation for the invasion of Iraq. Latin America itself was increasingly seen through the prism of these state interests. The area bordering Argentina, Brazil and Paraguay[10] was cited as a possible funding source for international terrorism; an attempt was made to link Cuba to the proliferation of weapons of mass destruction;[11] and illegal migration to the United States – most of which is from Latin America and the Caribbean – was re-evaluated in the light of the terrorist threat.

Leaders in the region watched these developments with great concern. The financial crisis in Argentina at the very end of 2001 was met with a deafening silence from Washington, as the new government in Buenos Aires was told it could not count on any assistance from the United States. The invasion of Iraq was deeply unpopular, as it trampled on one of the most sacred tenets in Latin America's independent history – non-interference in the affairs of a sovereign state. The efforts by the Bush administration to coerce Chile and Mexico (at that time members of the UN Security Council) into supporting the invasion were strongly resented.[12] Support was only forthcoming from Colombia, which was dependent on the United States for the success of its counter-insurgency strategy,[13] and from a handful of small states.

Anti-Americanism, present in the region in various forms since the mid-nineteenth century, reached startling proportions. It was also fuelled by the rise of the left in South America, since the anti-American tradition in the region has usually been stronger on the progressive wing of politics.[14] The rhetoric was pumped up several degrees by President Hugo Chávez of Venezuela, following the attempted coup against him in April 2002. Although the United States did not plan the coup, it seems highly likely that the Bush administration had advance knowledge and failed to inform the Venezuelan authorities. Certainly, unlike many South American governments, the United States did nothing to condemn the attempted overthrow of a democratically elected leader.[15] This left a sour taste, which President Chávez has ruthlessly exploited ever since.

The low point was reached in September 2008, when President Evo Morales in Bolivia expelled the US ambassador for allegedly interfering in Bolivia's internal affairs. Venezuela followed suit. Not to be outdone, President Manuel Zelaya of Honduras, one of the few countries in the region on whose support the United States can usually count, refused to accept the credentials of the US nominee for ambassador. This humiliation brought only the mildest of rebukes from the Bush administration, as it grappled with a series of domestic and international problems of far greater moment.

George W. Bush left the White House as the most despised US president in Latin America for decades. Yet his record in Latin America and the Caribbean, although not good, was not as bad as his reputation would suggest. Preferential Trade Agreements (PTAs)[16] were reached with Central American countries and the Dominican Republic (CAFTA-DR) as well as with Peru (those with Colombia and Panama were left pending). A strategic partnership began to take shape with Brazil on the basis of energy security and other shared interests. Support was given to the new government in Mexico as it struggled to gain the upper hand against drug-traffickers. And Bush remained a strong supporter of the Colombian government's fight against the guerrilla Revolutionary Armed Forces (FARC) and the drug-traffickers.[17]

THE NEW CONTEXT

The negative perception of the Bush administration in Latin America might seem to have provided President Barack Obama with an opportunity to improve relations. However, the situation is not so simple. Latin American leaders are looking for more than a change of rhetoric, and, when it comes to substance, there are serious obstacles. On the issues that matter to the region, it will not be easy for the Obama administration to deliver.

This became clear during the presidential campaign in 2008. Neither candidate wanted to talk about immigration policy – an issue of major importance to the region – because of its sensitivity. Senator John McCain did not want to be reminded of his failure to broker a deal in Congress on comprehensive immigration reform, while his opponent preferred to steer clear of a subject that resonates so badly with many voters. Obama was also vulnerable on trade agreements, since his call for stronger labour and environmental standards was seen in Latin America as code for increased US protectionism.

In fact, neither candidate paid much attention to the region in his detailed policy plans. A search for Latin America and the Caribbean on McCain's website produced little more than rhetorical support for Cuban exiles and evidence of the frequent misspelling of Colombia.[18] Obama at least made some specific commitments, including removing all restrictions on visits and remittances by Cuban-Americans to their families on the island.[19] However, Obama's policies also included some that were of dubious utility to the region such as doubling the size of the Peace Corps and employing US immigrants in public diplomacy while casting doubt on the fairness of Colombia's elections and opposing a PTA with that country on the grounds that trade unionists there are routinely assassinated.

Obama also insisted that the United States restore its 'traditional leadership in the region – on democracy, trade and development, energy and immigration'. Given past US support for dictatorships, distortion of trade through farm subsidies, limited development aid, incoherent energy policy and increasingly draconian immigration control, this may have seemed like a strange reading of history to many people from Latin America. Nevertheless, it raises the question of whether President Obama will be able to shift US policy so that it is more closely aligned with Latin American interests. It is to this that we now turn.

The region to which President Obama must address himself over the next few years has changed dramatically from the one faced by his predecessors. Latin America and the Caribbean countries are now much more assertive, less subservient and more determined to seek a new relationship with the developed world – including the United States – than in the period after the Second World War. There are, of course, nuances (examined below), but almost all countries in the region – and there are 20 republics in Latin America and an additional 13 independent countries in the Caribbean – are disinclined to return to a 'business as usual' approach.

At the same time, the levers of US power have been greatly weakened in recent years. Although in a geographical sense the countries south of the Rio Grande are still in the US sphere, geography no longer determines destiny. The region sells its commodities and services around the world and receives inward investment from a growing array of countries, while bilateral PTAs link the countries of the region to a large number of partners outside the Americas. For the first time in decades, Latin America enjoyed a prolonged period of fast growth from 2003 to 2008, with low inflation and a balance-of-payments surplus.[20]

This exceptional economic circumstance, though ending temporarily in 2009, has meant not only that direct US influence has fallen, but also that its ability to use proxy levers has declined. Following the 1982 debt crisis, the United States was able to use its own considerable muscle to influence policy but it also did so through international and regional bodies over which it exerted great power. The international institutions included the International Monetary Fund (IMF) and the World Bank, while the regional ones included the Inter-American Development Bank (IDB) and the Organization of American States (OAS).

These international institutions now have much less influence in Latin America. That could change, but it is likely that countries in other regions will make far more pressing demands on the limited resources of these institutions in the next few years. Latin American countries have used the recent economic bonanza to repay loans, and the IMF in particular has become a despised institution in many quarters (not just Venezuela).[21] The World Bank is not held in such contempt, but the middle-income countries of the region still would not figure very high on its list of priorities even if their demand for loans were to be greater than it has been.

In contrast, the Latin American regional institutions have acquired much more autonomy. The brilliant stewardship of the IDB under Enrique Iglesias gave the Bank a higher profile in the region, but only because it no longer acted as a US surrogate (as it tended to do after its launch in 1961). The United States is still the largest shareholder, but it is no longer so simple to find other shareholders that will turn this into a majority. Meanwhile, the OAS – a Cold War institution totally dominated by the United States after its creation in 1948 – has become almost insubordinate. Member states favoured the Chilean socialist José Miguel Insulza over the US-backed candidate from El Salvador in the last election for secretary-general.

The favourable economic circumstances that the region has enjoyed since 2003 have now deteriorated, even if there is every reason to expect that growth will return from 2010 onwards. It could be argued that this decline might provide a near-term opportunity for the United States to reassert its authority. However, the economic circumstances have deteriorated even more dramatically for the United States itself, so it is not clear how it could turn this situation to its own advantage. In any case, such a view takes no account of the changed political circumstances in Latin America.

To understand this change, we must go back a generation to the debt crisis in 1982. That was a traumatic episode for Latin America. Today, in the rich countries of Europe and North America, governments and voters worry about a recession that – at worst – will lead to a drop of 5 per cent in GDP per head. During Latin America's debt crisis, however, GDP per head dropped by 20 per cent in several countries, with the fall concentrated in one or two years. It occurred at a time when 17 of the 20 Latin American republics were one-party states or military dictatorships (only Costa Rica, Colombia and Uruguay were democracies). The swing of the pendulum therefore favoured the return of democracy.[22] Yet, despite the dire economic circumstances and the rise of extreme poverty, the return of democracy did not in fact favour the left.

The reason was simple. The debt crisis was attributed to two factors with which the left in Latin America was deeply associated: import-substituting industrialization (ISI) and debt-led development through state-owned enterprises (SOEs). The left failed at first to dissociate itself from these policies and was also slow to recognize the new reality: globalization.

Thus, democratization favoured the right and the centre-right. They were no longer supporters of ISI and had always been uncomfortable with state-led development. Furthermore, they were willing to adopt the policies of reform favoured by the IMF, the World Bank and the US government – all institutions based in Washington. That is why these policies – privatization, trade reform, financial market reform, etc. – became known as the Washington Consensus.

After a shaky start, these policies were quite successful. Countries that had not already done so joined the General Agreement on Tariffs and Trade (GATT) and later its successor, the World Trade Organization. Rather than waiting for others to lower tariffs, some countries adopted trade liberalization unilaterally. Regional integration schemes were revived or new ones started.[23] Inflation, the scourge of Latin America before the debt crisis, was brought under control. Fiscal deficits were reduced and capital inflows surged.

Between 1990 and 1997, Latin America was among the fastest-growing regions of the world, but the growth rate was unsustainable. The Asian financial crisis in 1997 marked the beginning of the end. From then until 2003, Latin America experienced a major recession dubbed the lost half-decade. Capital, which had flowed into the region, now flowed out. Poverty rates rose again. As in the 1980s, Latin America looked once again like an economic disaster zone.

The swing of the pendulum spelt disaster for the right and centre-right governments that had implemented the Washington Consensus. The beneficiaries this time were the left and centre-left. By now, these parties, movements and leaders had jettisoned the old ideas of ISI and SOEs and they understood the need for tough anti-inflation policies. They offered economic reform with a gentler face, giving more space to social policies that would help the poor.

The first indication of a swing to the left was the election of Hugo Chávez as president of Venezuela in December 1998. This was followed by the election of Ricardo Lagos in 2000 as the first socialist president within the ruling coalition that had governed Chile since the return of democracy in 1989.[24] Then came the victory of Luiz Inácio Lula da Silva (at the fourth attempt) in the presidential elections in Brazil in 2002. Since then, the swing to the left has gained force and secured its most recent – and in some ways most remarkable – scalps in Paraguay in 2008[25] and El Salvador in 2009.[26] At that point, 17 of the 20 republics had left or centre-left governments and only three (Mexico,[27] Colombia and the Dominican Republic) had right or centre-right governments.[28]

This swing was brilliantly timed from the point of view of the left. From 2003 to 2008, Latin America enjoyed a spectacular period of economic expansion that – as already mentioned – is almost unprecedented in its history. It is not so much the growth of GDP per head, although that has on average exceeded 3 per cent per year. It is more that Latin America has enjoyed at the same time balance-of-payment surpluses thanks to high commodity prices for its exports and has kept inflation low through prudent fiscal policies.

This phase of growth after 2003 was due primarily to the improvement in Latin America's terms of trade – the price of its exports divided by the price of its imports. Oil exporters benefited, of course, but net oil importers did so as well because of the rise in the price of the non-oil commodities on which their economies depend. High energy prices and high food prices – the two issues about which North Americans and Europeans have both fretted in recent years – helped Latin America greatly.

High commodity prices strengthened government finances and allowed a big increase in social spending.[29] That is why the left continued to win elections in countries as varied as Argentina, Brazil and Venezuela. Poverty rates fell sharply and social indicators improved. Centre-right governments have followed suit with social programmes that involve a large role for state spending.

There are clouds gathering on the horizon for incumbent governments and doubtless some will succumb in the next few years. First, the recession in the

United States is bad for Latin American growth because of the impact on the region's exports and will also lead to a reduction in remittances on which so many countries depend.[30] Mexico is the most vulnerable and a decline in the value of remittances was already recorded by the end of 2008. Recession in Europe and North America will also lower commodity prices – indeed, it has already happened – and a slowing of growth in other parts of the world (particularly China) will do the same.

Secondly, incumbents have struggled to contain inflation, notably in Argentina and Venezuela, and this is very unpopular. After a number of years in power, the left and centre-left are now the subjects of accusations of corruption – previously aimed mainly at right-wing politicians. There are also problems of fragile institutions in several countries. The indigenous population is now better organized and – in those countries where it represents a large share of the population – is demanding a greater share of resources.[31]

We should not, exaggerate, however. This is not 1982 or 1997.[32] Latin American economies are expected to return to growth, helped by Asia (assuming it stays out of recession), commodity prices that have fallen but will still be high by historical standards, and recovery in the United States, Japan and the European Union. Nevertheless, it would be surprising if there were not a swing away from the left in the next few years in some countries even if the parties that replace the left are likely to keep many of the social policies now in place.

It is often said there are two lefts in Latin America: a moderate left led by Lula in Brazil and a radical left led by Chávez in Venezuela.[33] This is very misleading. Chávez's Venezuela is really unique in both economic and political terms. The power given to him by oil is exceptional in the region and has been used to promote Venezuela's interests in the region through PetroCaribe and ALBA (the Bolivarian Alliance for the Peoples of Our America).[34] Politically, also, Chávez is unusual. He shot to prominence as an army officer in a failed military coup in 1992 against a democratically elected (albeit very corrupt) government. His instincts are deeply authoritarian, although he has – just about – played within the democratic rules of the game.[35]

More important is that Chávez and Lula are not hostile to each other. Venezuela was invited to join MERCOSUR at Brazil's instigation, and the two countries are the driving force behind a new development bank for South America (designed to replace the IMF), a project for political integration (whose unstated goal is an alternative to the OAS) and a plan for regional defence (intended to replace the Inter-American Treaty of Reciprocal Assistance).[36] Whether these projects come to anything is another matter, but they do demonstrate the ability of Brazil and Venezuela to work together across a broad range of interests, the sub-text of which is to reduce US influence in South America and to enhance the capacity of the sub-region to resolve its own problems without external interference.

This is the new political reality in Latin America with which the US administration must now deal. There will be changes of government and some of these will be welcomed in Washington, but it would be a mistake to assume that the status quo ante can be restored. Even a defeat for Lula's Partido dos Trabalhadores in the 2010 presidential elections would not end Brazil's strategic pursuit of a South America designed to further the country's regional and global ambitions.[37]

It is true that if Hugo Chávez loses the presidential elections in 2012 and quits the political scene at the end of his current term of office (2007–13), there is every likelihood that anti-Americanism in the region, though still present, will become less shrill. Chávez's bellicose rhetoric is something of an embarrassment for most Latin American leaders, and they would prefer it to be toned down. They seek a more mature relationship with the United States, based on a partnership rather than on US leadership, and they know that public manifestations of anti-Americanism make this more difficult.

THE OBAMA ADMINISTRATION AND LATIN AMERICA – THE RECORD SO FAR

President Obama came to office in January 2009 with very few specific commitments towards Latin America other than relaxing restrictions on Cuban-Americans, closing the prison camp at Guantánamo Bay and being opposed to the proposed Preferential Trade Agreement with Colombia. Nonetheless, expectations were high – much too high – that his election would mark a new beginning.

The personnel nominated for key positions in the State Department, the Treasury, the Pentagon and the choice of National Security Advisor were reasonably well received in Latin America, but there were no special envoys as there had been in the case of the Middle East and Afghanistan/Pakistan. Hardly surprisingly, this looked like a team whose priorities would be found outside the region.

The first issue Obama had to address was the prison camp at Guantánamo Bay. It soon became clear that closing it within one year – a firm promise – would be much more difficult than anticipated owing to the unwillingness of any US state to take any of the inmates. US leverage over other countries was therefore reduced and pressure on weaker countries (e.g. Bermuda and Palau) to receive some of the inmates made the United States look desperate. Latin American governments, however, were relaxed about the issue as they could see the Obama administration was making a serious effort to meet its promises and the eventual outcome was not really in doubt.

More troubling for the new President was the prospect of united opposition to US policy towards Cuba at the Summit of the Americas in Trinidad and Tobago in April 2009. This was defused to some extent by the announcement shortly before the summit that Cuban-Americans would no longer face restrictions on travel or on remittances sent to the island, while the prospect of US investment in telecommunications in Cuba was held out.[38] However, pressure was reapplied by Latin American governments at a meeting of the Organization of American States where a face-saving formula was crafted under which

Cuba was invited to apply for membership of a body from which it had been expelled in 1962.[39]

Other than Cuba, the first major headache for the Obama administration in Latin America has been the flow of illegal drugs from Mexico to the United States and the sale in the opposite direction of weapons for the traffickers. Apologies to Mexico from both President Obama and Secretary of State Clinton for the US share of responsibility in the drugs trade were well received there, but little has happened subsequently to change it. Drug consumption has not abated, money-laundering in the US continues and the transfer of weapons has not stopped. Meanwhile, the number of monthly deaths associated with the efforts of the Mexican police and army to curb the activities of the drug gangs remains very high.

The second problem for the United States has been the decision of the Ecuadorian government not to renew the lease on the US airbase at Manta. An arrangement was quickly reached with the Colombian government under which US military personnel could operate out of seven Colombian bases, but this was not well received in the rest of Latin America. The United States was placed on the back foot as it did its best to reassure a very sceptical region that there was no hostile intent and that this was purely designed to help the Colombian government fight drug-trafficking and the guerrilla movement.

There then followed one of those incidents that most US presidents have had to face at one point or another in their administrations. This was the removal by the Honduran armed forces of President Zelaya on the grounds that he had violated the constitution. This was not the view of the OAS, including the United States, which meant that Zelaya's removal amounted to a military coup. After the dust had settled, it became clear that Zelaya could only be restored if the United States was willing to flex its muscles. This, however, was precisely what President Obama had said he did not want to do at the Summit of the Americas in April 2009. The world was then witness to a bizarre situation in which the anti-American left in Latin America, including Hugo Chávez, were calling on President Obama to 'do something' to restore Zelaya, while the pro-American right preferred him to do nothing on the grounds that Zelaya was a left-wing menace![40]

After nearly a year, one is left with the strong impression of an administration that has no clear policy towards Latin America and is simply reacting to events in the region as they occur.[41] This is not particularly surprising, given US priorities elsewhere, but it does fall far short of the high expectations at the time of the inauguration. Yet it is not too late to change. Obama could have another term in the White House and the region may receive more attention once the US recession ends and healthcare reform is finally settled. It is therefore worth considering what future shape policy towards Latin America might take.

RECOMMENDATIONS FOR FUTURE US ENGAGEMENT

There are many policies open to the Obama administration that will have an impact on Latin America even though they are not specifically aimed at the region. Perhaps the most important of these is the US climate change framework that eventually emerges out of Washington following the UN Climate Change Conference in Copenhagen held in December 2009. Whatever the international frustrations from the limited achievements of the Copenhagen meeting, this is likely to provide opportunities for US firms to buy carbon credits through supporting projects in developing countries that lead to a reduction in emissions.

Beyond this specific issue, many of the recommendations that President Obama made with regard to Latin America during the presidential election did not apply exclusively to the region. Here, however, I concentrate on those policies that need to be designed specifically for Latin America rather than those that will apply more globally.

The analysis in the previous section suggests that the ambitions of the new US President in relation to Latin America should not be excessive. Above all, the Obama administration should put aside talk of re-establishing 'traditional US leadership' and instead focus on building a partnership. This semantic change may be difficult, given the history of US relations with the region, but it is essential. Indeed, President Obama's visits in 2009 to Mexico and Trinidad suggest that this lesson may well have been learnt.

Partnerships require partners and the United States cannot be expected to give equal weight to all countries in the region. The countries that are likely to be of particular importance for the United States are Brazil and Mexico, while in due course a new approach – perhaps eventually leading to a reconciliation – will need to be forged with Cuba. This means that the United States will need to be cautious about building a strategic relationship with other potential partners. Argentina, a country with which the United States has had a difficult relationship on frequent occasions in the last 150 years, is most unlikely to furnish the complementarity of interests that Washington needs. Colombia, on the other hand, will continue to need US support in its counter-insurgency campaign, but the United States would be unwise to imagine that this unequal relationship could serve as a model for the rest of the region. In any case, the relationship has been negatively affected by the unwillingness of the Obama administration to push for ratification by the Senate of the US-Colombia Free Trade Agreement.

A partnership with Mexico is so obvious that it might be felt to require little comment. Mexico, after all, is a member of NAFTA, and Mexico and the United States depend heavily on exports to each other. Migration and remittances tie the United States more closely to Mexico than to any other country in the world. Many US citizens now retire to Mexico on their social security payments and Mexican health services are in growing demand by those close to the border. US criminal networks, including youth gangs, span the border and environmental changes affect both countries for better or for worse. Mexico for its part is a leading actor in Central America, with which it has a relationship that at times mirrors the United States' own relationship with Mexico.[42] Yet Mexico is a better partner of Central America than the United States is of Mexico. The language of the United States is still steeped in the past, the actions of the US Congress are often humiliating for Mexico and executive behaviour is at times capricious. This needs to change and there is no better place to start than NAFTA itself.

NAFTA was sold to a sceptical US public by President Clinton on the assumption that Mexican export growth would lead to job creation and a reduction in illegal migration. That has not happened. NAFTA needs to be strengthened ('deepened' in the language of regional integration) so that it reduces the pressures to migrate. This means borrowing some of the policies used in the European Union to ensure that the average income of poorer countries rises quickly towards the regional average. Mexican incomes do not need to reach parity with those in the United States to curb outward migration, but they probably do need to reach half the US level. That is very far from the case at present.

The current US recession is forcing many Mexicans to return to their country of origin. This may lead the US administration to think that the migration problem has been solved, but that is clearly not the case. It will return with US growth. So the breathing space provided by recession should be used to shape, together with Canada, the new instruments that are needed to bring about greater income equality among the NAFTA partners. The EU is a good place to look, but of course it does not have all the answers (and some of its answers are too expensive). If the NAFTA countries can do it more cheaply and more efficiently, so much the better.

A true Mexican partnership can start with NAFTA, but it needs to go beyond it to embrace the environment, criminality and the drugs trade. Mexico has no monopoly on these problems, and the United States must take its share (a large one) of the blame. Mexico, for its part, can do much to help build a Central America that is less economically unequal, more socially cohesive and more politically mature; Central America is still the only part of the region where many political parties are little more than temporary arrangements to further the ambitions of one or another business leader. All of these developments would be very much in the interests of the United States.

A partnership with Brazil is indispensable for the United States, although it needs to have a different basis. Brazil and the United States are not joined at the hip by trade or investment, but neither can achieve its regional ambitions without the other. The Bush administration understood this better than some of its predecessors, but there is still a long way to go.

Brazil wants an unequivocal demonstration of US support for its global ambitions. These include a permanent seat on the Security Council. To demonstrate its bona fide credentials, Brazil led the UN mission to Haiti (MINUSTAH) and has peacekeepers elsewhere.[43] Brazil sees global warming as an opportunity to exploit its comparative advantage as an exporter of ethanol and protector of the Amazon forest. Above all, Brazil wants to be treated as a responsible player on the global stage.

These are all aspirations the Obama administration should welcome and embrace. It will mean abandoning its ambiguity towards Brazil's global ambitions and eliminating the tariff distortions that prevent Brazilian ethanol from reaching the United States. In return, the United States has every right to expect that Brazil will help to restrain immoderate behaviour and anti-Americanism by its neighbours (including Venezuela) as well as supporting the United States wherever it can outside the region. The United States should also do everything in its power to encourage Brazil's growing presence in the Caribbean – not just in Haiti.

Last but not least is the question of Cuba. A face-to-face meeting between Presidents Barack Obama and Raúl Castro would no doubt be historic, but it is unlikely to make a dramatic difference. The current Cuban leadership is interested in improved economic efficiency, even a greater role for the private sector, but it is not interested in multi-party democracy and is not in a position where it can be forced to offer it. If it did not do so in the dark days following the collapse of the Soviet Union, it will certainly not do so now when its economic circumstances are more favourable.[44] And without multi-party democracy, President Obama would be hard pressed to justify dropping the trade and other restrictions the United States currently imposes on Cuba.

However, there is one issue on which the United States could act unilaterally that would have a dramatic effect on the bilateral relationship and would reverberate round the world. That issue is Guantánamo Bay. Not the closing of Camp X-Ray and the transfer of its inmates, which can be taken as a given, but the termination of the indefinite lease under which the United States holds the territory in the first place. This lease was agreed to by Cuban politicians after independence in 1902 under the terms of the humiliating Platt Amendment, which Cuba was forced to accept in order to end the US military occupation (1898–1902). It was justified in US eyes by the need for coaling stations for its navy at a time when the United States was preparing to launch its audacious bid to build a transoceanic canal.

The US navy long ago ceased to use Guantánamo Bay for its original purpose, but the Cuban government cannot cancel the lease unilaterally. The return of the territory would be as dramatic an illustration of a change of policy as the decision by President Roosevelt to return Bahía Honda to Cuba in 1934 as part of the Good Neighbour Policy.[45] If President Obama is looking for a spectacular gesture that would demonstrate to the whole world a break with the past, he could do no better than start with Guantánamo Bay.[46]

NOTES

1 This war had begun in 1895 as Cuba's Second War of Independence, but following US intervention in 1898 it became known as the Spanish–American War since it led to the US occupation of Cuba and Puerto Rico (Spain's last remaining colonies in the Americas).

2 Batista fled from Cuba on the last day of 1958 (as viewers of *The Godfather* will know).

Fidel Castro entered Havana in triumph a few days later.

3 This intervention, which drew its inspiration from the Anglo-American coup against Prime Minister Mossadeq in Iran the previous year, ushered in nearly 40 years of state-sponsored terrorism against the Guatemalan people during which over 100,000 people died.

4 War was finally declared on 4 April 1945, by which time this had no military significance. See R. Humphreys, *Latin America and the Second World War, 1942–5* (London: Athlone Press, 1982), p.196.

5 The Cuban missile crisis in 1962 had been ended when the USSR agreed to dismantle its nuclear installations on the island and the United States committed itself not to invade.

6 The Preferential Trade Agreement between Canada and the United States in 1989 was broadened to include Mexico in 1994 and the name was changed to NAFTA.

7 President Aristide, elected in 1990, had been overthrown by the Haitian military in 1991. The United Nations had brokered a deal in 1993 under which Aristide would be restored. When the Haitian military reneged on the deal, the United States intervened. See P. Hallward, *Damning the Flood: Haiti, Aristide and the Politics of Containment* (London: Verso, 2007).

8 Outside Latin America, it is common to refer to Latin Americans in the United States as Hispanics. However, strictly speaking this refers only to those of Spanish descent so Latin Americans prefer to use 'Latinos'.

9 This took place during a state visit by President Vicente Fox. Those British officials present were said to be in a state of shock!

10 The epicentre of this area is Ciudad del Este, a Paraguayan city with many merchants of Middle Eastern descent and a reputation for black market activities. However, efforts to establish a firm link between these activities and the funding of international terrorism were not successful.

11 In an effort to diversify its exports, Cuba has developed with some success a bio-science industry. There has never been any evidence, however, that this has been used to produce biological weapons.

12 Since the vote on the second resolution was never held, we cannot know whether US efforts would have been successful. However, the fact that it was not held and the subsequent statements of the Chilean and Mexican Presidents suggest that US coercion had not worked.

13 This support is now channelled through *Plan Colombia* and is part of the reason why Colombia has been able to turn the tide in its counter-insurgency operations. An end to US support would be a major blow and Colombia has been understandably grateful.

14 Not always, of course. Under President Carter (1977–81), it was right-wing military governments that sometimes displayed anti-Americanism.

15 Nor, to its shame, did the British government. Indeed, a junior foreign minister publicly celebrated the demise of Chávez during the 48 hours he was ousted.

16 These agreements are referred to in common parlance as 'Free Trade Agreements'. However, this is misleading since they do not involve free trade and simply give preferences to a partner or partners across a range of goods and services.

17 The United States at first had tried to delink its support for the war on drugs from the counter-insurgency operations but the close connection between the two made this impossible. The United States now explicitly supports the two struggles, recognizing that in many respects they are one and the same.

18 'Columbia' (*sic*).

19 These had been tightened by President Bush. However, Obama's proposed relaxation went beyond the status quo ante.

20 This period began in 2003, since when Latin American GDP growth has averaged over 5 per cent per year. See ECLAC, *Preliminary Overview of the Latin American Economies* (Santiago: Economic Commission for Latin America and the Caribbean, 2008). It is not possible to say at this stage what the impact of US and European recession will be on the region.

21 It is particularly loathed in Argentina, where it is widely blamed for the depth of the financial crisis at the beginning of this decade.

22 It is correct to speak of a 'return' to democracy since many countries had been democracies before they became military dictatorships (e.g. Brazil).

23 Those revived include the Central American Common Market (CACM) and the Andean Pact (now renamed the Andean Community). The new ones were MERCOSUR (the Common Market of the Sothern Cone), whose first members were Argentina, Brazil, Paraguay and Uruguay, and of course NAFTA.

24 Since the return of democracy and until 2010, Chile has been governed by the *concertación*, a coalition of centre-right and centre-left parties. However, the president was always a Christian Democrat until the election of Lagos.

25 Paraguay had been ruled through the Colorado Party by General Alfredo Stroessner from 1954 to 1989. Then there was a managed transition that left the Colorado Party in charge. It was stretching a point to call it democracy, but the fiction was accepted by the US and other outside powers. When a radical former Catholic bishop was elected president in 2008 in free elections, Paraguay entered uncharted territory.

26 The FMLN, the political expression of the former guerrilla movement, seemed condemned after the end of the civil war to perpetual opposition. Yet their candidate Mauricio Funes, not himself a member of the party, succeeded in winning the presidential election in 2009.

27 And Mexico, it should not be forgotten, came within a whisker of electing a radical left-wing president in August 2006.

28 Subsequently, the centre-left were defeated in the Panamanian presidential elections in May 2009 and in the Chilean presidential elections in January 2010. This marked perhaps the beginning of the swing of the pendulum in favour of the right or centre-right.

29 The increased social spending has often taken the form of Conditional Cash Transfers (CCT), increasing its impact and reducing the risk of both corruption and capture by non-poor groups.

30 Their fall in 2009 is estimated at 11 per cent.

31 Not only in Bolivia, but also in Chile, Colombia, Ecuador, Guatemala and Mexico.

32 These were the years that ushered in financial crises that led to economic stagnation.

33 This argument has been developed by, among others, Jorge Castañeda (*Foreign Affairs*, September/October 2008) and Michael Reid (*Forgotten Continent: The Battle for Latin America's Soul* (New Haven, CT: Yale University Press, 2007).

34 PetroCaribe allows countries in the Caribbean to pay for oil imports at concessionary rates through subsidized loans. All net energy importers in the region except Barbados have joined. ALBA is a more formal institution created originally by Venezuela, Cuba and Bolivia, but which has been joined by several countries in Central America and the Caribbean. It emphasizes social solidarity and barter is often used in place of commercial transactions. Both PetroCaribe and ALBA are highly dependent on Venezuela receiving a high price for its hydrocarbon exports.

35 He was defeated in a plebiscite in December 2007 in his attempt to amend the constitution, including a proposal to remove the limit on the number of times a president
could be re-elected. Subsequently, however, the amendment was passed.

36 This treaty, signed in 1947 at Rio de Janeiro, has always been regarded with suspicion
by the left in Latin America because of the risk that it might be used by the United
States to justify intervention.

37 Brazil began a campaign in the 1990s, during the presidency of Fernando Henrique
Cardoso, to deny the relevance of 'Latin America' and to emphasise instead 'South
America' – a sub-region in which it can legitimately aspire to hegemony. It has been
very consistent (and quite successful) in pursuit of this goal despite changes of government.

38 There was a much publicized handshake between Obama and Chávez in which the
Venezuelan President handed over a book by Eduardo Galeano, a devastating critique
of US imperialism in Latin America. This book became required reading among the
anti-American left many years ago.

39 Cuba then saved the Obama administration from any subsequent embarrassment by
saying it had no intention of applying to join. It is fair to say that this had more to do
with the tricky question of Cuban conformity with the OAS Charter than sensitivity
to US concerns.

40 In September 2009 the Obama administration suspended the issue of visas. One
should not underestimate the importance of this to a country such as Honduras,
where the elite and their spouses are accustomed to travel frequently to Miami and
other parts of the United States. Nevertheless, it was inevitable that the United States
would have to do more or risk the charge of hypocrisy. In the end, the Obama administration broke with most Latin American states and recognized the presidential
elections in November 2009 despite the fact that President Zelaya had still not been
restored to power.

41 A good illustration of this is the reaction of the Obama administration to the tragic
earthquake in Haiti in January 2010. The reaction was swift and largely effective, but
there was no long-term plan for the reconstruction of the country.

42 Mexico is home to many migrants from Central America, who send remittances back
to their countries of origin. Mexico has PTAs with all Central American countries
except Belize and has promoted an ambitious scheme (Plan-Puebla-Panama) to link
Mexico with its southern neighbours through improved infrastructure.

43 However, the swift response of the Obama administration to the crisis in Haiti after
the earthquake and the major role taken by the US military have left unclear what
role MINUSTAH will now have.

44 Rationing became harsher in Cuba for some goods in 2009 as a result of foreign
exchange shortages, but the Cuban economy is not enduring the kind of existential
crisis it faced in the early 1990s.

45 This naval base had also been acquired after 1902 under the terms of the Platt Amendment.

46 I cannot therefore agree with the otherwise sensible recommendations of the Brookings
Institution (*Obama Administration and the Americas: Agenda for Change* (Washington,
DC, April 2009) that the US should invite Cuba to negotiate a future for the naval
base under which it would become internationalized. No international lawyer has ever
disputed Cuban sovereignty over Guantánamo Bay, so it is implausible that the Cuban
government would agree to anything that compromised the island's territorial integrity.

2

The Middle East: changing from external arbiter to regional player

Claire Spencer

REGIONAL PERCEPTIONS OF THE UNITED STATES

Relative to other regions of the world, the Middle East attracts a dispropor-tionately large part of America's foreign policy attention, presenting successive presidents with some of their most enduring challenges. Rarely, if ever, do new presidents inherit a clean slate for launching new policy initiatives in this region, and the options facing President Barack Obama from the start of his adminis-tration were no exception to this general rule.

More than ever since January 2009, pursuing the interests of the United States in the Middle East – above all, confronting the rise of Iran as a dominant regional power and its illicit nuclear activities, securing the Persian Gulf region as a major source of America's and the world's energy and protecting Israel as a key international ally while trying to broker a resolution to the Israeli–Palestinian conflict – has been complicated by the continuing presence of US forces in Iraq and the interrelated nature of sub-state and intra-state relations within the region.

Relations between the United States and Israel have already begun to adjust to a new post-Bush era, in which the first steps undertaken by the Obama administration have been neither successful nor warmly received by the Israeli public.[1] Changes both within the United States (above all the advent of the new pro-Israeli and pro-peace lobby J-Street, which takes a different stance from AIPAC, the American Israel Public Affairs Committee) and in the right-leaning configurations of Israeli politics make longer-term prognoses of where this relationship will go particularly hard to make so early in the Obama presi-dency. Yet we can be confident that it will not remain a static relationship, despite the stresses already encountered in forging any kind of bilateral consensus over how to re-engage the peace process and, in turn, to normalize Israel's relations with the rest of the region.

However, US relations with Israel always take a different form from US relations with the Arab and Muslim states of the Middle East. In assessing the challenges and changes the Obama administration faces in this region, the focus in this chapter is principally on the dynamics of the broader Arab and non-Israeli context of regional opinion. Understanding this context will be vital to the success of the Obama administration's policies in the region.

From the perspective of Arab and Muslim opinion towards the United States, one thing was clear from January 2009: the Obama administration inherited some of the most negative ratings in local opinion polls the United States has ever experienced. The critical starting date for this shift was March 2003, when the US-led military invasion of Iraq provoked widespread debate not only in the United States itself but across the wider expanses of a region stretching eastwards from Morocco to Iran and south as far as Sudan.

Of all the statistics arising from the 2008 University of Maryland/Zogby International poll of six Arab states (Morocco, Egypt, Jordan, Lebanon, Saudi Arabia and the United Arab Emirates), the most striking was that 88 per cent of respondents considered the United States to be one of two states that posed 'the biggest threat' to them. This percentage only narrowly followed that for Israel, which 95 per cent considered to pose the biggest threat. Asked how much confidence they had in the United States, 70 per cent responded that they had 'no confidence', 25 per cent that they had 'some confidence' and only 4 per cent that they had 'a lot of confidence'. Questioned about attitudes towards the United States in general, 64 per cent were 'very unfavourable', 19 per cent 'somewhat unfavourable', 11 per cent somewhat favourable and only 4 per cent (again) 'very favourable'. Perhaps less discouragingly in a survey that otherwise appears resolutely anti-American, these attitudes were based more on American policy in the Middle East (80 per cent) than on American values *per se* (12 per cent).[2]

One of the first tasks facing President Obama, therefore, was to promise change: not only in US policy towards the Middle East, but in the manner in which the region itself is perceived and dealt with in American policy circles. Three significant speeches – remotely to the Iranian people in March 2009 and in person in Turkey in April and Cairo in June 2009[3] – reinforced the inclusive and respectful tone in which relations with Muslims and minorities had already been discussed in Obama's pre-electoral campaign and inauguration speeches. Unsurprisingly, and before rhetoric could be judged against actions, this articulation of a new approach was almost immediately reflected in a shift of mood in Middle Eastern opinion. As the new administration promised to balance its support for Israel with concrete support for the creation of a Palestinian state, a new atmosphere of optimism was reflected in the first of 2009's regional opinion polls.[4]

Regional opinion nevertheless remains volatile, as became evident by late summer 2009 in the slipping away of support for the Obama team's first forays into the region. The main objectives of the new administration – namely, to propel Israelis and Palestinians towards peace and put relations with Iran on a new footing – were swiftly met by the intransigence and evasiveness of regional leaders on all sides. Following the disappointments of the UN General Assembly meeting of September 2009 (when the launch of a detailed Obama-led regional peace plan was widely anticipated), the regional debate then revolved around whether the Obama administration would indeed be able to move beyond the traditional obstacles to reorienting US policy in the Middle East. These obstacles, it became clear, are still as much rooted in American politics as in the ability of the new administration to exert leverage and authority over regional actors. As the limits to persuasion and public diplomacy became evident by October 2009, further doubts were raised in the region about the capacity of the administration to formulate a strategy capable of translating any of its aspirations into significant actions.[5]

The fact that such statistical snapshots of public, as well as elite, opinion over these developments have been produced is significant in a region usually noted for its lack of freedom of speech.[6] Polls generally conducted from outside the region have nevertheless failed to capture the growing immediacy of opinion shifts that has come to characterize the Middle East in recent years. Apart from in Israel, and to a lesser degree Turkey and Morocco, the region's press and state-owned media channels can rarely be deemed to reflect an accurate or uncalculated view of majority opinion. What is new is the upsurge in online blogging and instant commentary that increasingly large numbers of people can access and engage in. Likewise, region-wide access to a growing range of satellite television channels has shaped opinions and reactions to events across the Arabic-speaking world. The social and political effects have been such that the Arab League and the region's guardians of Islamic moral order have belatedly been trying to regulate and contain these developments.[7]

The rise in both open-source and covert debate nevertheless emphasizes one of the current paradoxes of the Middle East. Freedom of speech is no longer as constrained as it was, despite the continuing arrests of bloggers and journalists in Egypt, Tunisia, Syria, Saudi Arabia and elsewhere. The problem lies in the lack of accountability, both of those disseminating their unedited views and of the central state authorities that online and on-air opinion-formers seek to critique. The growth and articulation of public opinion, in other words, have no more opened the door to greater popular engagement in the real affairs of state than did the relative silence and silencing of public debate in earlier years.

The polling data on regional views of the United States should be seen against this background, not least since the lack of local accountability only encourages the tendency to blame the United States for not fulfilling more of the expectations once held of the world's most powerful democracy: to liberate the peoples of the region from authoritarian rule. In response to the past decade's disappointments, the standard line of popular argument across the region (with the obvious exception of Israel) has been only partially shifted by the advent of the Obama administration, and is in danger of slipping back into place if no progress is made on any of the core issues endangering the stability of the region.

The pervasive popular argument is that the United States invaded Iraq to secure its hold over the region's oil, to preserve its regional and global dominance, to defend Israel's occupation of the Palestinian territories and to subject Muslims (both Sunni and Shia) to their will. America's promotion of democracy is not genuine, but rather a smokescreen for the pursuit of the country's 'global war on terror' under a different guise by the Obama administration. 'Proof' of this thesis lies in the US government's preference for strengthening alliances with authoritarian regimes that detain and interrogate terrorist suspects on their behalf, rather than liberating the majority of Arab and Muslim peoples, or accepting Islamism as a legitimate form of political expression. The widespread use of US military force, the unaccounted-for deaths of thousands of Iraqis, and the symbolic resonance of Abu Ghraib and Guantánamo Bay all confirm the Americans' double standards, whereby invoking the security imperatives of themselves, their European allies and Israel allows them to ignore the miseries they and their local allies inflict on Arabs and Muslims.

A failure to close the Guantánamo Bay facility within a year, as President Obama promised in January 2009, and the direction taken in managing relations with Islamist groups, above all in relation to the Palestinian Hamas movement now controlling the Gaza Strip, will be judged as litmus tests for the credibility of the changes proposed in the Ankara and Cairo speeches of the first half of 2009. The identification of people in one part of the region with events taking place elsewhere or over wider issues of Muslim politics often provides a substitute for the limited political openings that Arab citizens enjoy locally. It also constitutes a complicating factor for US policy. Secretary of State Hillary Clinton's public praise in early November 2009 for Israeli Prime Minister Binyamin Netan-yahu's 'unprecedented' concessions over the issue of West Bank settlements, for example, may well have been intended for an American and Israeli audience. However, it was circulated widely throughout the Arab and Muslim world as evidence that the Obama administration was no different in its unconditional support for Israel from its predecessor.[8]

To some degree, venting public anger over Israel-Palestine reflects popular knowledge that speaking out against the United States and Israel is officially acceptable. It is also an oblique way of criticizing local leaderships for being so closely allied to US policy in the region. In Egypt, for example, public protests and journalistic denigrations of Israel are actively encouraged, just as senior officials often articulate their own public criticisms of US policy in the region. Yet officially Egypt is a partner of the United States in the pursuit of Middle East peace, at peace with Israel, and a recipient of an annual $2 billion in American aid.

Scepticism about America's grasp of the realities of the region is also expressed over the perceived failure of US policy-makers to distinguish between the different political and social contexts giving rise to a wide range of expressions of Islam and the desire for more accountable governments. The speeches and policy statements of President Obama have gone some way towards addressing this scepticism, but Muslim populations are still awaiting the actions that will back up his words. For better or worse, the related issues of securing a state for the Palestinians and reining in Israeli construction of settlements on the West Bank carry huge symbolic weight in popular opinion across the Middle East, where discrimination against Muslims is still perceived to underlie America's *modus operandi* in the region. For example, anger persists over the Gaza conflict of December 2008–January 2009 and is exacerbated by the blockade on the reconstruction efforts for the Palestinians of Gaza that is largely downplayed in American and European policy circles.

The question of how US diplomacy engages with the region's Islamists is also one of underlying rights and identities for the majority, rather than necessarily reflecting popular sympathy for Islamist ideologies and movements themselves. Even Arabs and Muslims opposed to Hamas's agenda and recent actions in Gaza have felt uneasy about the consequences and implications of the US-led international rejection of Hamas's electoral victory in 2006. The associated inference that all Islamists are potentially 'radical' and thus susceptible to the transnational enticements of al-Qaeda also sits uneasily with the more conservative majority of Muslims, and ignores the regional re-emergence of, *inter alia*, Sufist movements that explicitly reject violent action.

Even though, unlike its predecessor, the Obama administration no longer speaks so directly of the region in terms of threats, violence and civilizational divides, its apparent inability to decouple itself from the authoritarian governments of the Muslim Middle East continues to divide even the most moderate of political reformers in the region. The dilemma for 'secular' (i.e. Muslims who are not Islamists) opposition groups is particularly acute. If identified or given external support as the 'true democrats' against the perils of unfettered Islamism, they lose local credibility for having denied their own cultural and Islamic heritage. If supported by US or other external funders, these 'democrats' are also suspected of working on behalf of the West and of being in the same camp as the regimes they are ostensibly seeking to challenge.

A cursory glance at the different programmes supported by the US State Department under the Middle East Policy Initiative (MEPI) or the Broader Middle East and North Africa (BMENA) demonstrates that American officials are only too aware of the regional, national and local differences between political movements across the Middle East. What is at issue is how the more civic focus of these initiatives meshes with the perceived thrust of what the White House, the Pentagon, the US military and the ubiquitous CIA are really seeking to achieve across the Middle East. In a region replete with conspiracy theories and top-down forms of centralized leadership, it is not the complexity and diversity of US policy initiatives that are held under scrutiny. It is what the President and his closest aides say and do that counts.

Through this prism, a misplaced word, bullet, drone attack or handshake are all taken to mean that confronting terror and backing selected Arab allies and Israel are the only considerations that matter. If the actions of the US military in Iraq (as well as in Afghanistan, and now Pakistan) appear to confirm this perception, then the most reductionist of explanations for US policy ambitions will suffice.

Welcome as the efforts of President Obama to mark a rhetorical distance from his predecessor have been across the Middle East, he has set his administration on the difficult path of appealing simultaneously to America's traditional ruling allies and, beyond them, to their increasingly disenchanted citizens. At some stage, the Obama administration will have to face a clear choice between the aspirations of the former to stay in power at all costs and of the latter to play a greater role in shaping the future of the region. So far, it has steered clear of attempts to reconcile the different agendas inherent in these aspirations. The risk is that this will accelerate the noticeable drift away from the popular optimism invested in the 'Obama effect' early in 2009.

THE DILEMMAS FACING REGIONAL LEADERSHIPS

For the Arab ruling elites of the Middle East, the task of adjusting to post-2003 realities has been harder than for their populations. The main challenge facing them has been to adapt swiftly to the changes to a regional balance that they had all but taken for granted since the Gulf war of 1990–91. For the subsequent decade, the United States played the role of external security guarantor for its regional allies, particularly the Gulf states and Israel. Since the 2003 invasion of Iraq, the assumptions underlying this regional balance have been unsettled, with a number of consequences for America's position in the Middle East.

The first is that the use of US military force is no longer seen as the ultimate external sanction on actors, both state and non-state, seeking to upset the regional balance. The very fact that the United States acted as it did in Iraq has broken the spell that held most Middle Eastern actors in check. For the leaders of the Arab states closest to Iraq this has been particularly unnerving, on a scale corresponding to how openly or materially (such as through providing military bases) they supported the US-led campaign in Iraq. Leaders in the Gulf in particular had to balance their continuing strong dependence on the US security guarantee with less vocal support for the invasion and its consequences when addressing their publics. It was perhaps no coincidence that the most outspoken warnings that a 'Shia Crescent' had been unleashed by the war in Iraq came from America's closest allies in the region: King Abdullah of Jordan, President Hosni Mubarak of Egypt and Prince Saud al-Faisal, Foreign Minister of Saudi Arabia.[9]

The second consequence is that the taboo on 'regime change', and pre-emptive military action to bring it about, has been broken. Under the presidency of George H.W. Bush (1989–93), American actions in the Middle East explicitly stopped short of interfering in the domestic political arrangements of regional states. The decision not to unseat Saddam Hussein at the end of the Gulf war in 1991 did more than reassure the Ba'athists of Iraq; it also comforted other less-than-transparent leaderships in the region that they risked nothing if they stayed within the frontiers of their own states. Even though the US military subse-quently became so engaged in Iraq as to preclude a large-scale military invasion elsewhere in the region, the precedent has been set, at least in the eyes of the region's wary leaders. For this reason, many of them have been highlighting to their publics the benefits of stable, if authoritarian, leadership in the face of the chaos and bloodshed that gripped Iraq after 2003. The spectre of al-Qaeda has also been used to alert the largely conservative populations of the Middle East to the consequences of seeking to unseat their own rulers through violent means.

35

A third consequence of the Iraq war is that, to a large extent, the United States is now perceived as an internal regional actor, constrained by its continued presence in Iraq from intervening at will or with impunity elsewhere in the region. Even with only a residual advisory US capacity foreseen for Iraq following the withdrawal of combat forces scheduled for August 2010 and of the remaining 50,000-strong training corps by December 2011, the reinforcement of US forces in Afghanistan will continue to mark the United States out as a regionally embedded actor rather than as an external arbiter. The caution with which the Obama administration approached the disputed outcome of the Iranian elections in June 2009 and its aftermath is seen as consistent with the United States' new role as a quasi-regional actor. In struggling to counter the more volatile actions of Iran through engagement over the nuclear issue, the United States has appeared weaker in regional eyes, even if most Arab regional leaders continue to fear any form of escalation over Iran. The inability of the United States and its European and Russian allies to pin down the Iranian leadership to concrete commitments over its nuclear strategy has reignited Arab Gulf anxieties that negotiations will be allowed to drift on inconclusively, or will be abruptly terminated at will by the Iranians. In keeping with the disbelief that many felt at the lack of US planning for managing post-Saddam Iraq, Gulf leaders now also fear that the Obama administration has no clear strategy for bringing the Iranians to task if they continue to prevaricate over their nuclear intentions in public and build up their capacity in private. At the same time, the Arab states of the Gulf Cooperation Council (GCC) do not have the capacity to defend themselves, either collectively or individually, should Iran seek to extend its influence over its immediate neighbourhood, as still feared by some of the smaller states such as Bahrain. The confrontational approach of the previous US administration heightened concerns that Iran would retaliate in its immediate hinterland to any increase in international pressure. Now the seemingly less robust approach of the new American administration has unnerved the Arab leaderships for different reasons, not least over how reliable the US security umbrella over the Gulf might eventually prove to be. The challenge they face thus remains an uneasy juggling act between managing their own bilateral relations with Iran (with which they all continue to trade) and encouraging the United States to take sufficient, but not excessive, action over Iran to avoid the realization of their greatest regional security nightmares.

A fourth consequence, which disproportionately affects America's Arab allies in the region, is that they have been forced into filling gaps in regional diplomacy to counter the fragmentation of the Middle East along an unusually stark fault-line between rampant anti-American and anti-Israeli sentiment, on the one hand, and the opportunistic exploitation of this sentiment by the traditional opponents of the United States and Israel (Iran and Syria, in particular) and newly resurgent non-state actors (al-Qaeda, Hamas and Hizbullah), on the other. To counter this, since 2003, the Gulf states, Egypt, Jordan and Turkey have tried to broker deals between different Palestinian factions, between competing political forces in Lebanon, and between Israel, Hamas and Syria.

The Arab states (including Syria) have also launched one of the Arab League's most impressive (because rare) joint platforms, the Arab Peace Initiative, which proposes region-wide normalization with Israel for the first time in the League's history.

With the advent of the Obama administration, however, much of this activism has been diverted, if not dropped altogether, in favour of awaiting the outcome of the US administration's own bilateral pressures on Israel to cease settlement activity as a precondition for a return to peace negotiations. In tactical terms, this has also meant that America's Arab allies have resisted US pressures on them to make up-front concessions to Israel, such as overflight rights, as an incentive to return to the negotiating table. In trying to draw on moderate Arab support, as the Bush administration also tried to do in its last year, the Obama administration has misjudged the sequencing of events. From the perspective of the Arab world, the underlying logic of the Arab Peace Initiative has always been that Israel has to make the requisite moves to withdraw from the occupied Palestinian territory before reaping the rewards of full diplomatic recognition.[10]

The fifth consequence of the presence of America and its allies in Iraq is that the opponents of the United States and Israel in the Middle East have enjoyed unparalleled success in drawing on the latent anti-colonial sentiments that still prevail across the region. The reinforcement of the view that external forces have always intervened to pursue their own ends and prevent the region from following its own path may well be far from the outcome that recent US actions in the Middle East were intended to create. Thus opponents of the United States from President Mahmoud Ahmadinejad of Iran and Hassan Nasrallah of Hizbullah in Lebanon to the networks of al-Qaeda sympathizers across the Middle East have tapped into this vein of anti-interventionism to present US intentions as being far from benign. The inconsistencies of American policy have merely enhanced the coherence of the counter-arguments. Compounding this are the shock and surprise felt in elite Arab circles that America – not traditionally a colonial or interventionist power in the region on the scale of the United Kingdom or France – should have considered the invasion of Iraq without planning for the inevitability of having to govern the country, directly or otherwise, for some time to come.

President Obama has shown every sign of being fully aware of these dilemmas, but undoing the reputational damage caused by the crisis of US authority in the region will take more than minor steps. However, following a brief honeymoon period in the first half of 2009, the Obama administration continues to labour against the popular suspicions stoked up by America's opponents in the region. Every setback to diplomacy, however small, runs the risk of being taken as confirmation of continuity, not change, in US policy in the region. Moreover, and given the deliberate search by the Obama administration for compromise and agreement rather than confrontation, these opponents now present the failure to overcome obstacles to progress on the interrelated tracks of US Middle East diplomacy as a sign of its weakness, or even of the declining US commitment to engaging seriously with the underlying problems of the region.

The strength of opposition sentiment has nevertheless only led to passing and unsustainable success for the region's self-appointed champions. It has been one thing to condemn the presence of US forces in Iraq, or Israel's very existence in the region as an 'illegitimate' arm of American policy, but entirely another to translate this condemnation into concrete achievements for the people and overall stability of the Middle East. The polling data in this respect are quite ambivalent: the regional anti-heroes that have emerged since 2003 do not, over time, command uniform or majority support as viable alternatives to the status quo.[11] Hizbullah's failure to win a majority in the Lebanese elections of June 2009 left it with the ability to block the formation of a new government over ensuing months, but not to shape any consensus over the future of the country, much less the region. The inability of Hamas to conclude a 'national unity' agreement of any kind with Fatah has also done little to promote its popularity in a region more concerned with the creation of a Palestinian state than with the divisions that continue to beset the Palestinian leadership. As for Iran, and the newly re-elected President Ahmadinejad, the scenes of protest and violence that succeeded the June 2009 elections only served to delegitimize his role as a regional champion and promote popular regional identification with the 'Green Revolution' movement contesting the election results and denouncing the repressive measures used against it.

In terms of countering Iran's and Hizbullah's influence across the region, it is notable that in early 2007 none other than King Abdullah of Saudi Arabia spoke openly of the US presence in Iraq as 'illegal' and unacceptable in the longer term.[12] The alternative vision implied by this statement, and in the statements of other conservative leaders, is of the region taking charge of its own destiny to pre-empt worse being imposed from outside. On the political front, as noted above, there is little sign of sustained diplomatic action to back up this vision, but economically the wealthier, conservative Gulf states have been reinvesting their oil wealth at home and more widely across the region. Whether the rapid, but somewhat elite-focused infrastructural and economic investment projects undertaken from Morocco to Dubai over the past five years will limit popular discontent constitutes the essence of the challenge facing much of the region in coming years. The fallout from the continuing sovereign debt crisis in Dubai is likely to rein in the kind of bold policy initiatives required to invest in education and business development across the region.

What this type of regional shift also illustrates, however, is the final and most enduring legacy of the US invasion of Iraq. This has been to link all the region's crises and challenges into a single web of interrelationships. Before 2003, it was possible for the United States to conduct policy over the Israeli–Palestinian conflict in parallel and relative isolation from other policy tracks, such as bilateral military cooperation in the Gulf and the dual containment of Iraq and Iran. The disturbance of the regional balance now means that state and non-state actors alike have the ability to influence and upset policy outcomes across several policy tracks at once. This makes the sequencing and cross-referencing of US policy endeavours critical to the success of any and all of them. So far, this new reality has been reflected more in principle than in the far more difficult translation into practice of the Obama administration's regional ambitions, and it is here that most attention will need to be paid in coming years.

As America's Gulf Arab allies, and indeed Israel, have already demonstrated, compliance with US initiatives in the region is not a one-way street, nor is it free from the conditioning environments of domestic politics and the broader Middle East. Nor have US allies been susceptible to the kind of zero-sum game calculations engaged in by the Bush administration, which frequently acted on the assumption that there were net losses and gains to be made in the region and, with them, net losers and winners to defeat or bring over to the US side. The calculations of all Middle Eastern leaders, including those of Israel in making overtures to the moderate Arab states to join the fight against Islamic extremism, are based on maximizing their regional leverage and potential alliances, rather than finding themselves trapped irrevocably on one externally determined side or another.

Despite these reservations, the pro-American elites of the region do not see any alternative to maintaining their strong alliances with the United States for some time to come. The defence and security imperatives are still there, especially in view of the recent increase in US arms sales to the Gulf, Egypt and Israel. Even with France and other military powers making openings to the Gulf states,[13] the operational imperative to act in concert with the world's largest military power remains intact. Bilateral trade and investment relations with the United States are still highly important, as are the bilateral cultural and educational links that have been built up over the years. What the Arab leaders are working to change is the way the relationship with the United States is managed, within a context that has already been transformed radically since the 1990s. It is no longer a question of complying with US requests in an 'anything for a quiet life' fashion. What has been truly revolutionary in recent years is the extent to which previously reticent leaders have publicly criticized US actions in the region.

The Arab world is forging stronger commercial and political relations with China, India and even Iran, not so much to displace the United States but as a reflection of the new reality that China and India are increasingly influential players on the world stage as well as growing clients for the energy resources that the Gulf states and others can supply. Iran will remain a neighbour long after the United States has left Iraq and found a solution for its bilateral differences with the Iranian regime. The same might be said of links being forged beyond the region: inviting President Hugo Chávez of Venezuela or President Nicolas Sarkozy of France to discuss nuclear energy contracts or resource nationalism over tea is not an attempt to substitute them for the United States in the region, but rather evidence of the increasingly globalized nature of the Middle East's trade and diplomatic relations.

THE CONTINUING CAPACITY OF THE UNITED STATES TO
EXERT INFLUENCE IN THE MIDDLE EAST

Although diminished in regional eyes, the United States is nevertheless a key player in the Middle East, if not *the* key player in the spheres of energy investment, security and strategic relations for the foreseeable future. Policy options still exist for the Obama administration to restructure American approaches towards the Middle East in ways that reflect the very different Middle East that the United States now encounters from that which existed five years ago.

The first challenge consists of the likely shape of the longer-term US role in Iraq. The shift of the Obama administration's attention to Afghanistan and Pakistan does not mean that, for the Middle East, Iraq constitutes finished business. For as long as the US military presence in Iraq endures, the future configuration of Iraqi politics and its regional role will not be settled, even with the notable improvements in the overall security and investment climate since 2007. The bomb attacks in central Baghdad in August, October and December 2009 demonstrate that only a sustained transfer of powers and real capacity to Iraq's own security forces will ensure normalization over the longer term, and only then if the still fragile federal and national unity of the country can be maintained. Iran, Turkey and Iraq's Arab neighbours are thus all closely monitoring events as the competing political forces within Iraq position themselves for the 'day after' the formal withdrawal of all US forces in December 2011.

The main question, then, remains what form a more permanent US presence in Iraq might take, and whether residual training and support bases, even in the more sympathetic northern Kurdish region, will continue to provoke the anti-interventionist forces in Iraq and beyond. The best approach might be to evaluate the threat as the drawdown proceeds; what should not drive the decision is the desire to retain a US presence in Iraq at any cost. If a minority of Iraqis continues to resist the idea of foreign occupation, however minimal and benign in intent, and if al-Qaeda affiliates are able to regroup in any numbers in Iraq, resistance to that presence will continue until the foreign forces and associated administrations withdraw. Foreign bases cannot be sustainable over the longer term in Middle East states where borders are porous and local populations, as in Iraq, are divided enough to focus insurgencies against the main external allies of their local adversaries. The exception has been in the Gulf states, where local populations are small, less internally divided and under heavy centralized surveillance. In the larger society of Saudi Arabia, the presence of American bases played a key role in galvanizing local and regional recruitment to al-Qaeda, with consequences for Iraq and beyond that have already been well documented since 2003.

The second challenge relates to the unavoidable US role in re-engaging Israelis and Palestinians in a process of sustainable peace. The Obama administration appeared temporarily to have abandoned this as a diplomatic priority in the second half of 2009, but the one lesson learnt by all American presidents over the past 40 years is that the persistence of the Israeli–Palestinian conflict overshadows all other policy initiatives in the immediate region. With

Iran, Afghanistan and Pakistan close at hand, the overspill effects are felt in the broader Muslim world too. The solidity of the US–Israeli relationship represents both the key opportunity and the biggest hurdle to overcoming the current impasse and to fulfilling the obligations to the Palestinians that President Obama articulated in his Ankara and Cairo speeches. Here, the underlying strategy laid out was undermined in the first half of 2009 by an unfortunate choice of initial tactics, but there is still time to take stock and learn from this experience.

One unlikely starting point might be to examine the mistakes made by the United States and its European and UN Security Council allies in relation to Iran over the past five to six years. In this instance, the attempt to impose on Iran the precondition that all its nuclear enrichment activities be suspended before negotiations could take place and international sanctions be lifted has merely allowed the Iranian government to prevaricate, delay and continue enrichment virtually unhindered since 2005. If preconditions are such that governments clearly have neither the political will nor the domestic backing to fulfil them, then defining a more focused set of parameters, unhindered by preconditions, is the next best option for limiting their margin for manoeuvre and avoidance of the core issues. In the case of Iran, the Obama administration's preference for suspending preconditions in favour of direct engagement to iron out the details of a nuclear deal has not so far answered the challenge of how to monitor and ensure Iran's adherence to more than an agreement in principle. In practice, however, the options open to the Obama administration, including securing the sustained compliance of other UN Security Council members such as Russia and China in votes at the International Atomic Energy Agency (IAEA), have increased through this still evolving strategy, even though nuclear break-out by Iran remains a significant risk.[14]

As regards Israel and Palestine, it is not only in the Middle East but closer to home that the Obama administration's first steps towards restarting peace negotiations are perceived as having faltered badly.[15] The main tactical mistake was to try to bolster the position of Palestinian President Mahmoud Abbas by insisting that the Israeli governing coalition, led since February 2009 by Prime Minister Netanyahu, suspend all West Bank settlement activity as a precursor to returning to the negotiating table. Not only has the Israeli government been politically unwilling and constrained by its domestic support base from offering more than a curtailed and temporary 10-month undertaking to suspend new building permits, but the Palestinians have rejected anything less than a full settlement freeze as falling short of the necessary precondition for them to return to the negotiating table.[16] A more fruitful strategy might be to concentrate on creating the conditions for all sides to gain more from peace than from the unsustainable status quo. This may well mean rethinking how to engage with the Palestinians, including with leaders such as Marwan Barghouti who may be one of the few capable of commanding respect on both sides of the Fatah–Hamas divide. A number of commentators have also pointed to the Obama team's lack of direct appeals to Israeli public opinion as a critical missing element in this strategy.[17] Others, including the former US ambassador to Israel Daniel Kurtzer, have advocated setting out the parameters for a final peace settlement, rather than focusing on ways to restart negotiations without an end solution in sight.[18]

However the Obama administration re-engages with the Middle East peace process, its progress will be monitored by the rest of the region for evidence of a new balance being struck between America's traditional alliance with Israel and its promise of new openings to the peoples of the region. For the first months of Obama's presidency, regional opinion accorded him the necessary leeway to reorient relations with regional leaders towards supporting his new initiatives on Iran and the Israeli–Palestinian conflict. Subsequently, and in the wake of the renewed personal expectations invested in President Obama on his being awarded the Nobel Peace Prize in October 2009, regional opinion will be increasingly likely to focus on the missing ingredient so far in his strategy: the renewal of American support for regional democratization. In forging links across the region, it has not gone unnoticed that the Obama team has given scant attention to engaging the leaders of Egypt, Saudi Arabia, Jordan and other countries in a critical dialogue over human rights and democracy.

This neglect will not go without comment or action for long.[19] What most in the region have been expecting of the Obama administration, and some indeed feared, was a break with the top-down, elite- and personality-driven approach to regional deal-making that characterized the Bush era. The advent of President Obama promised a place on the agenda for the aspirations of ordinary people, and this can only mean a move away from the procedural and election-based approaches to democracy promotion favoured by the Bush administration. In terms of exerting renewed American influence in the region, the good news from the polling data is that the region's Muslim populations see no contradiction between their Islamic traditions and accountable democratic governance.[20] The majority are in favour of significant political and institutional reform in this direction. What they object to is outside interference that impedes the emergence of genuinely democratic forces and the legal frameworks to protect and promote democratic rights.

Responding to the region's democratic aspirations thus constitutes the third challenge, and the best opportunity for the United States to renew and reinvigorate its influence in the Middle East. The main regional criticism of US programmes designed to promote democracy, however, is that they seek to change the content of the political debate but not the context. US democracy promotion bodies tend to select and train political parties (often excluding groups and political figures deemed to be too radical), while other US actors and agencies turn a blind eye to the manipulation of electoral processes by incumbents. Unlike the policy positions adopted with respect to the post-communist states of Eastern and Central Europe in the 1990s, Arab Middle Eastern leaders have not been required to present themselves for free election under the rule of law, or in the case of dynastic rulers to accept the restraints of constitutional monarchy. Instead, and including into the Obama administration, the United States is perceived to have strengthened the region's authoritarian leaders in recent years in ways that have stifled the growth of democratic alternatives.

The opportunity that presents itself is for a review of policy that situates democracy and the rule of law at the heart of a US security strategy for a region hitherto perceived primarily in military, policing and intelligence terms. Such a policy could seek, above all, to create a new climate for constructive change, rather than supporting the specific parties or politicians capable of taking on this change. It would also require focusing on the details of country- and context-specific reforms needed for realizing longer-term changes in the overall security environment of the Middle East. So long as the US regional agenda is dominated by short-term security goals – namely, the containment of terrorist networks and forestalling Iran's nuclear ambitions – then the democracy agenda will suffer. The extra-judicial measures employed by governments in policing against terror are by nature restrictive in contexts where the police and security forces primarily serve to protect the interests of the existing regime, rather than those of the broader population.

With the spread of new technology, however, encouraging signs have emerged in recent years of local attempts to hold security services to account. This includes, for example, the use of mobile phones to provide photographic evidence of the abuse of detainees in Egyptian prisons. If US policy were to rebalance priorities towards the promotion of good governance, the strengthening of legal regimes to protect basic rights and the encouragement of local initiatives to impose limits on the impunity with which local security forces currently act, then a strong signal would be sent to the region that democracy and security are elements of the same policy, rather than (as currently widely perceived there) separate and largely contradictory objectives.

The Obama administration's decision to discard the language and umbrella approach of the 'global war on terror' – the most potent symbol of this contradiction – has been a very positive step. Now, however, the administration needs to implement policies that put the incentives for positive change for the majority of Middle Eastern populations at the heart of its strategy. More public acknowledgment of the US administration's awareness of the very different currents of Islamism would help defuse tensions, as would a focus on the country-specific injustices that underlie much of the attraction to anti-American alternatives in the region. The absence of any specific or visible initiatives to this end is beginning to sap the goodwill evoked by President Obama's Cairo speech. The danger in the aftermath of the commitments he made in this symbolic capital of the old Middle East is that the emergence of the new Middle East will be stifled by continuing US support for President Hosni Mubarak and the ruling elites of Egypt. The populations of Cairo and beyond to whom the speech was more directly addressed are still waiting for tangible, not symbolic, change.

To date, however, President Obama has not been personally involved in specific policy initiatives relating to individual countries and issues in the region. Reserving his political influence for critical future moments may be one of the best cards the administration still has to play, but this is also risky. The lack of clear and coordinated leadership across the different tracks of US regional diplomacy in 2009 undermined the coherence and standing of the whole when the administration met its first setbacks barely six to eight months into its term. The impression that President Obama is personally engaged for the long term will need bolstering by more than interim gestures and words in a region swift to make negative judgments about the ability of American officials to understand the region's complexities. Regional commentators may continue to question the administration's status and understanding of the region, through the kind of trivializing debate that emerged over whether or not President Obama bowed to the Saudi King Abdullah in April 2009.[21]

A final requirement is to reassess how the military track of US policy feeds into its economic and political tracks to ensure that they are mutually supportive. The use of military force is necessarily a blunt instrument that almost inevitably creates innocent victims. In regional cultures that hold the principles of dignity and justice dear, the use of force invokes notions of retribution. This means that external actors have to exercise extreme caution on the ground, especially in situations of asymmetric warfare, as in Iraq and Afghanistan.

There is growing doubt in the United States, as in allied European countries, whether armed campaigns against militants of the al-Qaeda or Taliban complexion will ever result in conclusive victory. At a time when the American and global economies are still undergoing severe and protracted contraction, it is also unlikely that a military-focused security strategy towards the Middle East can be sustained over the longer term. However, the recent increase in the volume and value of US arms contracts concluded with friendly regimes in the Middle East raises local concerns that the United States might seek to ensure its military capability and political presence in the region by proxy. There may well be economic imperatives to seeing these contracts through to fruition. However, the signal they send to the local opponents of American interests in the region are extremely dangerous in terms of perpetuating the pretexts for terrorist and insurgent activity in arenas stretching beyond the Middle East into the conflict zones of Asia.

CONCLUSION

American policy in the Middle East over the past decade has undoubtedly provoked the law of unintended consequences across the region, and the Obama administration has been trying to change tack to deal with the resulting fallout. Many of the negative repercussions can be traced back to the US-led intervention in Iraq, but others – above all the Israeli–Palestinian conflict – predate this. As the greatest symbol of perceived injustice across the Arab and Muslim Middle East, the resolution of the conflict should continue to take pride of place in the overall US Middle East policy agenda, as much for the future security of Israel as for the Palestinians themselves.

The changing US policy direction observed in 2009 still needs to take greater account of the new political environment in the region. Middle Eastern diplomacy and external alliances have become much more diversified, not only with regard to India and China, but also in relation to the new regional activism of states such as Turkey. This reality requires a further change in America's diplomatic style to counter the prevailing image in the region that the policy of successive administrations tends to move by U-turns between greater confrontation and deeper engagement – with Syria or Iran, for example. The traditional pattern whereby each new administration produces a new policy template for the Middle East is unsustainable. Not only are regional actors less compliant with and convinced of the authority of the United States, they also enjoy more policy options of their own. This is not an entirely bad situation for the United States. If American policy-makers cannot always prevail, they can nevertheless point to the need for regional actors to assume more responsibility for their own future, and structure regional relations accordingly. In increasingly substantive ways, the United States now enjoys more opportunities to engage in the region via the multilateral avenues promoted by others, even if this means adopting a supportive, rather than leading, role.

A clear repositioning of US policy in the direction of settling regional disputes through multilateral negotiations would also help promote a greater sharing of regional burdens. Such an approach would place the United States within the mainstream of regional and international thinking about unblocking regional deadlocks through consensus, rather than through external leadership.

One area of policy that could be assisted by this approach is the Israeli–Palestinian conflict itself. The Obama administration needs to look beyond the narrow confines of the bilateral security concerns of the Israelis and Palestinians and towards regional supporting mechanisms. The current deadlock in the peace process is caused as much as anything by domestic dynamics within Israel and the Palestinian community, and may be impervious to American bilateral diplomacy alone. In fact, much of the debate surrounding the failed Annapolis process of 2008 and the Obama adminstration's own diplomatic endeavours in 2009 hinges on bilateral security conditions and guarantees that neither side has been able or willing to provide without outside help. The United States may still be the main political broker for peace but others, such as the EU, Norway, Canada and other former members of the now defunct multilateral processes of the 1990s, need to be brought back in to foster an incentive-based, rather than precondition-based, resolution to the conflict.

Helping to create a more explicit regional framework within which the emergence of a two-state solution could be supported multilaterally could pay dividends, therefore, especially for Israeli public opinion, which is reluctant to make unilateral compromises. Current Arab regional initiatives are by no means as antipathetic to Israel and its role in the region as they are often portrayed outside the region. The Arab Peace Initiative, for example, which has the endorsement of the Arab League and fits well with the road map and UN resolutions regarding the Palestinians, needs to be revisited by US policy-makers as a vehicle for the longer-term stability of the region as well as for its specific proposals regarding the Arab world's normalization of relations with Israel.

In respect of Iran, appealing to the segments of Iranian society currently contesting the legitimacy of President Ahmadinejad's re-election is a much more problematic proposition for the Obama administration. For the foreseeable future, the Iranian nuclear programme and the need to maintain the IAEA's access to Iranian nuclear facilities is the greater priority. Nevertheless, as for Israel and the Palestinians, the opportunity to explore multilateral means to find a more balanced role for Iran in the Middle East should not be ruled out. The internal political dynamics of Iran are likely to evolve, perhaps faster than currently anticipated, and while the Obama administration has been wise not to intervene for the time being, outside regional support for what may emerge as a movement for longer-term change in Iranian society may require some flexibility in the way the United States and other international actors engage with individual groups within Iran.

Finally, despite the region's reputation for unrest, most societies in the Middle East are deeply conservative and weary of long-standing conflicts. The advent of the Obama administration appealed directly to the majority seeking a more balanced set of roles and identities within a globalized world. But the time for engagement with this middle ground is running out. In 2009, the American strategy appeared to be one of confronting the largest issues (Iraq, Iran, Israel–Palestine) before turning to more locally rooted grievances. The most important shift the Obama administration could make from 2010 would be to rethink the involvement of the region's populations in making the necessary changes to ensure that any high-level agreements reached will stick. This means appealing to Arabs and Israelis not only directly in words, but in conditioning the kind of support the United States gives to the current leaderships of the Middle East. Real leadership for change and reform can only emerge from within the region itself. The United States is the most influential actor both outside and within the region. As such it remains best placed to shape the context for gradual and positive change, rather than continuing the debilitating crisis management of recent years. If regional actors other than the local elites with which the United States has traditionally chosen to partner are given more say, the drain on American political, human and financial resources could be significantly reduced in coming years. This may mean that the United States will also need to adapt to a less prominent role in influencing the future direction of Middle East politics. But many Americans will be grateful if, as a result, the Middle East proves capable at last of assuming its own responsibilities.

NOTES

1 A December 2009 New America Foundation survey of Israeli attitudes found that 'Overall, Obama has a 41 per cent favorable /37 per cent unfavorable rating among Israelis, which is notably stronger than opinion toward the Israeli Defense and Foreign Ministers, and his unfavorable rating is only four points higher than the unfavorable rating for George W. Bush, who is routinely characterized as very popular among Israelis.' See http://asp.newamerica.net/sites/newamerica.net/files/profiles/attachments/NAFExecutiveSummary.pdf.

2 University of Maryland with Zogby International, '2008 Arab Public Opinion Poll', http://www.sadat.umd.edu/surveys/2008%20Arab%20Public%20Opinion%20Survey.ppt#348,84,Slide 84. See also note 5 below.

3 Transcripts of the speeches can be found as follows: Remarks on the occasion of the Iranian New Year (Nowruz), 20 March 2009, http://www.whitehouse.gov/the_press_office/Videotaped-Remarks-by-The-President-in-Celebration-of-Nowruz/ Remarks to the Turkish Parliament in Ankara, 6 April 2009, http://www.whitehouse.gov/the_press_office/Remarks-By-President-Obama-To-The-Turkish-Parliament/; and Remarks at Cairo University, 4 June 2009, http://www.whitehouse.gov/the_press_office/Remarks-by-the-President-at-Cairo-University-6-04-09/.

4 See University of Maryland with Zogby International, '2009 Annual Arab Public Opinion Survey', in which 51 per cent of respondents in the states surveyed were 'very hopeful' and 'somewhat hopeful' about US policy towards the Middle East within a few weeks of the arrival of the Obama administration. This rose to 59 per cent when figures for Egypt were excluded: http://www.brookings.edu/~/media/Files/events/2009/0519_arab_opinion/2009_arab_public_opinion_poll.pdf.

5 See Rami G. Khoury, 'Nine months of inconclusive US diplomacy', *The Daily Star* (Beirut), 24 October 2009, http://www.dailystar.com.lb/article.asp?edition_id=10&categ_id=5&article_id=107889.

6 Since 2003, Zogby International, the Pew Research Center, the University of Maryland, the BBC and ABC have all sought to measure Middle Eastern views on a variety of topics, above all on how the United States is regarded in the region. For 2008, most figures reflected the negativity of the Zogby/University of Maryland polls. By the first half of 2009, where gauged (as above), the tide of opinion had turned upwards.

7 See Daoud Kuttab, 'Satellite Censorship Arab League Style', *Arab Media & Society*, March 2008, http://www.arabmediasociety.com/?article=651.

8 Khaled Amrayeh, 'America's old ugly face', *Al-Ahram Weekly* (Cairo), 5–11 November 2009, http://weekly.ahram.org.eg/2009/971/re2.htm; Craig Nelson 'Obama betrays hope in the Cairo speech', *The National* (UAE), 2 November 2009, http://www.thenational.ae/apps/pbcs.dll/article?AID=/20091103/FOREIGN/711029816; Ian Black, 'Arab anger as Hillary Clinton backs Israel on settlements', *Guardian*, 2 November 2009, http://www.guardian.co.uk/world/2009/nov/02/arab-anger-clinton-backs-israel.

9 For a commentary on the fears underlying the emergence of a regional Shia–Sunni divide, see Amr Hamzawy, 'Adventurism versus submission', *Al-Ahram Weekly*, 27 July–2 August 2006, http://weekly.ahram.org.eg/2006/805/op121.htm.

10 For the most eloquent expression of the moderate Arab position on this in the immediate aftermath of the Gaza conflict, see Saudi Prince Faisal al-Turki's injunctions to the new Obama presidency in January 2009: 'Saudi Arabia's patience is running out', *Financial Times*, 23 January 2009, http://www.ft.com/cms/s/0/a11a77b0-e8ef-11dd-a4d0-0000779fd2ac.html?nclick_check=1.

11 See data in University of Maryland with Zogby International, '2008 Arab Public Opinion Poll'.

12 Hassan M. Fattah, 'US Iraq role is called illegal by Saudi King', *New York Times*, 29 March 2007, http://www.nytimes.com/2007/03/29/world/middleeast/29saudi.html.

13 See Richard Spencer, 'Deal making Sarkozy aims to capitalise on tarnished British image in the Middle East', *Daily Telegraph*, 15 November 2009, http://www.telegraph.co.uk/news/worldnews/europe/france/6575134/Deal-making-Sarkozy-aims-to-capitalise-on-tarnished-British-image-in-Middle-East.html.

14 Laura Rozen, 'IAEA vote seen as vindication of Obama approach', *Politico*, 27

November 2009, http://www.politico.com/blogs/laurarozen/1109/IAEA_vote_seen_
as_vindication_of_Obama_approach.html.

15 See commentary of US analysts in Robert Zeliger, 'Middle East Political Uncertainty
Stymies Peace Process', PBS Online Newshour Update, 13 November 2009, http://
www.pbs.org/newshour/updates/middle_east/july-dec09/mideast_11-13.html.

16 See 'Israeli settlement move helps peace talks – Clinton', Reuters, 25 November 2009.

17 See Aluf Benn, 'The communicator's challenge', *Bitter Lemons International*, 31:7 (13
August 2009), http://www.bitterlemons-international.org/previous.php?opt=1&id=
285#1165.

18 See Rozen, 'IAEA vote seen as vindication of Obama approach', for views of Daniel
Kurtzer and Robert Malley (former Clinton era peace negotiator), *inter alia*.

19 Regional bloggers are already picking up on the missing democracy dimension in
President Obama's policy; see, for example, 'Middle East: Where the US treads,
democracy does not spread', http://www.iran-resist.org/article5712.html.

20 See data in University of Maryland with Zogby International, '2008 Arab Public
Opinion Poll'.

21 See YouTube, 'Did Obama bow to Saudi King Abdullah or was he cleaning the floor?',
2 April 2009, http://www.youtube.com/watch?v=LEUif1--r38. This is the downside of
instant news reporting that now affects Middle East opinion as much as that of other
global observers.

3

Sub-Saharan Africa: providing strategic vision or fire-fighting?

Alex Vines and Tom Cargill[*]

The election of Barack Obama as president of the United States in November 2008 raised expectations around the world about the emergence of a more consistently and strategically engaged US policy approach to diplomacy and international relations. Given his own mixed African and American ancestry, these expectations were especially strong among pro-African communities within the United States, just as they were in cities and villages across sub-Saharan Africa.

Importantly, American awareness of the strategic importance of Africa had taken root during the administration of George W. Bush, providing a platform upon which he could build. As with other dimensions of his foreign policy, however, President Obama inherited a set of existing US policies towards Africa and a set of perceptions among African leaders and societies that would constrain his scope for action. In sub-Saharan Africa, the Obama administration also confronted a number of festering conflicts that threatened to break out and swamp its intentions to push forward a determined policy mix of diplomacy and development across the sub-continent. At the same time, the return to a more strategic US approach to Africa raised suspicions among African leaders that, despite downplaying the democracy promotion agenda of his predecessor, Barack Obama would begin to interfere in African politics in ways that carried the sorts of post-colonial echoes few would have expected from an African-American US president.

As a result, the Obama administration ended its first year with a mixed record in sub-Saharan Africa. The announcements of positive humanitarian initiatives and of support for improved levels of local governance have won him support on the African street and among reform-minded politicians. But this positive change agenda has also clashed with the entrenched political priorities

* Material from this chapter appears as Alex Vines and Tom Cargill, 'Obama's Sub-Saharan Africa Policy: Implications for Europe', in Álvaro Vasconcelos and Marcin Zaborowski (eds), *The Obama Moment: European and American Perspectives* (Paris: European Institute for Security Studies, 2009), pp. 213–23. Elizabeth Donnelly and Markus Weimer of Chatham House assisted with research for the sections on Nigeria and Angola in this chapter.

of a number of key African governments, as well as with some of America's own long-term strategic interests in the sub-continent.

MORE THAN HUMANITARIANISM?

Historically, the United States has rarely considered sub-Saharan Africa as being of great significance to its national interests, and most US presidents have had very little direct engagement on policy in Africa.[1] Even during the Cold War, the proxy conflicts that played out with Soviet- and Chinese-backed enemies across the continent from Angola to Ethiopia were generally never more than side-shows to the larger Cold War stand-off.[2] Sub-Saharan African countries were seen as uniformly poor and of limited commercial interest, had little impact, positive or negative, on the world stage, and did not offer any significant threats or opportunities to the United States. It was assumed that former European colonial powers that in any case happened to be NATO members, such as Britain, Portugal, Italy, Spain, Belgium and France, could be expected to carry the main responsibility for their former colonies.

On the other hand, in common with European countries, the United States has a long history of humanitarian interest in sub-Saharan Africa, based initially on missionary activity and later on an ideological commitment to the international promotion of democracy and human rights. These interests traditionally have been non-governmental in nature, grounded in the churches, civil rights movement and campaigning communities across the United States. Elected American officials have consistently been motivated to pay attention to their concerns, both out of genuine commitment and through the lobbying skills of these groups. However, from the 1990s onwards, the humanitarian lobby for Africa began to grow. Private philanthropy and remittances from the United States to the developing world in 2006 amounted to around $105 billion a year, dwarfing the $23 billion worth of official US assistance – and the growing amount of attention paid by successive US administrations to countries in the region has reflected this growth.[3]

In parallel, awareness of the strategic importance of sub-Saharan Africa for the United States has also grown since the 1990s, particularly because of concerns over terrorism and the radicalization of young Muslims, especially in the Sahel and eastern Africa. One of the earliest, most serious attacks by al-Qaeda on US interests was against the US embassies in Nairobi, Kenya, and Dar es Salaam, Tanzania, in 1998. The fear that Somalia is at risk of falling into the hands of anti-American extremists has driven US interest in that region for some years, as has the fact that some al-Qaeda operatives have originated from the Comoros and Tanzania. The establishment of an Africa Command (AFRICOM) in 2008 for the US military (discussed further below) is partly tied to this interest, though this is more of a rationalization of current organization than many of its more conspiracy-minded African critics will admit.

Energy security has been another driver of a more focused US policy on sub-Saharan Africa. The United States imports around 22 per cent of its oil from Africa (15 per cent from sub-Saharan Africa), more than it does from the Middle East, which provides around 17 per cent.[4] The presence of a US embassy in Equatorial Guinea, and the size of the Angola and Nigeria lobbies in the United States, are partly attributable to this fact. However, in comparison to the amount of national resources, both political and physical, invested in the Middle East, Africa has received only minimal attention in Washington to date – but this is likely to change.

A third driver of increased awareness of strategic interest has been the need to win the votes of African countries at the United Nations and to counter attempts by others to do so. Africa has more countries, and therefore UN General Assembly votes, than any other continent. In key decisions, such as over sanctions on Iran, or on climate change, winning the votes of African countries is crucial. In the past, either General Assembly votes were peripheral to US interests or it was considered pragmatic to secure the necessary African votes by inducement. In recent years, however, UN votes have become more important just as African states have become more effective at caucusing, both among themselves and within the broader G77 bloc of developing countries. Moreover, other countries such as Iran and China have increased their own coalition-building efforts, forcing the United States to do likewise. This driver for US interest in Africa is still less developed than the others mentioned above, and until recently both the United Kingdom and France had been more proactive in working to gain support for their positions in the General Assembly than has the United States.

African politicians have a history of skilful diplomacy and playing great-power suitors off against each other in order to secure special concessions for themselves. A key reason for support by African leaders for US policies in the recent past has been a pragmatic calculation of self-interest based on the acceptance, however reluctant, of a unipolar world order in which the United States stood as the world's only superpower. The dramatic increase in China's economic and diplomatic activities across Africa during the last five to ten years may yet change this, particularly as commercial and cultural links between African states and China grow. For Europe and the United States, the growing presence in Africa of 'emerging powers' such as China has helped push African issues higher up the policy agenda. This is something that most African governments are aware of and are keen to exploit. It is possible that the global economic downturn will slow down this contest for influence and access to natural resources in Africa, but it is also possible that a perception that the Chinese are taking advantage of American and European economic weakness to penetrate even more deeply into African markets and politics could further exacerbate tensions between them.[5]

Unlike those from China and a number of European countries, American firms have lagged behind others in seeking new markets in Africa. But although US investment in Africa outside the energy sector has remained almost static over the past decade, the cumulative level of investments in sub-Saharan Africa as a whole has not yet been superseded by Asian investments, and the United States remains Africa's largest trading partner. In fact, some American investors are already doing well in Africa. Washington-based Emerging Capital Partners (ECP) has raised more than $1.6 billion and has made more than 50 investments in 40 countries on the continent in the last nine years. The case of ECP is a rare one as American business does not have a historical presence in Africa beyond iconic brands such as Coca-Cola, and the largest US commercial presence is still in South Africa, where some 700 US companies operate subsidiaries.

Sub-Saharan Africa accounts for less than one per cent of overall US foreign direct investment although Commerce Department figures show US direct investment increased by 5 per cent between 2006 and 2007, to $13.3 billion, including in non-oil producing countries, such as South Africa, Mauritius and Liberia.[6] This relative lack of private-sector investment undermines US policy effectiveness on the continent. It means that American relations with African countries lack the complex business links that are so essential for cementing political ties and that could contribute to a more nuanced and sympathetic African view of American intentions and values.

THE GEORGE W. BUSH LEGACY ON AFRICA

George W. Bush faced withering domestic criticism for doing too little to end conflicts in Africa, especially in Sudan. But, unlike other areas where his administration's shortcomings overshadowed his positive policies, President Bush is acknowledged to have made progress on HIV-AIDS relief and democratization in Africa by rewarding well-functioning democracies with additional aid. In contrast to the relatively low levels of US commercial investment in Africa, there has been a very strong record of official US humanitarian support and aid over recent years.[7] As a result, the Bush administration was praised by activists and development analysts for its humanitarian commitment to Africa, and, in the end, President Bush met with more African heads of state than any previous American president.

American policy towards Africa in the last five years has fallen under two broad categories. The first sought to build the local governance and development capacities of African states. Policies under this category included the President's Emergency Plan for AIDS Relief (PEPFAR), the Africa Growth and Opportunity Act (AGOA), the Millennium Challenge Corporation (MCC) and the African Education Initiative, along with other programmes designed to improve standards of living across Africa. PEPFAR became the Bush administration's flagship policy in Africa. Signed into law in 2003, it committed the US government to spend $15 billion over five years to combat the global AIDS epidemic.[8] The MCC was also established as an independent agency providing development investment to countries whose governments 'govern justly, invest in their people, and encourage economic freedom'. By the end of President Bush's term, the MCC had signed $4.5 billion of aid agreements with African countries.

The second category of US policies sought to improve the security capacity of African states. Policy under this category included Africa Contingency Operations and Training and Assistance (ACOTA), the Trans-Sahara Counterterrorism Initiative, the founding of AFRICOM and the semi-permanent basing of US Marines and special forces in Djibouti.

Two factors underpinned Bush administration security policy in Africa. The first was a belief that the United States had become over-dependent on oil supplies from the Middle East and Venezuela, and that Africa represented an opportunity for diversification. This view was further driven by increased numbers of significant oil discoveries in Africa and by the volatility in the price of oil. Cutting across and influencing this was the increasing demand for oil and natural resources by emerging economies, particularly China.

The second driver was the fear that al-Qaeda-type organizations could become established in African states that have a significant Muslim population, or, even worse, that al-Qaeda could establish bases in a failed African state such as Somalia. It was this fear that led to the most controversial aspects of US policy in Africa under President Bush, generating a level of suspicion and opposition that President Obama must now counter. Aspects of US security policy towards sub-Saharan Africa were controversial because they led the United States into new alliances with African governments that have poor human rights records. Moreover, accusations were made that many of these governments subverted and co-opted the US anti-terrorism agenda to suppress democracy and silence legitimate dissent. This, in turn, allowed extremist voices to gain greater legitimacy by pointing to the futility of democratic opposition.

The best defence of US policies in such cases is that they often took place in the context of fast-moving events and grave threats, with limited specific expertise or intelligence available. The most tragic case of such a blunder occurred in Somalia. Ill-thought-through US policy during the Ethiopian overthrow of a popular Islamic revolutionary movement that had brought stability to Somalia for the first time in over a decade facilitated renewed violence in the country. This strengthened extremists there, delegitimized moderates and led directly to the chaos and piracy that are now increasingly disrupting trade and threatening wider terrorist activity in the region.

Partly as a response to concerns over the effectiveness of American security policy, the creation of AFRICOM constituted a recognition that US national interests in the region had reached critical mass. AFRICOM became operational in October 2008; the command incorporates the base in Djibouti as well as the Trans-Sahara Counterterrorism Initiative; and the initial annual budget is $266 million. While AFRICOM is an indication that the United States perceives African security within a more strategic framework, its implementation and the public relations surrounding it have been extremely poor.[9]

Announced in 2007 during a period when international criticism of US military methods and motives was high, AFRICOM's role and function in Africa were expounded in mixed messages to African leaders by different sections of the American government. The impression quickly emerged of internal confusion and uncertainty regarding the mandate and organization of AFRICOM. Different branches of the US government, principally the Department of Defense and the State Department, briefed different lines to African officials and others according to their perceived interests and perspectives. On the one hand, it was asserted that AFRICOM was a straightforward organizational military reshuffle with no real implications for non-US actors. On the other hand, it was asserted that AFRICOM would revolutionize the way in which the United States engaged with African states. There were also separate and contradictory briefings around where AFRICOM would be based – Tampa in Florida, Stuttgart in Germany or some African country. Combined with growing African concerns about the perceived militarization of US foreign policy in Africa, these contradictions in the public diplomacy surrounding AFRICOM meant that America's intentions quickly became lost in a sea of conspiracy theories.

The unnecessary confusion over AFRICOM's purpose is illustrative of the major problem the US government faced during the Bush years in trying to win a sympathetic hearing for its foreign policy abroad, one that is not unique to Africa.[10] There were simply too many American agencies with too many different roles and agendas that had a hand in defining and implementing foreign policy, and a lack of coordination between them. There was also fuzzy thinking and a lack of consistent cost-benefit analysis over the trade-offs between core American values and interests.

AFRICA POLICY UNDER OBAMA

In engaging with sub-Saharan Africa, the Obama administration has inherited a complex legacy from its predecessor. Increased levels of US financial assistance, especially to fight HIV/AIDS, have been welcome, as has the growing awareness of the strategic importance of building closer political relations with governments across the region. On the other hand, the Bush security agenda had awakened latent suspicions of a return to US post-colonial or Cold War-style interference that cut directly across African leaders' growing sense of their own independence and freedom of action – which has been fed by rising commodity prices and new players, such as China and India, starting to compete with the United States and with each other for access to African resources.

In this context, the Obama administration has attempted to mix continuity on the security front (reflecting its assessment of the continuity of US strategic interests in the region) with some important adjustments to the development agenda and to the coordination between the two. Thus, aggressive counter-terrorism operations have continued in Somalia through President Obama's first year and, although a review of policy is under way, no change is yet visible. At the same time, in the speech that he gave during his visit to Ghana in July 2009, Barack Obama sought to reassure his audience by stating that 'our Africa Command is focused not on establishing a foothold in the continent, but on confronting these common challenges to advance the security of America, Africa and the world'.[11]

The Obama administration has also stepped up efforts to rebalance and better delineate the different roles of the State and Defense Departments. For much of the Bush administration, the State Department, which should have been responsible for coordinating between and imposing sense upon the myriad initiatives and agencies involved in a more proactive Africa policy, was under-staffed, under-funded and under-valued. The Department of Defense ended up being elevated to a position where too much non-military activity was expected of it, including the reluctant exercise of public diplomacy. While these problems are not unique to Africa policy (or indeed to the United States), they have had a disproportionately negative impact on a continent where so much remains to be done.

Central to this rebalancing has been the rapid appointment early in 2009 of an experienced Africa team at the State Department with strong links to the National Security Council (NSC) in the White House and to the UN, another body with which the need for better US coordination on Africa policy is especially acute. Secretary of State Hillary Clinton made her Africa priori-ties clear during her confirmation hearing before the Senate Foreign Relations Committee early in 2009, insisting that Darfur, natural-resource conservation, the war in Congo, 'autocracy in Zimbabwe', African democracy and working to reach the Millennium Development Goals would receive her attention. She can now draw on a team with more Africa experience than many previous admin-istrations. Appointed as US ambassador to the UN at the outset of Obama's administration, Susan Rice served as Assistant Secretary of State for African Affairs in the administration of Bill Clinton and can now serve as a valuable ally to Hillary Clinton in this important forum. Gayle Smith, the NSC Director for Africa under Clinton, has been appointed as President Obama's NSC Senior Director for Reconstruction, Stabilization and Development.[12] The Africa team has Michele Gavin leading efforts at the NSC and Johnnie Carson as Assistant Secretary of State for African Affairs at the State Department. The State Depart-ment has also appointed Howard Wolpe, a former Michigan congressman who directed the Africa Programme and the project on leadership and building state capacity at Washington's Woodrow Wilson International Center for Scholars, as President Obama's Special Advisor to the Great Lakes Region.[13] His brief is to tackle a web of conflicts that have affected eastern Congo for 15 years.[14]

As part of its overall approach to the exercise of US foreign policy, the Obama administration has committed itself to strengthening the State Depart-ment and also centralizing aid policy under USAID. A review of the State Department's Bureau of African Affairs by the Office of the Inspector General made a blistering assessment and worryingly advised that some of its responsi-bilities be assigned to AFRICOM.[15] One of Assistant Secretary Johnnie Carson's initial priorities, therefore, has been to improve the morale and effectiveness of his Africa Bureau. However, as Princeton Lyman highlighted in his testi-mony on Africa to the Senate Committee on Foreign Relations in April 2009, 'no amount of staffing nor resources can make up for competing or confused policies' on Africa. He highlighted how thinly spread the State Department had become in Africa, especially in non-conflict countries.[16] During the same hearing, Howard Wolpe also drew attention to overstretch and to the lack of training in African languages for foreign service and intelligence staff.[17] As it appoints special envoys and rolls out new bilateral commissions to deal with key African countries, the Obama administration needs to give careful consideration to the objectives of these initiatives and to their sustainability in terms of human and financial resources.

President Obama also sent members of his campaign team to Europe prior to the US presidential elections to assess best practices from European development agencies, such as the United Kingdom's Department for International Development (DFID) and the German Agency for Technical Cooperation (GTZ). Drawing lessons from these should assist reform of US aid efforts.

All in all, a number of positive initiatives towards sub-Saharan Africa have emerged over Obama's first year:

- A commitment to review policy on Somalia is important given US mistakes there in recent years. There are no easy or short-term correctives, but a more inclusive, pragmatic approach to engagement would be helpful.
- In eastern Congo, the aspiration to reinvigorate the 'tripartite plus' process will also help, if done with sensitivity.
- The commitment on the Niger Delta is to become 'more engaged'; and the United Kingdom, Netherlands and other EU members are looking to coordinate their efforts with the United States.
- The assertion that AFRICOM 'should realize its potential' is a positive recognition of the problems the command has faced in defining its mission and structure in the face of fierce hostility across Africa.
- The Obama administration's $3.5 billion commitment to an African food security initiative could be a stimulus to greater investment in the agriculture sector. American food giants Dole and Chiquita are already exploring opportunities in Angola and Mozambique to supply European markets. Clearly, US firms will need more incentives to mitigate the perceived risks of investing in Africa and this is something that the Obama administration could focus on.
- A Global Energy and Environment Initiative that is a radical change from Bush policy will go some way towards promoting a changed public face for the United States in Africa, particularly in South Africa, which is so central to US objectives on the continent and yet has had a difficult relationship with the United States in recent years. By accepting both the need for carbon limits and that Africa has the most to lose if present environmental trends continue, the Obama administration has gained some additional political capital.
- The Obama administration is also paying more attention to multilateral institutions in US interactions with Africa. The September 2009 special meeting with African presidents at the UN General Assembly reflected this multilateral engagement. African perspectives were also being sought in the run-up to the Doha trade negotiations and the Copenhagen climate change summit. There is also more emphasis on the UN

Millennium Development Goals, which the Bush administration did not take seriously.

- The Obama administration is looking to merge PEPFAR into USAID to ensure that AIDS policy and development policy are better coordinated. Under the Bush administration, development assistance became heavily focused on spending to combat AIDS, at the expense of programmes in other areas essential to economic growth. Recently renewed by President Obama for another five-year term, PEPFAR now has an expanded budget of $19 billion, of which $11.5 billion will be spent in Africa. Its second-generation health policies place a greater emphasis on combating a wider range of disease, including malaria, as well as building health systems.

Plenty more remains to be done. According to Obama aides, the MCC could also benefit from coming under the control of USAID for the sake of better policy coordination and the more effective use of scarce resources. Of the 40 countries that have qualified at some level for the programme, 20 are in Africa. Certainly AGOA and the MCC provide a strong base from which the Obama administration will build further US engagement in Africa.[18]

Most importantly, the goal of improving US trade links and those of other countries with Africa should not be neglected; in the long term, greater US private-sector engagement in Africa will clearly assist a more rounded, regular Africa policy, drawing it away from its primary current focus on energy security, humanitarianism and counterterrorism. In this context, it is notable that Hillary Clinton led a 300-strong delegation in July 2009 for talks on AGOA in Nairobi with officials from 38 African countries: this is part of the US plan to reform trade policy, cut agricultural subsidies and expand markets at the same time.[19] The US Trade Representative, Ron Kirk, attended the AGOA meeting and then visited Ethiopia and Senegal. While in Dakar he signed an agreement with Senegal to provide $540 million to help that country rebuild its transportation and irrigation infrastructure.

Given that only one year has passed since President Obama's election, the nature and number of initiatives that have been launched towards sub-Saharan Africa are very promising. The challenge, as ever, will be to put these policies into practice, not just within the US inter-agency and congressional process, but also in terms of building support from and engaging with governments and civil society across this diverse region. It is to this aspect of the administration's policy that we now turn.

PUTTING POLICY INTO PRACTICE: STRATEGY AND FIRE-FIGHTING

In early July 2009, some six months into his administration, President Obama made his first trip to sub-Saharan Africa (he had already visited Egypt). The trip was brief: over the course of just 22 hours on the ground in Ghana, the President visited a maternal health centre, gave a keynote address on Africa to the Ghanaian parliament and visited a slave-trade castle. White House officials portrayed this stopover at the tail-end of summits in Russia and Italy as an indication that Africa was being mainstreamed, and becoming a routine foreign policy discussion item for the Obama administration.

A short Africa stopover by Obama early in his administration was probably appropriate, given that the detail of his Africa policy was still being defined. As a result, his speech had few specific pledges other than a promise to cut down on funding American consultants and administrators. Instead, President Obama's Ghana trip was mostly about symbolism, offering an effective backdrop for a sharp critique of corruption and repression on the continent, and advocating home-grown good governance and stronger institutions as remedies. Ghana was chosen to illustrate an African country that enjoys political pluralism and a growing economy.[20]

Likewise, the first African head of state to be received by President Obama in the Oval Office was President Jakaya Kikwete of Tanzania in late May 2009. He had been carefully chosen for his technocratic and democratic credentials and, according to the White House, the two presidents 'exchanged views on approaches to enhancing the US–Tanzanian partnership, improving development policy in the fields of health, education, and agriculture, and working with other partners in the region to solve some of the most pressing conflicts on the African continent'.[21] These conflicts include Sudan, Somalia, the Democratic Republic of Congo and Kenya.

Until his Ghana trip in July 2009, President Obama made few statements on Africa, limiting comments to addressing individual African conflicts, for example Sudan (which is a high priority for a number of domestic US advocacy groups close to the Democratic party), Somalian piracy (which has captured US media attention) and Zimbabwe (which stands out as an example of the bad local governance Obama has sought to criticize). Indeed, in late November 2009, President Obama presented at the White House the Robert F. Kennedy human rights award to leaders of a Zimbabwean women's rights group, Women of Zimbabwe Arise (Woza). The Obama administration has decided to play hardball with President Robert Mugabe and his supporters, hoping that this will weaken his grip on power.

The broad thrust of Obama's Africa policy was outlined in his Ghana speech: the buttressing of democracy and good governance, smart development assistance, strengthening public health, and support for conflict reduction and resolution.[22] He stated: 'Development depends upon good governance ... and that is a responsibility that can only be met by Africans'. The wider world must 'support those who act responsibly and isolate those who don't ... Africa's future is up to Africans.' Interestingly, he never mentioned the word 'terrorism'.[23]

Hillary Clinton's first trip to Africa as Secretary of State in August 2009 reinforced the message from Obama's Ghana visit. As she emphasized, 'we start from a premise that the future of Africa matters to our own progress and prosperity'.[24] She spelled this point out further in her October 2009 address to the US Corporate Council on Africa by highlighting trade, development, energy security, public–private partnerships and good governance, transparency and accountability as priorities for US policy in Africa.

But this long-term US agenda of promoting good governance and local responsibility for national development in the region must sit alongside important near-term challenges of conflict management. In this context, the situation in Sudan is near the top of the list of US priorities. The appointment in March 2009 of retired Air Force General J. Scott Gration as US Special Envoy on Sudan, even before the Assistant Secretary of State for Africa was in place, emphasized the importance of Sudan for the new administration. He has shifted American emphasis away from an exclusive focus on Darfur to an attempt also to stave off the disintegration of the Comprehensive Peace Agreement (CPA) between Northern and Southern Sudan by 'rekindling the same passion' that infused the original signing of the CPA. He hosted a meeting in Washington in June 2009 intended to boost political will to address some of the unresolved issues and to help prepare a 'soft landing' if the South votes in its scheduled secession referendum in January 2011.

The announcement in mid-October 2009 of a new Sudan strategy came after months of internal debate inside the administration, and mounting impatience among US activist groups.[25] It was a welcome recognition on the part of President Obama that the administration needed to focus on diplomatic engagement and 'mixing incentives and penalties' to secure cooperation on the part of the Sudanese, rather than oscillating between appeasement and aggression. The strategy also placed the United States in greater alignment with international partners concerned with Sudan such as the United Kingdom, the European Union, Canada and France, and opened the way for greater consensus-building with China and other key powers. Importantly, State Department documents acknowledge previous incoherence in US Sudan policy, and warn that US intelligence cooperation with Khartoum should not trump progress on Darfur and the implementation of the CPA which it is hoped will result in a peaceful post-2011 Sudan, so that Sudan does not 'provide a safe haven for international terrorists'.

By 'mixing incentives and penalties', US policy towards Sudan introduced for the first time benchmarks for progress and slippage, as well as a matrix of potential pressures, although these remain classified. It is not insignificant that the Obama administration for the first time also favourably mentioned the International Criminal Court (ICC) arrest warrant for President Omar Hassan al Bashir.

This policy shift towards 'engagement' fits Obama's efforts to reach out to the Muslim world, but it also reflects the ambiguity of the different constituencies that Obama has to accommodate at home. The administration's strategy does not guarantee success, and US groups will be impatient to see concrete results. President Obama himself may have to manage these expectations to allow time for this newly defined engagement strategy towards Sudan to be tested.

Elsewhere too 'fire-fighting' responses to other crises have preoccupied the Obama administration's Africa policy during its first year. Political developments in Madagascar, Guinea-Bissau and Guinea have drawn the attention of key officials away from their longer-term policy objectives, although fear of a repeat of Kenya's disputed election results in early 2008 meant that the US focus on Malawi's June election contributed to a non-violent outcome there. The administration seems to be concentrating on an effort to end or prevent the escalation of key conflicts through more forceful diplomatic initiatives after years of perceived drift by the Bush administration on these powder-keg situations.

For this reason Kenya also remains central to US regional policy, but it has added significance because of President Obama's personal commitment to the country, deriving from his family ties. He is able to speak out on Kenyan political issues much as former US presidents with Irish ancestry did on Irish politics. An indication of his harder policy towards Kenya came when, on 23 September 2009, Assistant Secretary Johnnie Carson sent a letter to 15 prominent Kenyans raising concerns about their role in blocking political reform. A number of them had already been banned from visiting the United States, prompting President Mwai Kibaki to write to President Obama to complain about this breach of diplomatic protocol.

During her 11-day visit to Africa in August 2009 (the longest ever to Africa by a US Secretary of State), Hillary Clinton visited six other African countries – South Africa, Angola, Nigeria, Liberia, the Democratic Republic of Congo and Cape Verde.[26] The choice of countries reflected the two themes – good governance, as in the case of Cape Verde, and the need for the United States to be involved in regional peace and security, as in the case of the DRC and Liberia. The choice of South Africa, Angola and Nigeria, however, pointed to a further priority of the administration in its Africa policy – the need to establish good relations with what are likely to be the three 'anchor states' of sub-Saharan Africa because of their size, economic potential and military capability, and in the case of Angola and Nigeria their vital roles as energy exporters. Each of these countries is undergoing significant internal political change, and the United States needs to upgrade its bilateral relations with them as quickly and effectively as possible. In so doing, however, the risk is that it may need to be ambiguous, at best, or to compromise, at worst, on its agenda of promoting good governance across the sub-continent.

THE UNITED STATES AND NIGERIA

Nigeria supplies 11 per cent of US oil imports, representing around 46 per cent of the country's daily production. This makes it the United States' largest trading partner in sub-Saharan Africa. In addition, there are an estimated one million Nigerians living the United States and over 25,000 American citizens living in Nigeria.[27] Recognizing this level of interaction, a US Act of Congress in May 2009 called for the establishment of a bilateral commission with Nigeria.[28] The last such commission (the US–Nigeria Economic Cooperation Commission) existed during Nigeria's transition back to civilian rule in 1998–99. And, soon after being elected, President Obama phoned his Nigerian counterpart

President Umaru Musa Yar'Adua, in a signal of the importance the United Sates attaches to the country.

However, signs confirming that engaging with Nigeria is never straight-forward became visible after President Obama chose Ghana instead of Nigeria for his first visit to Africa. With the largest population in sub-Saharan Africa (one-fifth of the continent's people), and as a significant player in the African Union and the Economic Community of West African States (ECOWAS), Nigeria sees itself as a key player and has in the past vied with South Africa for the role of leader of Africa in the international community.

Although officially the US President's bypassing of Nigeria was described as a non-issue by the Nigerian authorities it was widely described as a 'snub' in the Nigerian media.[29] And when President Obama stated in his speech that 'No country is going to create wealth if its leaders exploit the economy to enrich themselves. ... No business wants to invest in a place where the government skims 20 per cent off the top or the head of the Port Authority is corrupt,'[30] many in Nigeria believed he was speaking directly to their government. Obama's visit to Nigeria's friend but competitor, Ghana, was painted as a form of punish-ment for Nigeria's apparent backsliding on corruption and governance in recent years.[31]

But it was Hillary Clinton's visit to Nigeria in August 2009 that really upset the Nigerian government. The visit was troubled from the start over issues of protocol and security. Even before she arrived, the Secretary of State was critical, commenting on Nigeria during her stop in Angola. When she arrived in Abuja, she was received by a junior protocol officer from the Foreign Ministry and no senior government officials were present. Despite the smiling photographs of the visit, Clinton's comment about 'failure of governance at all levels, misman-agement and corruption and concentration of wealth in few hands'[32] ruffled the feathers of government ministers. The Nigerian media picked up on these comments with headlines like 'Clinton Knocks Federal Govt on Corruption', 'Clinton – Leadership has failed Nigeria' and 'Corruption Erodes Yar'Adua Legitimacy'. The ruling People's Democratic Party (PDP) was swift to condemn the comments on corruption and leadership, stating that they were based on 'misinformation'.[33]

Those in Nigeria who do not belong to or are not linked to the government took quite a different perspective. Though most Nigerians would agree with Assistant Secretary Johnnie Carson that theirs is the most important country in sub-Saharan Africa – and so in their view they should be respected accord-ingly – any opportunity to show up their distant, disconnected and apparently faltering ruling elite is welcome. Indeed, a Nigerian commentator stated that 'Mrs Clinton's comments about the sorry state of affairs in the country, which the PDP found detestable, if truth must be told, are not really original'.[34] The Nigerian Bar Association welcomed her remarks, stating that 'The NBA wishes to align itself with the statement credited to the US Secretary of State, the summation of which was that corruption, amongst other factors, [has] caused failure of governance in Nigeria.'[35] Clinton's remarks garnered support on forums such as 234next.com, with comments such as 'They keep reminding us the truth we should tell ourselves', and 'It is heart-breaking because we have, through our own actions and inactions and abiding selfish and narrow thinking, nurtured and elevated thieves to the levels of leadership.'[36]

Intentionally or not, President Obama's visit to Ghana acted as a catalyst for increased conversation and debate within Nigeria on the state of its democracy, which was only heightened by Secretary of State Clinton's visit. Though the Nigerian leadership may brush off such incidents and the chatter that follows, inevitably they do touch a nerve when they garner such domestic civil society support and also when their country, a dominant regional force for so many years, is negatively compared with its peers Ghana and Angola.

In the near term, therefore, it appears that bilateral relations will remain frosty. Nigeria became front-page news in the United States on 25 December 2009 when Nigerian Umar Farouk Abdul Mutallab tried to blow up a transatlantic flight preparing to land in Detroit. In January 2010 the US added Nigeria to its list of countries that sponsor terrorists, meaning 'enhanced screening of all holders of the Nigerian passport'. This has further soured relations.

While Washington appears to be ready for ribbon-cutting on the proposed new US–Nigeria Commission, the Nigerians had made little progress by late 2009, although the Nigerian Foreign Minister has agreed to it in principle.[37] Indeed, in addition to President Yar'Adua's health issues, official displeasure at Hillary Clinton's conduct in Nigeria may have also contributed to the Nigerian President's decision not to attend a lunch for 25 African heads of state and African Union Commissioner Jean Ping, hosted by President Obama on the first day of the opening session of the UN General Assembly in New York in September 2009.[38]

As of late 2009, therefore, the emphasis of the US policy on Nigeria remained firmly diplomatic, trying to focus the Yar'Adua administration on the issues of poverty, endemic corruption and environmental devastation that underpin the Niger Delta crisis. US officials believe their hard message has contributed to the recent focus by the government in Abuja on trying more actively to engage on the Niger Delta issue. US officials are also concerned about northern Nigeria and are looking to improve their understanding of this region by reopening a consulate in the state of Kaduna that was closed in 1994. But it seems at this stage that the Obama administration has little if any more leverage in promoting structural change in Nigeria than its predecessor, though this is a problem not uncommon among Nigeria's international partners. The Nigerian government will continue to court China, Russia and others as it seeks to diversify its international relations, as so many African states are doing. If Washington wishes to exert influence over developments in Nigeria, policy-makers will have to develop ever more nuanced and creative modes of engagement with it, without emotional reactions to claims of growing influence from other powers in the country.

THE UNITED STATES AND SOUTH AFRICA

The bilateral relationship with South Africa had been awkward during the Bush administration, following a fairly constructive period during the transition from apartheid until the late 1990s. In November 1993, a US–South Africa Business Development Committee was established, and Vice-President Al Gore, when attending the inauguration of Nelson Mandela in May 1994, proposed that the United States establish a high-level bi-national commission (BNC) to deepen the relationship between the two countries – similar to commissions that had been inaugurated with Russia and Egypt. This BNC was launched in 1995 under the chairmanship of Gore and South African Vice-President Thabo Mbeki, and comprised subcommittees at cabinet level on a range of issues. It was hoped that the commission would increase the coherence of US assistance to South Africa, but it depended almost exclusively on USAID funding, not departmental budget commitments. As the USAID programme declined, so did funding for the BNC.[39]

At the outset of the Bush administration, the future of the BNC was in doubt, although the administration initially signalled that South Africa, Nigeria and Kenya were the 'natural partners' of the United States in Africa.[40] Ultimately, the Bush administration replaced the BNC with a US–South Africa Cooperation Forum, but it met irregularly and not at the vice-presidential or even cabinet level.

During the Mbeki presidency, the bilateral relationship became unexceptional, not helped by the unpopularity in South Africa of the US intervention in Iraq and by Mbeki's equivocal stances on HIV/AIDS and Zimbabwe. The fumbled public relations around the establishment of AFRICOM offered easy ammunition to those in South Africa who had steadily formulated a rather two-dimensional (if, in the context, understandable) view of a rapacious United States seeking only to secure mineral and security interests across Africa, and using humanitarian and developmental concerns as a front.

These underlying tensions might have been expected to ease with Mbeki's departure from office in late 2008 and Barack Obama's election. Yet, so entrenched had the suspicion become that, in some quarters, Obama's African heritage was seen somehow as a threat to South Africa's self-perception as the leader of Africa bringing the authentic African voice into world discussions (which is deeply disputed and resented in many parts of Africa). Reflecting this ambivalence, President Obama's first conversation with then President Kgalema Motlanthe at the end of January 2009 did not go particularly well, according to insiders; there were concerns in South Africa that the new administration might signal a return to the Bill Clinton style of outspoken engagement that had so irritated many in South African governing circles in the past.[41]

Hillary Clinton's first visit to South Africa in August 2009 was thus a test of whether both countries understood the nature of the tensions between them and could overcome them. This was particularly important because the combined impacts of the global financial crisis and a complex global political agenda (including the rise of the G20 in which South Africa is an important player) meant that the need to re-engage and build on the extensive common interests between the two countries was long overdue.

As an indicator for future engagement the visit was hopeful. Clinton largely avoided the critical and outspoken language deployed in either Kenya or Nigeria, and repeatedly went out of her way to emphasize South Africa's regional and global importance and to praise its government.[42] On Zimbabwe, she took pains to urge greater South African leadership while praising the approach taken to date. Only on HIV/AIDS was she slightly more outspoken, obliquely criticizing the former Mbeki policy by referring to 'lost time' that had to be made up.[43] This was easier for the South African side to digest as the new government of President Jacob Zuma had disavowed the former Mbeki AIDS policy. Clinton also offered to resuscitate the US–≠South Africa BNC, thus upgrading the relationship from the ineffective Bush-era US–South Africa Cooperation Forum. Clinton described a meeting in Durban with President Zuma at the end of her South Africa visit as 'extremely helpful', and the South African President reciprocated: 'The two countries have always had good relations and we are taking that relationship higher.'

Despite these positive diplomatic statements, the visit was not easy. There was a sense of detachment on the South African side,[44] and media criticism despite the careful diplomacy.[45] There is some sense that US interest is simply a reflection of its great-power rivalry with China's increasing interests in Africa, itself an impression that reflects a peculiar defensive insecurity in South African self-perceptions.[46] Treading a path through these prickly sensibilities will be a difficult task for US diplomats, but vital if this important bilateral relationship is to be rebuilt.

THE UNITED STATES AND ANGOLA

Hillary Clinton's mission in Angola sought to build a strategic partnership between the two countries and followed a visit by the Angolan Foreign Minister to Washington in May 2009. In Angola, Clinton spoke of the two countries as 'partners, friends and allies'.[47] When the United States established diplomatic relations with Angola in 1993, during the Bill Clinton administration, the relationship was initially warm.[48] Following the collapse of the Lusaka peace process and the resumption of war in the second half of 1998, the United States backed away from an active involvement in the search for peace in Angola. Instead, a concerted effort was made to strengthen the bilateral relationship through the establishment of the US–Angola Bilateral Consultative Commission, which met formally three times during 1999–2000 to discuss a wide range of issues.

The election of George W. Bush was initially viewed with some trepidation in Angola because of the Republicans' previous association with Jonas Savimbi and the National Union for the Total Independence of Angola (UNITA). But, despite the fact that the US–Angola Bilateral Consultative Commission was inactive during the following years, the Bush administration pursued a policy of active engagement with the Angolan government, driven principally by the recognition of US long-term energy needs. Angolan oil is plentiful and accessible, and is also the type of high-quality crude the United States needs. In 2008, the United States imported just under 4 per cent of its oil from Angola.

Hillary Clinton's decision to visit Angola on her first Africa trip was seen in Luanda as proof that the United States wanted to work constructively with the government of President José Eduardo dos Santos. Confirming this impression, the United States and Angola plan to resuscitate their bilateral consultative commission and the Angolan Foreign Minister reported that he had found Washington open to solving African problems and to strengthening bilateral relations.

Clinton's references during her Angola visit to the need for good governance and to hold presidential elections soon were perceived by the Angolan government as appropriate in the context of the country being in transition. This was in contrast to her reception in Nigeria. It was also noted, however, that she was not directly critical of the government, rather stating that the United States was 'satisfied' with and would encourage further efforts to promote transparency, and that she was convinced that presidential elections would occur 'in due course' after ratification of the new constitution. This was perceived as a pragmatic line to take towards the Angolan government.

Times have changed. The Popular Movement for the Liberation of Angola (MPLA), a former Soviet-backed Marxist-Leninist resistance movement, is now the Angolan interlocutor for the US government, while the opposition UNITA – a former Cold War US client – expressed 'frustration' that it was not granted an audience with Clinton. Other opposition members and civil society groups felt equally sidelined.[49] Academic Mario Pinto de Andrade claimed that Clinton's speech undermined opposition parties and civil society organizations that were critical of the government. A letter by civil society activists to the US Secretary of State, highlighting concerns about corruption, bad governance and human rights violations, apparently went without public comment or mention.[50] Recognizing that public criticism eroded engagement opportunities, Hillary Clinton's trip to Angola was designed to pave the way for increased dialogue.

The approach that Hillary Clinton took towards each of these three 'anchor' countries in Africa differs significantly. A critical approach to corruption and low standards of governance in Nigeria annoyed the host government while vindicating civil society. In Angola, the situation was reversed, with opposition groups being critical of the Secretary of State's generally supportive approach to the MPLA government. In South Africa, American signals appear carefully designed to engage all key partners and upgrade the bilateral relationship at all levels, from government to civil society. Yet South African suspicion has remained and will take some years of cautious diplomacy to overcome.

The diversity of US approaches towards each of these so-called 'strategic partners' in Africa might be understandable given the differing US national and security interests that relations with each country evoke. But this emerging pragmatism can also open up US policy in the African sub-continent to charges of inconsistency, even while it can improve diplomatic freedom of manoeuvre and therefore leverage in specific instances. Such pragmatism needs to be placed within a broad, consistent, positive vision of the kind of democratic values and prosperity agenda the United States must support if it is to remain a leading voice for reform-minded engagement in sub-Saharan Africa in the face of ever-growing competition for influence and access from the world's other economic powers such as Brazil, Russia, India and China. As the Obama administration crafts a more coherent process and infrastructure for developing and implementing its Africa strategy – in contrast to the Bush administration, despite its specific successes – the risk is that a plethora of diverse US approaches to specific countries will undermine the central message of the need for better governance across the region and overwhelm the policy-making process in Washington.

CONCLUSION: BREAK WITH THE PAST?

A higher visibility and better coordinated policy towards Africa, relative to that of its predecessors, was inevitable at the start of the Obama administration. Ahead of his Ghana visit, Obama suggested in an interview to AllAfrica.com that the US government had lacked a well-coordinated aid-to-Africa effort in the past. 'Our aid policies have been splintered among a variety of agencies, different theories embraced by different people depending on which administration, which party is in power at any given time.'[51] Since then, in terms of avenues opened and proposals made, President Obama has not disappointed. At the L'Aquila G8 summit in Italy in July 2009, for example, he announced $20 billion in pledges for the developing countries, including $3 billion from the United States to improve food security for the poorest around the world. In his Ghana speech, he said his administration was also committing $63 billion to address global health crises.[52]

However, the level of US commitment to the region, and the quality of that commitment, remain uncertain, not just objectively but, just as importantly, in the eyes of African leaders and their peoples. The state of the US economy given the current crisis could hold the administration back from financing many of its most ambitious plans, and it is worth remembering that Vice-President Joe Biden commented during the 2008 election campaign that a Democratic administration would probably have to moderate its commitment to double foreign assistance.[53] There has been much lobbying against such a pull-back since the comment was made, but levels of funding will be as important an indicator of the administration's long-term commitment to Africa as have been the good ideas on policy coordination and the appointment of a strong team to carry out these policies. As discussed above, the Bush administration invested seriously in Africa, but many of its programmes were too narrowly focused and inflexible to be of much use in addressing the root causes of bad governance and institutional deficits in a sustainable way, and in offering real incentives for reform. With limited new funds to create major new programmes, and the option of redefining the existing ones being complex and time-consuming, it will be hard for the Obama administration to chart a new path, especially as one year has already passed.

There is little doubt that the process of US policy-making towards Africa should continue to improve in this administration, but the content will be the test. In this context, despite President Obama's African heritage, Africa policy is not a priority for his administration. Pressing domestic issues, such as reviving the economy and reforming health care, in addition to major foreign policy challenges such as the Middle East, especially Iran, and Afghanistan and Pakistan, will continue to be the focus of much of the administration's efforts over the next three years.

NOTES

1 Jimmy Carter was the first US president to make a state visit to sub-Saharan Africa. Prior to that only Franklin D. Roosevelt had visited Africa, during the Second World War, although Richard Nixon had attended Ghana's independence ceremony in 1957, as vice president. George H.W. Bush made two trips to Africa, both in 1982 as vice president, before Bill Clinton became the first US president to visit Africa twice while in office. George W. Bush also visited twice, and met more African heads of state than any of his predecessors.

2 An exception to this was the Angola civil war when, for some time, the National Union for the Total Independence of Angola (UNITA) was the second largest recipient of covert US support in the world. It is also worth noting that within five years of the 1959 opening of a US embassy in Guinea, 30 more had been opened across the continent.

3 Hudson Institute, *Index of Global Philanthropy and Remittances* (2008). See http://gpr.hudson.org/. The reasons for the growth in US domestic concern are complex, but partly driven by the fast-growing links between churches in the United States and across Africa.

4 Energy Information Administration (EIA) statistics, 2009. See http://tonto.eia.doe.gov/dnav/pet/pet_move_impcus_a2_nus_epoo_imo_mbbl_m.htm.

5 Princeton Lyman and J. Stephen Morrison, *More than Humanitarianism: A Strategic US Approach to Africa* (New York: Council on Foreign Relations, 2006).

6 Witney Schneidman, 'Africa/USA: A Cautious Look Beyond the Recessionary Gloom', *The Africa Report* 19 (October–December 2009), http://theafricareport.com.

7 Ray Copson, *The United States in Africa* (London: Zed Books, 2007).

8 PEPFAR did come in for criticism, however, for its religiously inspired restrictions on the way funds could be distributed; they favoured programmes that sought to promote abstinence as opposed to condom use.

9 Lauren Ploch, 'Africa Command: US Strategic Interests and the Role of the US Military in Africa', *Congressional Research Service Report for Congress*, 28 July 2009.

10 'Experts wary about Africom', *The Times*, 1 October 2008. See http://www.thetimes.co.za/News/Article.aspx?id=854378.

11 'Africa: Barack Obama's Address to Ghanaian Parliament – As Delivered', *allAfrica.com*, 11 July 2009. See http://allafrica.com/stories/printable/200907110013.html. There has not been much debate about this in 2009 although Jendayi Frazer, Assistant Secretary of State for African Affairs from 2005 to 2009, wrote in August 2009 in

the *Wall Street Journal* that she believed AFRICOM should be moved from Germany to Liberia. See Jendayi Frazer, 'Four ways to help Africa', *The Wall Street Journal*, 25 August 2009.

12 Samantha Power, also an Africa specialist, has been appointed as the NSC's Director for Multinational Affairs and David Goldwyn as Coordinator for International Energy Affairs at the State Department. For an assessment of Clinton on Africa, see J. Stephen Morrison and Jennifer C. Cooke (eds), *Africa Policy in the Clinton Years: Critical Choices for the Bush Administration* (Washington, DC: Center for Strategic and International Studies, 2001).

13 Wolpe previously served as an envoy to the region from 1996 to 2001 for President Clinton and more recently advised the Obama presidential campaign on African issues.

14 Chris McGreal, 'Obama adopts interventionist Africa strategy', *Guardian*, 11 July 2009.

15 United States Department of State and the Broadcasting Board of Governors Office of Inspector General, Report of Inspection: The Bureau of African Affairs, Report Number ISP-I-09-63, August 2009.

16 'Testimony of Princeton Lyman Before the Senate Subcommittee on Africa', Senate Committee on Foreign Relations, Subcommittee on African Affairs, Hearing on Strengthening US Diplomacy to Anticipate, Prevent and Respond to Conflict in Africa, 21 April 2009, http://www.cfr.org/publication/19147/prepared_testimony_on_strengthening_us_diplomacy_to_anticipate_prevent_and_respond_to_conflict_in_africa.html?breadcrumb=/bios/2373/princeton_n_lyman.

17 'On Strengthening US Diplomacy in Africa: Testimony of Howard Wolpe Before the Senate Subcommittee on Africa' Senate Subcommittee on Foreign Relations, Subcommittee on African Affairs, 21 April 2009.

18 'Interviewee Johnnie Carson, Seeking a New Path to Stability in Sudan, and Africa', 20 October 2009, http://www.cfr.org/publication/20461/seeking_a_new_path_to_stability_in_sudan_and_africa.html?breadcrumb=/region/143/africa.

19 'United States/Africa: Obama Launches his Agenda', *Africa Confidential* 50(14) (10 July 2009).

20 President John Atta Mills and Barack Obama are also newly elected heads of state and were legal professionals.

21 'Statement on White House Visit of Tanzanian President Kikwete: Leaders to Discuss Economy, Regional and Bilateral Issues', 19 May 2009. Available at: www.america.gov/st/texttrans-english/2009/May/20090519174952xjsnommiso.4865338.html.

22 'Africa: Barack Obama's Address to Ghanaian Parliament – As Delivered', *allAfrica.com*, 11 July 2009. See http://allafrica.com/stories/printable/20090711013.html; Tim Hughes, 'US-Africa Relations: The Modest Foundations of Obama's Four-Pillar Platform', *Business Day*, 14 July 2009.

23 Libby Purves, 'Treat Africans as part of the human jigsaw', *The Times*, 13 July 2009.

24 'Remarks by Secretary of State Hillary Clinton at CCA's 7th Biennial US–Africa Business Summit', Walter E. Washington Convention Center, Washington, DC, 1 October 2009.

25 Jennifer Cooke and J. Stephen Morrison, 'The Administration's Sudan Strategy', CSIS blog, 21 October 2009, http://csis.org/blog/obama-administration's-sudan-strategy.

26 During her Kenya visit, Hillary Clinton also met Somali President Sheik Sharif Sheik Ahmed.

27 US Department of State, Background note: Nigeria. http://www.state.gov/r/pa/ei/bgn/2836.htm.

28 http://www.thomas.gov/cgi-bin/query/F?c111:3:./temp/~c111CBUEWA:e380052.

29 http://news.onlinenigeria.com/templates/?a=3805.

30 http://www.america.gov/st/texttrans-english/2009/July/20090711110050abre
tnuho.1079783.html.

31 'I hope it is a big lesson to the Nigerian leaders that democracy can truly work in
Africa with total commitment and will of the leaders and the citizens alike. Whether
Obama comes or not, Nigeria is still the giant of Africa. It is okay for Obama to
encourage Ghana's democracy. In spite of our current woes we still have a profound
influence across Africa,' commented a reader of BBC reporting on the visit. See
http://news.bbc.co.uk/1/hi/world/africa/8138641.stm.

32 Paul Arhewe, Daniel Kanu, Francis Iwuchukwu (Lagos) Chesa Chesa, Rafiu Ajakaye
and Kemi Yesufu (Abuja), 'Clinton demands further action against corruption', *Daily
Independent*, 13 August 2009, http://allafrica.com/stories/200908130001.html.

33 Abdu Labaran Malumfashi, 'Mrs Clinton and PDP's sour grapes', *Sahara Reports*, 15
August2009,http://www.saharareporters.com/index.php?option=com_content&view
=article&id=3470:mrs-clinton-and-pdps-sour-grapes&catid=81:external-contrib
&Itemid=300

34 Ibid.

35 NBA President, Mr Oluwarotimi Akeredolu (SAN), quoted in Chuks Okocha,
Davidson Iriekpen and Martha Eigbefoh, 'PDP, Mark Tackle Clinton Over Nigeria',
This Day, 14 August 2009, http://allafrica.com/stories/200908140005.html.

36 Reader Comments, 'Nigeria is Heartbreaking Says Clinton', *Next,* http://234next.
com/csp/cms/sites/Next/News/National/5466351-147/Nigeria_is_heartbreaking_
says_Clinton_.csp.

37 When he spoke at the Brookings Institution in Washington on 30 September on
'The Nigeria–US Partnership', the foreign minister, Chief Ojo Maduekwe, provided
no substance on how this commission would be rolled out.

38 President Ellen Johnson-Sirleaf of Liberia spoke on youth and jobs, President Paul
Kagame of Rwanda spoke on investment, and Tanzania's President Jakaya Kikwete
spoke on agriculture at this lunch.

39 Princeton Lyman, *Partner to History: The US Role in South Africa's Transition to Democracy* (Washington, DC: United States Institute of Peace Press, 2002), p. 255.

40 Walter Kansteiner, Assistant Secretary of State for African Affairs, as quoted in
e-mails from the US–South Africa Business Council, 14 June 2001.

41 See 'Clinton Visit Should be a Debate, Not a Lecture', *Business Day*, 6 August 2009,
http://www.businessday.co.za/Articles/Content.aspx?id=77847.

42 See, for example, Clinton's press conference with the South African Minister of International Relations, http://www.state.gov/secretary/rm/2009a/08/127006.htm, and its
coverage, 'Breathing Life into Rocky Relationship', *Business Day*, 11 August 2009,
http://www.businessday.co.za/Articles/Content.aspx?id=78130.

43 Remarks at PEPFAR event with South African Minister of Health Dr Aaron Motso-
aledi, http://www.state.gov/secretary/rm/2009a/08/127008.htm.

44 http://www.nytimes.com/2009/08/08/world/africa/08diplo.html?_r=1.

45 'Yankees Go Home', *Business Day*, 12 August 2009, http://www.businessday.co.za/
Articles/Content.aspx?id=78301, and 'What Hillary wants from SA', *Mail & Guardian,*
8 August 2009, http://www.mg.co.za/article/2009-08-08-what-hillary-wants-from-
sa.

46 See also 'China shoves US in scramble for Africa', *Mail & Guardian,* 6 August 2009,
http://www.mg.co.za/article/2009-08-06-china-shoves-us-in-scramble-for-africa.

47 'Chefe de Estado fala de cooperação com Hillary Clinton', *Angop*, 11 August 2009.
48 See José Partricio, *Angola-EUA: Os Caminhos do bom-senso* (Lisbon: Publicações Dom Quixote, 1997).
49 'Líder da FNLA discursa na Assembléia por ocasião da visita de Hillary Clinton', FNLA Press Release, 9 August 2009.
50 'Sociedade civil angolana apresenta carta aberta a Hillary Clinton', Club-k.net, 7 August 2009.
51 'Africa: US Wants to Spotlight "Successful Models" and Be an "Effective Partner" – Obama', *AllAfrica.com*, 2 July 2009. See http://allafrica.com/stories/200907021302.html.
52 'Africa: Barack Obama's Address to Ghanaian Parliament – As Delivered' (see note 22 above).
53 'Transcript of Palin, Biden Debate', *CNNPolitics.com*, 3 October 2008. See http://www.cnn.com/2008/POLITICS/10/02/debate.transcript/.

4

East Asia: searching for consistency

John Swenson-Wright

INTRODUCTION

Asia, and in particular Northeast Asia, is critically important to the United States. This observation has been a truism in post-1945 international relations, but now, perhaps more than ever, the region looms large for decision-makers in Washington. A variety of factors explain why. Economically, the Asia-Pacific generates some 30 per cent of global exports and provides two-thirds of the world's foreign exchange reserves; and its annual bilateral trade with the United States is of the order of $1 trillion.[1]

From a security perspective, China's continuing military expansion, with some 14 per cent per annum growth in its annual defence budget, coupled with recent decisions to acquire two conventional and two nuclear-powered aircraft carriers, suggests that Beijing is steadily acquiring a power-projection capacity that will eventually challenge the maritime supremacy long enjoyed by the United States and its East Asian allies.

Persistent regional tensions, whether over China's desire to reassert its sovereignty over Taiwan or the provocative development by the Democratic People's Republic of Korea (DPRK) of its ballistic missile capabilities and its fledgling nuclear weapons programme, threaten to destabilize relations by fuelling an arms race among major and middle-ranking regional powers.

Apparently intractable territorial disputes, whether over the Northern Territories (the disputed islands to the north of Hokkaido, claimed by Japan but occupied by Russia), the Senkakus or Daiyoutai Islands, the Spratly Islands, or the Takeshima/Tokto dispute dividing Japan and South Korea, remain powerful irritants limiting regional cooperation. Allied to this are new, non-traditional security challenges, including the rising threat of piracy, natural disasters, pandemic diseases and the long-term danger of climate change, as well as more fundamental risks associated with the rise of beggar-thy-neighbour trade policies exacerbated by the current global economic crisis.

Given the substantive importance of these issues to the United States, it is surprising that it has not formulated a clear and coordinated set of responses. Since 1990, US governments have issued no fewer that four East Asian Strategy

Reports setting out the country's priorities in the region and specifying the necessary policy tools for meeting these priorities. However, the last such report was issued in 1998 and during the George W. Bush administration there was little evidence of any integrated American thinking on the region.[2] Indeed, to its critics the Bush White House approach to Asia was too sharply focused through the lens of 9/11 and the 'Global War on Terror'. As a consequence, vital US alliances, according to this interpretation, were neglected, or, in the case of the US–Japan relationship, weakened, potentially seriously. In addition, key sub-regions, such as Southeast Asia, were overlooked or apparently taken for granted. Adversaries, most notably North Korea, were handled inconsistently and in a manner that heightened tensions and undermined anti-proliferation measures, weakening the credibility of America's extended nuclear deterrence. Additionally, Washington's approach was coloured by an ideological agenda, rooted in the promotion of democratic values, which clashed with the pragmatism of many of the region's governments and had delivered few, if any, tangible political results.

As a general assessment of US policy towards East Asia between 2000 and 2008, much of this critique is well grounded. However, in certain key particulars the argument may have been overstated. For example, Sino-American relations were generally positive under President Bush and have continued to evolve in a pragmatic and constructive direction. North Korea policy, while inconsistent and erratic between 2000 and 2006, began to take on a much more pragmatic character in the last two years of the Bush administration and seemed close to delivering a managed, albeit incomplete, solution to the nuclear issue in August of 2008. Alliance relations with both Seoul and Tokyo were largely constructive and mutually advantageous, and President Bush enjoyed positive relations with a succession of Korean and Japanese leaders. Popular and elite-level criticisms of US policy in Iraq were arguably more muted in Asia than in Europe and, while the abuses at Abu Ghraib and Guantánamo Bay proved damaging morally to the United States, they did not appear to have generated a comprehensive backlash against neo-liberal notions of democracy, human rights and the rule of law with which the United States has recently been associated.[3] Importantly, the United States was able to secure some significant policy successes in key areas – for example, in putting together an ad hoc coalition to manage the humanitarian disaster associated with the Southeast Asian tsunami in 2004, and more generally in avoiding any immediate, obviously destabilizing security or political crises in the region.

Notwithstanding these important qualifications, for the Barack Obama administration sustaining existing relationships and avoiding crises is arguably not a sufficient basis for developing policy towards East Asia. Above all, this is because the region is subject to so much change and uncertainty – a leitmotif that helps to explain the worries of local elites and their desire to see the United States continue to play a leading role within the region. Specifically, Asia's leaders worry about a number of factors including:

- the shifting power relationship between China and the United States, not only regionally but also globally;
- the risk that existing security challenges, most notably that over North Korea, as well as territorial disputes and nationalism-fuelled inter-state rivalry, will produce greater regional instability; and
- the ability of the United States to manage and refocus its existing alliance partnerships to tackle a broader range of security and economic challenges, both traditional and non-traditional.[4]

High on the list of concerns for regional elites is the question of generational and leadership changes in some of the key states in the region. In North Korea, the recent illness of Kim Jong-il has led to much speculation regarding a possible leadership transition and the potentially destabilizing consequences of the transfer of power to Kim's likely successor, his son Kim Jong Un – at 27, a relatively unknown, inexperienced and untested figure. In Japan, the ending of some 54 years of virtually unbroken rule by the Liberal Democratic Party (LDP), and the inauguration of a new Democratic Party of Japan (DPJ) administration pledged to developing a more Asia-centric diplomacy and a policy of greater independence from the United States under the leadership of Hatoyama Yukio, have led some to point to a fraying of ties between Washington and Tokyo.

In China, as Kerry Brown's chapter notes, although leadership change is not imminent, any future generational transfer of power will involve a degree of uncertainty, now that communism has been eclipsed by nationalism as a basis for regime legitimacy. More broadly within the region, especially in Southeast Asia and notably in Thailand and the Philippines, there are concerns about the stability of local governments in the face of either separatist movements or sharp internal political conflicts. There are also signs of an effort by some states, such as Australia and Japan, to take the lead in devising competing policy blueprints to address this growing regional uncertainty – in the case of Australia, an Asian Pacific Community;[5] in the case of Japan, an East Asian Community. All these developments explain why there is added urgency within the Obama administration to be seen to be reasserting US involvement in Asian affairs and to devise a more strategic approach to the region.

The following analysis provides an overview of what the Obama administration has achieved during its first year in office in developing its policy towards the region, as well as the response of Asian states to America's effort. It not only assesses progress to date, but also considers what more concrete policy initiatives the administration might usefully wish to consider in the near to long term. For now, the record of achievement, while relatively modest, is nonetheless positive. President Obama's rhetoric and his inclusive approach have helped him build up a deep reservoir of popular and elite positive opinion in the region. Coupled with the high-profile visit by Secretary of State Hillary Clinton to Japan, South Korea, China and Indonesia in early February and the President's own visit to the region in November 2009, this has inspired confidence and allowed

Washington to project a positive image of calm reassurance, while minimizing, for now, disruptive tensions with potential adversaries.

Such progress represents at best a first step. Much more will need to be done in the immediate future if the United States is to continue to play a major role in the region and to advance its national interests in a manner that converges with and reinforces the interests of its core alliance partners. It will require considerable policy ingenuity and innovation, and some carefully calibrated changes in the way the United States does business and defines itself as an active participant in Northeast Asia. The resource implications of maintaining America's regional role are not inconsequential. With a forecast government deficit well in excess of $1 trillion for 2009,[6] the United States finds itself increasingly stretched financially as it seeks to sustain already expensive global commitments. Consequently, the Obama administration will need to reach out to a widening network of allies and friends, both old and new, to ensure that the burden of policy innovation is broadly and equitably shared.

ASSESSING OBAMA'S ASIA POLICY

It is arguably premature to say precisely how the Obama administration views the region. The White House has yet to release a formal official policy statement outlining its overall position. Nonetheless, there are enough early indicators, most notably Secretary of State Clinton's Asia trip and President Obama's own meetings with a number of his Asian counterparts and most notably his November visit to the region, that suggest that East Asia will rank high among the administration's foreign policy priorities and will be handled shrewdly and with considerable tact and ingenuity. Critically important will be how successfully the White House coordinates any new initiatives so as to allow a harmonized and coherent approach to the region.

Hillary Clinton's Asian tour de force

The new Secretary of State's decision to make her first overseas trip to Asia, visiting in rapid succession Japan, Indonesia, South Korea and China, unambiguously highlighted the administration's desire both symbolically and substantively to underline its commitment to the region. Prior to her departure, Clinton was careful, through a speech at the Asia Society in New York, to acknowledge the general perception that the United States had been giving insufficient attention to the region. The new administration, she spelled out, was committed to taking Asia seriously and planned to strengthen its collaboration with its allies in preventing nuclear proliferation and in meeting a broad range of challenges. Importantly, her trip would be an opportunity to learn, rather than to lecture, and as part of this, she wisely stressed the importance of meeting a broad section of Asian society – not merely traditional national elites but ordinary Asian citizens.[7] Stressing the importance of allied cooperation reflected continuities with the Bush administration, but the focus on dialogue and listening appeared to signal a change of both tone and substance on the part of the new administration.

In *Japan*, Clinton was careful to reiterate the country's primacy as the 'cornerstone' of America's alliance partnerships. She also bolstered alliance ties by signing a bilateral agreement reconfirming the relocation to Guam of US marines based in Okinawa, as agreed in the 2006 US–Japan Roadmap for Realignment. Clinton also sought to limit some of the negative political fallout associated with the Bush administration's decision from August 2008 to revoke the designation of North Korea as a state sponsor of terror – a decision that, by suggesting that Washington was insufficiently committed to resolving the fate of Japanese citizens abducted by North Korea in the 1970s and 1980s, had seriously antagonized elite and public opinion in Japan.[8]

Where relations with *Korea* were concerned, Clinton's visit to Seoul had been foreshadowed by an early February meeting in Washington between the Republic of Korea's National Security Adviser Kim Seung-hwan and his US counterpart Jim Jones, in which the Obama administration had carefully stressed its commitment to the Six Party Talks as well as alliance coordination with the South Koreans in dealing with North Korea. The same tone was reflected in Clinton's meetings with President Lee Myung-bak and then Prime Minister Han Seung-soo, and the Secretary of State was careful to acknowledge Seoul's important contribution in providing support in both Iraq and Afghanistan.[9]

In *China*, Clinton won plaudits from local commentators for stressing the importance of a 'positive' bilateral relationship, including her willingness to broach new and atypical elements in it, and for her repeated thanking of the Chinese leadership for their continuing purchase of US treasury bills. Choosing, for example, to include in her delegation an adviser on climate change appeared to signal a break from past negotiations when military issues have often been uppermost in discussion. By contrast, Clinton's approach to human rights and the sensitive issue of Tibet was muted and understated, exposing her to some criticism from the international human rights community but at the same time reassuring her hosts.[10]

In *Indonesia*, Clinton broke with precedent by visiting the headquarters of ASEAN (the Association of Southeast Asian Nations) – the first time that a US secretary of state has done so. She also helped to correct some of the impression of neglect associated with the previous administration when she pledged to attend the July 2009 meeting of the ASEAN Regional Forum. Condoleezza Rice, Clinton's predecessor, had failed to attend this important regional security forum twice in the previous four years, leaving Indonesians – rightly or wrongly – with the impression that America's interest in their country and the wider Southeast Asian region was shallow and insubstantial.[11] Appearing on national television and meeting with ordinary Indonesians was also a shrewd way for Clinton to convey an image of accessibility and engagement, and allowed her to capitalize on the huge popularity enjoyed by President Obama among young Indonesians. Obama had spent formative years between the ages of six and ten attending local school in Jakarta and his personal connection with the region has been an important source of unexpected and historically all too rare political goodwill for the new administration with the world's most populous Muslim nation.

President Obama's meetings with Asian leaders

Clinton's tour of the region helped to win local hearts and minds by stressing the application of America's 'smart' power and the importance of acknowledging the contributions of America's regional partners. This is a message that President Obama reinforced in his own meetings with senior Asian leaders. On 24 February, then Prime Minister Taro Aso of Japan was the first foreign leader to have a formal face-to-face meeting with the new President, who took pains to thank the Japanese leader for his government's contributions in Afghanistan while avoiding any impression of pressuring Tokyo to provide additional military assistance.[12] A similar message was conveyed to the Australian premier, Kevin Rudd, in a meeting in Washington on 24 March. President Obama very publicly and effusively thanked him for Australia's past efforts in Afghanistan, and both leaders emphasized their 'excellent meeting' and the importance of the bilateral relationship.[13]

Formal communiqué language such as this may seem relatively insignificant but it helps to set the tone for a positive relationship. A similar approach was taken by President Obama at the G20 London summit in early April 2009. His meeting with Chinese President Hu Jintao was important in allowing both countries to stress their commitment to 'strengthen ties at all levels' including economic issues and combating global terrorism, and Obama was quick to accept 'with pleasure' Hu's invitation to visit China later in the year.[14]

Also at the G20 summit, President Obama had the opportunity to meet with South Korea's President Lee. Significantly, the official communiqué from this meeting talked of both sides' desire to make progress in realizing the Korea–US Free Trade Agreement (KORUS FTA), while avoiding 'protectionism and economic nationalism', a position that Obama reiterated in his visit to Seoul in November. Given Asian fears during the US presidential election contest that Obama was tilting in a protectionist direction, this message – albeit relatively modest in terms of what it offers – has provided some reassurance that both countries were committed to managing, and defusing the tensions associated with past KORUS negotiations and reaching a final agreement at some point in 2010. However, the mid-term US Congressional elections in the autumn of 2010 may also throw up a number of complicating political issues; some Representatives are likely to push for greater access to the South Korean market for US auto companies – a concern that might well derail efforts to settle the KORUS FTA. In a separate context in his dealings with China, President Obama has already been willing to give a nod in a protectionist direction, endorsing punitive trade restrictions on Chinese tyre imports to the United States, and there is a risk that he might feel compelled to embrace similar measures *vis-à-vis* the Republic of Korea.[15]

The clearest test and expression of President Obama's commitment to Asia was his high-profile eight-day tour of the region in late November when he visited Japan, Singapore, China and Korea. This was not only a chance to meet with key US allies and the region's most important rising power, but also an unusual opportunity to participate in a full ASEAN summit meeting – a powerful and unmistakable indication that the United States is committed to re-engaging in Southeast Asia. His Singapore visit also included a meeting of APEC (Asia-Pacific Economic Cooperation) – an opportunity to engage with an organization that has perhaps the broadest and most diverse memberships of any of Asia's many multilateral bodies. Overall, the focus of the President's Asia visit was on re-emphasizing America's commitment to the region and demonstrating the centrality of Asian issues to the United States. Although the White House appeared to have been relatively unconcerned to secure concrete policy outcomes or 'deliverables' during the trip, it did succeed in reassuring Asia's elites that the United States remains firmly engaged in the region, with President Obama noting memorably during his visit to Tokyo that he is America's 'first Pacific president'.[16]

CRITICAL ASIAN POLICY CHALLENGES FOR THE OBAMA ADMINISTRATION

Summit meetings and overseas visits offer useful background reassurance to America's allies and its key regional interlocutors and there is little doubt that the Obama administration has, to date, appeared sure-footed and confident in the way it has managed its diplomatic presentations. Yet the impact of this new approach remains unclear, and it is likely to be tested by major regional policy challenges. Some of these are relatively easy to identify, whereas others may emerge unexpectedly and with little warning. The following section sets to one side America's bilateral relations with China and its immediate neighbourhood, including Taiwan and North Korea, which are covered in Chapter 8. Rather, it focuses on the potential future US role in promoting security and stability in East Asia more generally, through its other key bilateral regional relationship – with Japan – and through its support for the broadening and deepening process of regional integration.

Sustaining the US–Japan Alliance

The DPJ's success in replacing the LDP as Japan's new government in August 2009 – the first time that a non-conservative party has been able to form an independent administration in Japan since 1955 – has prompted speculation that the US–Japan Alliance may be under threat. During the general election, the DPJ stressed the need for a more Asia-centric foreign policy and greater equality in Japan's relations with the United States.[17] However, it would be wrong to view this rhetorical recalibration as a sign of incipient anti-Americanism or a desire on the part of the new government to redefine its relationship with the United

States in a radical way. The DPJ's new, assertive language was partly driven by electoral calculations and a wish to distinguish itself from the outgoing administration. It also reflects a desire for greater transparency and debate within the bilateral relationship – a point underlined by the new government's commitment to declassifying important archival material relating to post-war US–Japan relations.

Important practical issues are complicating the management of current ties – most notably surrounding long-standing plans to relocate US marine corps facilities at Futenma in Okinawa; the decision by the new government to end Maritime Self-Defense Force deployments to the Indian Ocean as part of Operation Enduring Freedom; and the wider question of burden-sharing and Japanese Host Nation Support for US forces in Japan. However, these are, in effect, managerial issues rather than fundamental disagreements. Public and elite opinion in Japan towards the United States remains very positive.[18] Prime Minister Hatoyama received his graduate training at Stanford University, and Okada Katsuya, the new foreign minister, is well connected in policy and political circles in Washington.[19]

A change in tone in characterizing the bilateral relationship may also extend into a re-examination of the precise way in which Japan chooses to support US security initiatives both regionally and globally. This is partly a consequence of Japan's domestic economic difficulties, which limit its ability to engage actively overseas; it also reflects a philosophical difference of emphasis from the outgoing LDP administration. Active employment of Japan's military assets in support of US security efforts in East Asia and further afield – a trend that had become more pronounced since the mid-1990s – is likely to be qualified by greater reliance on Japan's financial resources to support non-traditional security measures, for example through the provision of targeted developmental assistance such as the recently announced $5 billion aid package to Afghanistan. Moreover, when Japan does choose to deploy its military assets directly it may be more inclined to do so in an explicitly international context rather than via the traditional framework of the US–Japan Alliance – for example, by dispatching Maritime Self-Defence Force ships to assist in anti-piracy actions off Somalia (a measure for which the DPJ has already expressed its support). All of this adds up to a difference of emphasis rather than a domestic retreat, a dilution of support for the broader alliance with the United States or a questioning of US global security initiatives. Indeed, Prime Minister Hatoyama was quick to express his support for President Obama's expanded deployment of troops to Afghanistan in early December. Consequently, the critical claim in some quarters that the US–Japan relationship is 'structurally strong, but functionally weak' seems overstated.[20] The alliance will almost certainly experience some important practical changes in the immediate future and will therefore require careful management and negotiation by policy-makers on both sides of the Pacific, but it would be a mistake to assume that this is a partnership that is either in doubt or experiencing severe strain.

Enhancing regional and global economic coordination

With East Asian economic growth projected to slow sharply in 2009 – falling from a forecast rate of 4.4 per cent in November 2008 to an estimated 2.7 per cent in February 2009[21] – the Obama administration assumed office with a strategic approach to the region that needed to be couched in broad, inclusive terms looking beyond narrowly defined military issues and taking economic concerns into account.

America's reputation as a leader on international economic policy has been dented in East Asia as a result of the global financial crisis, but, as a recent report by the Chicago Council on Global Affairs has made clear, the 'Washington Consensus' model of modern capitalism remains largely secure and there is no alternative Asia-centric developmental strategy emerging to challenge it.[22] Nevertheless, the differential impact on individual countries of the economic slowdown in the region is adding to uncertainty, particularly regarding the continuing ability of individual countries to contribute to local and global economic prosperity.

With Japan anticipated to see its GDP shrink by 6 per cent in 2009 on the back of a sharp fall in its exports,[23] past certainties of continuing regional growth are in doubt and the regional balance of economic power appears to be shifting in critical ways that require a new strategic approach to regional economic policy-making by Washington.

Although China has continued to enjoy healthy economic growth rates, with 2009 growth anticipated to have been 8.4 per cent, any subsequent slowing of growth would risk producing potentially destabilizing internal tensions as unemployment rises, causing an even wider divergence between the material conditions of Chinese urban and rural workers. The risk that rising populism, whether in China or in other East Asian states, might spill over into more assertive economic nationalism and calls for economic protectionism is not insignificant. Linked to this are worries, expressed by US Treasury Secretary Timothy Geithner in past Senate testimony, that China may be manipulating its currency as a means of encouraging greater export growth and offsetting some of its current economic difficulties.[24]

Given America's exclusion from the East Asian Summit (EAS) and the slow, consensus-based decision-making character of many of the region's key economic institutions – including both ASEAN and APEC – the Obama administration will need a coordinated policy to sustain a central role in regional economic policy-making. It will also need to find a mechanism to encourage leading Asian economic powers (most notably China, Japan and South Korea) to play an active role in regional and global coordinated economic policy-making, in close partnership with the United States – particularly in promoting economic stimulus measures to deal with the shortfall in global demand.

Some measures are already being taken. China, for example, enacted early in 2009 a $586 billion stimulus package, boosting growth at home and among its neighbours. Similarly, Japan has passed two substantive stimulus packages totalling some $320 billion and, in November 2008, Prime Minister Aso pledged a bridging loan of $100 billion to the IMF.[25] There is a risk, however, that such initiatives will be overlooked or insufficiently acknowledged by the United States. It was conspicuous, for example, that Treasury Secretary Geithner failed publicly to acknowledge Japan's efforts earlier in 2009. It would not be surprising if resentment deepened in some Asian quarters about the United States dictating terms, or at the very least lecturing Asia rather than working genuinely in partnership to promote a coordinated response to the current economic crisis. Asian economies have, in fact, demonstrated a willingness to take their own regional initiatives in addressing the current economic crisis. Most strikingly, in February 2009 the finance ministers of China, Japan and South Korea agreed to expand the Chiang Mai initiative (ASEAN's multilateral currency swap arrangement) from $80 billion to $120 billion in order to help with regional liquidity problems.[26]

At the same time, any economic slowdown raises fears about a possible rise in beggar-thy-neighbour trade protectionism. But for now the risk of this does not seem particularly high, in part thanks to the reassurance that the Obama administration has recently provided that it supports key trade-enhancing initiatives in the region. President Obama announced during his visit to the region in November that the United States is willing to re-engage with the Trans-Pacific Partnership trade negotiations. The talks are important because of their broad, inclusive role involving a diverse collection of states including Australia, Brunei, Chile, New Zealand, Peru, Singapore and Vietnam. As such, they provide another opportunity for the United States to underscore its continuing centrality to effective economic initiatives in the region. What is less clear is what impact such a broad initiative might have on existing efforts to secure bilateral free trade agreements, for example between the United States and Thailand or Malaysia, as well the anticipated reaction of the US Congress, which may prove nervous about participating in a new region-wide grouping that includes states such as Vietnam.

Fostering both a regional and an extra-regional approach to climate change

In discussing the Obama administration's strategic choices in Asia, it is important not to be too conditioned by past initiatives. New policy challenges such as the threat of climate change and global warming do not neatly fit into the geographic boundaries of Northeast Asia that have shaped policy in the past, particularly given the prominence of both India and China as two of the world's leading emitters of greenhouse gases. In the light of President Obama's commitment to tackling environmental challenges, his administration will need to work closely with some of its regional partners – most notably Japan, given its impressive technical skills in this area – in devising responses to environmental challenges both within and outside the region.

In the run-up to the December 2009 Copenhagen summit, there were signs of encouraging developments, at least in the willingness of individual states to make a commitment to challenge the problem of global climate change. Japan's Prime Minister Hatoyama, for example, indicated that Japan was willing in principle to endorse a radical cut in its carbon emission levels by some 25 per cent relative to 1990 levels, subject to other countries embracing comparable targets. China talked of a 40–45 per cent cut in the energy intensity of its economy by 2020, and the Obama administration embraced quantifiable targets, talking explicitly of a 17 per cent cut on its 2005 output levels. While Copenhagen failed to deliver a legally binding international agreement to replace the Kyoto Protocol, scheduled to expire in 2012, the meeting did establish a global accord to reduce greenhouse gas emissions in a manner intended to prevent a rise in global temperatures in excess of 2°C above nineteenth-century levels. While critics see this as an agreement without teeth, the accord not only introduces important mandatory reporting requirements for individual countries but also provides valuable financial assistance (to the tune of some $100 billion per year by 2020) to ensure that developing nations can meet more ambitious emission targets.[27] Much more detailed agreement will be required to realize these targets, but the willingness of both America and a number of prominent states in Asia to agree in principle on the desirability of realizing substantial emission cuts provides at least the foundation for substantive progress in the future.

Promoting democratization, human rights and the rule of law

Rightly or wrongly, the perception in many Asian countries of the United States as the world's pre-eminent 'soft power' has suffered because of the Bush administration's sanction of torture as part of the Global War on Terror and the related perceptions of inconsistency and hypocrisy in the application of American values to authoritarian and non-authoritarian states. Some states, such as Japan, responded positively to the 'values-based initiatives' of the Bush administration by talking, for example, of the merits of promoting an 'arc of freedom and prosperity'[28] in the region; but others, such as Australia, were far more cautious, fearing that placing democratization at the heart of alliance strategy risked alienating China by creating the impression that the West was seeking to devise a new anti-Chinese political containment strategy.[29]

For the Obama administration to adopt a more pragmatic approach to promoting democratic values internationally has much to recommend it in terms of addressing underlying concerns among many in Asia about past US high-handedness, but it also exposes the new President to charges of weakness and inconsistency from his critics at home and more widely in the West. He was accused, for example, of pandering to China for not meeting with the Dalai Lama ahead of his November visit to Beijing and for failing to insist on addressing the Chinese public directly on television during his November visit. Nonetheless, a close look at his public statements during his visit to the region suggests that President Obama did not dilute the message about US values and human rights, but rather presented it in a way that was less overtly antagonistic to some of his Asian hosts.[30]

For example, in meetings both with senior Chinese officials and with students, the President was careful to stress the universal nature of fundamental human rights and his belief that such rights should be available to all. A similarly pragmatic approach was evident in the President's summit with the leaders of the ASEAN ten in Singapore, at which he signalled a shift towards a policy of pragmatic engagement with Myanmar by meeting with Prime Minister Thein Sein – a sharp departure from the Bush administration's uncompromising position of sanctions and rhetorical condemnation, including pushing for regime change and labelling Myanmar 'an outpost of tyranny'.[31]

As a result, ASEAN leaders (with their stress on non-intervention and respect for national sovereignty) and the Obama administration have established more common ground in dealing with Myanmar, albeit still with important differences of emphasis. ASEAN has been willing to stress the need for 'free, fair, inclusive and transparent' elections in 2010, but has been reluctant to speak out publicly on the fate of the prominent Myanmar opposition leader Aung Sang Suu Kyi. By contrast, President Obama has been much more forceful in calling directly for her release from house arrest, while presenting his argument in a context that acknowledges the need for dialogue and discussion even with regimes that fall substantially short of international human rights norms.

More generally, the Obama administration has demonstrated an astute regard for the importance of diplomatic protocol and expressions of respect when interacting with Asian states (for example, the President bowed in his meeting with the Japanese Emperor). Such small but nonetheless important symbolic gestures may rankle with certain sectors of the American media, but they arguably help to mitigate the earlier image of moral certitude and national superiority that at times limited the Bush administration's appeal within the region.

The Obama administration will want to retain the issue of values and democracy promotion as part of its strategic agenda in the region, both to satisfy its own political constituencies at home and to promote constructive change in East Asia, but it will need to do so carefully and in a manner that harmonizes with its other strategic priorities and the interests of its regional partners, both old and new.

Nevertheless, in trying to calibrate the US position between respect for the sovereign prerogatives of authoritarian governments and encouragement for their opening up to more representative forms of political governance, the Obama administration could find itself on the back foot with respect to two of the region's more long-standing democracies. Separatist instability in Thailand and the Philippines is an increasing source of concern. Pro- and anti-government militancy within Thailand has convulsed the Thai political system over the course of the last year, and the operations against Muslim separatist militants in the south of the country have exacerbated the political situation. In the Philippines, the activities of the Moro Islamic Liberation Front (MILF) have precipitated a major humanitarian crisis in Mindanao.

POLICY OPTIONS FOR ADVANCING US STRATEGIC OBJECTIVES

East Asia contains in its expansive geographic spread a range of complex challenges for the Obama administration. Each will require careful consideration over the coming years and a combination of policy focus and flexibility if the United States is to retain its past levels of political influence. Nevertheless, if there is one area where the Obama administration could invest significant effort with prospects for long-term benefit, it would be in helping promote deeper integration among the region's diverse countries and peoples, particularly in the security sphere, where a range of regional collective initiatives could address non-traditional security concerns including maritime security, drug- and human-trafficking, piracy and environmental issues.

In trying to enhance regional cooperation, it might, at first glance, be tempting to seek to launch new organizations or formal arrangements. However, Asia already has a plethora of institutions with multiple, often overlapping and sometimes conflicting roles. The alphabet soup of acronyms is bewildering: APEC, ASEAN, ARF (the ASEAN Regional Forum), ARF plus 3, SAARC (the South Asian Association for Regional Cooperation), the EAS, the Shanghai Cooperation Organization (SCO) and the Six Party Talks (SPT) process on North Korea.

Rather than seeking to supplement these bodies, it would be preferable for the United States to focus first on function rather than form.[32] Historically Southeast Asian nations have been fiercely protective of the concept of sovereignty and hostile to any treaty commitment or form of intervention that might weaken this norm and require them to act collectively in support of general goals. Southeast Asian states have been reluctant, therefore, to support previous US calls for more explicit collective security undertakings. Combating piracy in Southeast Asia, for example, is something that many of the regional players have chosen to view as a local policing initiative rather than as a more ambitious collective undertaking.[33]

Assembling ad hoc groups of states to deal with specific tasks that fall outside existing multilateral regional frameworks is the easiest option, as with the response to the 2004 tsunami, for example. In this regard, the US track-record of assembling and mobilizing local coalitions provides a potentially useful starting point for similar initiatives. This approach has the disadvantage, however, of requiring new coalitions to be formed on each occasion, with the risk that experiences cannot be shared and built upon and that responses will be sub-optimal.[34]

As a means of taking a somewhat more systematic approach to encouraging regional security cooperation, the Obama administration could start by building on the successes of the Bush administration in promoting closer trilateral and quadrilateral cooperation between the United States and Japan, Australia and India, dating from the key agreements of 2007 and 2008 and on existing proto-regional security structures such as the SPT. In this context, the Obama administration could consider reactivating earlier mid-level security dialogues such as the Trilateral Coordination and Oversight Group (TCOG) between Japan, South Korea and the United States. It could build on the apparent success of more global innovations such as the Proliferation Security Initiative (PSI) – which has played a direct role in trying to limit the opportunities for North Korea to proliferate – in order to link regional players in East Asia with other key players. Other fruitful areas for regional security cooperation might include joint peacekeeping activities involving China, Japan, South Korea and the United States. The United States might also look favourably upon new 'minilateral'[35] regional initiatives in which it is not formally involved, such as the December 2008 Fukuoka agreement by the leaders of China, Japan and South Korea to enhance trilateral security and economic cooperation, as well as the follow-up Sino-Japan-Korea trilateral meeting in Beijing in October 2009.

Increasing US support for greater regional integration should not and need not come at the expense of the United States maintaining and strengthening its existing bilateral alliances and also a significant US forward-deployed military presence in East Asia. In this context, security relations with both Japan and the Republic of Korea will need to remain central to US regional strategy, despite the fact that domestic politics in both countries is shifting quite fundamentally in ways that are likely to diminish US influence over their strategic policy decisions.

Despite the underlying strength of the US–Japanese relationship, governmental relations are likely to be difficult over the coming years, given the uncertainty surrounding the outcome of the next Japanese upper house elections, scheduled to take place in July 2010. The Obama administration must also prepare for the handover of joint military command authority to the Republic of Korea in 2012. However, President Lee's activist international agenda offers opportunities for the two countries to cooperate, whether through his new 'Asia Initiative' launched in March 2009 or the existing US–ROK Strategic Cooperation for Alliance Partnership Talks. Bilateral cooperation could also be extended to embrace a wide range of human security initiatives, including the coordinated provision of developmental assistance and support for regional peacekeeping, as well as common environmental goals – an area where the Lee administration's new 'green' agenda offers fruitful scope for cooperation.[36] The Obama administration should work to complete the KORUS FTA and, if it is successful, consider opening similar negotiations with Japan to promote a Japan–US FTA.

A third area of focus for the Obama administration should be the establishment of a more consistently visible presence for US officials in Asian organizations, particularly those in Southeast Asia. By emphasizing the continuing relevance of ASEAN in his November visit to Singapore and by inviting ASEAN's leaders to Washington for a second summit in 2010, President Obama has earned a considerable amount of political goodwill that should stand his administration in good stead in the future. This means that senior US officials should now reinforce the administration's publicly expressed commitment to attend and participate regularly in ASEAN meetings. Having signed the ASEAN Treaty of Amity and Cooperation (TAC), the administration has removed a major obstacle to US participation in EAS meetings too, but it will still be important to continue to look for other concrete opportunities to sustain its presence in the region.

For now, the United States retains a dominant position regionally in terms of its 'soft power'. American educational institutions, especially at the graduate level, continue to attract record numbers of Asian students; American popular culture, film and music continue to have wide appeal globally and within East Asia. However, Asian states are not being laggards in their own efforts to promote their respective cultures – Korean and Chinese cinema and television are attracting growing audiences both regionally and globally, China is investing heavily in its new Confucius Institutes as a means of promoting Chinese culture internationally, and there are indicators that more students within the region, for example from South Korea, are beginning to view China as an attractive destination for tertiary education.[37]

In this context, US leaders should keep in mind that soft power is not an inexhaustible or permanent asset. Careful cultivation and application of its diplomatic, educational and communications resources can help to sustain America's reputation in the region while also helping indirectly to advance specific policy goals. Wider American educational initiatives – particularly those that involve engagement with states with which the US does not currently have formal diplomatic relations (for example the DPRK) – expanded congressional/parliamentary exchanges, technical training programmes on public administration and legal governance, both in the United States and in the region, as well US support for historical reconciliation projects, can all help to alleviate regional tensions while reinforcing US influence in the region.

CONCLUSION

Despite the magnitude of the domestic and international challenges facing the Obama administration, during the past year its emphasis in East Asia on listening and dialogue, coupled with signs of a pragmatic desire to work collectively to address some of the region's and the world's most important challenges, suggests that there is reason to be optimistic about the prospects for a successful and long-term renewal of American influence in this most critical region. Nowhere else in the world will the rise of two of the twenty-first century's new world powers – China and India – be more directly felt. Regular, consistent and direct engagement by Obama administration officials combined with diplomatic flexibility will be needed if the United States is to leverage the goodwill generated in 2009 into meaningful influence for the next three to seven years. While careful attention to America's closest allies in the region will remain important, the Obama administration needs to engage directly in the process of creating a more transparent and predictable institutional security architecture for East Asia, without which the changing balance of economic, political and military power, as well as competition for natural resources, may increase levels of insecurity in the long term.

NOTES

1 Ralph A. Cossa, Brad Glosserman, Michael A. McDevitt, Nirav Patel, James Przystup and Brad Roberts, *The United States and the Asia-Pacific Region: Security Strategy for the Obama Administration* (Honolulu, HI: Pacific Forum CSIS, February 2009), p. 3.

2 Ibid., pp. 12–13.

3 For an extended discussion of this theme, see Michael J. Green, 'The Iraq War and Asia: Assessing the Legacy', *Washington Quarterly* 31(2)(Spring 2008): 181–200.

4 Thomas J. Wright, *Implications of the Financial Crisis for Soft Power in East Asia – Special Report* (Chicago, IL: Chicago Council on Global Affairs, 2009), p. 8.

5 For more on Australia's new proactive approach to regional security in East Asia, see Rory Medcalf, 'Squaring the Triangle: An Australian Perspective on Asian Security Minilateralism', in National Bureau of Asian Research, *Assessing the Trilateral Security Dialogue*, NBR Special Report No. 16 (Seattle, WA: National Bureau of Asian Research, 2008), pp. 23–32.

6 Office of Management and Budget, *A New Era of Responsibility. Renewing America's Promise* (Washington, DC: US Government Printing Office, 2009), p. 35.

7 Brad Glosserman and Carl Baker (eds), *Comparative Connections* 11(1)(2009) (Honolulu, HI: Pacific Forum CSIS), p. 3.

8 Ibid., p. 16.

9 Ibid., p. 37.

10 Ibid., pp. 4 and 26.

11 Ibid., p. 54.

12 Ibid., pp. 17 and 21.

13 Ibid., p. 6.

14 Ibid., p. 32.

15 For a useful discussion of the influence of the US Congress on Obama's Asia policy, see Edward Gresser and Daniel Twining, *Shock of the New: Congress and Asia in 2009*, NBR Analysis (Seattle, WA: National Bureau of Asian Research, February 2009).

16 'Remarks by President Barack Obama at Suntory Hall, November 18, 2009', The White House, Office of the Press Secretary, available online at: http://www.whitehouse.gov/the-press-office/remarks-president-barack-obama-suntory-hall.

17 Leif-Eric Easley, Tetsuo Kotani and Aki Mori, 'Electing a New Japanese Security Policy? Examining Foreign Policy Visions within the Democratic Party of Japan', *Asia Policy* 9 (January 2010): 46; available online at: http://www.nbr.org/publications/asia_policy/AP9/AP9_C_DPJ.pdf.

18 A joint Yomiuri Shinbun-Gallup poll of November 2009 revealed that 48% of Japanese characterize the US–Japan relationship as 'good', almost double the number who view it as 'bad' (some 26%). 'Only 17% say Hatoyama will improve ties with U.S.', *The Daily Yomiuri*, 12 December 2009, p. 3.

19 Telephone interview with senior Japanese Ministry of Foreign Affairs (MOFA) official, 15 September 2009.

20 Cited in Michael Finnegan, *Managing Unmet Expectations in the U.S.-Japan Alliance*, NBR Special Report No. 17 (Seattle, WA: National Bureau of Asian Research, 2009), p. 25.

21 'Asian Growth Losing Steam Fast Amid Global Downturn', IMF Survey Online, 3 February 2009. Available online at: http://www.imf.org/external/pubs/ft/survey/so/2009/CAR020309B.htm.

22 Wright, *Implications of the Financial Crisis*, p. 6 (see note 4 above).

23 Ibid., p. 4.

24 Jackie Calmes, 'Geithner hints at harder line on China Trade', *New York Times*, 22 January 2009. Available online at: http://www.nytimes.com/2009/01/23/business/worldbusiness/23treasury.html.

25 'Aso pledges $67 billion to Asia', *Nikkei Weekly*, 25 May 2009; 'Latest economic package to address credit crunch, job fears,' *Nikkei Weekly*, 15 December 2008, p. 6.

26 'Joint Media Statement. Action Plan to Restore Economic and Financial Stability of the Asian Region', *Report from the Finance Ministers of the ASEAN + 3 to Heads of State/Governments*, Phuket, Thailand, 22 February 2009. Available online at: http://www.aseansec.org/22158.htm.

27 'Copenhagen Accord Faces First Test', *Strategic Comments* 16 (January 2010). Available online at: http://www.iiss.org/publications/strategic-comments/past-issues/volume-16-2010/january/copenhagen-accord-faces-first-test/.

28 The 'arc of freedom and prosperity' concept was first formulated in November 2006 by Taro Aso in his capacity as foreign minister to then Prime Minister Shinzo Abe. For an extended discussion of this idea, see Taro Aso, *Jiyu to Hanei no Ko* (Tokyo: Gentosha, 2007).

29 Aurelia George Mulgan, 'Breaking the Mould: Japan's Subtle Shift from Exclusive Bilateralism to Modest Minilateralism', *Contemporary Southeast Asia* 30(1)(2008): 64.

30 As Obama noted during his visit to Shanghai, 'We do not seek to impose any system of government on any other nation, but we also don't believe that the principles that we stand for are unique to our nation. These freedoms of expression and worship – of access to information and political participation – we believe are universal rights. They should be available to all people, including ethnic and religious minorities – whether they are in the United States, China, or any nation. Indeed, it is that respect for universal rights that guides America's openness to other countries; our respect for different cultures; our commitment to international law; and our faith in the future.' See 'Remarks by President Obama at Town Hall Meeting with Future Chinese Leaders', The White House, Office of the Press Secretary, 16 November 2009. Available online at: http://www.whitehouse.gov/the-press-office/remarks-president-barack-obama-town-hall-meeting-with-future-chinese-leaders.

31 David Steinberg, *Burma/Myanmar: What Everyone Needs to Know* (Oxford: Oxford University Press, 2010), pp. 117–20.

32 For an extended and persuasive discussion of this argument see Evan A. Feigenbaum and Robert A. Manning, *The United States and the New Asia* (Washington, DC: Council on Foreign Relations, 2009), p. 9 and passim.

33 National Institute for Defense Studies, *East Asia Strategic Review, 2009* (Tokyo: National Institute for Defense Studies (NIDS), 2009), pp. 176 and 272; Sheldon Simon, 'The United States, Japan, and Australia: Security Linkages to Southeast Asia', in National Bureau of Asian Research, *Assessing the Trilateral Security Dialogue*, p. 52 (see note 5 above).

34 Feigenbaum and Manning, *The United States and the New Asia*, pp. 14–15.

35 The term 'minilateral' has become increasingly widespread in discussing new regional security initiatives in East Asia and elsewhere. With its focus on developing cooperative policy initiatives involving an intentionally restricted number of national participants,

this approach is in marked contrast to 'multilateral' solutions that are much broader and more inclusive and, therefore, in the view of critics, more inclined to fail. For a discussion of the concept, see Stephen M. Walt, 'On Minilateralism', *Foreign Policy*, 23 June 2009. Available online at: http://walt.foreignpolicy.com/posts/2009/06/23/on_minilateralism.

36 Scott Snyder, *Pursuing a Comprehensive Vision for the U.S–South Korea Alliance* (Washington, DC: Center for Strategic and International Studies, 2009), pp. 2, 7, 29.

37 South Korean interest in China as a provider of tertiary education has increased dramatically in recent years. See Jason Cohen, 'The Dragon Next Door: Republic of Korea–People's Republic of China Relations', in J. J. Suh et al., *SAIS U.S.–Korea Yearbook 2007* (Washington, DC: Johns Hopkins University Press, 2007), p. 141: 'Between 2003 and 2007, the number of South Korean university students studying in China jumped more than 50 per cent, from 36,000 to 54,000. South Koreans now constitute more than one third of the 162,000-plus foreign students in China, outnumbering students from any other single country. Indeed, while the U.S. remains the number one destination for South Korean students, with 70,000 studying there in 2006, China is catching up fast as a preferred study-abroad destination. At the same time, 24,000 Chinese students were enrolled in South Korean schools, making China the largest contributor of foreign students to the ROK.'

5

South Asia: navigating minefields

Gareth Price

INTRODUCTION

South Asia has presented President Barack Obama with his greatest foreign policy challenge. In both Pakistan and Afghanistan he inherited a situation in which the United States was the most important external actor and enjoyed, superficially at least, good government-to-government relations. But he also inherited a substantial amount of historical baggage that makes many in the region suspicious of US motives and intentions.

The biggest problem any American leader would face is an underlying disbelief in any long-term US commitment to the region. Pakistan's economic collapse in the 1990s stemmed partly from mismanagement by a succession of short-lived civilian governments. However, many in Pakistan blame the United States for treating its ally during the 1980s period of opposition to the Soviet occupation of Afghanistan almost as a pariah state on account of its nuclear programme (of which many believe the US was aware) as soon as the Soviet Union withdrew and Pakistan's strategic importance declined. The subsequent drying up of US financial inflows that had kept the country afloat during the 1980s left a strong and lasting impression of US short-termism in Pakistan. Doubts over America's motivations also stem from its willingness to radicalize Afghanistan and Pakistan's tribal belt during the 1980s in order to undermine the Soviet occupation. In the early 1980s USAID funded the University of Nebraska-Omaha to produce millions of textbooks 'filled with violent images and militant Islamic teachings, part of covert attempts to spur resistance to the Soviet occupation'.[1] To most in the West, such Cold War stories seem to belong to the distant past. But memories (and textbooks) last longer in South Asia.

Consequently, political elites in Pakistan are polite to their US counterparts, thankful when they provide financial support, but doubtful that the good times (whether as in the 1980s or as in this post-9/11 period) will necessarily last. And the 'masses' are simply suspicious. Short-termism has bred short-termism: during the good times, Pakistan's economy improved, but huge sums were simply co-opted by elites. Under President George W. Bush, there seems to have been little if any accountability in the assistance provided to Pakistan's military. Here

89

was a situation that could not continue indefinitely – increasing inequality and visible corruption were working to strengthen the Islamist opposition, not the government, creating instability rather than stability. Yet when President Obama came to recalibrate US policy towards Pakistan it inevitably stirred up animosity among much-needed allies.

An even greater challenge presented itself in Afghanistan. As Obama took office, it was clear that the conflict with the Taliban had reached a stalemate. No obvious solution presented itself and whatever strategy was followed bore the risk of failure. The Taliban were slowly consolidating power in rural Afghanistan, the poor security situation made it difficult for the Afghan government to operate in large parts of the country and there were not enough foreign troops to reverse these trends. With questions looming about whether foreign troops were part of the solution or the problem, President Obama launched a major strategic review of policy towards Afghanistan.

In contrast, with India the Obama administration inherited a rapidly improving relationship. India's middle class consistently expresses admiration for the United States, and the previous two administrations had worked to 'de-hyphenate' India from Pakistan. The Bush administration's decision to strike a deal with India on supporting its civilian nuclear programme was the most definitive signal of the shift in US policy.[2] Rather than seeing South Asia as a zero-sum region of 'Indo-Pakistan conflict', the United States had attempted to improve bilateral relations with India while maintaining a close relationship with Pakistan.

This policy was driven by growing trade links with India, by the growing political influence of the Indian diaspora in the United States and the perception that India (along with Japan and Australia) can become a key buffer against the rise of Chinese influence in Asia. This has manifested itself in an acceptance of India's dominant position within South Asia, with the United States happy to follow India's lead in terms of policy towards the smaller countries in the sub-region.

But President Obama came to power just weeks after the terrorist attacks of November 2008 in Mumbai that left almost 200 people dead and India's relations with Pakistan at their lowest ebb since 2002. This highlighted the difficulty of maintaining the strategy of de-hyphenation at times of heightened tension between India and Pakistan, given the overriding need for a continued good relationship with the latter.

Many in India were already sceptical about the notion of de-hyphenation. Instead, they felt that for the first time the United States was taking India seriously. It was not, they would argue, that India was hyphenated to Pakistan; it was that Pakistan was America's Cold War ally and India was, to all intents and purposes, sidelined. Such concerns were highlighted by the admission that the majority of US military assistance to Pakistan following 9/11 was used not to undertake military operations against Taliban-linked groups in Pakistan, but to buy armaments intended for war against India.[3] As President Obama noted during a press conference during the official state visit of Indian Prime Minister

Manmohan Singh to Washington in November 2009, 'There have probably been times in the past in which we were so single-mindedly focused just on military assistance in Pakistan that we didn't think more broadly about how to encourage and develop ... civil society in Pakistan.'[4]

That this was the case was already well known in India. Calling on the United States to monitor properly its assistance to Pakistan, India's Minister of State for External Affairs, Shashi Tharoor, earlier commented, 'We support countries helping Pakistan fighting against terrorism, but we do not expect the aid turned against us.'[5]

While US relations with India remained generally solid in the first year of the Obama administration, there have been teething troubles. India was initially offended by the inclusion of Kashmir, along with Afghanistan and Pakistan, in the US conception of the theatre of war against radical Islamist groups. The American strategy later morphed into what the US Special Representative to the region, Ambassador Richard Holbrooke, frequently termed as 'Af-Pak'.[6] These teething problems were then exacerbated by the Obama administration's early prioritization of its strategic relationship with China, particularly given that Sino-Indian relations deteriorated (as a result of renewed Chinese territorial claims) during 2009.

DE-HYPHENATION AND RE-HYPHENATION

To the extent that the United States has constructed a theoretical prism through which it conducts policy towards South Asia in recent years, it has been one of de-hyphenation. The notion of de-hyphenating US policy towards India from that towards Pakistan was successful in the early 2000s in building up US links with India, specifically. Economic links grew rapidly, as two-way trade – just $5 billion in 1990 – reached $14 billion in 2000 and rose to nearly $50 billion in 2008,[7] and the United States gave far greater prominence to its relations with Indian politicians. Yet the ensuing US focus on bilateral relationships in South Asia appeared to conceal key linkages within the region from the eyes of US policy-makers. This was most obvious in the time it took the Bush administration to appreciate the extent of the linkages between developments in Pakistan and Afghanistan after 2001.

Moreover, de-hyphenation only worked when relations between India and Pakistan were relatively calm. Even then, many in India doubted the extent to which India had truly been 'de-linked' from Pakistan, given how Pakistan used US military assistance. As the Council on Foreign Relations noted:

> In June 2008, the US government reported that nearly $11 billion in military and economic assistance grants have been delivered since 2002, the vast majority channeled through Pakistan's military for security-related programs. A report by the Center for Public Integrity finds that in the three years after 9/11, military aid to Pakistan from the Coalition Support Fund – created after the attacks to assist US allies in the global fight against terrorism – was nearly $3 billion, ten

times the amount received by Poland, the second-highest recipient of cash from the fund. Pakistan has used the money to purchase helicopters, F-16s, aircraft-mounted armaments, and anti-ship and antimissile defense systems – weapons that Indian officials and others have deemed of questionable relevance to the counterterrorism mission.[8]

While cooperation between India and Pakistan in the aftermath of the November 2008 terrorist attacks in Mumbai has been relatively good, and there have been no significant further Islamist attacks in India since then, India remains acutely sensitive to the ambivalent Pakistani attitudes to the violent Islamists on it soil, notably its failure to prosecute those linked to Lashkar-e-Toiba, responsible for the Mumbai attacks. One further major attack could rapidly scupper relations with Pakistan.

For its part, in the past Pakistan had demanded US and Indian support for a solution to the dispute over Kashmir, arguing that, once this occurred, improved bilateral relations would follow swiftly. India, conversely, suggested that confidence-building measures should be introduced first, to create a more conducive environment for resolving the Kashmir dispute. Since 2002, India and Pakistan have started a 'composite dialogue', attempting to address a range of confidence-building measures and the status of Kashmir simultaneously. While this enabled some progress on the confidence-building measures, unsurprisingly the issue of Kashmir remains unresolved. Pakistan halted progress on the other measures because of the lack of movement over Kashmir, refusing to grant India most-favoured nation trading status in 2007, for instance.[9] And, following the Mumbai attacks, India has also stalled the process.

For now, positive US relations with the two countries have been helped by India's reluctance to undermine the new civilian government in Pakistan. But bilateral relations between India and Pakistan remain poor and vulnerable. At the heart of the problem lies the Pakistani government's need to maintain the support of the military. On the one hand, the military is the main tool with which Islamabad is fighting Islamist militancy. But appeasing the military (by, for instance, releasing Pakistan's disgraced nuclear scientist, A. Q. Khan, from house arrest in February 2009) brings Pakistan into conflict with both India and the United States. President Obama may find that conducting relations with the countries of South Asia continues to be more zero-sum than win-win.

PAKISTAN MOVES UP THE AGENDA

Throughout 2009, the parlous security situation in Pakistan deteriorated further, raising the spectre of the emergence of a failed, but nuclear-armed, state. This instability was not just dangerous in itself, but directly threatened the US capacity to act in Afghanistan; already, the vast majority of NATO supplies traverse Pakistan's tribal districts on their way to Afghanistan. Pakistani military operations to keep the supply lines open often appeared to be designed to demonstrate Pakistan's continued tactical importance to the United States rather than to tackle militancy in these areas in a sustainable and successful manner.

That President George W. Bush put too much weight on a personal relationship with General Musharraf is clear.[10] President Obama's administration stressed that, in contrast to its predecessor, it would work to deal more with institutions rather than individuals in its foreign policy as a whole. This shift was perhaps made easier in Pakistan by the fact that neither of its two dominant political figures – Asif Ali Zardari and Nawaz Sharif – is a particularly attractive ally for the United States. Yet finding the correct institutions with which to deal is easier said than done and the recognition of the limitations of past strategy does not necessarily mean that a better strategy presents itself for the future.

The recent US acceptance that Pakistan's active cooperation is essential to ensuring security in Afghanistan, coupled with the upsurge of violence within Pakistan itself, has pushed relations with Pakistan to the top of the American policy agenda. However, the limitations of President Obama's leverage as America seeks to deepen its engagement with Pakistan were revealed by an Al Jazeera-Gallup opinion poll in July 2009. When asked the question 'Some people believe that the (Pakistan) Taliban are the greatest threat to the country, some believe India is the greatest threat, whereas some believe US is the greatest threat. Who do you think is the greatest threat for Pakistan?', only 11 per cent answered the Pakistan Taliban. Instead, 18 per cent suggested India and 59 per cent the United States.[11] Equally problematically, Pakistan faces three distinct but interrelated internal threats or challenges, none of which can be solved in isolation and each of which will make the US strategy all the more difficult.

The first concerns the growing threat from the 'Pakistan Taliban', relevant to the United States because of the hospitality it shows to foreign fighters and to the leadership of al-Qaeda. Bomb blasts and brazen suicide attacks grew in frequency during 2009. The attack on the army headquarters in Rawalpindi in October 2009 was only the most audacious in a string of attacks that have killed hundreds, with at least 300 dead in that month alone. At the same time, the Pakistan Taliban remain in control of about six out of seven districts in the tribal areas[12] and appear increasingly aligned to various Islamist militant groups based in southern Punjab.

After initially ceding control of Swat to the militants, Pakistan eventually adopted a military approach which appears to have placed the Pakistan Taliban on the back foot, both in Swat and in Waziristan. The extent to which Pakistan's shift away from making peace deals towards a more kinetic approach stemmed from US criticism, from a realization within Pakistan that the state itself was at risk or from a desire, and need, for financial assistance, is unclear. What is clear is that military action against the Pakistan Taliban leads for the foreseeable future to yet more bomb blasts and suicide attacks elsewhere in the country.

Pakistan's second challenge is its economic crisis. Insufficient power supplies, insecurity and competition from China, in particular, since the ending of the multi-fibre agreement, have devastated Pakistan's textile industry, which provides more than half of the country's foreign exchange receipts.[13] In 2008 unemployment in Pakistan stood at 13.6 per cent, over double the previous year's rate,[14] and some observers place job losses in the textile sector alone in the hundreds of thousands.[15]

Rising economic assistance from abroad will struggle to counter the continued slump in exports[16] and capital flight, thought to average around $2–3 billion annually, as more affluent Pakistanis transfer their financial assets to more secure environments. One of the few features that sustain the economy is that the worse things get at home, the more Pakistanis move abroad for work. Remittances from Pakistanis living overseas have grown significantly in recent years, propping up the economy. They reached record highs during the second half of 2009, standing at $758.3 million in October alone as workers sent more money home from the United Arab Emirates, United States and Saudi Arabia.[17] While this can be seen as an economic success story, it equally reflects the failure of Pakistan's domestic economy to support its population.

Pakistan's third challenge is the fragility of its civilian government. The threat of a military coup hangs over it and were a general election held early in 2010 the current Pakistan People's Party (PPP) government would probably be ousted by the main opposition Pakistan Muslim League (Nawaz) (PML(N)). Consequently, the PPP government is focusing on constitutional mechanisms and traditional patronage politics as a means to perpetuate its rule, trying to entrench and enrich itself in the process, rather than on implementing policies to meet the more fundamental challenges that Pakistan faces.

The US administration has continued its long-standing, and generally unsuccessful, attempts to influence Pakistan's domestic political affairs.[18] In May 2009 officials said they had been reaching out to Nawaz Sharif, in the hope that he could work with President Zardari, despite a history of animosity between the two. The hope that a different leader or combination of leaders would work better seems misplaced. Islamabad has been dominated by a similar set of political groupings and machinations (unlinked to the lives of ordinary people elsewhere in Pakistan) for decades, and it seems hard to envisage that an alternative ruler is likely to do anything differently. The history of military coups in Pakistan makes every civilian ruler nervous and forces a focus on the short term. Breaking this cycle will take time, rather than any policy change from abroad.

This disconnection between politicians and people is a major concern, and is reflected in Pakistani concerns about the state of the economy and corruption. It is obvious, and understandable, why the United States sees Pakistan through a security prism. But security remains just one challenge for most Pakistanis as security is linked to more mundane issues such as their economic livelihoods, which in turn relate to overall questions about governance. A survey in late 2007 conducted by the International Republican Institute (IRI) asked Pakistanis what issues would determine their voting intention in the general election. Six per cent of respondents mentioned terrorism, 15 per cent unemployment and 53 per cent inflation. During 2008 the security situation deteriorated, yet when the same organization asked, in March 2009, what respondents saw as the most important issue facing Pakistan, the results were remarkably similar: 46 per cent cited inflation, 22 per cent unemployment and just 10 per cent terrorism.[19]

In the light of these three threats, many of the policies that the Obama administration has adopted in the past year appear sensible. Financial assistance is, in the short term at least, the best method of shoring up the economy. But much of the aid the United States gave to Pakistan following 9/11 disappeared without achieving any long-term impact.[20] Thus, the Obama administration decided to link future assistance to specific conditions. Conditionality and monitoring will be vital adjuncts to future US aid to Pakistan, not just in developmental terms. In the past, inflows of assistance have been squandered by Pakistan's leadership, either creating asset bubbles, notably in property, or simply lining people's pockets. As in Afghanistan, radical groups draw support through attacks on government corruption; by inadvertently feeding that corruption, the United States has undermined support for the government – not the Islamists.

Recognizing this dynamic, the Enhanced Partnership with Pakistan Act of 2009 (or Kerry-Lugar-Berman Act), signed by President Obama in October 2009, offers Pakistan $1.5 billion per year in economic assistance provided that the regime works to prevent nuclear proliferation and acts against terrorism, and that the military does not interfere in the political process. The deal was championed by the Zardari government, but the imposition of conditions was taken both by the military (for self-interested reasons as much as any other) and by the PML (N) to be a violation of Pakistan's sovereignty. A columnist in the *Pakistan Observer* spoke for many by arguing:

The secretary of state asserted that the legislation doesn't in any way interfere in Pakistan's internal affairs or erode its sovereignty. The reality, however, is that the Pakistani–US partnership has for decades been a conspiracy against the Pakistani people, in which Washington has used the Pakistani political and military leadership as linchpin of America's strategic designs in the Middle East, Central and South Asia.[21]

A recognition that 59 per cent of Pakistanis see the United States as the greatest threat to the country should be a vital, if depressing, starting point in US policy-making to Pakistan. The Kerry-Lugar-Berman Act puts into perspective several challenges faced by the West in dealing with Pakistan. Without continuous assistance, the country would rapidly default, causing further economic and political crisis. But Pakistan's civilian and military elite has come to expect continued disbursements, free from any conditions. While American lawmakers pointed out that Pakistan was under no obligation to accept the funding, Pakistani elites still railed against the infringement of sovereignty, and its military pointed out, not incorrectly, that Pakistan's army has lost many more soldiers, perhaps around 2,000, in the fight against Islamist groups than the United States and its allies in Afghanistan.

The focus on greater accountability in the use of assistance, and on targeting assistance at economic development rather than the military, puts in place a pattern which, if sustained in the long term, could begin to alter perceptions of US policy. But the starting point is low, and it is debatable whether focusing energy and US funds in those areas where there is most resentment towards the United States and its policies and which are the most insecure will be an effective approach. It may not make sense, therefore, for the United States to focus its efforts in Pakistan on initiating development projects in the tribal areas, to which few if any of its staff can travel. Just as the International Monetary Fund faces a challenge overseeing the accountability of the Pakistani government from meetings it holds with its officials in the Gulf, additional US development spending in the tribal areas is likely to be misspent without on-the-ground oversight. And were the United States to announce the establishment of 'Reconstruction Opportunity Zones' in the tribal areas, and in neighbouring districts of Afghanistan (as the Afghanistan and Pakistan Reconstruction Opportunity Zones Act of 2009 proposes), this would imply that much of the security problem had disappeared. These strategies might make sense in a post-conflict environment, but neither the tribal areas of Pakistan nor Afghanistan are yet in that state.

As in Afghanistan, it would have been encouraging to have seen a debate on whether development assistance is best spent on those areas where security is greater and more can be achieved, or on those areas where insecurity is greatest. In Afghanistan, the concentration of development assistance on the South had two negative impacts. First, it alienated many in the North who wondered whether they would receive greater attention if they were to take up arms. Second, because of the difficulties and high cost of carrying out development activity in the South, opportunities for misappropriation of funds were greater. Many Afghans see the current military intervention to be a means for the West to exploit them, and feel more alienated than placated by claims of assistance that appear to be intangible.

In retrospect, it might have been wiser to concentrate assistance in the north of Afghanistan and wait for positive messages to drift into the South. While this could have risked intensifying a Pashtun sense of victimization, it might at least have produced some results. If assistance to Pakistan is concentrated on the tribal areas, this same pattern could be replicated. Shoring up the more secure heartland of Pakistan – Punjab and Sindh – is a strategy at least deserving of greater US assessment.

Another aspect of US policy towards the tribal areas during the Obama administration's first year that would benefit from careful review is the increased use of unmanned aerial vehicles, or drones, targeting al-Qaeda or Taliban militants in the tribal areas. There may well be a strong military and counter-terrorism case for such attacks, but the downside for US policy in Pakistan is huge. It is not simply that the death of civilians as the collateral victims of such attacks adds another wider familial group to those willing to take up arms against the United States. Preserving the territorial integrity of Pakistan is also considered paramount to most Pakistanis, who have been brought up in permanent fear of Indian aggression. In the March 2009 IRI poll, 72 per cent of those surveyed opposed US military incursions into the tribal areas. The drone attacks reinforce underlying distrust of American motives which then permeates into attitudes to more positive US policy shifts towards Pakistan.

This puts the United States' Pakistani interlocutors in a very difficult position, forcing them to use double-speak with their population about the strength of the bilateral relationship. Criticizing the United States in public but supporting it in private makes the wider Pakistani population distrustful of their leaders, and in turn creates a situation in which the 'narrative' provided by radical Islam makes more sense than that provided by their leadership. While President Zardari and Pakistan's Chief of Army Staff, General Ashfaq Parvez Kayani, may genuinely want to halt the spread of militancy across the region, they are aware that they have to present themselves as more distant from the United States than did General Musharraf, whose alliance with that country alienated him from both extremists and moderates.

In turn, successive governments in Pakistan have sought to limit their reliance on the United States (not least because of the belief that US support may be transitory). Thus Pakistan is studiously attempting to diversify its sources of external political and economic support. Its links with the Gulf states are long-standing. Following the US imposition of sanctions through the 1990s, Saudi Arabia stepped in with its Saudi Oil Facility, later converted to a cash grant. Individuals from the Gulf have also provided funding for the plethora of madrassas that have emerged, notably in the Northwest Frontier Provinces. And Pakistan's most enduring ally remains China; Chinese funding of the construction of the blue-water port at Gwadar leading out to the Arabian Sea is the most notable example of the close relationship which works to dilute US leverage over Pakistan in the longer term.

BUILDING ON THE LEGACY OF THE NUCLEAR DEAL

President George W. Bush was held in relatively high regard in India, not least because of the bilateral agreement on civil nuclear cooperation. However, the country has yet to fully embrace President Barack Obama. While the general trend of closer cooperation between the United States and India has continued, a number of specific challenges have arisen in the bilateral relationship.

First, and potentially most damaging, has been the seeming priority that the Obama administration has given to its relations with China, especially in the wake of the global economic crisis that turned China into the world's market 'of last resort'. Fear of Chinese expansion into the Indian Ocean – into Burma, Sri Lanka and Bangladesh, as well as Pakistan – has grown in Indian policy consciousness in recent years.

India's relations with China deteriorated during 2009, and the Indian media have been ferocious in their criticism of China's strategy towards the disputed Indian state of Arunachal Pradesh that is adjacent to Tibet. These concerns intensified following the publication of an article in China entitled 'China can Dismember the So-called Indian Union with One Little Move',[22] and other unofficial Chinese statements which accompanied the Dalai Lama's visit to the state in November 2009.

Arunachal Pradesh may appear remote, but this small state in northeastern India may yet affect the dynamics of US relations with China and India. President Obama faced some criticism in the United States for failing to meet the Dalai Lama in October 2009, ahead of his own visit to China in November. Conservative opponents claimed it was a sign of weakness. But some Indian observers have also suggested that the United States is veering towards a policy of neutrality on Arunachal Pradesh. India's concerns about the sanctity of its borders were revealed in relation to Kashmir. That same sensitivity relates to Arunachal Pradesh.[23]

Under President Bush, the United States and India had held talks about conducting searches for the bodies of US airmen lost in Arunachal Pradesh during the Second World War. Progress in these talks appears to have slowed since the new administration took power. For the United States, either India or China will have to be offended in relation to Arunachal Pradesh, and, at present, it appears to be India that is taking offence.

Such concerns also undermine attempts to bring India into a semi-formal relationship, along with Japan and Australia, as key buffers against US perceptions of Chinese expansionism. While there is little support within India for a formal alliance with the United States, President Obama's language during Prime Minister Manmohan Singh's state visit to the United States in November 2009 was positive: his call for a 'global strategic partnership' and his acknowledgment of 'shared values' (in unstated contrast to those of China) went down better in India than might have been expected.[24]

Second, India was quick to criticize apparently protectionist measures built into President Obama's 2009 economic stimulus package, fearing that increasing numbers of skilled Indian workers would fail to get visas to work in the United States and that India's IT industry, much of which works on office functions outsourced from America firms, would suffer. While these concerns have dissipated somewhat, they dampened expectations at the very start of the Obama administration.

Third, regardless of President Obama's victory, American legislators have become more concerned about the lack of religious tolerance within India in recent years. The Chief Minister of Gujarat, Narendra Modi, has been barred from entering the United States because of alleged complicity in a pogrom against Muslims in 2002. In August 2009, the US Commission on International Religious Freedom, a bipartisan advisory panel, placed India on its watch-list, citing violence against Christians in Orissa and against Muslims in Gujarat. In October 2009, 21 American legislators wrote to the Chief Minister of Orissa calling on him to do more to prosecute those responsible for the deaths of more than 100 Christians in riots in 2008. India condemned the suggestion that its independent judiciary and media would not challenge and investigate any threat to the country's official secularism.

Fourth, even before President Obama was formally inaugurated, India's concerns grew that US policy would 're-hyphenate' India to Pakistan, and indeed to Afghanistan as rumours spread that Richard Holbrooke, with his reputation for aggressive crisis management, was to become the US special envoy to South Asia.

While the dispute in Kashmir is clearly connected to radical Islamist movements in Pakistan and Afghanistan, Indian sensitivity to the internationalization of Kashmir is well known. And although the Obama administration quickly adjusted its position and made Holbrooke its envoy to Afghanistan and Pakistan only, damage had already been done within India.

Despite these upsets, the general functioning of the US–Indian relationship remains sound: Secretary of State Hillary Clinton has described India as a global partner for the United States, and the first state visit to Washington of the Obama presidency was made by Prime Minister Singh in November 2009, relatively soon after his re-election.

Most substantively, the key drivers behind the rapprochement between India and the United States remain in place. The greatest asset of the United States in engaging with India (compared with the EU in particular) is that its model of development is more easily understood among elites in India than, for instance, the focus on human security that has characterized much of the EU's discourse with India. This has been reinforced by extensive US–India business links, built mainly around the outsourcing of various back-office functions, most notably IT, to Indian firms.

The linkages have been further strengthened in recent years as Indians have found it more attractive to study in the United States than (as in the past) in the United Kingdom. These 'people-to-people' linkages are a significant asset to the United States in dealing with India. The Indian diaspora in the United States is almost three million strong, and is the wealthiest single ethnic community. Until the last decade, apart from remittances to family members who remained in the home country, the diaspora in the United States was somewhat cut off from India itself. Rising economic opportunities within India, however, have changed the picture. Many US-educated Indians are now returning to India, taking business practices learnt in the United States back with them.

Partly as a result, concerns about possible American protectionism early in the Obama administration appear to have dissipated. Business support in the United States for outsourcing, coupled with the strength of the India caucus in Congress, seem to have limited any potential hindrances to Indian firms. The American strategy of engaging with a range of Indian professionals (rather than with a few super-rich oligarchs or self-appointed 'community leaders', as has been the case in the United Kingdom) appears to have paid dividends.

The 2009 Pew Global Attitudes poll suggests that 76 per cent of Indians had a favourable opinion of the United States. While the polling is biased towards urban Indians, this goodwill felt towards the United States among India's middle class is a powerful tool for the Obama administration, and one which is unlikely to fluctuate dramatically despite the not insubstantial hiccups in the political relationship described above.

Underlying this goodwill is the US–India nuclear deal, which for many Indians has demonstrated that the United States is more astute than the EU in focusing on its own and its partners' main strategic interests. The Obama administration has remained committed to the landmark agreement, despite internal and external opposition, and has argued that it contains sufficient safeguards even though India has not signed the Nuclear Non-Proliferation Treaty.

In October 2009, the United States and India held their biggest-ever joint war-games exercise. Whatever the recent tensions in the two countries' bilateral relations, they share a strategic concern about the rise of China, while India continues to seek US support to force Pakistan to take more steps to tackle militants operating in Kashmir and India itself. In turn, as the United States has begun to examine the regional dynamics in Afghanistan, it has recognized that rivalry between India and Pakistan in Afghanistan threatens its own stabilization efforts in that country.

While there are widespread and strengthening commercial links between the United States and India, therefore, the bilateral relationship has taken on more of a politico-military hue since the signing of the nuclear deal in 2008. In July 2009, for example, the two countries struck a deal allowing American companies to enter India's defence market. The subsequent war games provided an opportunity for these companies to showcase their wares.

The other driver of increased cooperation is that India clearly wants to be seen as a global player: as an investor in other countries and as a donor rather than a recipient of aid. Its improving economic position has given it a confidence and self-assuredness in global forums that had previously been lacking. Thus far, much of this has focused on trying to gain the facets of a global power – nuclear weapons, a space programme and a permanent seat on the UN Security Council. But Indian ambitions are in flux, and the United States can use the experience of the nuclear dialogue to engage with India on other issues of common concern.

Seeking support for a changing US policy towards Burma fits within this context. With Burma, as with North Korea and Iran, the United States has moved from isolation towards engagement. The United States has also recognized that it is not the prime actor in relation to Burma; dialogues with India, as with ASEAN (the Association of South-East Asian Nations) and China, are necessary in an attempt to effect change.

The civil nuclear deal was the first in-depth US–Indian political interaction. The United States should have noted that India's political system is slow and, at times, appears to act against its better interests as it tries to gain support from as many constituencies as possible. India is a democracy, and opposition parties, of whatever hue, will attack the government for any perceived diminution of sovereignty. This should serve to emphasize the need to maintain the diverse interactions that currently reflect relations between the two countries: India's slow-moving political class should not be the only point of interaction.

But this caveat aside, the nuclear deal should have demonstrated to the US government that, if it is patient, agile and determined, it can achieve results in partnership with India. The process by which the nuclear deal was resolved should be used to set a benchmark for future cooperation in other areas and issues – whether Burma, Afghanistan, UN reform or climate change.

With forethought, the challenges that India will present to the United States should not be insurmountable. India's politicians often seek electoral support at the level of the lowest (and most populist) common denominator. But, when in power, they act in the interests of India's businesses and its growing middle class, all of which want to strengthen ties with the United States. If the United States can apply the positive lessons from the nuclear deal to other areas, more constructive engagements may result.

Having largely ignored India throughout the Cold War in favour of military-dominated Pakistan, the United States should accept the fact that it is still the object of a persistent underlying suspicion in India. It also needs to accept that, although India is clearly flattered by the greater US attention it now receives, it is not currently willing to move towards becoming a fully-fledged ally of the United States or of the 'West'. Its policy towards China, for example, is nuanced and while many in India are concerned about the future dynamic of Sino-Indian relations, most hope to balance expanding trade links with China against their ongoing strategic concerns.

India's approaches towards other challenges of common interest will continue to be driven by pragmatic concerns about its national interests rather than by the desire to conform to the norms of a US-led, Western democratic club. When these interests diverge, an increasingly assertive India is unlikely to acquiesce to American wishes. But, one year into the Obama administration, there are more synergies than rivalries between the two countries.

THE BIGGEST CHALLENGE: AFGHANISTAN

Afghanistan is where the interests of India, Pakistan and the United States diverge, and it is also President Obama's most urgent foreign policy challenge. While there has been valid criticism of the time taken by the administration during its first year to complete its various reviews of US strategy towards Afghanistan, some of the implicit conclusions drawn demonstrate a better understanding of the complexities of the country and the limitations of US leverage despite the numbers of American troops present within it.

As with India and Pakistan, however well-intentioned current US policy may be, history for Afghans did not begin on 9/11. That event merely marked the latest stage in a civil war that had already run for two decades. And while most Afghans were pleased to see the departure of the Taliban, they remained cognizant of prior US support for the anti-Soviet mujahideen, parts of which subsequently morphed into the Taliban.

More concerning, however, was that few had seen the fruits of the claimed investment in Afghanistan from the West since the toppling of the Taliban. Distrust of both the Afghan government and the motives of the West had increased substantially in the subsequent seven years. After 30 years of conflict, most Afghans had grown accustomed to sitting on the fence. This failure to back the government in turn makes the reconstruction effort harder.

Two central conclusions have evolved from the strategy review. The first is that the primary actor in Afghanistan is not the US-led military force. Instead, the success of the mission to stabilize Afghanistan will stem from the impact and effectiveness of the government. This observation brought into greater focus the importance of the legitimacy of the presidential election process, and the pervasive impact of corruption. The latter did not just hinder attempts at development, but played directly into the rhetoric of the Taliban whose religious message, such as it is, focuses on the need to create some form of 'pure' and incorrupt society.

The second conclusion relates to the possible role of Afghanistan's neighbours in the conflict. However, as Afghanistan's neighbours primarily focus on their own divergent and mutually exclusive interpretations of national interest, the difficulties of such an approach are immense. Any 'regional solution' would have to surmount the challenge of forcing India and Pakistan to forge a common position on Afghanistan. The likelihood of this is close to non-existent.

America's recognition of the obstacles it faces in Afghanistan and of the need to win Afghan hearts and minds is positive, but it leaves some fundamental questions unanswered. Many Afghans have a trust deficit towards both their government and the Western forces, stemming from what they perceive as broken promises. Whether this trust can be regained is uncertain. Moreover noting, for instance, that there is widespread corruption in Afghanistan is not the same as preventing it.

The Taliban have been quick to exploit any disconnection between Western policy and practice. Following Barack Obama's appointment of Gen. Stanley McChrystal as the Commander of United States Forces in Afghanistan,[25] the US military has stressed the need to avoid civilian casualties; yet the more it claims to be avoiding accidental civilian deaths, the more forceful is the Taliban's claim of hypocrisy whenever civilian casualties do occur. The greater the number of Western troops sent to Afghanistan, the greater will be the likelihood that civilian casualties will continue, if not increase. The need to avoid civilian casualties has been noted frequently in the past few years. But avoiding civilian casualties in a climate of tribally motivated misinformation is easier said than done, particularly given Western governments' desire to minimize casualties among their troops.

The Taliban have also grown increasingly sophisticated. Whereas the threat in Pakistan is from terrorist-style bomb attacks, in Afghanistan the Taliban are reported to have produced a handbook for their soldiers aimed at not alienating local populations. As the conflict has continued, the Taliban have been able to tap into Afghan nationalism, particularly among the Pashtun population, and they have a range of tools – such as suicide bombers – with which they are trying to drive a wedge between foreign troops and the local population. It is imperative that the US-led coalition appears to be on the side of Afghans, and not an occupying force, but with public opinion turning against the conflict in both the United States and Europe, this will provide yet another challenge for President Obama.

Even without sophisticated Taliban propaganda, many Afghans now simply disbelieve claims made by the West. In more secure parts of the country many of the minority groups – Tajiks, Uzbeks and Hazaras – question why they have not benefited from the aid that has been pumped into Afghanistan. In the less secure, predominantly Pashtun areas, Pashtun nationalism is growing, a trend not assisted by the American notion of an 'Af-Pak' strategy. In this context, though expediting the development of the Afghan National Army (ANA) makes sense, the process adds a further complication if the army increasingly appears to be one of Tajiks and Uzbeks, rather than a truly 'national' army.

TO TALK OR NOT TO TALK?

The shift in the United States towards an acceptance of the likelihood of talks with 'moderate' Taliban appears profound and clearly reflects a more pragmatic approach that will frustrate proponents of improved women's rights and other core tenets of a more tolerant and democratic Afghanistan. But it also implies a strategy that may become a means of enabling an early exit by US and other Western forces.

A number of questions arise from this policy shift, the answers to which are likely to emerge in 2010–11. First, does the notion of 'moderate Taliban' make sense? A temporary shift in allegiance to the Kabul government by local-level commanders who are then ready to transfer allegiance back to the Taliban hardliners as soon as foreign troops have left would make little sense.

Second, is there any likelihood that the Taliban leadership, the so-called Quetta Shura, would consider holding talks? At present, the answer appears to be no. But, should a surge in foreign troops and increased ANA activity put it on the back foot, its interest in talks may well increase.

Third, the absolute minimum for any Western compromise with the Taliban would have to be their agreement to oust foreign fighters from Afghanistan. On this issue the evidence from Pakistan is not positive. There, successive governments signed a range of peace deals with Islamist groups in the tribal areas. Yet each deal collapsed as those groups involved in ceasefires would allow their territory to be used by groups from areas where ceasefires were not in force.

Many Pakistanis would argue that their cultural awareness of the tribal areas makes Pakistan better suited than the United States to tackle the problem of dealing with the demands of radical groups. The government in Pakistan would clearly prefer to negotiate with radical groups, believing that greater use of force leads to greater alienation. The IRI survey in March 2009 suggested that 72 per cent of Pakistanis supported a peace deal with the extremists. Since then, the greatest factor galvanizing Pakistani public opinion against the Taliban was their brief but memorable period of misrule in Swat which triggered the military campaign against them first in Swat and subsequently in South Waziristan. The shift in Pakistani policy stemmed less from US pressure than from an acceptance that the groups were so well entrenched that a military solution was inevitable.

Should Pakistan's military gain the upper hand, it is likely to press the government to shift back towards a policy of talks with militants. Pakistan's military has been quick to deny rumours of mutinies among troops refusing to fight fellow Pakistanis, but it is clear that the Pakistan military sees fighting against its own citizens as a last resort.

If the United States allows the Afghan government to talk to 'moderate elements' in the Taliban, many in Pakistan will claim that the United States has simply adopted its own long-standing policy. Despite clear differences between the Afghan Taliban and the range of groups that comprise the Pakistan Taliban, unless there is a shared strategy on both sides of the Durand Line (the *de facto* border between Afghanistan and Pakistan), it is unlikely to be successful. Past crackdowns in one area of Pakistan and Afghanistan have simply forced militants to relocate to safer havens. Pakistan has undertaken military action in the tribal areas, and simply shifted the centre of insurgency, and the military action by ISAF (the International Security Assistance Force) in Helmand province has led to rising militant activity elsewhere in Afghanistan.

RECOMMENDATIONS FOR FUTURE US ENGAGEMENT

Recognition of the limitations of US leverage – and of the limitations of US allies, whether Western partners in Afghanistan or the governments of Afghanistan and Pakistan – may appear a sign of weakness. But a more honest assessment of the starting point shows the way towards a more effective and realistic policy. In Pakistan and Afghanistan the most important actor is the national government. Without the active support of the government, both at a strategic level and in terms of being able to implement policy on the ground, the likelihood of US policy objectives being met is minimal.

The fact that almost 60 per cent of Pakistanis view the United States, rather than India or the Pakistan Taliban, as the main threat to their country ought to be uppermost in American minds. In the past there has been a tendency to privilege interlocutors who advance their own interests by telling the administration what it wants to hear, which may or may not reflect realities 'on the ground'. If the United States is to come to be seen as an ally of Pakistan (and not just the friend of its military and a small coterie of politicians), it will need to broaden its range of contacts to include those who disagree with its policies. And, in the first instance, it will have to review whether the military utility of drones in the tribal areas outweighs the negative impact on public opinion and on consequent steps by the Pakistani government.

One fear is that the United States will repeat in Pakistan errors made in its earlier Afghanistan strategy. One of the notable complaints by Afghans is that they have not seen any return from the billions that have been spent in their country. This is partly explained by the cost of security and the demand for high returns. But it also stems from corruption. The role of corruption as a driver of rejection of central government control and, ultimately, of radicalization and recruitment for Islamist groups (both in Afghanistan and in Pakistan) cannot be overerestimated.

Providing the Pakistani government with unconditional assistance has been a proven failure, fuelling corruption, increasing inequality and consequently increasing support for those who oppose the state. The shift towards conditionality has caused resentment within Pakistan, and some level of corruption will be impossible to prevent. But the United States should make it a priority to ensure that as wide a public as possible in Afghanistan and Pakistan benefit from development assistance. Encouraging the national governments to shift from a top-down to a bottom-up approach – asking people in the tribal areas or in Afghanistan to prioritize those issues from which they believe they would most benefit – could help gain local buy-in, when security conditions allow. And development assistance should be used to shore up those parts of Pakistan and Afghanistan that remain vulnerable to a rise or return to conflict but where, for ethnic reasons, there is little love lost for the Taliban.

Rebuilding President Hamid Karzai's relationship to the people of Afghanistan is another priority following the election débâcle, with widespread reports of electoral fraud and malpractice. The United States should support his efforts to convene a meeting of tribal elders and, potentially, to rewrite Afghanistan's constitution. While the last and current US administrations may traditionally have preferred the notion of a strong central leader, in multi-ethnic Afghanistan a centralized system is bound to create strains.

The current constitution has been shown to contain a number of flaws: parliament is frequently circumvented and itself comprises a number of former warlords and other flawed individuals whose role as lawmakers makes stability less, not more, likely. Afghanistan's constitution should not be held as a sacred relic but amended as required, with as much Afghan ownership as possible. If Hamid Karzai can be encouraged to decentralize power, the war may yet be won.

The need to move towards decentralization is a corollary of the lesson that should have been learned about the danger of focusing US bilateral relationships in the region on individual relationships between leaders. Under President George W. Bush, US relations with Pakistan were focused on the President's personal relationship with his counterpart, Pervez Musharraf. The failings of such an approach became apparent after Musharraf's party was almost wiped out politically in the 2008 general election. Subsequent revelations regarding the lack of accountability in US aid disbursements to Pakistan demonstrate the leeway that Musharraf had been given by the US administration.

Long-standing American concerns regarding President Zardari may make it easier to avoid a close president-to-president personal relationship but, even so, most institutions in Pakistan are weak. The United States could work to enhance the status of the prime minister *vis-à-vis* the president and army chief, and with institutions that uphold the rule of law, most obviously lawyers themselves. The media, and notably the vernacular media, in Pakistan are not averse to expressing virulent hostility towards the United States, as well as publishing a range of conspiracy theories. Rather than seeing such groups as enemies, US interests would be best served by engaging with them. Introducing a major programme allowing Pakistani journalists to visit or even receive private training in the United States could be a start.

During her October visit to Pakistan, Hillary Clinton said that America wanted to build a broad and deep partnership with Pakistan and expand 'official and people-to-people relations' between the two countries.[26] Increased financial support will help to do this, presuming it is spent wisely. Combating the tendency of US administration officials (whatever legislators and the media may choose to do) to question domestically whether US interests would be better served should the current (or future) leadership of Pakistan be replaced would also help shift the focus away from personalities. It should be for the people of Pakistan to determine whether or not President Zardari is deemed a success or a failure.

On the surface, the Obama administration's appointment of Richard Holbrooke as Special Envoy to Pakistan and Afghanistan has implied a return to diplomatic leadership by the State Department under Hillary Clinton. Ambassador Holbrooke has underscored since his appointment the importance of development assistance and improved political governance rather than an emphasis on military solutions. However, Holbrooke, nicknamed by some 'the bulldozer',[27] has a personalized style of diplomacy that may yet lead to a re-centralization of US decision-making alongside certain favoured Pakistanis if the political situation in Pakistan continues to deteriorate.

India should prove to be the easiest relationship for the Obama administration to manage among these three counties. The lingering concern in India that it risks being sidelined by the focus on Afghanistan and Pakistan in some ways highlights the importance India currently attaches to its bilateral relationship with the United States. Unless US protectionist impulses take more concrete form, it is difficult to envisage that the appeal of the United States to India's emerging middle class will be derailed.

The challenge with regard to India will be less about the bilateral relationship than about engaging India on third-party issues. The United States would prefer India to lead international policy should challenges arise within the smaller countries within South Asia – Nepal, Sri Lanka and Bangladesh – but historical distrust can reduce India's leverage over its neighbours. As China plays a growing role in the Indian Ocean, India's smaller neighbours now have an alternative to accepting Indian patronage and direction. This has created an emerging vulnerability within India, exacerbated by China's renewed border claims. This should help consolidate the US relationship with India, with one proviso: it remains inconceivable that India would consider any explicit or even seemingly formal alliance with the United States.

An informal strategic rapprochement between India and the United States will not necessarily translate to a more amenable India in relation to global issues, such as climate change or trade. India feels it deserves recognition as a key international actor, whether through a permanent seat on the UN Security

Council or through emerging institutions such as the G20. The greater role that it plays will be avowedly in its national interest. India is a 'rich/poor' country, and will position itself as one or the other as it sees its interests best served. India's agreement in international forums will stem from finding win-win solutions to global challenges. It will be imperative to persuade India that it will be affected worse than most by many emerging challenges, such as climate change.

The United States needs to keep its agenda open, engage inclusively and not become a tool in the hands of limited local interests in Washington or in South Asia. Such an approach would make it apparent to the politically astute people of South Asia that the United States has a longer-term commitment to building and reforming institutions, development and democracy, rather than a cynical short-term interest in getting what it wants out of South Asia. If President Obama can change that perception then he will have surpassed expectations.

NOTES

1 Joe Stephens and David B. Ottaway, 'From U.S., the ABC's of Jihad', *Washington Post*, 23 March 2002.
2 Under the deal India agreed to separate its civil and military nuclear facilities, and to place civilian nuclear facilities under International Atomic Energy Agency (IAEA) safeguards. In return, the United States agreed to full civilian nuclear cooperation with India.
3 In an interview in September 2009, former President Pervez Musharraf admitted the use of US assistance against India: http://news.bbc.co.uk/1/hi/8254360.stm. See also http://www.cbsnews.com/stories/2009/10/04/ap/asia/main5362064.shtml.
4 Quoted in http://www.denverpost.com/headlines/ci_13876202.
5 http://beta.thehindu.com/news/national/article19970.ece.
6 In March 2008 Holbrooke noted: 'First of all, we often call the problem AfPak, as in Afghanistan Pakistan. This is not just an effort to save eight syllables. It is an attempt to indicate and imprint in our DNA the fact that there is one theater of war, straddling an ill-defined border, the Durand Line, and that on the western side of that border, NATO and other forces are able to operate. On the eastern side, it's the sovereign territory of Pakistan. But it is on the eastern side of this ill-defined border that the international terrorist movement is located.' Quoted in http://www.world-widewords.org/turnsofphrase/tp-afp1.htm.
7 http://www.reuters.com/article/topNews/idUSTRE5ANoPD20091124.
8 http://www.cfr.org/publication/16644/.
9 http://www.expressindia.com/news/fullstory.php?newsid=79697.
10 See, for instance, Dan Froomkin, 'The end of the Bush-Mush affair', http://www.washingtonpost.com/wp-dyn/content/blog/2008/08/19/BL2008081901224.html.
11 http://english.aljazeera.net/focus/2009/08/2009888238994769.html.
12 The Pakistan Army is currently fighting the Pakistan Taliban in South Waziristan; see http://www.longwarjournal.org/multimedia/maps/FullImageWrapperLatestFullImage.php.
13 While the US has offered to bring down tariffs on cotton-product exports from Pakistan, the industry's problems run much deeper.
14 https://www.cia.gov/library/publications/the-world-factbook/geos/pk.html.

15 http://www.fibre2fashion.com/news/nylon-news/newsdetails.aspx?news_id=76058.

16 See, for instance, www.dailytimes.com.pk/default.asp?page=2009%5C10%5C11%5Cs tory_11-10-2009_pg5_1.

17 http://www.bloomberg.com/apps/news?pid=20601091&sid=aV5ZxhC7tKwU.

18 See for instance http://www.nytimes.com/2009/05/02/world/asia/02policy.html.

19 http://www.iri.org/newsreleases/pdfs/2009%20May%2011%20Survey%20of%20 Pakistan%20Public%20Opinion,%20March%207-30,%202009.pdf.

20 Between 9/11 and 2009, the United States provided Pakistan with around US$9bn in military assistance and a further US$3.6bn for economic and political support.

21 http://pakobserver.net/200911/07/Articles03.asp.

22 http://www.ft.com/cms/s/0/bbe4b39e-8764-11de-9280-00144feabdc0.html?catid=15 &SID=google.

23 China's claim to Arunachal Pradesh is based on the borders of Tibet. A visit by the Dalai Lama to Arunachal Pradesh in late 2009 could be seen as recognition by 'Tibet' that the region is now part of India, causing consternation in China.

24 http://timesofindia.indiatimes.com/home/opinion/edit-page/A-Natural-Alliance/ articleshow/5276333.cms.

25 In addition to his role as Commander ISAF (International Security Assistance Force).

26 http://www.dawn.com/wps/wcm/connect/dawn-content-library/dawn/news/world/ hillary-stressed-us-desire-for-broad-partnership-05-sal-03.

27 http://articles.latimes.com/2009/feb/02/world/fg-holbrooke2.

6

Central Asia: responding to the multi-vectoring game

Annette Bohr

'America's Eurasian policy is part of Washington's much broader global strategy designed to perpetuate America's domination in the world economic and financial system and its military-strategic superiority.'[1]

– Murat Laumulin, senior research analyst, Kazakhstan Institute for Strategic Studies under the President of the Republic of Kazakhstan, Almaty

'In general, US aid and investment have been viewed as strengthening the independence of the Central Asian states and forestalling Russian, Chinese, Iranian or other efforts to subvert them.'[2]

– Jim Nichol, US government specialist on Russia and Central Asia, Washington, DC

Formerly regarded as a regional backwater by US policy-making establishments, Central Asia[3] saw its strategic importance for the United States dramatically raised by the terrorist attacks on America of 11 September 2001. These placed the region at the vanguard of the fight against terrorism, religious radicalism and arms-trafficking. In the aftermath of 9/11, all of the Central Asian states provided assistance in one form or another to US and coalition military forces in Afghanistan, as a result of which the United States greatly expanded its strategic presence in Central Asia.

If in 2002 the United States was poised to play the leading great-power role in Central Asia, by 2005 American influence and prestige in the region were experiencing a precipitous decline as individual states drew closer to Russia and China. Some Central Asian political elites have attributed this decline in prestige to misguided policies formulated in Washington, including – in the words of one leading Kazakhstani analyst – 'the promotion of the idea of "managed democratization" of the post-Soviet regimes, unacceptable and unfounded political rhetoric in regard to the internal political processes of other countries and also the unpredictable and aggressive course of the US in the international arena as a whole'.[4]

Despite the limits to American power in the region, the Central Asian leaderships nonetheless continue to use relations with the United States to counterbalance Russia and, to a lesser degree, China. Perhaps the most salient example of this balancing has been the concessions by Russia and China to increase purchase prices for energy exports from Central Asia as a direct result of the interest shown by Western nations in diversifying export routes. Following Kazakhstan's lead, all Central Asian states have now explicitly or implicitly adopted a 'multi-vector' foreign policy approach in order to gain maximum manoeuvrability and bargaining power in their relations with Russia, China and the United States.

Nearly one year into the Barack Obama presidency, it is clear that his administration is confronted with Central Asian leaders who are not willing to take pointers on democracy and who retain a considerable degree of antipathy for a Western and, more specifically, American geopolitical agenda. Nonetheless, in so far as Obama's election victory demonstrated that citizen mobilization can lead to political change, the new US administration could enjoy an increased degree of credibility among Central Asians when advocating political reform in the region.

US POLICY IN CENTRAL ASIA

The Obama administration's policy priorities in Central Asia follow on consistently from those of the George W. Bush administration, concentrating on two main areas: the war on terror and energy interests. President Obama's revised strategy for Afghanistan is investing the United States more extensively in that country than at any time since the attacks of 9/11 in 2001. Since coming to office in January 2009, he has approved the deployment of an additional 30,000 troops to Afghanistan to address a growing insurgency – more than doubling the number present there at the time Bush left office. One consequence of the renewed focus on Afghanistan is the higher priority that the new US leadership is assigning to the Central Asian states in terms of military planning for this operation. In the energy sphere, the American government is likely to continue to assist US energy firms to explore for additional hydrocarbon reserves in Central Asia and to make headway in the struggle to secure pipeline routes that bypass Russia.

The 'Global War on Terror'

The most immediate interest of the United States in Central Asia has been gaining support for the US-led Operation Enduring Freedom and NATO's International Security Assistance Force in Afghanistan,[5] in that rooting out al-Qaeda and the Taliban remains a top priority on the American security agenda. Central Asian leaders were quick to show themselves as US allies in the Bush administration's 'global war on terror': Kyrgyzstan provided basing for US and coalition forces at its Manas airbase, Tajikistan hosted a small French force and provided a refuelling facility near Dushanbe, and Kazakhstan and Turkmenistan provided overflight rights and other support.[6] In a major display of solidarity, within one month of the 9/11 attacks Uzbekistan's President Islam Karimov had signed a bilateral agreement with Washington permitting the US military to use its base at Karshi-Khanabad (K2), just 60 miles from Afghanistan.[7]

To be sure, Washington's and Tashkent's interests in combating militant Islamist groups have converged in Afghanistan for well over a decade. President Karimov openly supported the anti-Taliban Northern Alliance – and the ethnic Uzbek warlord General Abdul Rashid Dostum in particular – during the 1990s,[8] and he gave permission for a CIA unit to use his country's territory to hunt Osama bin Laden as early as 1999.[9] Additionally, the outlawed Islamic Movement of Uzbekistan (IMU), whose stated aims are to overthrow the Karimov government and establish an Islamic state embracing all of Central Asia, is on the US State Department's list of global terrorist groups. The IMU was particularly active in the Ferghana Valley region of Central Asia in the late 1990s before relocating to Afghanistan. After sustaining many casualties, it was driven out of Afghanistan in 2001–02 during Operation Enduring Freedom, subsequently regrouping in Waziristan in Pakistan's Federally Administered Tribal Areas where it has maintained connections with the Taliban and al-Qaeda. Since 2001, the IMU's priorities are reported to have changed from overthrowing Uzbekistan's ruling regime to a broader, global jihadist agenda, in large part owing to the complex web of alliances IMU members have formed during the years they have been resident in Pakistan's tribal areas.

Despite initial hopes following the 9/11 attacks that the US would act as an external security guarantor for Central Asia and provide vast amounts of financial aid to regional governments, unmet expectations led to a deterioration in US–Central Asian relations from 2003. Following years of mounting tensions,[10] a final blow was delivered to Washington's relations with the Karimov government in May 2005 when Uzbekistani government troops opened fire on a group of armed and unarmed protesters in the Ferghana Valley city of Andijon. The US government accused Uzbekistani ruling circles of using disproportionate force and called for an independent, international investigation of the matter. In contrast to the barrage of criticism put forth by many Western governments, Russian and Chinese leaders offered their full support and approval to President Karimov.

President Karimov interpreted the unrest in Andijon as a warning sign that the 'virus' underlying the sweep of so-called coloured revolutions through Georgia (November 2003), Ukraine (December 2004) and Kyrgyzstan (March 2005) was about to infect Uzbekistan. Regional media ascribed a sinister role to the United States by arguing that the active presence of US-supported NGOs involved in democracy promotion in all three countries was at the root of the regime overthrows.[11] As one senior analyst in Kazakhstan's leading government think-tank has put it, 'the NGOs are openly integrated into Washington's general strategy aimed at America's global domination.'[12] From 2005, Uzbekistan shut down more than 200 NGOs, many of them US-based or US-supported.

The opinion that President Karimov was the next target for American 'democracy promotion' was by no means confined to Uzbekistan. A Kyrgyzstani security expert surmised: 'The film *Bringing Down a Dictator* (which documented the defeat of Slobodan Milosevic in 2000 by massive civil disobedience), the bible of "color revolutionaries", has already been translated into Uzbek.'[13] Russia and China actively supported this line of thought by disseminating the idea that the United States was the principal player behind the 'colour revolutions'.[14] Unsurprisingly, as US influence declined in Central Asia, Russian and Chinese-led regional initiatives incorporating the Central Asian states were significantly strengthened.[15]

In the wake of Andijon, Tashkent informed Washington in July 2005 that it was terminating the agreement permitting the US military to use K2, giving the Pentagon 180 days to evacuate the base. The loss of the airbase was a significant blow for Washington, given that the US air group stationed there handled an average of 200 passengers and 100 tons of cargo a day in support of Operation Enduring Freedom. Following the expulsion of US troops from K2, the Manas airbase in Kyrgyzstan has provided the main staging area for US and coalition military activity in Afghanistan. Since the mid-2000s, the Manas airbase has been under attack in the Russian and local press, which succeeded to a large degree in shaping public sentiment against the presence of the United States in Kyrgyzstan. As late as April 2009, Russian television broadcast a documentary alleging that Manas was a cover for a large-scale US spying mission on Russia.[16] To increase popular support for the base in the face of an anti-American backlash in Kyrgyzstan, US airmen have become involved in local volunteer work and community activities.[17]

Faced with a populist movement to close down Manas, the United States has managed to retain the use of the base primarily owing to the financial benefits it brings to the economy of Kyrgyzstan.[18] In 2005, as anti-American sentiment grew in that country, the government demanded a major increase in lease payments from the US government for the use of Manas, at the same time reaffirming Russia's free use of a nearby base. According to US Central Commander General David Petraeus, Washington was contributing $150 million annually to Kyrgyzstan's budget, $63 million of which was directly related to the air base.[19] Nonetheless, in February 2009, President Kurmanbek Bakiev signed a decree evicting the United States military from the base. Only after sustained diplomatic efforts, including appeals by Afghanistan's President Hamid Karzai and Turkey's President Abdullah Gul, was it announced in June 2009 that the United States would be allowed to continue operations at Manas – at more than three times the previous rent. Under the new terms of the agreement, rental fees for the base have gone up from $17.4 million to $60 million, in addition to $117 million that the United States will spend to upgrade airport facilities and combat drug-trafficking and terrorism.[20]

US energy interests

A primary driver of US policy in Central Asia has been the effort to gain access for American firms to energy exploration, refining and marketing opportunities in the region's three energy-producing states: Kazakhstan, Turkmenistan and Uzbekistan. The US government also seeks to moderate global energy prices through the development of reserves in the region and to promote US and European energy security by pursuing the diversification of suppliers and export routes.[21] Although not a second Persian Gulf, the Caspian Basin is one of only a handful of oil- and gas-producing regions with an interest in maximizing its exports.

Kazakhstan and its oil constitute the main focus of US energy interests in the region, particularly since American and Western firms have been relatively successful in gaining access to Kazakhstan's oil while they have had only limited success in making inroads into the less transparent and less investor-friendly regimes in the predominantly gas-producing states of Turkmenistan and Uzbekistan. While American strategists have seen some success in breaking Moscow's oil export monopoly with the construction of the Baku–Tbilisi–Ceyhan (BTC) pipeline,[22] which pumps nearly one million barrels of oil per day from Azerbaijan to Turkey and on to Europe, all gas exports to Europe from Central Asia flow through Russia.

Following the death in December 2006 of Saparmuat Niyazov, the long-time president of Turkmenistan, Washington used the opportunity provided by the regime change to lobby more intensively for the construction of a trans-Caspian gas pipeline. This pipeline would carry gas on the seabed from Turkmenistan to Azerbaijan and further to world markets through a Georgian–Turkish gas route parallel to the BTC oil pipeline, thereby weakening Moscow's control over gas exports from the region. To that end, in 2007 the US State Department created the post of Coordinator for Eurasian Energy Diplomacy (renamed the Special Envoy for Eurasian Energy in April 2009) in order to promote the development of hydrocarbons in the Caspian Basin and their transport to global markets. The new office is similar to the one that existed in 1998–2004 when, despite daunting obstacles, US pressure and diplomacy were instrumental in the construction of the BTC route. The key to US success at that time was the ability of American firms to secure access to energy reserves before putting in motion plans for transport routes.[23]

In addition to a trans-Caspian pipeline, the United States has also staunchly supported a planned trans-Afghanistan pipeline (the TAPI), which would export some 30 billion cubic metres of gas from Turkmenistan's Dauletabad field across Afghanistan to Pakistan and India. The TAPI would not only weaken Russia's stronghold on Turkmenistan's gas but also undermine the prospects for a parallel Iran–Pakistan–India pipeline, which the United States opposes. In October 2008, the long-awaited results of a preliminary, independent audit of Turkmenistan's major oil and gas reserves carried out by a British consultancy firm indicated that the South Yoloten–Osman gas fields in the southeast of the country contained enough gas to make it the world's fourth or fifth richest gas deposit in the world, potentially doubling Turkmenistan's export potential in the medium to long term and moving Turkmenistan ahead of Saudi Arabia in terms of proven gas reserves. The audit results were expected to lead to increased competition for Turkmenistan's uncommitted and undeveloped gas fields among Russia, Europe, China, the United States and South Asia.

However, despite American lobbying, natural gas pipeline projects that flow westward from Central Asia to Europe or southward through Afghanistan are beset by numerous obstacles, including political instability in Afghanistan, a lack of committed financing, the unresolved ownership dispute between Turkmenistan and Azerbaijan over certain offshore fields in the Caspian and the impasse over the determination of the legal status of the Sea itself. Not least, the Georgian crisis of August 2008 highlighted the political risk surrounding both completed and planned energy export routes through the Caspian for producer and consumer states alike,[24] thereby further discouraging the Caspian littoral states from opting for pipelines that directly challenge Russian influence.

In contrast to Europe and the United States, China is constructing pipelines and making investment deals at a rate that the former two cannot even approximate. By adopting an integrated approach to exploration, production, transport and marketing, China's National Petroleum Company (CNPC) succeeded in winning the first onshore production-sharing agreement awarded to a foreign company by the Turkmenistani government. Construction is under way on a Chinese-funded pipeline that will eventually move 40 billion cubic metres of gas annually from Turkmenistan across Central Asia to China,[25] and, in May 2006, Kazakhstan began delivering oil to the Xinjiang region of China through a newly constructed pipeline that will eventually link to Kazakhstan's Caspian Sea coast.

The problem of opposing perceptions

Particularly since 2005, the gulf between the self-perceptions of American policy-makers and the perceptions of US actions by Central Asian leaders has widened perceptibly. A potent example of this 'opposing perceptions dilemma' is the idea of a Greater Central Asian Partnership, which was set out by a leading US expert on Central Asia in 2005[26] and later embraced by American policy-makers.[27] This concept promulgated the integration of Central Asia, Afghanistan and ultimately South Asia into a regional whole through the development of transport, communications and trade ties. Accordingly, the 2006 US National Security Strategy declared that 'increasingly, Afghanistan will assume its historical role as a land-bridge between South and Central Asia, connecting these two vital regions'.[28] To underscore this goal, in 2006 Central Asia was moved from the Bureau of European and Eurasian Affairs to the revamped Bureau of South and Central Asian Affairs in a State Department reorganization. The Obama administration has continued this course by increasing the resources allocated in fiscal year 2009 for furthering the integration of the two regions, specifically affirming 'the importance of linking Central to South Asia through energy, trade, education, and media initiatives'.[29]

Despite a body of evidence to show that widening the definition of Central Asia would promote trade and support the integration of the region into the global economy,[30] many Central Asian leaders and political elites nonetheless interpreted the idea of a 'Greater Central Asia' as an American ploy 'to detach the extended region from the monopoly influence of the other great powers (Russia and China)' and ultimately 'connect it to the so-called Greater Middle East controlled by the West'.[31] They also viewed with suspicion America's stated objectives in using the Central Asian region as a staging area for activity in Afghanistan. Although welcoming assistance to counter security threats emanating from Afghanistan, Central Asian leaders perceive that the United States brought its military might to the region for the purpose of containing the expansion of Russian and Chinese military and economic influence, while establishing Western hegemony in Central Asia and elsewhere, as evidenced by 'NATO's strategy of drawing as many countries as possible into Western geopolitics'.[32] In the words of a Kazakh parliamentary official, the United States has used instability in Afghanistan 'to justify NATO's continued presence in Central Asia and its emergence outside the European zone'.[33] Some American policy-makers have argued that the United States should maintain military access to the region even when Afghanistan becomes more stable,[34] which has been interpreted in Central Asian circles as a clear sign that they would like to make its base there a permanent feature.

It is a widely held belief among ruling circles in Central Asia that the establishment of bases in Central Asia and Afghanistan is part of a larger American plan to carve out the foothold it needs to launch an attack on Iran. In Kyrgyzstan, in particular, the media and official sources have speculated on claims that the US intended to use Manas to launch air strikes against Iran. In 2007, the chairman of Kyrgyzstan's parliamentary defence committee declared unequivocally that 'I have no doubts that, if hostilities start, the United States will bomb Iran from the Manas airbase in Kyrgyzstan.'[35]

As in the sphere of counterterrorism, the 'opposing perceptions dilemma' comes into play in the energy interests sphere. A senior analyst in Kazakhstan's premier think-tank attached to the office of the president has asserted that 'the American administration views energy resources in Central Asia and the Caspian purely as geopolitical instruments to be used against Russia and China for the purposes of weakening their influence on the states of the region and, in contrast to Moscow and Beijing, not as a source to safeguard its own energy security.'[36] On the other hand, a leading US government specialist on Central Asian affairs has argued that 'Russia seeks to counter Western business and to gain substantial influence over energy resources through participation in joint ventures and by insisting that pipelines cross Russian territory.'[37]

THE CAPACITY OF THE UNITED STATES TO EXERT INFLUENCE IN CENTRAL ASIA

Democracy rhetoric

As the United States has remained bogged down in protracted wars in Afghanistan and Iraq, it has lost much of its credibility in the eyes of Central Asians and, consequently, has conceded a significant part of its capacity to influence and promote positive change in their region. In the aftermath of the 'colour revolutions' of 2003–05 in particular, American attempts at democracy promotion engendered suspicion among the region's authoritarian leaders, who have come to regard them as an integral part of an overall US strategy of subversion.

American criticism over the extent and pace of democratic reform in Kazakhstan, which came to a head in 2007 when US officials resisted Kazakhstan's bid to chair the Organization for Security and Cooperation in Europe (OSCE), has been a source of irritation for Kazakhstan since the early days of independence. Regular criticism of Uzbekistan's human rights practices also played a role in that country's turn to Russia and its decision to join the very Russian-led cooperation structures that it had either ignored or expressly rejected in the late 1990s and early 2000s, such as the Eurasian Economic Community and the Collective Security Treaty Organization.[38] Even Turkmenistan's new president made it clear during his first months in office in 2007 that Turkmenistan–US relations should not be 'politicized'.[39]

Nor do efforts by Western nations at democracy promotion in Central Asia appear to have been effective. Sanctions imposed on Uzbekistan by EU officials in the wake of the Andijon unrest failed entirely to influence domestic practices in Uzbekistan, in much the same way that the democratic reform pledges that the US extracted from Kazakhstan in connection with the its impending chairmanship of the OSCE in 2010 remain unfulfilled.[40] On the contrary, a 2008 study by Freedom House, a US-based NGO, found that new wealth has been serving to intensify authoritarian practices in the post-Soviet 'petrostates' of the former Soviet Union (Kazakhstan, Azerbaijan, Russia and Turkmenistan), since democratic reform necessarily requires a greater degree of transparency and accountability than the petrostates' leaderships are prepared to tolerate.[41]

Although the United States has lost much of its superpower leverage in Central Asia in recent years, the states of the region still regard the US administration as having an important role to play in helping them to integrate into the Eurasian and world economies. Kazakhstan, the region's economic and political powerhouse, relies in particular on Western energy companies for the technology and foreign direct investment it requires to develop its oil fields. The United States is also still regarded as a partner of choice for professional training and technical innovation. Additionally, a number of small and medium-sized US businesses in a variety of sectors are active throughout the region. Even economically weak Tajikistan has been attempting to break out gradually of its role as a Russian protectorate by reclaiming control over its Afghan and Chinese borders and presenting itself as a candidate for Western development.[42]

Indeed, the United States remains the top individual donor of humanitarian aid in Tajikistan, providing 64 per cent of the overall volume in 2007. Particularly since 2008, as the global financial crisis has dealt a blow to Russia's economy and diminished its value as an economic partner, the Central Asian states have turned more to China and, to a lesser extent, the United States to step into the economic breach.

A new opening for Washington?

While Kazakhstan has been able to maintain good relations with Russia, China and the United States throughout the entire independence period, Uzbekistan's foreign policy has been characterized by abrupt geopolitical shifts. If, after 9/11, Uzbekistan consolidated its unequivocal status as the United States' strategic partner in Central Asia, by 2005 that state had, in essence, eschewed relations with Washington altogether. Somewhat predictably, however, after a period of isolation from the West, Uzbekistani President Karimov was ready to make tentative moves at re-engagement, and, by 2007, both Washington and Tashkent were looking for ways to rebuild relations. Thus, when Commander of the US Central Command (CENTCOM) General David Petraeus visited Uzbekistan in February 2009, Karimov told him that 'we consider your visit to Uzbekistan as a visit of the first representative of the new administration of the United States, of President Obama, and as the United States' aspiration to establish closer, mutually beneficial relations with Uzbekistan.'[43]

Karimov's campaign to restore bilateral ties with the United States is predicated on two primary motivations: Uzbekistan's increasingly tense relations with Russia, and its position as a frontline state on the border with an insurgent and militarized Afghanistan. Uzbekistan's leadership has asserted the view that continued destabilization in Afghanistan is largely in Moscow's interest, in so far as Russia has used the conflict there to justify an expansion of its military presence in Central Asia. Uzbekistan has strenuously objected to the opening of a new Russian military base in the city of Osh in southern Kyrgyzstan, which is to be a key component of the new Collective Operational Reaction Forces (CORF) under the auspices of the Russian-led Collective Security Treaty Organization. In June 2009, the Collective Security Treaty Organization formally created CORF as part of its ambition to create forces 'on a par with NATO forces'[44] and in view of the unstable situation in Afghanistan, despite the objections of member states Uzbekistan and Belarus. Both states refused to sign the agreement to form the forces owing to multiple misgivings, including the concern that the forces could be deployed during an internal conflict within a member state or between member states, rather than simply to repel foreign aggression.[45] Additionally, Uzbekistan is likely to view a Russian-led military presence in the volatile Ferghana Valley – regarded as Central Asia's heartland – as a factor impinging on its ability to continue to exert its hegemony on its smaller Central Asian neighbours.

To be sure, President Karimov has made it clear that 'we in Uzbekistan are acutely aware that the decisive factor for security is the attainment of peace and stability in Afghanistan'.[46] Central Asia serves as a transit corridor for narcotics flows from Afghanistan north through Tajikistan and Kyrgyzstan to Russia, and west through Iran and Turkmenistan to Turkey and Europe. Furthermore, in spite of his misgivings regarding US motives in Central Asia, President Karimov values US-led efforts to curtail the activities of al-Qaeda and Taliban training camps in Pakistan's tribal areas, which contain militants believed by the Uzbekistani leadership to pose a threat to all of Central Asia and to Uzbekistan in particular. From early 2009, Obama administration officials began to refer to an 'AfPaK' strategy, according to which Afghanistan and Pakistan were considered an integrated theatre of operations against al-Qaeda and its Taliban allies. In line with this strategy, launching missile strikes against these targets using unmanned Predator aircraft, or drones, became the primary method of combating extremism in the tribal areas of northwestern Pakistan.

Although estimates of its number range vastly from a few hundred to 5,000, it has been reported that the ranks of the IMU have been expanding, primarily with new recruits from Uzbekistan's section of the Ferghana Valley. At the same time as new recruits have been arriving from Central Asia, Pakistan's campaign to oust extremists in its Northwest Frontier Province and the Federally Administered Tribal Areas has prompted many IMU fighters to flee Pakistan and either to seek new sanctuaries in the north of Afghanistan or, in some cases, to filter back to their countries of origin. While the ability of the IMU and other Islamist groups in Pakistan and Afghanistan to stage guerrilla operations in Central Asia itself remains unclear, since May 2009 a number of attacks and clashes with security forces have taken place in Uzbekistan, Kyrgyzstan and Tajikistan, all of which have been blamed on the IMU.

Although regional organizations that bring together the Central Asian states and Russia (and China, in the case of the Shanghai Cooperation Organization) have become more active in recent years, those multilateral groupings have thus far been unwilling to become involved directly in stabilization and reconstruction operations in Afghanistan, preferring instead to 'let the Americans waste their money and troops'.[47] Consequently, as the limitations of such regional organizations have become more evident, the Central Asian states have displayed a renewed willingness to facilitate US and NATO efforts in that South Asian state. As one Tashkent-based analyst put it, 'Everyone likes throwing Americans out of their bases and gloating about their failures, but [the Central Asian governments] realize that if the Americans leave Afghanistan, it will be a serious blow to all Central Asian countries, Uzbekistan in the first place.[48]

During unprecedented appearances at a NATO summit in April 2008,[49] the presidents of Uzbekistan and Turkmenistan offered logistical support for the ongoing battle in Afghanistan against a resurgent Taliban. Uzbekistan agreed to grant US military servicemen attached to NATO access to an air facility at Termez in southern Uzbekistan on a 'case-by-case basis' and also offered to sign an agreement with NATO on providing an overland transit corridor through its territory for the delivery of non-military cargo to Afghanistan, which would significantly reduce the cost of reconstruction efforts there. The German magazine *Der Spiegel* reported in May 2008 that the number of NATO supply planes landing at a military air base in Turkmenistan on their way to Afghanistan had increased following talks between the Turkmenistani government and NATO in April that year.[50] In 2009, the US Department of Defense confirmed that Turkmenistan allowed transport planes carrying non-lethal supplies on their way to Afghanistan to land and refuel at Ashgabat airport; in addition, a small contingent of US service personnel is stationed in Turkmenistan to assist operations.[51]

It is estimated that the additional troops sent to Afghanistan under Obama will require at least a threefold increase in supplies in 2010–11 as compared with 2008. Along with the increase in troops, repeated attacks by the Taliban on NATO convoys using the Pakistan supply route through the Khyber Pass have compelled US policy-makers to establish alternative supply lines to Afghanistan. To this end, they have given priority to opening the Northern Distribution Network (NDN) for the purpose of transporting supplies from Western Europe and the Baltic States to Afghanistan via Russia, Kazakhstan, Uzbekistan and Tajikistan. The establishment of the NDN has required the United States to conclude bilateral agreements with Russia, Kazakhstan, Tajikistan and Uzbekistan for the transit of lethal and non-lethal supplies. Uzbekistan plays a key role in this process; as Afghanistan lacks railway infrastructure, goods must be delivered by road from the border town of Termez to final destinations. Extending its cooperation further, in May 2009 – nearly four years after expelling US forces from its K2 airbase – Uzbekistan offered the use of the country's cargo airport at Navoi, which was being renovated under a long-term lease by South Korea. The involvement of South Korea allowed the Karimov leadership a way to 'save face' when resuming strategic cooperation with the United States.

While the NDN is engaging the Central Asian states as economic transit partners, it is not without its disadvantages: in similar fashion to the main Khyber Pass route, the second route through Central Asia could become a natural target for violence by Islamist militant groups.[52] Secondly, it is much more likely that Western payments related to the NDN will end up in the hands of ruling elites than trickle down to the broader population, thereby forming another source of corruption.[53]

THE ROAD AHEAD: RECOMMENDATIONS FOR FUTURE US ENGAGEMENT

The Obama administration has taken a pragmatic approach towards Central Asia that has de-emphasized democracy promotion in favour of securing the cooperation of the region's states as a crucial front for the war in Afghanistan. This task has been made easier by the willingness of Uzbekistan – a key transit state for US and coalition supplies to Afghanistan – to renew relations with Washington in part to counteract Russian influence in the region. However, should the Obama administration choose to re-emphasize political reform in the near future in Central Asia, it is unlikely to be any more successful over the next decade than it was during the last one. Calls for greater democratization will continue to create suspicion among the region's authoritarian leaders that the United States is prepared to promote movements whose aim is to overthrow the incumbent regimes. Moreover, the promotion of a democracy agenda under the Bush administration inevitably led to charges of a double standard since, as Central Asian leaders have pointed out, it is impossible to apply such a policy consistently around the globe. For their part, most Central Asians pay little heed to democracy, regarding it by and large as an empty ideological framework, and preferring instead to concentrate on traditional networks and informal structures. Consequently, any democratization efforts must be part and parcel of a long-term plan to foster development in relatively apolitical areas, such as education, communications, agriculture and healthcare.

As long as its mission in Afghanistan continues, the United States will maintain its interest in Central Asia as a crucial military transit and supply hub. Yet the Obama administration should desist from increasing military assistance to the Central Asian states outside the NDN, since such assistance is invariably coupled with calls to aggressively promote short-term democratization measures in order to avoid the appearance of supporting authoritarian regimes. In turn, an increase in such measures leads to greater levels of distrust from Central Asian states in their bilateral relations with Washington, thereby laying the groundwork for a repeat of the post-2001 cycle.

American policy in Central Asia has been hampered in recent years by the breakdown in the inter-agency process whereby the Department of Defense has pursued an interests-based agenda while the Department of State has promoted a values-based agenda. The 2005 unrest in Andijon brought the lack of a consistent approach to the fore: while State Department officials argued that the United States must press for an international inquiry, officials at the Department of Defense concentrated on the security-related advantages associated with cooperation.[54] Ensuring a convergence of views within the new administration would enable it to speak to Central Asian leaders with a united voice.

The US government is likely to continue to assist American energy firms to explore for additional hydrocarbon reserves in Central Asia and to make headway in the struggle to secure pipeline routes that bypass Russia. However, despite the recognition by the Central Asian states that the diversification of pipeline routes is a prerequisite for their economic security, Russia has far outdistanced the United States in pipeline diplomacy, primarily owing to a lack of incentives for Central Asian energy producers to abandon long-term gas supply contracts with Russia and China. Additionally, the Russian–Georgian war has made export routes from Central Asia crossing the Caspian even less viable than they were before.

While gas reserves from Turkmenistan's major onshore deposits will not be flowing to Europe via the Caspian Sea any time soon, the United States needs to refocus its efforts in Turkmenistan on the development of offshore fields there and the use of a subsea tieback to connect them to existing Azerbaijani infrastructure. These initiatives would enable the oil and gas that is produced to be carried by the BTC and Baku–Tbilisi–Erzerum pipelines to Europe.[55] To this end, the Obama administration should concentrate on facilitating negotiations between Turkmenistan and Azerbaijan on disputed Caspian oil and gas fields, which in turn would improve the prospects for a resolution of the legal status of the Caspian Sea.

American policies should acknowledge the need of the Central Asian leaderships to strike a balance between Russian, Chinese and US interests in order to preserve their sovereignty and, in the case of Kazakhstan, its ability to exert influence within the region itself. It is tempting for US policy-makers to harbour illusions that Kazakhstan – Central Asia's clear economic leader – will ultimately ally itself with the United States if the material incentives are great enough, forsaking in the process the balanced approach it has assiduously cultivated throughout its independence. However, US officials need to bear in mind that Kazakhstan will continue to welcome American attention and investment, all the while maintaining Russia as its priority partner. Demonstrating its extraordinary political skill in manoeuvring between Russia and the United States, Kazakhstan is the only Central Asian state to have negotiated an Individual Partnership Plan with NATO, while at the same time resolutely rejecting any suggestion that it host a US military base – a move that would be sure to incur Russian and Chinese disapproval.

Particularly during the years following the US invasion of Iraq, Central Asian leaders have discovered what much of the world had already learnt: they do not need to take their marching orders from Washington or respond to US advice on democracy-building unless they deem it is in their interests to do so. All five states are now adept, albeit to varying degrees, at the game of multi-vectoring, in which leaders play the main international actors against each other in order to maximize strategic gains. Consequently, the Obama administration has little option but to set aside or, at least, tone down any messages in favour of democracy and to focus on common interests, while pursuing a long-term strategy in Central Asia aimed at furthering socio-economic development and increasing the citizenry's general understanding of democratic processes.

NOTES

1 Murat Laumulin, 'US Strategy and Policy in Central Asia', *Central Asia and the Caucasus* 4(46) (2007): 46.

2 Jim Nichol, 'Central Asia: Regional Developments and Implications for US Interests', US Library of Congress, Congressional Research Service, CRS Report RL33458, September 2009, p. 2.

3 For the purposes of this chapter, 'Central Asia' comprises the five post-Soviet states of Kazakhstan, Uzbekistan, Tajikistan, Kyrgyzstan and Turkmenistan.

4 M.N. Namazbekov, 'Energetiicheskie interesy SShA, Rossii i Kitaia v Tsentral'noi Azii i Kazakhstana', conference paper published by the Kazakhstan Institute for Strategic Studies under the President of the Republic of Kazakhstan, Almaty, 5 June 2007, p. 276, http://www.kisi.kz/img/docs/3229.pdf.

5 Formerly, there were two different chains of command for Western forces operating in Afghanistan: the International Security Assistance Force (ISAF), controlled by NATO, and Operation Enduring Freedom, under the US Central Command. In June 2009 four-star General Stanley McChrystal was appointed the commander of both the ISAF forces and all US forces in Afghanistan with responsibility for strategy, while a separate, subordinate command was created to oversee day-to-day combat operations.

6 Nichol, 'Central Asia' (September 2009), p. 22.

7 President Karimov also provided a base for German forces at the southern city of Termez and a land corridor to Afghanistan via Termez.

8 Abdumannob Pulat, 'Mirovye derzhavy i Uzbekistan: Obshchie interesy i problemy', *Daidzhest 'Evraziiskogo doma'*, eurasianhome.org, 2 November 2007; Annette Bohr, *Uzbekistan: Politics and Foreign Policy* (London: Royal Institute of International Affairs, 1998), p. 55.

9 Steve Coll, *Ghost Wars* (New York: Penguin Books, 2004), cited in Vitaly Naumkin, 'Uzbekistan's State-Building Fatigue', *The Washington Quarterly* 29(3)(Summer 2006): 132–3.

10 In addition to other points of contention, the Uzbekistani government was unsuccessful in its attempts to persuade Washington to make payments for the use of K2 in line with US payments for the use of Manas in Kyrgyzstan. For accounts of events leading up to the collapse of Uzbekistani–US relations in 2005, see Eugene Rumer, 'The US Interest and Role in Central Asia after K2', *The Washington Quarterly* 29(3)(Summer 2006):141–54; and Roger McDermott, 'United States and NATO Re-engagement with Uzbekistan', Eurasian Home Analytical Resource, 1 October 2008, www.eurasianhome.org/xml/t/expert.xml?lang=en&nic=expert&pid=1748&qm onth=0&qyear=0.

11 Fiona Hill and Kevin Jones, 'Fear of Democracy or Revolution: The Reaction to Andijon', *The Washington Quarterly* 29(3)(Summer 2006): 115.

12 Laumulin, 'US Strategy and Policy in Central Asia', p. 50.

13 Leonid Bondarets, 'American Military Presence in Kyrgyzstan: Problems and Possible Repercussions', *Central Asia and the Caucasus* 4(46)(2007): 71.

14 Stephen Blank, 'US Interests in Central Asia and the Challenges to Them', Strategic Studies Institute, US Army War College, Carlisle, PA, p. 14, http://www.strategic studiesinstitute.army.mil/pdffiles/PUB758.pdf.

15 Roy Allison, 'Virtual Regionalism, Regional Structures and Regime Security in Central Asia', *Central Asian Survey* 27(2)(2008): 193–4.

16 'Uzbekistan signs transit route agreement', *Eurasia Daily Monitor*, Jamestown Foundation, 7 April 2009.

17 Joshua Kucera, 'Kyrgyzstan: US armed forces try to win hearts and minds', Eurasianet. org, 4 December 2007.

18 For figures of payments made by the United States for the use of Manas airbase before 2009, see Roger McDermott, 'Reflections on Manas', *Eurasia Daily Monitor*, Jamestown Foundation, 30 June 2008.

19 Deirdre Tynan, 'Kyrgyzstan: US forces appear to have deal to stay at Manas air base', Eurasianet.org, 1 June 2009.

20 Deirdre Tynan, 'Kyrgyzstan: US armed forces to remain at air base for Afghan re-supply operations', Eurasianet.org, 23 June 2009.

21 Jim Nichol, 'Central Asia: Regional Developments and Implications for US Interests', US Library of Congress, Congressional Research Service, CRS Report RL33458, July

2007, p. 26.

22 In May 2008 Kazakhstan signed into law a 2006 agreement to transport oil through the BTC pipeline, while making plans to upgrade its transportation network to connect its oil to the BTC route.

23 Joshua Kucera, 'US diplomats set their sights on Turkmenistan's Berdymukhamedov', Eurasianet.org, 29 January 2008.

24 John Roberts, 'Going for Gas', *The World Today* (October 2008):14–16.

25 In January 2008 China agreed on a competitive price for pipeline gas imports from Turkmenistan, marking China's emergence as a serious competitor for Central Asian gas. China's willingness to pay competitive prices poses an even greater challenge to the European Union than Russia's recent increases in gas purchase prices, since additional volumes of Central Asian gas delivered to Russia would eventually find their way to European customers.

26 S. Frederick Starr, 'Partnership for Central Asia', *Foreign Affairs* 84(4)(July/August 2005): 164–78.

27 Jim Nichol, 'Central Asia: Regional Developments and Implications for US Interests', US Library of Congress, Congressional Research Service, CRS Report RL33458, November 2007, p. 30.

28 *The National Security Strategy of the United States of America*, The White House, Washington, DC, March 2006, p. 40.

29 FY 2009 International Affairs (Function 150) Congressional Budget Justification: South and Central Asia: South and Central Asian Regional Overview, http://www. usaid.gov/policy/budget/cbj2009/101468.pdf.

30 Clemens Grafe, Martin Raiser and Toshiaki Satsume, 'The Importance of Good Neighbours: Regional Trade in Central Asia', in Richard M. Auty and Indra de Soysa, *Energy, Wealth and Governance in the Caucasus and Central Asia* (London: Routledge, 2006); Annette Bohr, 'Regionalism in Central Asia: New Geopolitics, Old Regional Order', *International Affairs* 80(3)(May 2004): 497–8.

31 Laumulin, 'US Strategy and Policy in Central Asia', p. 53. See also A. Kniazev, 'Bol'shaia Tsentral'naia Aziia – eto vpolne ochevidnyi geopoliticheskii morazm', interview on ferghana.ru, 5 July 2007, http://www.ferghana.ru.article.php/?id=5214. For a response by Starr to the debate within Central Asia engendered by his 2005 *Foreign Affairs* article, see S. Frederick Starr, 'In Defense of Greater Central Asia', Central Asia-Caucasus Institute & Silk Road Studies Program, Johns Hopkins University, September 2008, http://www.silkroadstudies.org/new/docs/Silkroadpapers/0809GCA.pdf.

32 Timur Shaymergenov, 'Problems and Prospects of NATO's Central Asian Strategy: The Role of Kazakhstan', *Central Asia and the Caucasus* 2(50)(2008): 63.

33 Ibid., p. 65.

34 Jim Nichol, 'Central Asia: Regional Developments and Implications for US Interests', US Library of Congress, Congressional Research Service, CRS Report RL33458, July 2007, p. 3.

35 Bondarets, 'American Military Presence in Kyrgyzstan', p. 65.

36 Namazbekov, 'Energetiicheskie interesy SShA, Rossii i Kitaia v Tsentral'noi Azii i Kazakhstana'.

37 Nichol, 'Central Asia' (July 2007), p. 8.

38 After joining the Eurasian Economic Community only in January 2006, Uzbekistan decided to suspend its membership in October 2008.

39 'Turkmen Leader Wants "Apolitical" Ties with Washington', News Briefing Central Asian Update, Institute for War and Peace Reporting, 29 June 2007.

40 Testimony of Andrea Berg, 'Promises to Keep: Kazakhstan's 2010 OSCE Chairmanship', US Commission on Security and Cooperation in Europe, Washington, DC, 22 July 2008.

41 Christopher Walker and Jeannette Goehring, 'Petro-Authoritarianism and Eurasia's New Divides', *Nations in Transit 2008* (New York: Freedom House, 2008), pp. 25–45.

42 Frédérique Guérin, 'Tajikistan's International Positioning: Between Nationalism and Geopolitical Realism', *Journal of International and Strategic Studies*, European Centre for International and Strategic Studies, Spring 2008, p. 23.

43 Roger McDermott, 'Uzbekistan playing renewed strategic role in NATO's Afghanistan mission', *Eurasia Daily Monitor*, Jamestown Foundation, 26 February 2009.

44 Pavel Felgenhauer, 'A CSTO rapid-reaction force created as a NATO counterweight', *Eurasia Daily Monitor*, Jamestown Foundation, 5 February 2009.

45 Roger McDermott, 'Russia's vision in crisis for CSTO military forces', *Eurasia Daily Monitor*, Jamestown Foundation, 30 June 2009.

46 John C. K. Daly, 'Central Asian leaders signal support for NATO corridor to Afghanistan', *Eurasia Daily Monitor*, Jamestown Foundation, 3 April 2008.

47 'Stealth move: American troops to return to Uzbekistan amid thaw', Eurasianet.org, 5 March 2008.

48 Ibid.

49 This was the first appearance at a NATO summit by a president of Turkmenistan. Uzbekistan attended NATO summits in 2002 and 2004.

50 'Geheime Allianz', *Der Spiegel* 21/2008 (19 May 2008): 103.

51 Deirdre Tynan, 'Turkmenistan: American military personnel set up shop in Ashgabat', *Eurasia Insight*, 12 July 2009, http://www.eurasianet.org/departments/insightb/articles/eav071209.shtml.

52 Deirdre Tynan, 'Afghanistan: Northern distribution network grapples with growing security threat', Eurasianet.org, 8 September 2009.

53 Laurie Rich, 'Afghanistan: new supply route may create fresh headaches', Eurasianet.org, 29 September 2009.

54 Blank, 'US Interests in Central Asia and the Challenges to Them'.

55 John Roberts, conference presentation at conference on 'Oil and Gas in Turkmenistan', London, 18 April 2008; 'Turkmenistan – EC: novye dogovorennosti', *Bol'shaia Igra*, consulting company LaTUK, Moscow, No. 2 (2008), p. 3.

7

The South Caucasus:
drama on three stages

James Nixey

INTRODUCTION

The three countries of the South Caucasus (sometimes referred to as the Transcaucasus) – Georgia, Azerbaijan and Armenia – form the most complex, combustible and unstable region in the former Soviet Union. Lying at the crossroads of Europe, Asia and the Middle East, they share deeply ingrained historical trauma, Soviet-era bad practice, economic mismanagement, corruption, social problems, weak institutions, conflicting tendencies towards authoritarianism and reform, inter-ethnic disharmony, border disputes and several low-intensity (or 'frozen') conflicts. Georgia, often the most visible of the three countries to the West, has undergone a brief but dirty 'hot' war with the major regional power, Russia, after years of Russian threats and pressure. This was a pivotal event, which carried consequences for the capacity, scope, emphasis and effectiveness of engagement by the United States across the region.

With natural borders, large neighbours and considerable cultural homogeneity at various points in its history, the South Caucasus is a distinct and interconnected region with a total population of around 16 million. However, the three countries differ considerably, both internally and in their geopolitical orientations. Ancient as nations, but new as self-governing states, they have each taken separate routes since the break-up of the Soviet Union and independence in 1991.

Georgia is located strategically on the coast of the Black Sea; it was a 'failed state' for at least the first half of the 1990s and then underwent a peaceful and democratic 'Rose' Revolution in 2003. It has a staunchly pro-Western foreign policy orientation. It is predominantly Orthodox Christian and desires NATO and EU membership. There is no significant Georgian diaspora community. It suffers from unpredictable foreign policy decision-making and was defeated (and, for some, discredited) in the war with Russia.

Azerbaijan is located strategically on the coast of the Caspian Sea; Baku was the world's first oil capital in the 1890s (and the world's first oil pipeline was built there in 1906). It is overwhelmingly Muslim, though nominally secular, and has a dynastic presidency. It currently performs a delicate balancing act between Russia and the West.

Landlocked Armenia has poor relations with – and is currently blockaded by – its neighbours Turkey and Azerbaijan. Its national assets are increasingly being bought up by Russia but it shares no border with that country. It has a large diaspora (more Armenians live outside Armenia than in it) and an influential (if diminishing) lobby in the United States. It was the world's first country to officially adopt Christianity as a state religion in 301 AD and it is developing an increasingly close relationship with Iran.

Of the six countries that lie within the South Caucasus or that directly border the region – Georgia, Azerbaijan, Armenia, Iran, Russia and Turkey – only Iran maintains embassies in each of the other five capitals.

Throughout the region, closed borders coexist with a relatively long history of federalism, while the interplay of geopolitical pressures and local politics at times creates a combustible mix. Although these are small countries, they can create big problems for great powers and, in consequence, could yet hinder the Obama administration in the conduct of its wider foreign policy.

US INTERESTS IN THE SOUTH CAUCASUS

With the demise of the Soviet Union, US policy in the Caucasus was essentially non-country-specific. The main aim during the 1990s was to manage a peaceful transition in the region as a whole, while other areas of the post-Communist world (the Balkans for example) took precedence. US policy broadly aimed to help construct market economies and promote democracy. Then, in the mid-1990s, the Caspian oil boom gave the region a new significance, mostly as an East–West conduit for energy supplies to Europe. The concept of a 'wider Black Sea region', incorporating the South Caucasus as well as Bulgaria, Romania, Moldova, Ukraine, Russia and Turkey, was envisioned by the United States in the 1990s to build regional cooperation and harness both strategic and democracy-building objectives.[1] All three counties joined NATO's Partnership for Peace (PfP) in 1994.

After the terrorist attacks of 11 September 2001, the American-led 'Global War on Terror' ensured that the South Caucasus became of military-strategic importance as a potential launch pad for US military forces en route to the Middle East or Afghanistan. It was also seen as a threat in terms of being a possible source of radicalized Islam (especially in parts of northern Georgia). These three states were among the first to support the United States in its 'new reality'[2] post-9/11 and they all offered it the use of their airspace for Operation Enduring Freedom in Afghanistan. As the first decade of the twenty-first century drew to a close, the historically influential regional powers of Turkey, Iran and particularly Russia grew more assertive with regard to the South Caucasus. They forged and broke bilateral allegiances with the three states, forcing American policy to become more tailored and differentiated.

American economic aid to the South Caucasus includes Freedom Support Act (FSA) initiatives, food donations, Peace Corps activities, assistance under the Millennium Challenge Corporation (MCC) and security assistance.[3] The major US security assistance programme to the region is known as the Clearing House – its purpose is to share security and some intelligence data among donor and beneficiary countries.

In September 2008, one month after hostilities in Georgia ceased, the then US Deputy Assistant Secretary of State for European and Eurasian Affairs, Matthew J. Bryza, articulated three objectives for the United States in the South Caucasus: supporting Georgia in particular, blunting Russia's strategic objective of undermining the southern East–West energy corridor, and shoring up friends and partners in the wider region.[4] These objectives remain largely intact, though slightly weakened, under the Obama administration.

Georgia

Until August 2008, it could have been said with confidence that Georgia had become more pro-American in the previous five years than any other country in the world. In the 1990s, relations between former Presidents Bill Clinton and Eduard Shevardnadze had been warm, but not as close as the bond that developed between Presidents George W. Bush and Mikheil Saakashvili. In part, this was due to Georgia's cooperation over the war in Iraq, where it had the third largest contingent of troops per capita until they were pulled out (in American aircraft) to return to Georgia for the war with Russia on 9 August 2008.[5] The relationship was further defined by the pipeline politics of Georgia's link position in the energy transit corridor to Europe and a shared increasing suspicion of Russia. Reflecting their hopes and appreciation of US political support, crowds waved American as well as Georgian flags during the Rose Revolution of 2003. Although the United States had supported Georgia through encouragement of its hopes of NATO membership and more generally as part of democracy-building, US policy nonetheless also initially encouraged post-Rose Revolution Georgia to work with Russia on peace settlements in the rebellious north Georgian provinces of Abkhazia and South Ossetia, not even objecting to Russian 'peacekeeping' operations there. This policy shifted to more overt support of Georgia as Russian provocations increased in 2008 and Georgia's territorial integrity was threatened.

It was a core US policy in the 1990s that aid to Georgia (and indeed to all the South Caucasus countries) was not military-related to ensure that it could not be misused in local ethnic conflicts.[6] The focus was on transforming the military. That changed with the 'Global War on Terror'. A new $64 million 'Train-and-Equip' programme in 2002–03 was designed to provide better capability for Georgia's border management (as a result of US concern about Islamic fundamentalist elements in the Pankisi gorge).[7] With the benefit of hindsight, of course, one might speculate that the training provided by the Americans for counter-insurgency operations would have been better employed for Georgia's homeland defence and conventional military threats, given the country's future relationship and, ultimately, conflict with Russia. However, at the time, it was perceived as worthwhile. Other security assistance included the Sustainment and Stability Operations Program (SSOP) from the US European Command (EUCOM).

In spite of all this assistance, many Georgians felt that the United States betrayed them in August 2008. For some, this sense of betrayal can be traced to America's defence of President Saakashvili following his harsh reaction to protests in November 2007, and its silence after two flawed elections in 2007 and 2008. It appeared that the United States was supporting Saakashvili rather than Georgia itself as a nascent, troubled democracy. For others, the frustration lay in the lack of strong American vocal support for Georgia in the first few days of the conflict. After the August 2008 hostilities ceased, many politicians were open in their criticism of US policy and questioned what they were getting from the United States. President Saakashvili went on record to claim: 'Frankly, my people feel let down by the West',[8] although this was not a line he then pursued in most of his interviews with the international media. Unsurprisingly, disillusionment with the United States is felt even more keenly in Abkhazia and South Ossetia. The Abkhaz 'foreign minister', Sergey Shamba, for example, has stated that, 'the US government and some EU countries should equally share responsibility for Saakashvili's military adventures'.[9]

The August 2008 conflict was devastating for Georgia. It lost lives, land, prestige and credibility with the West, including with the United States. It also seriously damaged what had been Georgia's top foreign policy priority since the Rose Revolution: NATO membership. Until then the country had made moves towards achieving that goal – turning the military over to civilian control and launching a successful fight against government corruption (largely by replacing Shevardnadze-era officials with younger personnel). These were impressive steps for a country that in Soviet times was essentially run by mafias. But this process has also led to a loss of institutional memory in ministries and subsequent immature decision-making, which has frustrated US and NATO officials.

Azerbaijan

Azerbaijan, 'a geopolitical pivot', as former US National Security Advisor Zbigniew Brzezinski has described it, is constantly performing a balancing act in its relations with the United States, Russia and Iran. The latter two share borders with Azerbaijan to its north and south respectively. There is significant competition between the United States and Russia over Azerbaijan, and President Ilham Aliyev is adept at accommodating the leadership of both countries, which is crucial for the country's sense of sovereignty. Relations with the United States have been classed as a 'strategic partnership'[10] – a devalued term nowadays, reflecting that the alliance is now confined to common interests and that there are few common values. The Bush administration gave Azerbaijan $3 million for the October 2008 elections, spent on NGOs, debates and monitoring[11] – steps that were not to the Azerbaijani leadership's liking. Yet Azerbaijan proved resistant to the Bush administration's 'democracy project', and the high levels of global anti-Americanism under President Bush – particularly in the Muslim world – compounded the sense of ambivalence at both political and popular levels.

In 1991, Secretary of State James Baker set out the United States' 'five principles' of democracy and human rights, which were to severely limit US relations with Azerbaijan as it moved from near chaos and civil war in the early 1990s to an increasingly autocratic regime once Gaidar Aliyev became president in 1993. Nonetheless, close relations were developed in the wake of Azerbaijan's 'contract of the century' in September 1994 for the giant Azeri–Chirag–Guneshli oil field; American companies secured major stakes in projects to develop Azerbaijan's hydrocarbon reserves, currently (and conservatively) estimated at seven billion barrels (one million tonnes) and 42.3 trillion cubic feet (1.2 trillion cubic metres).[12] Energy issues provided the foundation of the relationship and continue to do so today. The United States played a crucial role in the construction of the BTC (Baku–Tbilisi–Ceyhan) and BTE (Baku–Tbilisi–Erzurum) oil and gas pipelines. These arteries link the hydrocarbon reserves of the Caspian with the West via Turkey, thus breaking Russia's previous monopoly on Caspian oil and gas export routes to major world markets. Azerbaijan and Georgia do not therefore as a rule provide energy transit to the West via Russia, but rather through Turkey.

These pipelines were major achievements of US (and European) policy and enhanced America's influence in the South Caucasus more broadly. As a large producer of natural gas (BTE: 6.6 bcm per year) and with close to one million barrels of oil flowing through the BTC pipeline every day,[13] Azerbaijan has the potential to be a significant alternative to the monopoly transport systems of Russia. Despite initial fears that the Georgian war (which was accompanied by a brief cessation of Azerbaijani oil and gas exports through the BTC and BTE pipelines) would curtail development of transit pipelines through the South Caucasus, the expansion of BTC to a capacity of around 1.6–1.8 million barrels per day, to accommodate Kazakhstani as well as Azerbaijani oil exports to the West, is under active consideration. At the same time, Azerbaijan's gas exports through the BTE line are expected to climb to around 20 bcm per year in 2016–17.[14] The importance of the South Caucasus energy corridor for other Caspian states is also demonstrated by the fact that Kazakhstan and Azerbaijan are jointly exploring the possibility of a new South Caucasus oil pipeline to the Georgian coast, and Turkmenistan is assessing prospects for exporting some of its own gas to Western markets via Azerbaijan and Georgia.

Azerbaijan's military relationship with the United States differs in both size and style from that of Georgia and Armenia. Baku's defence spending ($2 billion in 2008, including some modest, targeted US assistance)[15] is by far the largest in the South Caucasus, mostly paid for with the petrodollars it generates, and is larger than Armenia's entire national budget. The United States has long expressed an interest in establishing an airbase outside Baku,[16] but progress has been sluggish. Azerbaijan has also been slow in implementing its military doctrine, essential for the country's Individual Partnership Action Plan (IPAP) with NATO.[17]

The country may have little ambition to join NATO but there are continuing discussions on compatibility, training and equipment standards.[18] The US State Department has attempted to link military assistance to democratic reform in Azerbaijan, but progress has been negligible. President Aliyev's visit to Washington in April 2006 drew widespread criticism, not least from Russia, which did not miss the opportunity to remark caustically that the Bush administration seemed to be putting energy before democracy. Meanwhile, the balancing act continues as President Aliyev stated in 2008 that the 'present standard of our cooperation with NATO suits us'.[19] After American troops were forced to evacuate the Khanabad airbase in Uzbekistan in 2005, Azerbaijani territory was considered as an alternative airbase location. A US-financed modernization of an Azerbaijani aerodrome for possible stop-overs by American aircraft en route to Afghanistan has been completed. However, Azerbaijan has not been comfortable with a US presence on its territory. So-called 'Cooperative Security Locations' (where there is no *permanent* US presence) aid American forces in mobilizing 'counter-proliferation operations' along the Iranian, Georgian and Dagestani borders. The term is more expedient for the Azerbaijani leadership than the politically charged 'base'. Since 2003, the relatively uncontroversial, US-financed 'Caspian Guard' initiative for extra security in the Caspian Sea (not only in Azerbaijan) and, since 2004, a separate US State Department-funded $20 million maritime border guard training programme (the SSOP) have escaped much internal criticism in Azerbaijan.

Nagorno-Karabakh

The so-called 'frozen conflict' in the disputed territory of Nagorno-Karabakh, involving the occupation of approximately 15 per cent of Azerbaijani territory by Armenia, has so far resulted in approximately 15,000 deaths and hundreds of thousands of refugees. It has entailed the largest build-up of military forces in the South Caucasus region. Successive US administrations have been assisting the efforts to find a settlement of the Nagorno-Karabakh dispute since 1992 in their capacity as a member of the Minsk Group. The Azerbaijani Foreign Ministry has warned that the country would 'reconsider' relations with anyone not supporting its position on Nagorno-Karabakh, namely that it should be returned to Azerbaijan.[20] Ultimately, though, Azerbaijanis believe that the process will be resolved not by legal rulings but by negotiation among the big powers. However, the high level of Azerbaijani defence spending is making Armenia nervous that Azerbaijan plans to retake Nagorno-Karabakh by force, and President Aliyev has consistently refused to rule out the option. As both Zeyno Baran and Svante Cornell have pointed out, the United States remains the only power in the region that both sides in the Nagorno-Karabakh conflict still trust.[21] This trust remains – just about – in spite of the fact that the Armenian lobby in the US, via section 907 of the Freedom Support Act that has prevented financial and military assistance to Azerbaijan except for certain non-proliferation and disarmament activities, has limited America's ability to play the role of impartial mediator at times.

Armenia

Armenia's large and vocal diaspora in the United States[22] and its unenviable position in the South Caucasus – possessed of neither hydrocarbons nor major transit pipelines, and sandwiched between Turkey and Azerbaijan, with which it has very poor relations – means that it values its relationship with the United States particularly highly. Armenia's greatest foreign policy problem is its lack of friendly neighbours. Reciprocal blockades with both Azerbaijan and Turkey have meant necessarily closer relationships with the geopolitically problematic alternatives of Russia to the north and Iran to the south.

An astonishing 69 per cent of Armenians believe that the 2008 Russo-Georgian war was ultimately in the interests of the US government – a far higher percentage than Armenia's South Caucasus neighbours.[23] But Armenia has a special resonance in the United States, which since 1991 has been principally concerned with encouraging Armenian independent statehood, partly through the FSA. Also, the US Millennium Challenge Corporation pledged $235.65 million to Armenia in 2005, although some of these funds have been held back owing to concerns over backsliding on democracy (in particular, the violent repression of peaceful demonstrations in Yerevan over the March 2008 elections, when several protesters were killed by Armenian security forces). Other areas of cooperation, such as the US–Armenia Economic Task Force and the US–Armenia Strategic Dialogue, were institutionalized in the last few years.

In 2004, American financial aid to Azerbaijan was significantly larger than to Armenia in acknowledgment of its more frontline position in the war on terror. Funding parity was then restored by the US Congress in 2005 after pressure from the Armenian lobby. This underscores the influence of the lobby in the United States – but it is also seen by US hawks as contrary to American security interests.[24] If anything, the large and widespread international Armenian diaspora has greater influence than the Armenian lobby in the United States. The former's economic success has provided the Armenian economy with much-needed additional capital through the high level of remittances from Armenians working abroad. President Serzh Sargsyan's week-long, 30,000-km international 'diaspora tour' in October 2009 placed a notable emphasis on the United States.

It is not the United States, however, but Russia that is the main guarantor of Armenia's security as lead nation of the Collective Security Treaty Organization (CSTO), of which Armenia is a member. Armenia's more critical stance towards US policy on Iraq (though it still has 44 troops deployed there) reflects this reality.[25] But while also expressing no interest in joining NATO,[26] President Sargsyan has stated that relations with NATO are 'beneficial, instructive and necessary, and not only in the military sphere'.[27] Armenia has participated in the PfP programme alongside the other South Caucasus states and Armenia has troops deployed in Kosovo and Iraq, and in bilateral partnership plans with NATO since 2005, including 'Command-and-Staff' and field exercises. This, the President has argued, gives Armenia a more modern defence system.[28]

Georgia

The war with Russia, the subsequent discrediting of the Saakashvili regime and the election of President Barack Obama have led to a cooling in US–Georgia relations. Even though President Obama singled out Georgia as a major point of difference between Russia and the United States, the 'tough love' delivered by Vice President Joe Biden in his speech to the Georgian parliament in July 2009 (including criticism of Georgia's democratic deficiencies and warnings against further military engagement in South Ossetia and Abkhazia to reclaim these territories) has somewhat estranged the two countries. There is a notable concern in Tbilisi that, despite the continuing statements of support, Georgia has been downgraded in the list of US priorities and the Georgian leadership is struggling to discern where it fits in American policy in the light of the 'reset' of US relations with Russia.

Yet there have been elements of continuity with the George W. Bush era as well. The US–Georgia Charter on Strategic Partnership, which was signed by the Bush administration, has been taken up by the Obama administration. This allows for further US military training of the Georgian army and improvement of interoperability with NATO, as well as greater trade and economic assistance. An Enhanced Bilateral Investment Treaty, a Free Trade Agreement and access for Georgia to the General System of Preferences have also been pursued.[29] The United States is also training Georgian police officers, judges, prosecutors and defence lawyers. These bilateral agreements sit alongside multilateral groupings such as the NATO–Georgia Council and the Annual National Plan in which the United States takes the lead roles.[30] Although the US administration has been clear that the Charter does not provide security guarantees, its provisions have angered Russia as it sees them as directly infringing upon its sphere of influence. In the face of strong Russian opposition, Georgia also hosted two NATO PfP exercises in May 2009. But Georgia has had to face up to the reality that there are limits to US support. Although there have been negotiations for a new US base on Georgian soil,[31] these have not yet produced any tangible results, and direct military assistance in the form of US troops on the ground will not happen under any circumstances.

Since August 2008, the United States has committed $30 million in humanitarian aid in its annual assistance programmes to Georgia, as well as a $1 billion multi-year package of economic aid for stabilizing the economy, helping refugees and democratic development.[32] In addition, US-funded Radio Liberty began broadcasting news to South Ossetia and Abkhazia in November 2009 with the explicit aim of decreasing anti-Georgian sentiment and countering Russian propaganda.[33] But the Abkhazian government's view is that this is 'Georgian propaganda' designed to promote Georgia as an attractive country for Abkhazia and South Ossetia; the breakaway republics have threatened to jam radio signals.[34] However, international aid is masking the serious effects of the economic crisis on Georgia. Foreign investment has fallen by just under 75 per cent since the beginning of 2008. More helpfully for the long term, Georgia's income from trade with the United States is currently $360 million a year.[35] In a sense, Georgia was lucky. The August war and subsequent aid promises came just before the global financial crisis. A few months later and the international community might not have felt so generous.

Azerbaijan

America's strategic commitment to Azerbaijan has diminished its ability to place the issue of human rights onto the bilateral agenda. Nonetheless, American policy-makers have stated that Azerbaijan will need to take democratic standards more seriously if it is to get what it wants from the partnership. If Georgia and Armenia have trouble running free elections, Azerbaijan has trouble in even understanding the concept – the country is almost totally depoliticized. Elections are held, but they are neither free nor fair. Azerbaijani officials are frustrated that there is little US recognition of the country's economic achievements (the increase in energy prices has made it the world's fastest-growing economy for the last three years) and political stability. Like Russia, Azerbaijan is quite happy to use historical precedent to accuse America of double standards. Slavery, gender barriers, racial discrimination and corruption in the United States have all been used by Azerbaijan to rebut criticism and soothe domestic irritation at the United States' 'interference in internal affairs'.[36] President Aliyev decided at the last moment not to join an energy summit in Batumi, Georgia in January 2010, partly in protest at the decision of the US Congress to provide $8 million in humanitarian aid to Nagorno-Karabakh.

In spite of this current downturn, the US–Azerbaijan relationship is unlikely to be significantly harmed in the long term. For Azerbaijan, a good rapport with the United States is useful to exert leverage in dialogues with other powerful nations – principally Russia, as Gazprom attempts to maintain its near-monopoly on gas exports from the region and ensure that gas from Azerbaijan, or delivered from other Caspian producers to international markets via Azerbaijan, does not become a serious alternative gas supply for Europe. To keep the Americans happy, Azerbaijan has a contingent in Iraq, and doubled its troop numbers in Afghanistan in 2009 to 95.

Armenia

Armenia remains one of the highest per capita recipients of American economic aid under the Obama administration. In 2009, Armenia received $48 million in assistance to Europe, Eurasia and Central Asia (AEECA) funds. The USAID–Armenia managed share was $31.85 million. However, US investment in Armenia ($21 million in 2007) is not as large as Armenian investment in the United States ($31 million in 2007[37]), despite the close cultural and business links described above. What little US investment exists is mainly in the hotel and IT industries.

The United States has also signed an agreement with Armenia to build a nuclear power plant in the country.

The Obama administration has expressed concern over Armenia's increased economic links with Iran – not least in the form of a Russian-backed pipeline sending Iranian natural gas to Armenia. Armenia's response is that increased ties with Iran will reduce its energy dependence on Russia. Ninety per cent of Armenia's energy currently comes from Russia and its $160 million of debt to Russia was cancelled in exchange for state assets. Much of the Armenian transport, energy and telecommunications industries are now controlled by Russia. Simply put, it is harder for the United States to play a role in Armenia because of the depth of Russian involvement there. Moreover, given the Turkish and Azerbaijani blockades, Armenia has little choice. The United States would still like the Armenian leadership to be a more active participant in dissuading Iran from acquiring nuclear weapons technology. Armenia's influence over Iran, like Russia's, is questionable, but Iran does enjoy closer relations with Armenia than with any of its other neighbours.

Finally, Armenia's relations with Turkey constitute the most positive progress that has been achieved in the region in 2009. The 2008 war in Georgia created the environment for the signing of protocols in October 2009 to establish diplomatic relations and open shared borders between Armenia and Turkey.[38] There was a major push on the US side to get the Turkish–Armenian protocols signed in April 2009 in time for President Obama's visit to Turkey later that month for the Alliance of Civilizations forum. This made Azerbaijani leaders angry with Istanbul and Washington, and the process was delayed until October. However, if all goes well with the necessary parliamentary ratifications – a big 'if' – Turkey will become an even more active player in the Caucasus region.[39] The Obama administration has welcomed this rapprochement, but has also learnt its lesson of the spring and kept its distance, preferring to let the bilateral dynamics take their own course. It should be noted also that, for fear of endangering any future agreement, President Obama did not use the word 'genocide' when referring to the events of 1915 in his address to the Turkish parliament in April 2009, as he had during his election campaign. Instead, he used the other term Armenians use, 'Mets Yeghern' – literally, the Great Calamity. As shown during Turkish Prime Minister Recep Tayyip Erdogan's visit to the United States in December 2009, Washington is now less able to influence Turkish foreign policy as Turkey has, at the time of writing, refused to de-link its own rapprochement with Armenia from the issue of a settlement between Armenia and Azerbaijan over Nagorno-Karabakh.

CAPACITY AND RECOMMENDATIONS FOR FUTURE US ENGAGEMENT

The Bush administration's policies towards the South Caucasus were contradictory and inconsistent. The desire to diversify energy supply routes around Russia meant that Azerbaijan was courted (Defense Secretary Donald Rumsfeld made four visits there on return trips from Afghanistan, but ignored Georgia and Armenia). Georgia, for its part, received favoured treatment because of its Western orientation and the personal relationship between the two presidents. The pressure from the Armenian lobby in the United States and international diaspora meant that Armenia also received preferential US treatment in relation to Azerbaijan. As a result of these three parallel and disparate policies, none of the South Caucasus states were satisfied. The challenge for the Obama administration is to achieve greater consistency of policy while allowing for the specificities of each country. Regional integration should therefore be encouraged, but it should be voluntary and should be driven by the economic interests of the states concerned rather than American geopolitical ambition. If the United States were to help facilitate this process – which is unlikely to succeed without some external impetus – this would constitute the foundation of a more coherent US policy and the beginning of more strategic thinking about the region as a whole.

To realize its aims, the Obama administration needs, first, to understand the limits of US power and come to a better understanding of how to use that power. The small countries of the South Caucasus are unable to defend themselves alone against an attack or pressures from their large Russian neighbour to the north, so they look to other external great powers such as the United States for support to balance Russia's influence. The resulting 'great game' sometimes makes the situation in the region resemble the early years of the twentieth rather than the twenty-first century. But, in terms of playing the 'great game', Russia is the best placed in the South Caucasus. There is not only an asymmetry of power between the United States and Russia in the region, but one of interests too, imposing powerful constraints on American policy – as was made clear in August 2008. The biggest danger is that the interests of the three small Caucasus countries, especially Georgia, will be sacrificed in tacit geopolitical deals or simply by default as a consequence of a strategic retreat by the United States from its earlier ambitious plans for the region and a new focus on 'resetting' US relations with Russia. One must hope that the principle of consent will not be forgotten when the United States makes its geopolitical calculations.

Russia's desire for influence in the region far exceeds its desire for stability. Therefore, US policy must first demonstrate to the countries there as well as to Russia that the latter's tactic of 'controlled instability' damages itself just as much as the South Caucasus states. True, Russia has gained tangible benefits from the recent instability by gaining explicit influence over territory in the South Caucasus (Abkhazia and South Ossetia), but at a huge financial cost and by incurring international disapproval. A related US aim should be to convince the Russians that a zero-sum approach to security in the region will be self-defeating and that the conflicts there do not have a military solution. Following the Georgian war, these points will be extremely difficult to communicate, not least because the United States has long under-estimated Russian power (soft as well as hard) in the region, but also because Moscow claims that the United States has taught it the opposite lesson since 1991.

To succeed in its objectives the Obama administration also needs allies in the wider region. And it must demand less from them and support them more. In this context, the situation in the South Caucasus underscores how important it is for the United States to consolidate its relationship with Turkey. The latter's Caucasus Stability and Cooperation Platform (CSCP)[40] is often criticized as being impractical at best and cosmetic at worst. But the Obama administration should not dismiss it out of hand, even though its launch was a surprise and does not involve the United States (which is why the Russians have given it attention, believing that it would help keep the United States out of its backyard and further isolate Georgia). Similarly, Turkey's possible reconciliation with Armenia will be an important part of this process and deserves US moral support at the very least.

In addition, the August 2008 crisis makes it imperative that the Obama administration reassess the security of Western-sponsored energy projects in the region. The Caspian produces about 4.1 per cent of the global trade in oil and around 9.3 per cent of the gas delivered across international borders.[41] Although the Georgian war initially looked likely to scare off fresh investment, projects to expand both oil and gas transit through the Caucasus gathered pace in 2009. Supplier states – Kazakhstan and Turkmenistan as well as Azerbaijan – looked for fresh markets to diversify their export options and reduce their dependence on routes through Russia. And the European Union and leading European energy companies looked to the Southern Corridor through the Caucasus as a way of diversifying energy supplies, particularly in gas. It is clearly in US interests to promote both regional and global energy security by ensuring such diversification of both suppliers and export routes, which should also contribute to energy price moderation. Consequently, new pipelines such as the Interconnector Turkey–Greece–Italy (ITGI), Nabucco (Turkey to Austria via Romania, Bulgaria and Hungary) and even a trans-Caspian pipeline all make strategic sense for the United States. Clearly, it is not possible for America or the countries concerned to defend every kilometre of exposed pipeline, but there are particular critical points in the region's existing energy infrastructure that could be better protected, and where US financial assistance and technical expertise would make a significant difference.

Next, the Obama administration needs to work with the EU to develop a new transatlantic South Caucasus strategy. American and European goals in the region, after all, are broadly identical: preventing a new anti-Western orientation, opening markets and improving the rule of law, diversifying the extraction and transportation of hydrocarbons, and promoting regional stability and democracy. The wealth of US political appointees now in the Obama administration with strong knowledge of the region should support the development of a coordinated US–EU policy towards the region. A key component of this strategy, however, is to accept the importance of the EU in driving long-term regional economic integration. The United States should play a strong supporting role here. Better and more liberal visa policies by both US and EU authorities towards the three South Caucasus countries, for example, would be beneficial, as would the completion of free trade agreements with the EU. The United States could also play a role in the EU's Monitoring Mission (EUMM) in Georgia, where it would add to stability and aid in the return of refugees. At a minimum, it is vital that there is no rift between the US and the EU on policies towards the region.

The starting point for future American engagement with Georgia must be recognition of what failed in recent US policy and why. The Bush administration relied too much on personal friendship between senior US officials and Georgian leaders, and too little on engagement with other factions in Georgia's policy elite or helping to build institutions. Although there is no political figure on the scene with President Saakashvili's charisma, popularity, experience and political muscle, there are many individuals who could form part of a national government and possibly help achieve greater consensus.

One of the other major American mistakes in the South Caucasus since 1991 has been its support for peace plans that have been deficient, not least because they did not tackle issues of final status on recognition of independence for disputed territories. But US backing for the plans made the governments believe they were sound when they were not. Territorial integrity, for example, is important, but not at the very outset of the process. Another past mistake lies closer to home. Contradictory American approaches towards the South Caucasus in the past can be attributed to the in-fighting between different arms of the US government – in particular, the executive versus the congressional branch. For example, the US Congress has allocated aid directly to Nagorno-Karabakh, which contradicts State Department policy in the region.[42] Now is the time for a major American push on Nagorno-Karabakh through the Minsk Group and in collaboration with the EU.

Georgia's desire to join NATO presents one of the biggest challenges to US policy. The view that NATO membership for Georgia will bring greater security for the South Caucasus might prove correct in the long term. But in the near term, the risks and liabilities far outweigh the gains for the West. In the military and security sphere, support for Georgia is critical. The Georgian National Security Council wants new equipment and weapons for the Georgian army, and for it to be trained to a greater level of preparedness.[43] Further military assistance, if it is to be given, should not be tank-for-tank replacements of those destroyed in the war, but better defensive capabilities, such as sophisticated air defence and command, control, communications and computer intelligence systems.[44] However, as Steven Pifer of the Brookings Institution has pointed out, there is no conceivable military assistance the United States can provide to Georgia that will ensure that the Georgians can defend themselves from a Russian attack or forcibly retake South Ossetia and Abkhazia.[45] Meanwhile, political and institutional safeguards must be devised to ensure that Georgia's forces will not be deployed in offensive operations again. Nonetheless, there remains a strong argument for anti-tank and anti-aircraft missiles and for increasing the level of performance of the top Georgian military leadership.

At the same time, there must be no question of closing the door to NATO membership, as this would have a catastrophically demoralizing effect on elites and society at large in Georgia. It would also diminish US influence where it is most needed (in promoting the democratic accountability of the armed forces and security structures) and embolden Russia. Nor should the Obama administration 'recognize the recognition' of South Ossetia and Abkhazia – for the very same reasons. Admittedly, Georgia is potentially more stable without South Ossetia and Abkhazia than with them (although this is because the majority of ethnic Georgians there were thrown out and the displaced have no voice). The Obama administration can help emphasize this point by highlighting the link between Georgia's internal economic success and political stability and the erosion of the divide between 'Georgia proper' and the 'independent' secessionist entities. The United States should make clear its belief that Georgia's long-standing policy of wooing South Ossetia through the building of trading outlets was steadily increasing the central government's control in various parts of the territory before the war and that it was the Georgian government's impatience with this slow but successful policy that helped trigger the war. It will be harder now to revert to this pre-war policy. But it is a worthwhile long-term strategy. This would also help to make Georgia more attractive for Abkhazia too one day.

Given that Georgia's recovery has been largely dependent on American support, the United States retains enormous leverage in the country, despite its past failings. The Obama administration now needs to conduct a sustained discussion with the Georgian elite and help it think through its interests and challenges. Most importantly, the United States can use its influence to ensure that economic recovery is supported by a broader, more solid (and more responsible) political framework than that which effectively allowed one individual to commit the country to war. As honest broker and one of Georgia's principal paymasters, the US administration should leave President Saakashvili in no doubt that diplomatic support, much-needed financial loans and the rebuilding of Georgia's armed forces, including assistance in rewriting their failed military doctrine, are conditional on political reform. At the same time, US financial aid needs to be targeted as accurately as possible.

The United States should broaden its engagement with Abkhazia and South Ossetia by all means and on all dimensions short of recognition. The United States, in fact, has no current policy towards the separatist states (except in terms of providing aid). It should develop one to engage and to accomplish over the long term in order to prevent decades-long situations such as the one in divided Cyprus. Aid is no substitute for a policy that allows these entities to escape from the trap that Russia has put them in. The US challenge is to undermine Russia's ability to define Abkhazia's and South Ossetia's engagement with the outside world and force us to choose between recognition on the one hand and isolation (and *de facto* annexation) by Russia on the other.

In the immediate post-Rose Revolution period, Georgia quite successfully countered Russian actions and influence simply by being more democratic. But this is no longer the case. President Saakashvili or his successors must actually behave like democrats and carry through their promises to the UN

General Assembly on the protection of private property, greater independence to parliament and the judiciary, trials by jury, and increased funding and better access to the media for opposition parties. In other words, the presidency must be weakened. Perhaps more than anything else, Georgia needs American pressure to prevent backsliding on its own commitments to greater democracy and improved human rights.

CONCLUSION

While not as important as Iraq, Afghanistan, non-proliferation or fighting international terrorism, the South Caucasus has become a vital concern for US foreign policy as a result of the Georgia war. August 2008 was the first time since the fall of communism that Russia sent its forces across an international frontier in anger. This in itself has massive implications not only for the South Caucasus countries but also for other major American partners in the former USSR, such as Ukraine, as well as for NATO members themselves. The South Caucasus matters in itself but also in relation to other policy areas for the United States such as energy and the war on terror. The balance between them must be constantly reworked for the United States to avoid being caught up too closely with the region.

As many have now observed, August 2008 was a proxy war for Russia, not against Georgia, but against the West and particularly the United States. To counter this dynamic, the Obama administration may have to rethink its military capabilities to cope with a third simultaneous crisis or conflict situation in addition to Iraq and Afghanistan. However, regaining its influence in the region will give the United States the best chance of achieving durable solutions and ensuring that the South Caucasus countries are less vulnerable to internal and external forces of instability.

In contrast, retreat from this region by the Obama administration would have far-reaching, short- and long-term negative consequences for American interests, including an inevitable further rise in Russian (and Iranian) influence. The Caucasus lies on the fault line in Western attitudes on how to deal with Russia. But Russia will react, whatever the United States does in the South Caucasus. And the United States will not be able to constrain it any more than it was able to in August 2008. At the same time, Russia will be similarly incapable of blocking all US policy actions. The South Caucasus states have all banked their autonomy, their legitimacy and their increasingly pro-Western orientation on a continuing American presence in the region. For some in South Caucasus, the United States has been just as unreliable in its principles as Russia and has lost some of its credibility. And today, even though the United States is the indispensable country for the independence of the South Caucasus states, we are entering a period of less American engagement there, not more. This has been made clear by the Obama administration. In itself, that may not be a wholly bad thing for a sensitive region riven by ethnic and civil conflicts. Nonetheless, to the extent that the United States will remain involved in the affairs of the three countries of the South Caucasus, future American engagement and leadership must be thoughtful and not fail them – or itself – a second time.

NOTES

1 This concept was further developed by Ron Asmus and Bruce Jackson. See 'The Black Sea and the Frontiers of Freedom', *Policy Review* (June/July 2004).

2 Kenneth Yalowitz and Svante Cornell, 'The Critical but Perilous Caucasus', *Orbis* 48(2) (2004).

3 Sources: US State Department, Congressional Justification for Foreign Operations, FY2010, 12 May 2009.

4 Testimony before Congress on Security and Cooperation in Europe (US Helsinki Commission), Washington, DC, 10 September 2008. Interestingly, Georgian opposition leader Salomé Zourabishvili argues that Bryza should be punished for the role he played in the August 2008 offensive – urging on Georgian President Mikheil Saakashvili and never saying stop. (Conversation with the author.)

5 In June 2009, Georgia announced that after US training, a company and a battalion of 500 troops would join the International Security Assistance Force (ISAF) Afghanistan in 2010. Two thousand Georgian servicemen served in Iraq. Source: BBC Monitoring, Caucasus, 8 December 2009.

6 The Millennium Challenge Corporation gave Georgia $295.3 million before the August war.

7 'Train' involved approximately 200 US military trainers teaching four Georgian battalions in infantry tactics for facing down *small*-scale security threats. 'Equip' included the provision of uniforms, small arms and light weaponry and communications equipment.

8 Interview with CNN, 13 August 2008.

9 Quoted in BBC Monitoring alert. Caucasus. 12 October 2009.

10 Azerbaijani parliament speaker Ogtay Asadov after meeting with US Ambassador to Baku Anne E. Derse, 8 January 2006.

11 Press conference with US Ambassador to Baku Anne E. Derse, Baku, 1 May 2008.

12 BP, *Statistical Review of World Energy*, June 2009.

13 BTC, http://www.hydrocarbons-technology.com/projects/bp/. http://europa.eu/rapid/pressReleasesAction.do?reference=SPEECH/07/368&format=HTML&aged=0&language=EN&guiLanguage=en.

14 Ibid.

15 http://www.eurasianet.org/departments/insight/articles/eav051308a.shtml and http://www.reuters.com/article/crisis/idUSL1597375.

16 Alman Air Ismail, *A Base or not a Base?* Eurasianet.org, http://www.eurasianet.org/departments/insight/articles/eav091205ru.shtml.

17 Individual Partnership Action Plans (IPAPs), launched in 2002, are designed to deepen cooperation with NATO in terms of interoperability and reform. Georgia became the first country to agree an IPAP with NATO in October 2004. Azerbaijan agreed one on 27 May 2005, Armenia on 16 December 2005. They must be distinguished from the Membership Action Plans (MAPs). No Caucasus country has officially been offered a MAP. Only Georgia openly desires it at the present time and it is not likely to be offered in the immediate future.

18 'Azerbaijan, US Discuss Military Cooperation', *RFE/RL Newsline*, 24 November 2003.

19 Interview with Russian news agency Interfax, 21 March 2008.

20 Azerbaijani Ministry of Foreign Affairs press release, 19 March 2008.

21 Zeyno Baran, 'The Caucasus: Ten Years after Independence', *The Washington Quarterly* (Winter 2002), p. 223; Svante Cornell, 'US Engagement in the Caucasus: Changing Gears', *Helsinki Monitor* 2 (2005), p. 118.

22 By one estimate, there are 1.4 million Armenians in the United States: http://www.armeniadiaspora.com/followup/index.html.

23 Hans Gutbrod, The Caucasus Research Resource Center program (CRRC). Poll conducted in November 2008.

24 S. Frederick Starr, *Resolving Karabakh: Strategic Options for the US Government*, (Washington, DC: Central Asia and Caucasus Institute, 2004). This has led to the FSA being waivered in every year of the Bush administration and in 2009. Jim Nicols, 'Armenia, Azerbaijan and Georgia: Political Developments and Implications for U.S. Interests', Congressional Research Service, 2009.

25 Jason Burke, 'Armenian agency analyses Yerevan's refusal to back Iraq campaign', http://www.eurasianet.org/resource/armenia/hypermail/200303/0057.shtml.

26 Interview with Russian *Kommersant* daily, 27 June 2008, http://www.armradio.am/news/?part=pol&id=13076.

27 Quoted in BBC Monitoring, Caucasus, 16 November 2009.

28 Mission of the Republic of Armenia to NATO, http://www.armenianatomission.com/index.php?cnt=3.

29 US Department of State, *US-Georgia Charter on Strategic Partnership*, 9 January 2009.

30 The Annual National Plan (sometimes Programme) of Georgia deals with military reform, media freedom and anti-corruption measures. It is seen by some as a diluted version of the NATO Membership Action Plan.

31 BBC Monitoring alert, Caucasus, 6 October 2009.

32 Announcement by US President George W. Bush, 3 September 2008; and Philip H. Gordon, Assistant Secretary of State for European and Eurasian Affairs. Testimony before the Senate Relations Committee, Subcommittee for Europe, Washington, DC, 4 August 2009.

33 BBC Monitoring alert, Caucasus, 23 November 2009.

34 BBC Monitoring alert, Caucasus, 6 November 2009.

35 US Census Bureau, Foreign Trade Statistics, 2009.

36 Chief of the Azerbaijani Presidential Administration Ramiz Mehdiyev in remarks quoted on 6 May 2008 by the daily newspaper *Yeni Azerbaijan*.

37 National Statistical Service of the Republic of Armenia.

38 This is a central point in Gareth Winrow, *Turkey, Russia and the Caucasus: Common and Diverging Interests*, Chatham House Briefing Paper, November 2009.

39 At the time of writing, the situation appears more pessimistic. The leaders of Azerbaijan and Turkey have gone as far as internal political pressure will allow in terms of accommodation, and Azerbaijan, which has always desired a Turkish–Armenian settlement to be linked to a resolution on Nagorno-Karabakh, has also objected. Azerbaijan is fearful that Armenia will 'pocket' this agreement, and not budge on Nagorno-Karabakh. In short, the siege mentality and the East–West divide in the Caucasus may continue.

40 The CSCP requires a resolution of the Nagorno-Karabakh dispute, the Russia–Georgia dispute and the normalization of relations with Turkey and Armenia. Many view it as an ineffectual talking shop.

41 I am grateful to John Roberts for these data, which are derived from *BP Statistical Review of World Energy*, June 2009.

42 Other examples of different arms of the US government working against each other in the South Caucasus can be found in B. Shaffer, 'US Policy', in Dov Lynch (ed.), *The South Caucasus: A Challenge for the EU*, Chaillot Papers No. 65 (Paris: Institute for Security Studies, December 2003).

43 Georgian National Security Council Head, interview with the author, 21 October 2008.

44 Jon E. Chickey, *The Russian-Georgian War: Political and Military Implications for US Policy*, Policy Paper, Central Asia–Caucasus Institute Silk Road Studies Programme February 2009.

45 Steven Pifer, 'Delivering Tough Love to Ukraine, Georgia', http://www.cfr.org/publication/19906/delivering_tough_love_to_ukraine_georgia.html.

PART II

Partners and Competitors

8

China: between global responsibilities and internal transitions

Kerry Brown*

INTRODUCTION

China's relations with the United States will be one of the most important, if not the single most important, relationships on the international stage in the coming decades. But there remain specific points of possible conflict and contention, the most noticeable of which are Taiwan and the skewed bilateral trade balance. Over these looms the broader issue of how the United States accommodates a re-emergent, increasingly competitive economic superpower, which China stands well placed to become before the end of the next decade. China's support for restructuring the global financial system is one area where it will be pushing against key US interests, and where the current international economic crisis has left the United States less able to assert itself. Another is the potential conflict between the two for commodities in the coming years. Nevertheless, the dynamic of the relationship depends as much upon developments within China as on American strategy. China's leadership realizes that overt conflict with the United States is in no one's interest. But it also understands that the global system needs to be more representative of China's importance, and that, in the years ahead, Chinese public opinion, which is becoming increasingly assertive, will not accept political elites that look as if they are selling China cheap.

The fact remains, however, that talk in the United States, China and beyond that the G2 (the United States and China) is now the only truly meaningful global partnership, rather than the G8 or the G20, will lack substance until China's leaders show greater clarity on what role they want it to play on the world stage in the future. At the moment, there is little evidence that it wishes to assume a global leadership position. It remains preoccupied with issues of internal development and maintaining its own territorial integrity, something that was forcefully underlined by the explosion of violence in the North West Xinjiang Autonomous Region in July 2009. And its leadership will be preoccupied until 2012 with a crucial transition to a new, fifth generation of leaders.

---

* The author is grateful for the input into this chapter of Guy de Jonquières, Gareth Price and Robin Niblett.

It has been widely noted that, in the first months of 2009, the administration of Barack Obama enjoyed a remarkably smooth initial period with the Chinese government. This bucks the trend for most previous administrations of having an initial testing period and then settling into more harmonious relations. Secretary of State Hillary Rodham Clinton paid an early, high-profile visit to Beijing where she declared that the key consideration was economic cooperation between the two countries, and that other matters, including contentious issues such as human rights, needed to be seen in that context. President Obama met President Hu Jintao at the G20 Forum in London in April 2009 and enjoyed wide-ranging and positive discussions. Both sides started to address the thorny issue of climate change and what sort of deal they could both live with after the UN Climate Change Conference in Copenhagen. Barack Obama is the first US president to have visited China within the first year of his presidency, something that was noted when he went to Beijing and Shanghai in late November 2009. And the Joint Statement issued as a result of this visit was one of the most complete and wide-ranging ever issued between the two countries.[1]

Conflict is a remote and unlikely prospect. But China's military build-up and future potential, its projection of military and political power into ever-increasing areas in the world where it is acquiring considerable strategically economic assets, and the fact that it looks likely to emerge from the current economic crisis faster, and in better shape, than any other major economy, all contain seeds for future bilateral tension. Dealing with these challenges of a rising China will be a key theme for the Obama administration. During his first year, the President showed extraordinary international ambition. With China, it is already clear that he will be seeking a historic concord on climate change and will attempt to forge a bilateral relationship with a new level of shared strategic aims. The question is just how far China, with its internal complexity, can go to meet him with these aspirations.

CHINA'S INTERNAL DYNAMICS

China is, by its economic size and the speed at which it is industrializing and developing, a global power. But it is a contradictory global power, and this makes it potentially both unstable and unpredictable. It is the world's second largest economy (in purchasing power parity terms), and, as of 2009, the world's largest exporter, and it has the largest foreign currency reserves. Over two decades of double-digit growth and massive investment have endowed large parts of the country, though far from all, with modern physical infrastructure. And, in the larger cities at least, an increasingly affluent, free-spending, property-owning middle class has emerged. But there are good arguments to show that the urbanization of China has been at the cost of its real entrepreneurial development.[2] The Chinese private sector thrived in the countryside in the 1980s. It has been controlled and, in some areas stifled, in the last decade of more urban, pro-state-sector growth.

For all the wealth creation of the last three decades, this is a country with perhaps as many as 200 million profoundly impoverished people, whose suffering was highlighted in the earthquake in May 2008 in Sichuan. One US report has called this the world's first 'rich poor country'.[3] Income inequality has grown rapidly in recent years, raising risks of social instability.[4] Despite increased spending on health and education, social service provision is rudimentary. Public institutions are weak and, while rule of law is improving (created in effect from scratch since 1978), it is still patchy. Notwithstanding an authoritarian system, the capacity of the central government to implement policy in any of China's 31 provinces or autonomous regions is often limited. The current leadership has put a lot of effort into dealing with corruption, and it inspired the current talk of 'harmonious society' and the attempt to implement more pro-poor policies, but corruption remains prevalent. All of these factors impede efficiency of government in China, eroding confidence and trust. As Premier Wen Jiabao has said, China's greatest challenges, and the greatest threats to its stability, come from within. This needs to be factored into any discussion of its relations internationally.

Because of their fundamentally different political systems, and the different cultural values they espouse, the interaction between China and the United States will be the key global relationship in the coming decades given the continuation of the United States as the world's superpower, whatever the extent of its relative decline, and the revival of China as a great power. It is clear from many statements by senior Chinese leaders that they see the United States alone as the key power for them to relate to in the coming years.[5] The European Union only features in their world-view as a trade partner.

For the United States, the challenge of accommodating a new, dynamic, but sometimes hostile power, with its own global aspirations and ambitions, will be significant. China is likely to continue to pursue the largely cooperative attitude that was enshrined in the famous '24 character statement' issued by Deng Xiaoping in the 1980s, in which he insisted that China be a biddable and positive member of the international community, seek to build relationships and friendships across the region, and build up its internal economic capacity, if it sees this as in the best interests of its stability and success. Both countries will want to avoid conflict, and conflict is, as noted, unlikely. But in two areas – economic competition and Taiwan – there is certain to be continuing tension and hard negotiation. This is the case even though, in the short term, the return of the long-ruling Kuomintang (KMT) to power after the 2008 elections in Taiwan has eased cross-Strait tensions considerably. Taiwan's potential to throw up unexpected problems should not be understated. President Obama's early decision to give Secretary of State Clinton ownership over policy towards Asia, and specifically China, means that he has avoided the long hiatus that occurred between the inauguration of the George W. Bush presidency and its decision of who had lead ownership over policy towards China. Secretary of State Clinton's high profile means that she is taken seriously in China. Her upgrading of the Special Economic Dialogue to embrace strategic issues was also welcomed (see below), though some in the previous administration criticized it for conflating too many issues into one vehicle. Even so, it showed that the administration was looking beyond just the economic relationship. In view of the complexity of the shared interests between the two countries, that is sensible. But will China be able to deliver on these expectations? This is the question addressed below.

THE HISTORICAL CONTEXT

Despite all the profound changes of the last four decades, the fundamental parameters of US relations with China are still those set by President Richard Nixon during his groundbreaking visit to China in 1972, a visit that predated the economic reforms after the death of Mao in 1976. Since these reforms started, the United States and China have largely sought mutual benefit, engagement and cooperation, but within boundaries. China has gained intellectual property and expertise from US investment in hi-tech industries, but American firms, like those of most other countries, have been careful to keep their most sensitive intellectual property to themselves, especially since Chinese firms have started to become international competitors. The general parameters that existed since the beginning of the rapprochement are unlikely to change without a major cause of disagreement or conflict. What is fundamentally different now is that, having constructed a major economy since 1978, there are increasing international concerns about China's external impacts and growing expectations about the sort of 'responsible' role it should play in the global economic and political system.

Until the presidency of George H. W. Bush, surveys (inasmuch as they have been allowed) indicated that most Chinese looked up to and wanted to emulate the United States, regarding it as a model they wished to use in their development.[6] Following the Tiananmen Square Massacre in June 1989 and again under George W. Bush, public opinion appears to have turned against the United States. The accidental bombing of the Chinese embassy in Belgrade by NATO during the Kosovo conflict in 1999 was another landmark in souring views. This is ironic because, in the mid-1970s, when his father was head of the US Liaison office, George W. Bush had lived in Beijing and could claim some understanding and knowledge of how China worked. However, a combination of international and bilateral events (the shooting down of a US spy plane over Hainan in early 2001 being the most striking) meant that, by the time of the terrorist attacks of 9/11, US–China relations were going through a particularly bad patch. President Bush seemed to be veering towards greater recognition of Taiwan and was keen to push China harder on human rights and trade issues. At a time when China was becoming increasingly open to the outside world, especially with its entry to the World Trade Organization (WTO) in 2001, Bush's administration was in danger of going down as one of lost opportunity with China.

All of this was changed by 9/11, which had a considerable effect on the dynamics between China and the United States. China's support for resolutions against Afghanistan at the UN led the United States to place one alleged Uighur secessionist group onto its terrorist list. There was also a reduction in lobbying on human rights issues. For China, disunity and instability are the ultimate bogeymen and are blamed for the most baleful periods of its history since 1850. Not wanting to see an unstable China, US policy has largely been sensitive to and cautiously supportive of the central government in its handling of restive areas in the west of China. Following this pattern, the Obama administration, like most Western governments, expressed concern about the July 2009 crackdown on violence in Xinjiang, but held back from stronger statements that could imply any desire to see China breaking apart. That would be a massive force for instability in the rest of the world.

MANAGING THE TRANSITION TO THE OBAMA PRESIDENCY

Hillary Clinton's first visit to Asia as Secretary of State, in March 2009, included a high-profile meeting with Chinese leaders in Beijing and dispelled many immediate worries on the Chinese side. Historical Chinese unease with US Democratic administrations as compared to their Republican counterparts, along with a general lack of understanding of President Obama's political instincts among Chinese officials during his campaign, were partly dispelled by Clinton's clear signal that the United States viewed its relationship with China as critical for the region and for the world, and that China's partnership in confronting problems in the global economic order was key. Perhaps most important, Clinton's willingness to talk of the relationship in broad terms, rather than focusing, as had been feared in China, on narrower issues of human rights and political differences, went down well. That she was willing to declare this approach openly to the American public via an interview on the way to Beijing helped too.[7]

The administration's creation of a 'Strategic and Economic Dialogue' to replace the previous purely economic dialogue, the first meeting of which was held in Washington in late July 2009, backed up Clinton's words with the institutional means to carry on this enhanced, broadened dialogue. Spats between submarines in the South China Sea (in what the United States claimed were international waters, and China claimed were in its territory) did not have much impact. Nor did the evidence of increasingly aggressive cyber-attacks from China, creating the need in Washington for a special office to deal with these threats (the United Kingdom has also followed suit). All of this good mood music was amplified when President Obama met President Hu for the first time (they had talked several times by telephone before their meeting) at the G20 in London in April 2009. Their agreement on the main strategies to deal with the global recession, with China even contributing US$40 billion for aid through the International Monetary Fund to developing countries, was a tangible outcome of this new partnership, especially their agreement, finally, over the treatment of tax havens after the raising of French concerns.

These positive steps do not negate the continuing potential for bilateral tensions. As the 2008 US National Intelligence Committee report *Global Trends 2025: A Transformed World* spelt out all too clearly, China's growing role in the global economy will push it into competition with the United States in other countries, especially in view of its major investments abroad and its continuing search for resources in areas like Africa or the Middle East.[8] The American concern was once that China's global role was too limited; now it is the reverse. Over the past decade, China has participated in international forums at almost every level, taken part in UN peacekeeping missions, played a more assertive role in the UN Security Council, and joined the WTO. But the United States, and the West in general, takes more notice of its involvement in countries such as Sudan. China buys around two-thirds of Sudan's oil, and has faced criticism for its support of the Sudanese government. In May 2007 China responded to the mounting criticism, appointing a highly respected diplomat, Liu Guijin, as its special envoy on Darfur, sending 3,000 peacekeeping troops from China to the region, and finally supporting a UN resolution on Sudan, albeit a softer version than had originally been proposed.[9]

Nevertheless, China's actions are clearly motivated by a precise definition of its national interest.[10] This definition revolves around the search for stability, which is based, in turn, upon the critical need for continued high rates of economic growth. Growth requires a peaceful international environment and, more specifically, increasing energy and raw material imports. But its booming demand for oil pushes China into long-term equity deals with a range of African and Middle Eastern countries, which leads, at times, to competition with US and other Western oil companies and, at others, to propping up authoritarian regimes. China has shown itself willing to transfer technology and to supply regimes in countries such as Sudan, Zimbabwe and Nigeria with military hardware (despite its stated support for non-proliferation of conventional and nuclear weapons) to curry favour with their leaderships.

In the specific area of relations with the authoritarian and nuclear-armed Democratic People's Republic of Korea (DPRK), China has a key role to play, both as a neighbouring country and as a major conduit of energy supplies. The importance of its role has been brought into sharp relief by the series of aggressive steps taken by the DPRK in the first half of 2009 (one nuclear test and several missile launches). As a result, China accepted tougher UN sanctions on the DPRK. The main questions remain, however, how far China's influence really goes with such a uniquely problematic country and to what extent the Chinese leadership wants to exert whatever influence it has on the regime in Pyongyang. China has been loath to declare its real strength with regard to the DPRK, but in view of the fact that it supplies 50 per cent of the aid to the regime, and 90 per cent of its energy, it is clear that it does have some real traction there. The next logical question, then, is how far the Chinese leadership is willing to use this potential leverage. The answer during 2009 was only to a very limited extent. The suspicion remains that, whatever the DPRK does, China does not want to walk away from its 'little brother' with all of the unpredictable regional consequences this would entail.

Competition over energy security and non-proliferation (halting the spread both of conventional weapons and of nuclear technology to 'rogue' states) are two very specific areas of potential conflict and misunderstanding in the US–China relationship, and clear ownership of the dialogue on these two issues, with the goal of articulating shared interests and near-term objectives, will be critical. However, as long as the United States can understand China's self-defensive definition of its national interest and how this is expressed through its diplomacy and action, it should not have grounds for systemic concerns in the medium term, whatever the near-term frictions.

CHINA'S RISING INTERNATIONAL IMPORTANCE

China's evolution from an inward-looking, isolated country has caused mixed reactions in the United States. Where to collaborate with and where to oppose this new China are questions that are working their way to the heart of the policy debate in the United States, and that the Special Economic Dialogue was partly set up to address in 2006. In many areas, particularly in Asia, China is clearly in competition with the United States, trying to exercise greater influence through the ASEAN-plus-three group, and through the Shanghai Cooperation Organization, a grouping the United States regards with suspicion (witnessing Russia and China trying to forge a united front again brings back bad memories). Some commentators say that China is starting to present itself as an alternative partner and even to offer an alternative model of state-led growth to replace the now discredited 'Washington Consensus'. At this stage, however, there is little evidence that China will aggressively promote its economic model internationally, and all the statements of its main leaders imply that this model is one that is most suitable for China at its current stage of development, nothing more.[11] Underscoring this point, in 2003 China's leading ideologue, Zheng Bijian, started to attempt to reassure outside observers, many of them in the United States, that China's rise was 'peaceful' (*heping jueqi*).[12] Since 2007, and the 17th Communist Party Congress in Beijing, the concept has evolved into one of 'peaceful development', largely because many observers outside China found the use of the word 'rise' somewhat ominous.

At the same time, as a result of skilful soft diplomacy, China capitalized on the fall in the reputation of the United States in the region after the invasion of Iraq in 2003. In Cambodia, Thailand and the Philippines, surveys have shown that the historical distrust of China has been replaced by an admiration for the Chinese economic model and the political stability that the Chinese government has achieved in the last two decades.[13] Growing Chinese political influence in the region and beyond has been backed up by a dramatic rise in the number of Chinese students studying overseas, by increasing amounts of Chinese development aid and by the establishment of Confucius Institutes in various parts of Asia, Africa and Europe, to promote cultural and educational ties.

There is controversy, however, about whether China's efforts to improve the reach of its soft power have been particularly successful. Although artfully embellished, China's foreign policies and foreign assistance are, at heart, driven primarily by its government's perceptions of national economic need. At its best, it has contributed to the development of poor resource-producing countries, notably in Africa, by increasing the value of their raw materials exports and through extensive Chinese-funded investments in modern infrastructure. At its worst, China's self-interested munificence has aroused growing local criticism. In Africa, critics complain that its policy of 'non-intervention' has often amounted to giving financial support to tyrannical regimes, that too little of its investments benefits local economies, that local producers are overwhelmed by waves of cheap Chinese exports and that Chinese lending could plunge African borrowers into unaffordable debt. Some also worry that the result will be excessive economic and political dependence on China.[14]

There is plenty of evidence in blogs (which have become massively popular in China) and in China's increasingly lively media that many in the Chinese government and media, as well as among the Chinese middle class, feel that their country is not being accorded the respect it deserves for its achievements over the last three decades. As the economic turmoil unleashed by the financial crisis spread around the world, governments in industrialized countries have been obliged to accept that the active involvement of China, and of other emerging economies, is no longer just desirable but indispensable to the restoration of global stability. That recognition was powerfully reflected in the decision by George W. Bush to invite their leaders to a first 'Group of 20' summit meeting in Washington in November 2008 to discuss the crisis and the subsequent G20 summit in London in April 2009, at which China was a central and active participant. In London, such was the importance of the two countries' joint agreement to any final global economic deal that the talk was of it being in fact a G2 summit, though both sides rejected the moniker.

One thing that the talk of a G2 did capture, however, is that solutions to almost all global economic, environmental and political challenges will depend critically on the quality of the relationship between Washington and Beijing. President Bill Clinton often talked about trying to build a strategic partnership with China. President George W. Bush attempted to construct a framework in which both sides could work together on areas of mutual benefit and interest (most prominently in the US–China Strategic Economic Dialogue). But now that China has moved away from its original position of complete 'non-interference' in the affairs of other countries, 'strategic partnership' needs to mean much more than a deepening of US–China bilateral understanding and cooperation. China now has clear overseas interests and, like the United States a century before, will want to defend and promote them. The Obama administration's enhanced 'Strategic and Economic Dialogue' goes some way to recognizing this new reality.

CHINA'S INTERNAL TRANSITIONS

But the management of this critical bilateral relationship is no longer something that the elite leadership of the Communist Party can decide upon alone. In the run-up to the next Communist Party Congress in 2012, the party will need to manage a transition from the leadership of Hu Jintao to that of a new group, the so-called 'Fifth Generation' of Chinese leaders. As always, China's civilian leaders will have to gain the support of the People's Liberation Army for this transition. However, this transition will also need to gather and carry popular support somehow – a particularly difficult challenge given the lack of explicit mechanisms for engaging popular input into the process. The fact is that there are increasingly influential and vocal constituent elements in Chinese society that the leadership will need to continue to buy in to the system – from a new middle class that might number over 100 million to a new group of entrepreneurs who are critical for the growth of the economy, were allowed into the party in 2001 and, according to the OECD, now account for over half of Chinese growth.[15] In addition, there are 3,000 civil society groups agitating on the environment and over 12 million petitions were submitted in 2008 alone from disgruntled citizens. More Chinese are aware of, and willing to exercise, their rights. A successful transition to a new group of leaders in 2012 will depend on their having support across this complex blend of constituencies and being seen as legitimate in their eyes and representative of their views.

The Hong Kong-based commentator and journalist Willy Lam has expressed concern at the very slow progress of political reform and transparency in decision-making in China in the face of this rise in greater civic activism and politically aware constituencies.[16] Even officials within the party admit that there is currently no clear road map to a more 'democratic' system of government, despite the government's declaration in 2005 that 'democracy is the common aspiration of mankind'. This slow pace of change is dangerous partly also because of the rise in Chinese nationalism, sometimes encouraged by the government, but increasingly citizen-motivated. Japan in particular, and sometimes the United States, appear to regard this nationalism as a source of external threat; this suggests that China needs to go it alone more often and stand up to what are seen as unreasonable external demands.[17]

The idea, therefore, of an elite leader such as Mao Zedong or Deng Xiaoping doing backroom deals with US leaders is no longer tenable. Leaders of China cannot afford, now or in the future, to seem weak or compliant in their international dealings or detached from public concerns. Nor is it acceptable from a Chinese perspective for the United States to appear to be handing down edicts or acting, as it often did in the 1990s, like the world's policeman. It no longer has the moral authority in China to get away with this kind of approach.

A different kind of approach may work, however. As noted by Mobo Gao, an Australia-based academic originally from China, survey after survey has shown that the Chinese still admire America and aspire to live lives similar to those in the United States, despite the damage done to its international reputation across Asia as a whole during the past decade.[18] President Obama has sought to take advantage of this latent goodwill and has consistently identified during his first year the need for the United States to live up to the values that it publicly espouses if it is to re-establish the potential to exert US global leadership.

In this context, the United States may be able to play a constructive role in China's need to address the hugely complex issue of its own process of gradual political reform. In view of the environmental, political and social challenges that China will face in the next decade, and the potentially cataclysmic fall-out if it fails to manage a smooth transition to a modernized system of political and legal governance, the United States, along with the EU and its member states, should seek to identify the areas where governmental and private or non-governmental initiatives could help indirectly in this process. These could include supporting the embedding of the rule of law, the growing influence of non-political civil society groups, the building of more professional media, and the construction of a financial services infrastructure. There will remain areas related to national security and sovereignty where engagement would be counter-productive and where China will need to face the challenges on its own. But for this long-term rapprochement to take place, both sides will have to overcome a great deal of historical suspicion as well as two more persistent areas of bilateral tension – the future of Taiwan and the imbalance in the bilateral economic relationship.

THE PROBLEM OF TAIWAN

The joker in the pack of US–China relations is Taiwan and the state of cross-Strait relations. This is an issue where the US position is critical. Taiwan's development as a democracy since 1996 has been remarkable. The peaceful transfer of power from the more pro-independence Democratic People's Party (DPP) to the KMT in the 2008 election was a process that was accorded international praise. The new president, Ma Ying-jeou, has promised to improve relations with the Mainland. He has talked of a greater China market, and indeed, in 2006, the first Mainland Chinese investment was made into Taiwan. In 2008–09, 'three links' (air, post and sea) between the two were established, and the People's Republic of China has assented to Taiwan joining the World Health Authority as an observer, after many years of Taiwanese lobbying. But even an improved relationship with Ma's government has not meant that China has granted Taiwan the diplomatic space for more than the most minimal forms of international participation. And Ma's government remains vulnerable to criticism about what tangible political and security benefits it has gained from China in the last year.

Under the 1979 Taiwan Relations Act, the US executive is required to report to Congress if Taiwan comes under attack, and then consult with Congress on a response. In the last decades, since the formulation of the One China policy, the United States, along with much of the rest of the international community, has avoided all talk of sovereignty. Even so, there are valid questions about how long Taiwan can develop as a democracy without at least moving closer to independence. Many in the generation born long after 1949, when the KMT fled to the island, feel that they are Taiwanese first and Chinese second. Mainland China has never given up the threat of military action if Taiwan were to declare outright independence. It has over 1,000 missiles pointed at the island and has increased its expeditionary military capacity over the last decade. The capacity for the Taiwanese issue to be a major cause of tension is clear. As long as China remains a one-party state and Taiwan is a democracy, then, in the event of an attack by China, it would be politically unfeasible for the United States not to defend Taiwan, no matter what the political stripe of the US administration controlling the White House.

The issue of Taiwan, therefore, exacerbates all of the concerns in Washington about China's military build-up. With an official increase in its annual military budget of 17 per cent, China's overall military spending is around US$50 billion, although the true figure may be as high as four times this.[19] Even though US military spending would eclipse this larger figure, the speed of China's technical progress and the increased professionalism of its forces have raised the stakes. With Taiwan, China has a clear unresolved strategic objective. The United States has to continue to walk a line between supporting Taiwan – but not tolerating any declaration of independence (which would be deeply destabilizing for the region and the world) – and showing that it will not stand by if China were to adopt a military solution to this problem. The Mainland Chinese leadership's legitimacy depends on not compromising on China's territorial integrity. Support for the status quo is therefore likely until Ma Ying-Jeou leaves office (he can stay in power until 2016 if he wins the next presidential election in 2012). The risks for US–China relations could resurface if the next Taiwanese administration decides to follow in former President Chen Shui-bian's footsteps and become more assertive of Taiwan's independent status.

ECONOMIC TENSION BETWEEN CHINA AND THE UNITED STATES

No recent event has symbolized more graphically the global implications of China's economic rise than the attendance by Hu Jintao at the hastily convened G20 summit in Washington in November 2008 and the follow-up summit in London in April 2009. After years of being singled out by Western critics as a source of international economic problems, China is now being greeted as an integral part of the solution and invited to take a place of honour at the top table.

Economically, of course, the United States still dwarfs China. Though the latter has grown rapidly to become the world's second largest economy in terms of purchasing power parity, its gross domestic product, measured on the same basis, was still barely half that of the United States in 2008, while its income per capita was less than one-eighth.[20] However, the gap is narrowing rapidly. If recent relative growth trends continued, China's GDP, on a PPP basis, might draw level with that of the United States by as early as 2015 – though rather later on a nominal basis.[21]

That prospect has led the economic relationship between the two countries often to be characterized as one of rivalry, especially by China's American critics. But it is also increasingly one based on interdependence. The United States remains China's largest national export market (although its relative importance has recently diminished), a valued source of technology and know-how and, above all, a central pillar of the global economic stability that Beijing prizes highly.

China's financial stake in the United States is also large. As the world's biggest foreign owner of US dollars – amounting to an estimated 70 per cent of its total foreign exchange reserves worth US$2,000 billion – and the largest holder of US government debt, it has a vested interest in America's national welfare. By the same token, the United States has relied heavily on credit from China to help finance its persistent fiscal and current account deficits and to support its currency. That reliance is set to grow as Washington is obliged to borrow further to fund its recent bank bail-outs and economic stimulus packages.

These factors mean that the two countries are to a considerable extent bound together in a marriage of necessity, the break-up of which would almost certainly inflict grievous costs on both, and on the rest of the world. But like many other such alliances, it is bedevilled by repeated frictions and disputes and by under-currents of mutual suspicion. Its survival depends less on a natural commonality of interests and more on their ability to cope with the inevitable differences and conflicts between them.

These tensions have ranged across a broad spectrum of economic issues, including China's treatment of intellectual property, its alleged discrimination against foreign competitors and its overseas investment strategy in the United States and elsewhere. But the most sensitive and recurrent source of friction has arisen from repeated US complaints about the substantial imbalance in bilat-eral trade and angry allegations that this is due to China's 'manipulation' of its currency. This issue reared its head during the confirmation hearings in Congress of Tim Geithner as Secretary to the Treasury in February 2009, when he was quoted as accusing the Chinese of currency manipulation.

The Special Economic Dialogue created by President Bush and headed by Treasury Secretary Hank Paulson from 2006 managed to keep dialogue open about these issues and to stop them boiling over into large-scale spats. Even so, some constituents in the United States are asking what the dialogue has achieved, especially since President Obama upgraded it at the start of his administra-tion. There is a perception that in the economic area, just as in the geopolitical realm, China is too much of a self-interested actor. Hopes that a more dynamic domestic consumer market would appear on the back of the Chinese stimulus package and specific government measures directed at enabling increased consumer spending in the early part of 2009 now look premature. According to one US official, a consumer market on anything like the scale of that in the EU or United States is as much as a decade away. The concentration of so much manufacturing capacity in China in such a short period since 2001 has created its own problems; the economic downturn saw many factories in South China close with millions losing their jobs, raising the spectre of social instability.

However, the greatest problem is one of perception. Since 2009, General Motors, now 80 per cent owned by the US taxpayer, has been manufacturing most of its cars in China. In the same year, China became the world's largest manufacturer and consumer of cars. The symbolism of US consumers spending their money to buy cars from a US taxpayer-owned company that has its main factories and employment in China will be potent.

Since China's economic reforms began, its policy-makers have viewed the United States as a role model and object lesson in how to structure a modern capitalist economy. China is obviously far from embracing that system in its entirety. But when undertaking change, it has often looked to America as a template, one it has then adapted selectively to its own particular needs and circumstances. That has been true both of reforms of its financial markets and of industrial policy, which has striven to create 'national champion' companies in the image of established US industry leaders. One Western analyst has characterized the approach as 'backward-looking and imitative'.[22]

However, as the financial crisis has brought venerable US financial institutions crashing down and sent shockwaves through the world economy, Chinese respect for the American way of doing things has turned to scepticism. Indeed, some officials have expressed open contempt for American faith in the efficiency of unfettered financial markets.[23] That Beijing has been gradually loosening direct state control over its banks, while Washington has been forced to step in to support troubled financial institutions, has added piquancy to their comments.

President Obama is therefore confronting a China that is less in awe of US economic might, but whose cooperation is even more necessary to the achievement of US national and global priorities. That shift could clearly increase Beijing's influence and bargaining power in its dealings with Washington and with the rest of the world. Much will depend on whether and how China decides to use its strength. So far, the indications are that it will be exercised cautiously, although commentators noted that, during President Obama's visit to Beijing in November 2009, the Chinese government showed very little flexibility, at least in public, on the trade deficit, the exchange rate of the Chinese yuan, and specific trade disputes.

The Chinese regime's dependence on delivering economic growth as the foundation of its political legitimacy means it is likely to be heavily preoccupied for some time with combating the slowdown of its national economy. In addition, though Chinese officials have some technical expertise in international financial and monetary affairs, it is relatively limited, as is their familiarity with the high politics involved. In such circumstances, launching dramatic initiatives could risk embarrassing failure. For the moment, Beijing seems to have opted for a safety-first approach, even though some high-level officials (in particular the Chinese Central Bank Governor Zhou Xiaochuan) have floated the idea of the dollar being replaced as a global currency with an alternative. But for that to happen, the government would need to face the problems of making the Chinese renminbi convertible, something they have resisted till now.

Another source of potential friction would be a misjudged hostile Chinese bid for a 'crown jewel' US company perceived, or popularly portrayed, as vital to US national security. Since Congress defeated the attempted takeover of the major oil company Unocal by China's National Overseas Oil Corporation in 2005,

China's attitude towards large American acquisitions has grown more cautious. Nonetheless, depressed stock market valuations – and a desire to diversify its US dollar investments – could cause opportunism to prevail over prudence.

There are, fortunately, some restraints in place that could limit the scope of confrontation. One is that it would be difficult for the United States to legislate unilateral trade sanctions against China without violating World Trade Organization rules and inviting a successful legal challenge by Beijing. In that event, the United States could face the choice between a humiliating climb-down and flouting a WTO ruling against it. Since the WTO's dispute procedures are the strongest lever that the United States possesses over China's trade policy, such a move could weaken its moral and political authority.

A second constraint is that American and Chinese economic interests are now so closely intertwined that rash or aggressive actions on trade would quickly backfire, with potentially serious consequences for both economies. While the United States remains China's largest national export market, plentiful supplies of cheap imports from China have contributed to US prosperity by enabling its economy – at least until recently – to grow at rapid rates without generating high inflation.

The fact that many of those imports are made in Chinese plants owned wholly or partly by US companies and sold under their brand names also changes the political equation. There is now a large, powerful and politically well-connected US business lobby with a vested interest in maintaining open trade with China and in fighting political attempts to restrict it. That is fundamentally different from the situation in the 1980s, when Japan was the target of bitter US complaints about its trade practices: because American companies had few investments in Japan, none had any incentive to oppose threats of trade sanctions. Indeed, in many cases, they led the charge.

Nonetheless, as long as serious imbalances remain on bilateral trade with China, they are likely to be a source of contention. Although undervaluation of the renminbi may have contributed to those imbalances, it is not their principal cause. The real culprit is the huge disparity between the two countries' savings rates. For a variety of reasons, China saves vastly more than it consumes or invests at home, generating persistent trade and current account surpluses and swelling foreign exchange reserves. Conversely, America's propensity for debt-financed consumption – by both government and households – has led to large external deficits, not just with China but with the world.

However, the current economic turmoil is changing the equation. As the credit crisis forces American borrowers to 'deleverage', and as American consumers cut spending in the face of recession, household savings are set to rise sharply. The result is likely to be a steady reduction in the US current account deficit and weaker demand for imports, from China and elsewhere. That might reduce one source of friction between Washington and Beijing – but at the risk of creating others.

CONCLUSIONS

The fundamental problem for the United States is that China remains a deeply complex actor. The interactions of its central and regional governments are highly particular: in some areas the central government can enforce policy implementation; in others the local government acts as a rule unto itself. In that sense, the United States is engaging not with one entity but with many different ones. A deal in Beijing does not necessarily carry any weight beyond the capital. The highly fragmented nature of the Chinese political and economic landscape is often forgotten because of the strong image that the central government likes to project. Beijing promotes a sense of unity, but this unity is highly vulnerable. Events in Tibet and Xinjiang, in 2008 and 2009 respectively, both prove that.

At the same time, the United States must try to encourage China to look beyond its immediate national interests and accept that its growing economic and political importance requires it to play a larger multilateral role. For most of the time since it joined the WTO in 2001, China has taken a back seat, although, along with India, its dispute with the United States over agricultural subsidies provoked the collapse of the 2008 Doha Round negotiations. This is ironic, because China has been perhaps one of the major beneficiaries of entry to the WTO.

However, if China is to become a 'responsible stakeholder', this would require the United States to share global leadership with it in those areas where each country has the greatest stake – from climate change negotiations and energy security to non-proliferation. It is far from clear that the full implications of such a development are grasped in Washington, including the degree to which it would be obliged to accommodate Chinese arguments and viewpoints that would often be radically different from its own.

In broad policy terms, there will be little change in US–China relations over the next five years in terms of grand strategy. The overall aims will remain the same: to identify common interests and work together, to acknowledge dependency – especially in the economic sphere – and to manage areas of potential conflict, such as Taiwan and trade policy. While the United States may dislike China's political system and their ideological differences will persist, the two countries are becoming increasingly mutually dependent.

The real challenge for the United States, however, will be to react to and accommodate a China that is increasingly proactive beyond its borders, whose influence in some parts of the world will start to outweigh that of the United States, and that, politically, will be articulating positions led by a clearly diverse and complex set of domestic constituencies within China. The United States must find a way to respond in the pursuit of its own interests, without creating conflict. One clear policy goal for the Obama presidency should be to rebuild US influence and credibility in China and among the Chinese people, and to show that the goals that the United States represents – freedom, dignity for the individual and the rule of law – are still fundamental for the future stable prosperity of the world community and also for China itself. The United States needs to continue building constructive bridges to the increasingly influential and diverse range of interested communities and constituents in China. It should be more willing to dare to talk of democratization and its connection to good decision-making and governance, something that is accepted by many in positions of influence in China despite the continuing demonstrations of ideological intolerance by the Chinese communist leadership.

It is imperative that the United States and China work together within an agreed framework on energy and environmental issues, as noted in other chapters in this book. The United States also needs to identify the very real constraints on China's development at the moment – from demographics (an ageing and increasingly male population) to its economic model and energy inefficiency. The United States should not expect China to be able to step up to the plate and become a global leader when it is so clearly preoccupied by internal issues. But it has no choice but to encourage China to be a strategic partner, and help spell out a shared strategy. To achieve that, the United States needs to work with others to change the architecture of multilateral forums such as the World Bank and International Monetary Fund so that they are more representative not just of China but of other developing economies (see Chapter 14). In this way, at least some of the miscommunication that has marred US–China relations in the past can be avoided in the future.

NOTES

1 Available at http://www.whitehouse.gov/the-press-office/us-china-joint-statement (accessed 3 December 2009).

2 See Yasheng Huang, *Capitalism with Chinese Characteristics: Entrepreneurship and the State* (Cambridge University Press, 2008), for an excellent demonstration of this.

3 C. Fred Bergsten, Bates Gill, Nicholas Lardy and Derek Mitchell, *China, the Balance Sheet: What the World Needs to Know about the Emerging Superpower* (Washington, DC: CSIS and Peterson Institute for International Economics, 2006).

4 The increasing inequality in China is evidenced in the UN Human Development Report issued in November 2008, and available at http://hdrstats.undp.org/countries/country_fact_sheets/cty_fs_CHN.html (accessed 15 November 2008).

5 See Wang Jisi, 'China's Search for Stability with America', *Foreign Affairs* 84(5), (September/October 2005): 'The United States is currently the only country with the capacity and the ambition to exercise global primacy, and it will remain so for a long time to come. This means that the United States is the country that can exert the greatest strategic pressure on China' (p. 39).

6 These are contained in Joshua Kurlantzick, *Charm Offensive: How China's Soft Power is Changing the World* (New Haven, CT: Yale University Press/New Republic, 2007).

7 See 'Clinton: Chinese Human Rights Can't Interfere with Other Crises', at http://www.cnn.com/2009/POLITICS/02/21/clinton.china.asia/ (accessed 3 December 2009).

8 See *Global Trends 2025: A Transformed World*, report by the National Intelligence Council, US, available at http://www.dni.gov/nic/PDF_2025/2025_Global_Trends_Final_Report.pdf, p. 29 (accessed 3 December 2009).

9 An eloquent exposition of China as a global collaborator and cooperative partner is contained in Bates Gill, *Rising Star: China's New Security Diplomacy and its Implica-*

tions for the United States (Washington, DC: Brookings Institution Press, 2007).

10 This is articulated in the Chinese White Paper on National Defense, issued in 1998: 'China unswervingly pursues a national defense policy that is defensive in nature, keeps national defense construction in a position subordinate to and in the service of the nation's economic construction, strengthens international and regional security cooperation and actively participates in the international arms control and disarmament process'. See http://english.peopledaily.com.cn/whitepaper/2forward.html (accessed 3 December 2009).

11 The argument of a newly emerging 'Beijing Consensus' was presented by Kissinger Associate Joshua Cooper Ramo in the Foreign Policy Centre paper, 'Beijing Consensus', Spring 2004, available at http://fpc.org.uk/publications/123 (accessed 15 November 2008).

12 His most notable exposition of this theory, at least outside China, is in 'China's Peaceful Rise to Great Power Status', *Foreign Affairs* 84(5) (September/October 2005): 9ff.

13 See Kurlantzick, *Charm Offensive* for these, especially chapter 9, 'America's Soft Power Goes Soft', pp. 176ff.

14 For the influence of China in Africa, see Kerry Brown and Zhang Chun, *China and Africa – Preparing for the Next Forum for China Africa Cooperation*, Chatham House Asia Programme Briefing Note 2009/02, June 2009, at http://www.chathamhouse.org.uk/files/14269_0609ch_af.pdf.

15 See OECD, *Economic Survey of China*, available at www.oecd.org/document/21/0.234 0,en_2649_34571_35331797_1_1_1,00.html (accessed 29 March 2006).

16 See Minxin Pei, *China's Trapped Transition: The Limits of Developmental Autocracy* (Harvard University Press, 2006); and Willy Lam, *Chinese Politics in the Hu Jintao Era: New Leaders New Challenges* (Armonk, NY: M.E. Sharpe, 2006).

17 This is well covered in Susan Shirk, *China: Fragile Superpower* (Oxford University Press, 2007). Shirk speaks with particular authority: she was the Undersecretary of State covering China and East Asia under President Clinton.

18 Mobo Gao, *The Battle for China's Past: Mao and the Cultural Revolution* (London: Pluto Press, 2008), Introduction.

19 This is contained in the *Pentagon Annual Report to Congress on China's Military* in 2008, available at http://www.defenselink.mil/pubs/pdfs/China_Military_Report_08.pdf (accessed 15 September 2008).

20 IMF statistics available at http://www.imf.org/external/country/index.htm (accessed 1 January 2010).

21 Angus Maddison, *Chinese Economic Performance in the Long Run*, 2nd edn (OECD, 2007).

22 Arthur Kroeber, editor, *China Economic Quarterly*, in conversation with the author, 2006.

23 *The Economist*, 8 October 2008.

9

Russia: managing contradictions

James Sherr

By the time new American presidents have settled into the White House, they usually understand one thing about Russia: it is a difficult country to live with. But it usually takes them a full term to discover something else: Russia is a museum of contradictory truths.[1] The country's power has always concealed anxiety. Its weaknesses have always shrouded ambition. Its Eurasian expanse and perspective instils, in equal measure, a sense of vulnerability and prominence, a 'right' to 'equality' in all regions to which it is proximate and a demand for pre-eminence in areas that are historically its own. Even during the relatively congenial mid-1990s, Russia was too distinct and too proud to 'simply dissolve into the schema of European diplomacy' (in the words of Boris Yeltsin's press secretary in 1994).[2] Yet apart from the period of Leninist messianism, it has never possessed the distinctiveness, self-confidence or cultural integrity to become, like China or India, 'the other' with respect to Europe. Like an only child needing company and fearing intrusion at the same time, Russia seeks a seat at the top table of today's European and Euro-Atlantic clubs, while claiming exemptions from the values and standards that make them clubs.

To the Russian mind, contradiction is part of life itself, and life's complexities and ironies call for contradictory thoughts and approaches. To the American mind, contradictory thoughts are a sign of stupidity and contradictory approaches a sign of guile. But this is an attitude that Russians find difficult to comprehend. The United States has been unique in its ability to dominate international institutions and stand apart from them. Long before the George W. Bush administration, Russians marvelled at America's apparently presumptive right to lead the world and, without any shame at the inconsistency, heap opprobrium on Russia for trying to remain 'leader of stability and security' over the finite territory that it once possessed. Russians have no difficulty adding colour to this picture. From their vantage point, the United States is a country absolute about defending its own sovereignty but strident in warning others that 'sovereignty is no defence'; carefree in equating itself with the 'international community' but ready to disregard that community (and the UN) the moment its national interests intervene; passionate in elevating democracy to a universal norm but assiduous in financing and arming autocratic, kleptocratic and despotic allies in the pursuit of 'energy security' or the 'war on terror'. From Russia's perspective, the United States has mastered the contradictions of life very well.

The Russian image of American hypocrisy, part parody but part reality, overlooks another reality: the widespread attractiveness of the United States and the alliances and institutions that it has formed, inspired or led. Since the end of the Second World War, the United States has occasionally led with bravado, but more often with sobriety and occasionally with reluctance. Some of its alliances (with Israel, Egypt, Saudi Arabia and Pakistan, for example) have added to the stock of antipathies and turbulence in parts of the world undergoing (for reasons that transcend US policy) convulsive clashes between modernity and its opponents. Yet America's core alliances in Europe, the Far East and Australasia have made a profound contribution to the security, stability and prosperity of regions and operate with a degree of collegiality that has few precedents in history. Its allies might wish the United States were wiser, but they rarely have wished it to be weaker. Since 1991, the Russian Federation has been spared many of the dilemmas and burdens that a global power faces. Its relationship with its own allies (and those who resist alliance with it) is burdened by the Soviet legacy – macabre and sanguinary by any comparison to American 'hegemonism' – by its ambivalences towards that legacy and by its very old-fashioned craving for respect.

Although Russian negative perceptions of the United States have a long pedigree, they have achieved an unusual piquancy in recent years, and it is no exaggeration to say that President Barack Obama took office at a uniquely low point in the post-Cold War US–Russian relationship. Ironically, this decline is less attributable to the Bush administration's policy towards Russia than to the resonances generated by its policies elsewhere: the western Balkans, Iraq and, not least, NATO enlargement and missile defence. So far, the last two have been regarded as 'anti-Russian' by definition, irrespective of any evidence provided or explanation offered, and this imperviousness to evidence and explanation already constitutes one of the main challenges facing the new US administration.

THE ELUSIVENESS OF TRUST

It would be entirely artificial to pick one defining moment that marked the deterioration in the US–Russia relationship since the last period of high expectations in the weeks and months following 11 September 2001. The Rose and Orange Revolutions of 2003–04 were clearly profoundly important watersheds. Midway between these two upheavals, President Vladimir Putin darkly hinted that Western governments were complicit in the slaughter of schoolchildren in the town of Beslan in 2004.[3] Nevertheless, the Western political class as a whole did not come to terms with the depth of the divide until Putin's speech at the 43rd Munich Security Conference on 10 February 2007. Since then, a key question on the minds of those who are now working in the Obama administration has been whether trust can be restored. For minimalists in that administration, the 'resetting' of relations is designed to explore the degree to which this is possible;

for maximalists, the restoration of trust is assumed to be possible, and the 'reset' is designed to restore it.

The beginning of wisdom is to recognize that there have been only two periods of mutual trust since 1991 and that both were based on unrealistic expectations. American expectations during the first period, which extended roughly from 1991 to 1994, were conditioned not only by triumphalist and historicist thinking, but by American experience. Political establishments in the United States and most European countries had long persuaded themselves that capitalism, prosperity and liberalism went hand in hand. Far too many politicians, officials and consultants ignored far too many warnings that in Russia, the absence of civic traditions and effective institutions would produce rigged markets rather than free markets, the transformation of unaccountable bureaucratic power into unaccountable financial power and illicit alliances between the state, business and organized crime. In their more hopeful beliefs the architects of Western policy were encouraged by the self-designated liberals and economic radicals who featured so prominently in President Yeltsin's initial policy team. Western triumphalism and Russian 'romanticism' reinforced one another in ways that became increasingly unwelcome to those outside this magic circle. Far from helping Russia through the 'birth pangs of democracy', the pronounced character of Western support for Boris Yeltsin's reformers and their narrowly macro-economic model of reform made the United States an inadvertent protagonist in a process that, not for the first time, gradually persuaded much of the country, 'not for the first time in Russian history, that Western models and values are irrelevant, if not downright harmful, to their peculiarly Russian circumstances and predicaments'.[4]

Western governments were also wrong to assume that, once the dust settled, Russia would be reconciled to the post-Cold War status quo. In 1992, Russia acquired borders that it had never possessed before and which, to much of the country, made no sense in economic, security or civilizational terms. Far from regarding these realities as a new and legitimate status quo, the 'liberal' leadership regarded them as temporary.[5] The first Foreign Ministry report on the subject in September 1992 defined the integration of the former Soviet space as a 'vital interest' to be pursued by 'all legitimate means', including 'divide and influence policies'.[6] Very few at the time regarded this as an anti-Western interest. To the contrary, Foreign Minister Andrei Kozyrev and others believed that Russia's integration into the West would prove to be the antidote to Soviet disintegration and provide the basis for reintegration on 'democratic', post-Soviet terms, with US support.[7] The 'Russia first' policy prevalent in Washington and other Western capitals until the mid-1990s did nothing to discourage them. Nor did it discourage the hopes of Russia's liberals that the end of confrontation would lead to an 'equal' position for Russia in Europe: in other words, veto-wielding prerogatives in decision-making on matters of pan-European importance.

By the time the liberals, pejoratively dismissed as 'romantics', were moved aside by the more traditional 'centrists' of the Russian establishment, warnings of a divergence of perspective between Russia and its Western partners had become not only evident but 'loud'.[8] It was not in 2004 but 1994 (at the start of NATO's *UN-sanctioned* bombing campaign in Bosnia) that Boris Yeltsin told the Foreign Intelligence Service that 'ideological confrontation is being replaced by a struggle for spheres of influence in geopolitics' and warned that 'forces abroad' wanted to keep Russia in a state of 'controllable paralysis'.[9] Five years later, NATO's intervention in the Kosovo conflict (which was not UN-sanctioned) entrenched these views across the political spectrum.

By the close of the Yeltsin era, US policy-making circles were coming to terms with the re-emergence of four elements of continuity in the 'new' Russia:

- a growing emphasis on geopolitics, which, with its emphasis on power and 'struggle', had begun to fill the intellectual vacuum left by the demise of Marxism-Leninism;
- displacement of the Western priority (and priority of integration into Western institutions) by integration of the post-Soviet 'near abroad' as a vital and irreducible interest, no longer predicated on Western support;[10]
- increasingly open designation of the external CIS borders as the defence perimeter of the Russian Federation itself;[11] and
- the considerable recovery of influence by the country's military and security establishments, which in their mentality and working culture remained Soviet establishments in all but name.

The chronic economic dislocations inside Russia, the deepening of tensions between state and society, the *de facto* privatization of state institutions by sectoral and clan interests, and continued *mnogogolosiye* ('multi-voicedness') in the formation and execution of policy sharply constrained the potential of these trends and limited their visibility abroad. Nevertheless, a considerable souring of relations had set in well before Vladimir Putin came to office.

Today it is easy to forget that many US policy-makers (not least President Bush) saw Putin's accession to power as a fresh start. His candour about Russia's past mistakes,[12] his elevation of a new generation of technocrats and reformers, his assault on the oligarchs 'as a class', his streamlining of regulations and lowering of taxes; his emphasis on foreign trade and investment, and his pronounced emphasis on 'pragmatism' as the basis for foreign relations (even the hint that Russia might entertain NATO membership) secured a broadly favourable image for Putin in the West until the onset of the YUKOS affair in 2003. Yet outside the post-Soviet 'near abroad', the more significant departures from the Yeltsin era were discerned by few:

- The restoration of the state, and the transformation of security services, armed forces, the defence-industrial complex and the energy sector into instruments of national power and pillars of national revival.
- The emergence of a strong geo-economic impulse to policy and, with the restoration of the 'administrative vertical' in Russia, politically usable economic power. The *Energy Strategy of Russia to 2020* (published in 2003, before the rise in global energy prices) stated that 'the role of the country

in world energy markets to a large extent determines its geopolitical influence'.[13]

- The coming of age of a new, post-Soviet class – moneyed, self-confident, European in outlook but nationalistic and illiberal; and, in parallel with their maturation, a state-fostered restoration of national pride on the basis of a selective, but potent fusion of pre-Soviet, Soviet and post-Soviet values.[14]

- A shift in emphasis in the new foreign policy *Concept*[15] from the strengthening of mutual interests towards the 'firm promotion of national interests'.[16]

- In the 'near abroad', a similar shift away from 'fraternal' ties towards a policy described as 'clear', 'specific', 'cold' and 'far tougher'[17] – and, with this, a 'more active' utilization of hard and soft power to 'promote in neighbouring countries groups of influence orientated towards Moscow and a gradual weakening and neutralization of pro-Western circles'.[18]

Were it not for the events of 9/11, more might have been made of these tendencies by policy-makers in the West. Instead, to all intents and appearances, they vanished in that carnage. President Putin immediately grasped that the attack had changed the coordinates of world politics, and he rose to the occasion over the stationing of US military forces in Central Asia and the resumption of cooperation with NATO. Yet he never lost sight of Russia's core interests. Whereas Western governments viewed the post-9/11 world with foreboding, he viewed it as an opportunity. It was the West that now needed Russia. With fair justification, he assumed that the new partnership would untie his hands against 'Islamic extremism' in the north Caucasus, which was juridically part of Russia. With little justification, he assumed that the West would also acquiesce in Russia's dominance over newly independent states, which were not. He also assumed that by conceding Russia's right to its own policies towards Iraq and Iran, the West had forfeited its right to criticize these policies and ask how they furthered partnership. Within little more than a year, old differences reappeared, and the second, brief period of trust dissipated. Even before the coloured revolutions of 2003–04, a fresh round of recriminations was under way.

Yet it was the Rose Revolution in Georgia and, even more, the Orange Revolution in Ukraine that launched Russia on the trajectory that reached its nadir with the Russia–Georgia war of 2008. To Russians persuaded that *samostoyatel'noy Ukrainiy nikogda ne budet* ('Ukraine will never be able to stand alone'), these were Western 'special operations' from beginning to end. Not only were they seen as marking an ominous turn in an intensifying geopolitical rivalry, they were also seen as a major intensification of the West's *Kulturkampf* against Russia and its political order. After the post-9/11 partnership with the United States and years spent cultivating the EU, these developments were seen as nothing short of a betrayal.

To be sure, NATO enlargement played a major role in this dynamic. To the Russian military establishment and by now the overwhelming majority of the political establishment, NATO was and remains an anti-Russian military alliance. Claims that it has become a political-military alliance dedicated to the strengthening of common security are regarded as risible and insulting. These views have at least two sources. The first is the geopolitical determinism of the military establishment, which has acquired influence well beyond this narrow milieu. Whereas Western security elites define threat in terms of intention and capability, their Russian counterparts define it in terms of space: by the presence of foreign forces in areas in the vicinity of Russian territory, whatever their ostensible purpose and irrespective of whether the host countries have invited them or not.[19] Within this schema, the Russian defence perimeter includes the former Soviet space, whether or not the countries that inhabit this space agree. The second source of Russian views is NATO's policies, which have hardened perceptions about its aims and character. The 1999 Kosovo conflict was a turning point in this context.[20] It removed any pretence that NATO was a strictly defensive alliance. The war in Iraq (wrongly seen in Russia as a NATO operation) only reinforced this conclusion.

Yet within two years of the Orange Revolution, there was a new element to Russia's estrangement from the West: self-confidence. As Putin said at Munich in February 2007, 'we have a realistic sense of our own opportunities and potential'. He also had a realistic sense that the United States and its allies had become globally overextended, that NATO programmes of cooperation in Russia's 'near abroad' lacked teeth, that the weaknesses of NATO's partners were chronic and that NATO itself was profoundly divided about its future course. NATO hoped that the formula agreed by its heads of state at their summit in Bucharest in April 2008 – no formal offer of Membership Action Plans (MAP) to Ukraine and Georgia, no timetables, but an existential commitment that 'Ukraine and Georgia will become members of NATO' – would lower the temperature. Instead, it raised it. By then, the gap between Western aspirations and capability had all the appearance of bluff. In August 2008 the bluff was called.

Had the West been willing to learn more lessons from the Soviet collapse and teach fewer of them, it might have been possible to avoid illusions, anticipate (and articulate) differences and diminish resentment. Had the West been less reassured by its own good intentions and more conscious of the precedents its actions would create in the minds of others (as over the independence of Kosovo), it still might have acted as it did, but been better prepared for the consequences.

Nevertheless, the West did not 'lose' Russia, and it is naïve to suppose that it could have 'won' it.[21] Unlike post-war Germany, post-Cold War Russia was not in the West's trusteeship. It was not defeated in war and occupied. It was not governed by Western authorities and administrators. No Western policy could have spared Russia economic trauma. No Western agency could have reconstructed the elites of the country or persuaded Boris Yeltsin to dismantle the iron core of the military and security system. No Western policy or power could have induced Russia to abandon the myths of a 'common history' with Ukraine or to come to terms with the actual legacy of Soviet power in the former USSR.

Although the West might have given more substance to its magnanimity – by cancelling the USSR's debt, for example – it is Russia's leaders who must answer for their failure to make the historic choice to establish a state (like Adenauer's Germany) that based its legitimacy on a repudiation of the state that preceded it. Instead, they chose to have it both ways: to create a 'successor' state based on rejection as well as continuity with the state that preceded it. Inevitably, many of Russia's neighbours viewed this stance as an attempt to reclaim some of the prerogatives of the Soviet past while denying responsibility for it. It is unrealistic, not to say unreasonable, to expect former adversaries, as it were overnight, to grant 'equality' to a state that was so historically ambivalent about a predecessor that had extinguished their independence.

The anti-Enlightenment philosopher Joseph de Maistre once said, 'we do not invent ourselves'. In a not entirely different spirit, T.S. Eliot once remarked that 'mankind cannot cope with much reality'. The post-Cold War years vindicated both of these warnings. The collapse of Communism could not restore an Enlightenment heritage that Russia never possessed or dispose of the imperial mentality in a country where state and empire were never distinguishable. After too much reality, it was not surprising that Russia did not find itself 'at the end of history', but at the beginning, 'rediscovering the historical, cultural and geo-political imperatives that make Russia Russia'.[22]

NATIONALISM, RESENTMENT AND DISORIENTATION

One year before Barack Obama took office, Russia's policy towards the West was based on three foundations: nationalism, resentment and self-confidence. Today, it is based upon nationalism, resentment and disorientation. The global financial crisis – which some in Russia predicted would be visited upon others only – accounts for much of this disorientation. But there are two other factors: the unhealthy configuration of power in the country and the failure to secure pre-eminence in the former Soviet Union after the Russia–Georgia war.

There have been several waves of official reaction to the financial crisis since the summer of 2008: first, denial and a public front (based on an ardent wish) that Russia would remain an 'island of stability' and a 'safe haven' in the turmoil; second, behind-the-scenes panic as the real economy slid rapidly downhill; and third, relative calm as oil prices began to rebound in early 2009. But only now has genuine disorientation set in, as the truth dawns that even as oil prices recover, the economy recovers less. The explanation for this truth, well expressed by a number of Russian experts, is that the strategy of commodity-led growth ignored and repressed structural flaws in the economy that have now assumed malignant proportions: monopolization (which explains why prices rise even when income falls); a level of bureaucratic sclerosis and corruption not seen even in the Yeltsin era; and chronic underinvestment in the domestic energy market (which consumes as much oil and gas as Japan, India, the United Kingdom and Italy combined).[23] To these realities, one half of the Russian policy-making elite has been deaf and the other half apprehensive, anxious and blocked by the first half.

Given the realities of power in Russia, it is not difficult to understand why. Vladimir Putin, who as prime minister bears overall responsibility for the economy, lacks an economist's understanding of it. Having convinced himself that the restoration of the 'vertical of power' restored Russia's economic prospects, he cannot now accept that it is the single greatest factor that hinders them. President Dmitry Medvedev might be able to accept it, but in the words of one Russian expert, he has 'no appetite for tough decisions' and has a 'lack of character that cannot be compensated by social skills'.

Yet there are deeper reasons than these. Those who run the country now own it. Whereas 50 per cent of Russia's GDP was controlled by seven relatively independent bankers in the 1990s, by 2006 five senior Kremlin officials chaired companies that produced 33 per cent of national wealth. These individuals are most unlikely to champion a reform that would deconstruct the system they constructed. Moreover, that system could only have been constructed by emasculating the representative institutions that made their appearance in the chaos of the 1990s. Legislators, judges and bureaucrats who are drummed into submissiveness do not act when factories and social services shut down in their localities. They await instructions. Flying visits by Putin and his deputies now substitute for the normal workings of government. This absence of democratic normality – scrutiny, feedback, argument and the countervailing powers that compel leaders to pay heed to them – has aggravated every unhealthy characteristic of an inbred, opaque and self-referential elite. It is not surprising that, while Medvedev and Putin remain trusted by the public at large, informed circles now openly express a sense of futility and foreboding.

Foreboding would also be a rational response to the change in relations between Russia and its neighbours after the war with Georgia in August 2008. One month after that conflict, President Medvedev boasted to members of the Valdai Club (the annual gathering of international experts on Russia) that his country was no longer 'weak and defenceless' and would no longer 'tolerate' the West's 'unfair and humiliating' policy in 'traditional areas of interests' defined by 'shared, common history' and the 'affinity of our souls'.[24] Yet, one year later within those 'traditional areas', that affinity is less reciprocated than at any time in recent decades. Russia's use of armed force against Georgia has profoundly alarmed its other neighbours. No member of the Commonwealth of Independent States[25] has followed Nicaragua's example and recognized the independence of South Ossetia and Abkhazia. To add insult to injury, four heads of state failed to attend the August 2009 CIS summit; Belarus (a member alongside Kazakhstan of a 'Union State' with Russia) has accepted an invitation to join the EU's Eastern Partnership that Russia condemns and has instructed its citizens to respect Georgian laws in the newly 'sovereign' states; Tajikistan has issued a decree downgrading the status of the Russian language; Kyrgyzstan has restored basing rights to the United States (and charged Russia a heavy tariff for new bases); Turkmenistan has declared its support for the Nabucco pipeline project (which Russia reviles); Uzbekistan's officials openly express disquiet about Russia's motives to American visitors;[26] and the Russian-sponsored mediation effort over the disputed enclave of Nagorno-Karabakh has fallen apart. As Boris Nemtsov (a former Acting Prime Minister of Russia) lamented: 'we have no remaining friends, only enemies … To put it simply, we have fallen out with everyone'. If in August 2008, Russia could plausibly blame the West for its difficulties, that is no longer possible.

Yet instead of following Nemtsov's advice to look in the mirror and draw conclusions, on 11 August 2009 Medvedev took an aggressive step backwards. His very public letter to President Victor Yushchenko of Ukraine reiterated every Orwellian utterance that fills even Russophile Ukrainians with apprehension. Russia and Ukraine are 'two sovereign states'.[27] Yet 'for Russia, Ukrainians since the dawn of time have been and remain not only neighbours, but a brotherly people', from which it follows that Ukraine, in contrast to other 'sovereign states' is obliged to maintain 'tight economic cooperation' and 'solidly kindred, humanitarian ties' with Russia. Although less than two years had passed since Putin called Ukraine's statehood into question at the NATO summit, and barely a month since he termed any attempt to separate Russia and 'little Russia' a 'crime', Medvedev saw fit to remind Yushchenko that a 'Russian threat to Ukraine's security … as you perfectly well know does not exist and never will'. Barely a year after Russia went to war in response to Georgia's 'barbarous assault' against South Ossetia, Medvedev declared that Ukrainians who supplied arms to Georgia 'fully share responsibility with Tbilisi for these absolute crimes'. Inevitably, his letter was read not only as a clumsy attempt to influence Ukraine's presidential elections, but also as a warning of trouble in the future.

CURBING ENTHUSIASMS

On the face of it, the dynamics and discourse on display in Russia's neighbourhood could not stand in greater contrast to the principles set out in Russia's proposals for a new European Security Treaty (EST). Analysis of these proposals from their initial articulation by President Medvedev in Berlin on 5 June 2008 to the publication of a draft EST on 29 November 2009 raises a number of questions.

This is most notably the case with regard to the cardinal principle that President Medvedev set out on 8 October 2008 at the World Policy Conference in Evian: the creation of an international system 'equal for all states … without zones with different levels of security'. Set against his condemnation of the 'NATO-centric approach', the clear premise behind the call for equality is that it does not yet exist. For it to emerge, the 'strengthening of the positions of the Russian Federation in international affairs' must be accepted (in short its role must be enhanced), while other actors must not overstep their 'legitimate' interests and scope of activity (in short their role must be diminished).[28] The United States must adhere strictly to international law and accept the reality of a 'polycentric international system' not 'ruled from a single capital'. However, it must decline calls for assistance from other national capitals.[29] 'Equality' must replace the 'NATO-centric approach' but Russia has a right to maintain ('like other countries in the world') regions of 'privileged interests', i.e. 'with our close neighbours'.[30] NATO must halt its 'mechanical enlargement', even when it occurs by invitation. It must confine itself to issues of 'hard security' within the 'geographical limits of the alliance', even if within these geographical limits no issues of hard security exist. The EU and the Organization for Security and Cooperation in Europe (OSCE) must eschew 'double standards, respecting the national and historical peculiarities of each state'; but must raise no objection when Russia fails to respect them in the former USSR.[31] Gazprom must (in the words of its CEO, Alexei Miller) be recognized as a 'global energy leader', and the EU has no right to use anti-monopoly regulations to block its 'legitimate ambitions' even where the pursuit of these ambitions violates the laws of member states and international best practice.[32]

President Obama gave a distinctly guarded welcome to President Medvedev's proposals during their first meeting on the eve of the G20 London summit in April 2009. Since June 2009 the so-called Corfu process, under the OSCE chairmanship of Greece, has institutionalized the dialogue with Russia on Europe's security architecture. But it has done so on the basis of three principles at variance with Russian proposals:

- The OSCE, as an inclusive body of 56 states, should remain the framework for this dialogue.
- The dialogue should cover all aspects of security, including human rights, democracy and the rule of law.
- The dialogue must not presuppose a conclusion or lead *a priori* to a 'binding' security treaty.

In response, the Russian Ministry of Foreign Affairs asserts that EST and Corfu are 'mutually overlapping but not mutually replaceable approaches'.[33] Russia will be satisfied with nothing less than an entirely new process, leading to a binding security treaty. Otherwise, as Foreign Minister Sergei Lavrov warns, there will be a full-scale renationalization of security (which can only mean *by Russia*, since NATO and the EU make decisions by consensus).[34] The continuity between Medvedev's initial proposals in Berlin and the draft EST demonstrates a striking imperviousness to the ideas, principles and concerns of Russia's supposed partners.

The inescapable question that follows is what chances the US 'reset' initiative has of overcoming this imperviousness. The Moscow summit on 6–8 July 2009 produced one significant commitment – to conclude a successor to the July 1991 Strategic Arms Reduction Treaty (START-1), which lapsed on 5 December 2009 – and one significant agreement (to allow lethal military equipment to transit Russia by air to Afghanistan).

Now both of these initiatives are foundering. The follow-on to START has aroused the anxiety and suspiciousness of Russia's military establishment. Critics warn of a net diminution of Russia's deterrent capacity in the face of a new, phased US missile defence programme (which replaced the February 2007 Bush missile defence initiative in September 2009), the unrestricted development of US precision-guided conventional munitions, the progressive obsolescence of Soviet-era strategic nuclear forces and the calamitous setback to Russia's sea-launched ballistic missile programme caused by the latest failure of the Bulava missile in December 2009.[35] The Obama administration's substantial concessions over conventional warheads, nuclear missile modernization and inspection have done little to alter mindsets, and on 29 December Prime Minister Putin firmly established the link between a new offensive arms accord and ballistic missile defences.[36]

The Afghanistan transit accord has also run into the buffers of the system. Thanks to unspecified 'technical problems', instead of 12 heavy US transports transiting Russia to Afghanistan on a daily basis as envisaged at the July summit, only one test flight had taken place by 31 December 2009. Those who heard Lavrov express Russia's worries about a NATO defeat in Afghanistan might find this surprising.[37] Yet Lavrov has not expressed support for a NATO victory, and this is not a trivial distinction. Much of the military and security leadership fear that a stabilizing, consolidating Afghanistan under NATO auspices would complicate Russia's relations with China, India, Pakistan and Central Asia (where it already finds itself under pressure), as well as providing a further impetus for energy transit projects to bypass Russia. It would compromise Russia's self-perceived pivotal role and set back its ambitions for the CSTO (Collective Security Treaty Organization)[38] and SCO (Shanghai Cooperation Organization) to become the pre-eminent security bodies in Central and Southwest Asia.[39] It would also set back Russia's ambitions to have a decided influence in Afghanistan itself, not as a US partner, but as an independent actor, with its own breadth of experience and hard-earned wisdom and without the 'democratic' baggage that comes with US support.[40]

In the aftermath of the Moscow summit, Washington did not claim any breakthrough on the second issue of global importance, Iran. This is not surprising. Until recently, Moscow's operative principle was the 'great game', not partnership with the United States. The interests of powerful financial groups in Russia possibly take precedence over both. Economic ties with Iran are of structural importance: greatly beneficial to the high-technology sectors of the Russian economy, which Moscow believes the West seeks to weaken. In the boardrooms of Gazprom and Rosneft, the continuation of tension between Iran and the West is preferable to Iran's re-emergence as a full player on global energy markets. Moreover, Russia has strong reasons to ensure that Iran continues to show restraint with regard to Azerbaijan (where there are ethnic ties), Armenia (where there are historical ties) and the states of Central Asia (where there are elements of both). It is equally keen that Iran, like Russia, should continue to oppose the construction of a trans-Caspian gas pipeline to supply Nabucco. There is, in short, a complex of interests at work and a complex of players inside Russia.

Nevertheless, Moscow has recently demonstrated marked concern at Tehran's defiance of the International Atomic Energy Agency (IAEA) and shown greater willingness to act in concert with the Western members of the 5+1 group (notably, in securing an IAEA resolution censuring Iran and transferring the issue to the UN Security Council). How much this is due to the US reset is, for the moment, unclear. In summer 2009, Israel provided a sharp reminder of its ability to act independently and in ways that could prove damaging to Russia. The seizure of the Russian vessel *Arctic Sea*, most likely by Israeli commandos, and the messages subsequently conveyed in Prime Minister Netanyahu's semi-secret visit to Russia caused at least a minor panic in Russia's security establishment.[41] It is too early to say whether Moscow's tougher position is an isolated episode, a tactical repositioning or the start of a trend towards closer cooperation with Washington.

So far, the US administration has been sober in its expectations about the reset. Nevertheless, in his interview with the *Wall Street Journal* on 25 July 2009, Vice President Biden came to a sound conclusion and a questionable one. The sound conclusion, as noted above, is that Russia's problems are serious and 'over the next fifteen years … not sustainable'. The questionable one is that the gravity of these problems will induce Russia to accommodate itself to the interests of others. Biden's qualification – that in the short term, Russia could become more belligerent – should not be a qualification, but the focal point of near-term attention. Long-term forecasts can be skewed out of recognition by wilfulness, ingenuity and miscalculation in the near term. The emphasis on the need for 'calculated decisions' in Russia begs the question: who calculates? Important as it is to understand the art of the possible over the next 15 years, the more urgent task for Washington and Brussels is to understand what Putin and Medvedev might do during the next two. It would be prudent to proceed from three assumptions.

First, the financial crisis does not create a 'need' for moderation in Russia's policy. It creates pressure. In January 2009, Russia's response to this pressure was to lock in its comparative advantage with Ukraine and make aggressive use of residual margins of strength. Whatever Ukraine's responsibilities for the winter gas crisis, financial pressure on Gazprom produced immoderation rather than moderation. The November accords between Putin and Ukrainian Prime Minister Tymoshenko – and the likelihood of a reset initiative by the new Ukrainian president – make it likely that a repetition of this scenario will be avoided. But for how long? Financial, market and production conditions now make it ever more uncertain that Russia's flagship pipeline projects will be financed or that there will be enough gas to fill them. These constraints only increase the importance of Ukraine's Gas Transit System and its management. Sooner or later, that system could come under assault as Ukraine, burdened by an economic crisis far more dire than Russia's, finds that it cannot pay its gas bills. The dynamics of tension and the risks of harsh action are not alleviated by the financial crisis, but worsened by it.

Second, Russia's priority in its own neighbourhood is not stability but influence, and this has been evident under all three Russian presidents since the Soviet collapse. While homilies about the danger of Ukraine's destabilization are issued at regular intervals by part of the policy-making elite in Moscow, the fact is that

Russia has invested heavily in the tools of destabilization and identified every nodal point of fragility in that country. In the states of the south Caucasus (and Russia's own republics in the north), Moscow's policy of 'divide and influence' has been pursued with malign and damaging effect for these states and Russia itself. Outside initiatives (e.g. the EU's Eastern Partnership) that do not envisage a 'privileged' role for Russia are vehemently opposed, whatever their intended or real benefits. It would be imprudent to suppose that the structural deficiencies of the Russian economy, which become ever more plain as time advances, will alter this priority. But it might for a time recede. Such an interregnum, if it arises, will buy time for systemic change in neighbouring countries, should local elites and their Western partners be prepared to take advantage of it. For countries which value their independence, qualitative change – of public institutions, administrative cultures and the relationship between business and the state – will be the only way to defeat this post-Soviet syndrome until systemic change in Russia finally cures it. As a Russian interlocutor of the author said in 2009, 'we would love to interfere in Poland, but we can't find any way of doing it'.[42]

The third prudent assumption is that intra-elite relationships will be the principal determinant of change inside Russia and in its foreign policy. To be systemic, such change would have to be political as well as economic. Today, economic pressures are being managed within the conventions of the system by the groups that define these conventions and benefit from them. So far, the crisis has not been deep enough to alter paradigms about Russia's political or economic model, or its model of relations with the outside world. One could do worse than to accept Stephen Blank's verdict that 'Russia's problem is a structural one, inherent in the Russian system and Russia's ongoing efforts to carve a larger role ... than it can sustain'.[43] Or, as Ira Straus put it with a less deterministic edge:

> If Russia wants a strong and stable influence in the post-Soviet space, it will try to do it together with the West. If instead what it wants is pride in its influence against the West, it will keep on running into bad news, and manic-depressive mood swings between moments of triumph and moments of despair.[44]

In sum, while external factors set the scene, systemic, intra-elite and temperamental factors produce the play. The West is not doomed to be a spectator. Its challenge is to set the scene. But this requires a degree of purpose and fibre that has not always been present in Western policy.

IMAGINATION AND REALISM

Imagination and realism are required in three areas. First, it is time to face the uncomfortable truth that we are rarely seen by others as we see ourselves, and this is certainly the case for the United States *vis-à-vis* Russia. NATO enlargement, military intervention in Kosovo (and subsequent recognition of its independence), the Iraq war (perceived by many in Russia as a NATO operation), the establishment of military bases and facilities in former Warsaw Pact countries and support for Georgian President Mikheil Saakashvili vindicate, in

Moscow's eyes, the core premises of the Putin–Medvedev policy. Yet the main explanation for Russian attitudes is Russia. Without understanding the way the Darwinian system of power relations, undiluted geopolitics and aggressive geo-economics interact and reinforce one another, Western governments will not understand why their policy has been interpreted so negatively or why so many of their Russian interlocutors are deaf to explanation and argument.

A second, more uncomfortable truth is that, although the West possesses an abundance of policy instruments in Russia's neighbourhood, for the first time since the early 1990s it has no effective policy there. The previous US administration often acted as if Russia had no legitimate interests in the former Soviet Union. Some policy-makers pushed to the limit the sound principle that non-member states be afforded no 'right of veto' over NATO's future enlargement, excluding any accommodation or discussion about the modalities of the process. At a number of levels, US diplomacy was as professional as it could be. But public diplomacy, which was often shrill and moralistic, was undiplomatic. The tone of US policy failed to take into account not only the sensibilities of Russians but the anxieties of Ukrainians, most of whom see NATO as an anti-Russian instrument. The tone of NATO's public diplomacy – bland, formulaic and clichéed – came across in the local environment as elusive and dishonest despite the best efforts of NATO's local representatives to enliven and give substance to the discourse. Russians and Ukrainians 'know' that Russia's Black Sea Fleet will have to leave Crimea before Ukraine joins NATO and that Ukraine–Russia defence-industrial cooperation will end. But NATO does not know these things and does not necessarily believe them. Most of its members are distinctly open-minded on these subjects and predisposed to find acceptable solutions, but how many in the region know this?

Yet these issues, which deserved articulation in 2005, have been overtaken by the Russo-Georgia war. Today the issue is fundamentally more serious. How does NATO re-establish credibility with those in partner countries who now believe that war is possible, who perceive that the former Soviet borders are no longer sacrosanct, who fear that questions long regarded as settled (e.g. the status of Crimea and Sevastopol) can be reopened at any moment, who grasp that 'civilizational' and 'humanitarian' factors (e.g. the status of the Russian diaspora) can constitute a *casus belli* and who are now convinced that where there is no Article 5, there is no collective defence? If NATO does not address this question, it will forfeit influence. If the United States does not lead this exercise, it will not take place.

To many, a failure by NATO to rebuild its influence in the former USSR would simply be a belated recognition of geopolitical reality. Yet these realities can no longer be understood in nineteenth-century terms. We are no longer living in a world where small powers quietly accept what great powers dictate. Empire, spheres of influence and the balance of power – principles long associated with the European international order between 1648 and 1914 – had by the early twentieth century become synonymous with international and internal disorder, not to say misery, and no explanation of the origins of the First World

War has standing if it ignores the fact. Ignoring this history is the surest way of repeating it.

Third, we need to ask whether the institutions that *we* deem central to the relationship between Russia and the West – NATO, the EU and the OSCE – are fit for purpose. The first two display a combination of common interests, shared values and collective capacity that does not exist elsewhere and would be uncommonly difficult to replicate. But neither they nor the OSCE have succeeded in reconciling Russia to the post-Cold War system that these institutions have largely created.

For one thing, the core premises of the NATO–Russia relationship have not been reassessed in an explicit or concerted fashion since the 1990s, and the Alliance is possibly no longer capable of adopting such an assessment. The Russia–Georgia war did not change paradigms. It only deepened divisions. NATO's emerging New Strategic Concept, the first since 1999, may extract some coherence from these divisions, but the NATO–Russia Council, which did not meet once between the April 2008 Bucharest summit and the start of the war in Georgia, plainly failed to rise to the occasion. Although some lessons have been learnt, Russia is no longer prepared to believe that the Council will give adequate weight to its interests or status.

The EU, for its part, has defied sceptics by developing security-enhancing capacity alongside NATO rather than at cross-purposes with it. With predictable detours and inhibitions, it is also adopting a strategic and proactive approach to energy security, to Russia's neighbourhood and to Russia itself. Yet its terms of engagement do not engage Russia. Russia retains its proclivity for bilateral relations with European states, as opposed to deepening relations with the European Union, and this proclivity is displayed more flagrantly now than at any time since the end of the Cold War. Moscow oscillates between indignation towards the European Commission and smug confidence that its core bilateral partnerships will reduce disagreeable initiatives (e.g. the Eastern Partnership) to impotence. It is equally confident that new member states can be marginalized, intimidated or bought.

The OSCE has also defied sceptics. Contrary to apprehensions in the mid-1990s, it has not become Russia's chosen instrument. Its three specialized institutions and 19 field operations have acquired substantial autonomy, have concentrated overwhelmingly on the Helsinki Final Act's soft security 'baskets' and have done so largely east of Vienna, in defiance of blunt Russian warnings.[45] During the three rounds of voting that demarcated the stages of Ukraine's Orange Revolution, the OSCE's Office of Democratic Institutions and Human Rights (ODIHR) became a *de facto* guarantor of peaceful regime change. This evolution explains Putin's outburst at Munich in 2007 at those who were 'trying to transform the OSCE into a vulgar instrument designed to promote the foreign policy interests of one or a group of countries'.[46] At the same time, Russia set stringent constraints on ODIHR's election monitoring in Russia's presidential and State Duma elections – constraints that were swiftly adopted by Russia's partners in the CSTO – and in 2008 Russia terminated the

OSCE field operation in Georgia.

Russia no longer accepts the centrality of these institutions. Its preoccupations of the 1990s – enlarging its prerogatives inside NATO and securing a pre-eminent role for the OSCE – have been overtaken, as both Medvedev's security proposals and Russia's tough termination of the OSCE's mission in Georgia demonstrate. Russia's representatives lament the fact that 'twenty years after the end of the Cold War, there still is no reliable, comprehensive and integrated security architecture throughout the area extending from Vancouver to Vladivostok'.[47] But NATO and the EU have brought peace to a large part of Europe in large part because their members accept common standards as to what takes place within these jurisdictions. Whose security will benefit if others are denied the right to embrace these standards and join these institutions? Why should liberal democracy be excluded from a discussion of European security when it has brought so much security to Europe? Russia's draft EST is not only unsound but impractical.[48] It is a flawed document that calls for discussion and scrutiny. This is because it sums up everything that is problematic about Russia's relationship with Europe. Russia's rejection of established institutions also raises a compelling question: how can it find security in a system with which it refuses to integrate? Russia has brought this conundrum upon itself, and it cannot avoid responsibility for it. But the Euro-Atlantic community cannot walk away from it either.

US CAPACITY: POSSIBILITIES AND LIMITS

No country can assess the adequacy of its capacity until its objectives are defined. The United States is a global power, and it must think globally. It remains the only country with the means to deploy hard and soft power in almost any part of the world. Within its purview are threats that are highly unconventional and potentially apocalyptic in character. The most intuitive conclusion to reach is that, where Russia is concerned, the top US priority must be to enlist that country's help in addressing those global threats where it enjoys influence: Afghanistan, Iran and, more generically, counter-terrorism, counter-proliferation and missile defence. A number of distinguished observers have made this point forcefully.[49] Yet for three reasons, the argument is open to question:

- It conflates global US priorities with the priorities that should govern the US–Russia relationship. If Russia could make the difference between success and failure in Iran or Afghanistan, the argument for doing so might be strong. But it cannot, at least not at an acceptable cost to itself. Its own national interests place stringent limits on the degree to which it would either support or obstruct US policy. Russia's capacity also has limits.
- There are other areas of long-standing US interest – not least on the Eurasian continent – where Russia has greater capacity to be helpful or cause harm. If Russia is to sacrifice important interests of its own in Iran or Southwest Asia, it will demand a price in areas of primary importance

to itself: its 'near abroad' and Europe. If the United States is not willing to pay that price, then its policy will lack realism.

• If the United States *is* willing to pay this price, it will lack wisdom. The precondition of the US ability to act globally is not cooperation with Russia, but stability and security in Europe. Those who claim that this is no longer so need to ask how the United States would meet its global challenges if conflict returned to Central and Eastern Europe and if the West's core institutions, NATO and the EU, were not only divided but in disarray or on the point of dissolution.

With respect to Russia, the challenge for the United States is to achieve three objectives in a way that makes them mutually reinforcing. The broad and primary objective must be to advance Western interests in Central and Eastern Europe, the Black Sea region and across Eurasia. It has been rightly said that:

The main aim of Western policies in the late 1980s and early 1990s was to manage a peaceful transition in Europe as a whole. Policy towards Russia fitted into this wider picture, but could not be, for the West, its sole or determining preoccupation.[50]

Similarly today, the United States and other Western actors have an interest in consolidating the outcome of the 1990s transition in Central Europe, maintaining the security and self-confidence of NATO's newer members, providing Russia's neighbours with the assistance and support they need to remain independent *de facto* as well as *de jure*, strengthen energy security, support a safe and predictable environment for trade and investment and diminish new and existing regional threats in the form of terrorism, weapons proliferation and transnational organized crime.

The second objective is to find sustainable and mutually beneficial accommodations with Russia. The West will not be able to do so unless it is willing to live with Russia as it is. That will entail a mature understanding of differences between Russian interests and those of the West, a dispassionate acceptance of differences of political culture, a disciplined understanding of the realities of power (which in the former Soviet Union do not always favour us) and prudent expectations. Where US capacity is essential but insufficient (as is arguably the case in Ukraine and the South Caucasus), the West must consider how to rebuild it. But it should never again allow toughness to become a substitute for strength. Firmness, prudence and patience are required in equal measure if we are to diminish misunderstanding, limit tension and identify areas where we can cooperate with Russia to mutual advantage. Under Russia's present political dispensation, these areas are likely to be limited.

The third objective should be to transform the West's relationship with Russia, because in the long run Europe will not be fully secure, let alone 'whole', until Russia feels secure in Europe. The pursuit of this objective is likely to outlast the efforts of one US administration because it depends upon a far from simple task: changing thinking and practice in Russia. Russia's current security paradigm is 'outmoded, distrusted, damaging to Russia's neighbours and harmful to every tendency in Russia that we seek to encourage'. It will not change if the West legitimizes it. If we inadvertently legitimize it, we will create demoralization, uncertainty and instability across the Black Sea and Caspian regions.[51] We will also be encouraging Russia to devise roles that are beyond its capacity to sustain and which damage its own well-being as well as that of others.

The tension between the second and the third objectives is obvious. But it is not insurmountable. Russia's current security paradigm is not unchangeable, and there is a distinguished corps of politicians and thinkers inside Russia who understand that, by maintaining its present course, Russia is isolating itself. The recent past provides examples (e.g. the Gorbachev and early Yeltsin years) where the premises governing state policy changed radically and for the better. As of today, it is impossible to determine whether the current economic crisis will change Russia for the better, for the worse or not at all.

What Americans can determine is the policy of the United States. That policy will not accomplish its objectives by means of what Lavrov has called a 'messianic' approach, let alone by reverting to the norms of containment. Neither will it succeed by adopting the unhistorical and morally desensitized approach of the neo-realists.

The realization of these objectives has two prerequisites. The first is the articulation of principles that are clear and defensible. In place of the presumptively evangelical notion of a 'Europe whole and free', the United States and its European partners would achieve greater dividends by upholding the right of every sovereign state to choose its own model of development and its own partners. That right is reflected, at least in principle, in the Russia–Belarus Union State and the CSTO, as it is in NATO and the European Union. By denying that right to Ukraine, Georgia and Moldova, it is Russia, not the West, that maintains a double standard. The second principle should be that Russia's values are Russia's business as long as they remain Russia's business. Once they undermine the West's values-based institutions, they become our business. Russia has a right to its choice, but it must accept the consequences. The West cannot allow it to compromise the integrity of Western laws and regulatory structures or export to Europe the 'system of understandings' that characterizes the relationship between business and the state in Russia. Neither can it concede to Russia a right to undermine new democracies in the common neighbourhood.

The second prerequisite is a two-track policy. The first track, consistent with the reset initiative, would develop cooperation with Russia and explore the limits of it. It would address issues of importance to the United States (which should include the Treaty on Conventional Armed Forces in Europe (CFE) as well as strategic arms, the High North as well as Afghanistan), issues of mutual importance, such as energy security, and issues of particular importance to Russia, such as relations with NATO and Europe's security architecture. We have nothing to fear from a discussion of the latter issue. But we must be prepared for it. If Russia demands that the discussion takes place outside the OSCE, it should be asked why. If it insists that discussion be confined to hard security, we should explain why that would not advance security. We should not be bullied into accepting the desirability of a new treaty until its desirability is demonstrated. We also should be prepared to have our own ideas tested, and we should be open to persuasion. As Joschka Fischer famously said, 'in a democracy, you have to make the case'. The same holds true for a negotiation.

The second track, as already discussed, should complement the 'reset button' with what Samuel Charap has called a 'recommit button' in relations with Russia's neighbours, particularly Ukraine and Georgia.[52] But if this effort is limited to rhetorical reiteration of support for independence, territorial integrity and 'open doors' it will only arouse cynicism. Many countries in the former Soviet region are traumatized by the Russia–Georgia war and its dispiriting aftermath. If the United States and its allies cannot rebuild confidence in tangible ways, the internal equilibrium of these countries will suffer, as will their external security. Beyond these two traditional partners, the United States must also explore fresh opportunities, which surely are present, to develop more beneficial relationships with Belarus, Moldova, Armenia and Azerbaijan – and, with due care, the countries of Central Asia.

Both tracks should aim to foster an accurate understanding of US motives and interests, encourage cooperative approaches and instil prudence. At the same time, they should aim to foster an awareness of the international resonances generated by Russia's domestic choices and arrangements. *In extremis*, Russia like any state might need to act decisively and unilaterally. But US policy will fail if Russia acts on the basis of an erroneous reading of US interests or without a proper understanding of the likely consequences.

The capacity of the United States to achieve these objectives will depend upon:

(1) the adequacy of its resources (financial and political as well as military) and the prestige that accrues to any country from the intelligent management of its own affairs;

(2) the solidity of its relationships with old and new allies and, within these alliances, the ability to live with differences and manage disagreement;

(3) the extent to which it is prepared to treat Russia as a priority in its own right, rather than a 'variable' requiring attention only in the context of other strategic issues;

(4) the ability to demonstrate the appeal, effectiveness and adaptability of Western models by example – very difficult after the financial crisis – rather than by rhetoric.

(5) the ability to demonstrate clarity and consistency, particularly in providing timely and well-targeted support to friends and allies who come under pressure.

Above all, US capacity, and that of the West as a whole, will not reach its potential until enough people in the West realize that Russia's future will affect their own.

NOTES

1 Although I am guilty of abusing this phrase, its author is the poet and critic Remy de Gourmont.
2 Vyacheslav Kostikov, *Trud*, 22 February 1994.
3 'On the whole, we have to admit that we have failed to recognize the complexity and dangerous nature of the processes taking place in our own country and the world in general. In any case, we have failed to respond to them appropriately. *We showed weakness, and the weak are trampled upon. Some want to cut off a juicy morsel from us while others are helping them. They are helping because they believe that, as one of the world's major nuclear powers, Russia is still posing a threat to someone, and therefore this threat must be removed*' [author's emphasis]: President Putin's Televised Address to the Nation, 4 September 2004 (*BBC Summary of World Broadcasts: Former Soviet Union*, 28 April 1994; hereafter *SWB*).
4 James Sherr, 'Living with Russia in the Post-Soviet Era', Camberley: Soviet Studies Research Centre, paper F31, July 1992, p. 8.
5 In the words of State Secretary Gennadiy Burbulis, an overtly pro-Western liberal, 'there is a logic that will bring the former Soviet republics back again our way. The West will not take them as they are'. Cited in Jeff Checkel, 'Russian Foreign Policy: Back to the Future?', *RFE/RL Research Report*, 16 October 1992.
6 Deputy Foreign Minister Fedor Shelov-Kovedyayev, *Strategy and Tactics of Russian Foreign Policy in the New Abroad* [*Strategiya i taktika vneshney politiki Rossii v novom zarubezh'ye*], government memorandum, September 1992, p. 4 (author's copy).
7 Hence in February 1993, Yeltsin called upon the United Nations and other international bodies to 'grant Russia special powers as guarantor of peace and stability' in the former Soviet Union – and did so in the hope that such support would be forthcoming.
8 As Kostikov said, 'Russia is a great power and has begun to say this loudly' (see note 2 above).
9 At a closed address on 27 April 1994, excerpted (and partially paraphrased) by ITAR-TASS, *SWB*, 27 April 1994.
10 As early as October 1992, Foreign Minister Andrei Kozyrev stated, 'in the future our foreign policy will continue to defend Russia's vital interests, even in these cases where it is contrary to the interests of the West' (*Izvestiya*, 8 October 1992). On replacing Kozyrev in January 1996, Evgeniy Primakov defined Russia's top foreign policy priority as 'the strengthening of centripetal tendencies on the territory of the former USSR'. Transcript of press conference [*Zapis' Press-Konferentsii Ministra Inostranniykh Del Rossii E.M. Primakova*], 12 January 1996 (author's translation).
11 Although this emphasis appeared as early as the draft military doctrine of May 1992, which stated that 'Russia starts from the assumption that its security and that of other CIS states are indivisible' and defines the 'presence' and 'build-up' of foreign forces in adjacent countries as a 'military danger'.
12 Vladimir Putin, 'Russia at the Turn of the Millennium', speech, December 1999.
13 Energy Strategy of Russia to 2020 [*Energeticheskaya strategiya rossii na period do 2020*], Government of the Russian Federation, 28 August 2003, No. 1234-g.
14 As Putin declared in his 'Millennium' speech, 'Russia was and will remain a great power. It is preconditioned by the inseparable characteristics of its geopolitical, economic and cultural existence. They determined the mentality of Russians and the policy of the government throughout the history of Russia, and they cannot but do so at present.'

15 The *Concept of Foreign Policy* was approved on 28 June 2000 and published on 7 July (and in English on that date in *SWB*) – hereafter *Concept*.

16 Foreign Minister Igor Ivanov, Address to the National Press Club, Washington, DC, 27 April 2000.

17 For example, by the state-controlled ORT television on 18 April 2000: 'Kyiv is sure that from now on Russian–Ukrainian relations are going to be on a much tougher and more pragmatic footing than before'; and *Izvestiya* the same day: 'It seems that the new Russian President is prepared to be far tougher towards the Commonwealth countries than his predecessor was. ... The warm style of contact between the "brother Slavs" is being replaced by the cold, businesslike style of contact between foreign policies linked to one another by legal obligations'.

18 As Dmitry Trenin wrote in 2004, 'Resting on strengthening economic links, Moscow will definitely be able to secure political loyalty from the CIS countries. ... The principal instrument for realizing the "CIS project" will be the achievement of understandings with the governing elites of the CIS. This will demand long-term and painstaking work to create and promote in neighbouring countries groups of influence orientated towards Moscow and a gradual weakening and neutralization of pro-Western circles'. 'The CIS Project – The New Priority of Russian Foreign Policy?' [*Proyekt SNG'– noviy prioritet rossiyskoy vneshney politiki?*], February 2004 (author's copy).

19 Thus the November 1992 Concept of Foreign Policy states that Russia 'will vigorously oppose all attempts to build up the politico-military presence of third countries in the states adjoining Russia', adding the 'urgent' task of strengthening 'the unified military-strategic space' (Interfax, 2 November 1992).

20 See James Sherr and Steven Main, 'Russian and Ukrainian Perceptions of Events in Yugoslavia', Conflict Studies Research Centre, RMA Sandhurst, 25 April 1999: 'The most serious consequence of the Kosovo crisis is likely to be the legitimisation of anti-Western perspectives which Russia's moderates have thus far kept under control. ... In the worst, but far from implausible case that an anti-Western leadership comes to power [after Yeltsin], four axes of breakout would arouse interest: (1) "reviving Russia" by a "strong", regulated economic policy and by a stronger and larger "Slavic core" (to Ukraine's possible peril); (2) a serious long-term commitment to revive Russia's military power; (3) the Balkans, where "intelligence struggle" will be enlisted to undermine Western allies and clients; (4) a search for "strategic partnerships" with India, China and possibly Arab countries and Iran'.

21 In this view, I am very much in agreement with Sir Andrew Wood, who recently stated that Russia has been 'very much the main actor here, and Western policies towards the country have been a contributory rather than a principal factor in determining what has happened'. 'Reflections on Russia and the West', REP Programme Paper 08/01, November 2008, www.chathamhouse.org.uk/files/12710_1108russia_west.

22 James Sherr, 'The New Russian Intelligence Empire', *Problems of Post-Communism* 42(6) (November–December 1995): 11–17.

23 See, for example, Vladimir Milov, President of the Institute of Energy Policy (and former Deputy Minister of Energy), 'The Power of Oil and Energy Insecurity', Moscow: Institute of Energy Policy, April 2006; *The EU-Russia Dialogue: Competition v Monopolies* (Paris: IFRI, September 2006); Vladislav Inozemtsev, 'The Resource Curse and Russia's Economic Crisis', Russia and Eurasia Programme Roundtable Summary, Chatham House, London, March 2009.

24 Author's notes from Valdai Club lunch, Moscow, 12 September 2008.

25 The members of the regional organization of former Soviet republics are Armenia, Azerbaijan, Belarus, Kazakhstan, Kyrgyzstan, Moldova, Russia, Tajikistan, Turkmenistan and Uzbekistan. Although Ukraine initially joined the CIS, its Foreign Ministry insists it is not a member, as it never signed the organization's charter. Georgia left the CIS after the war of 2008.

26 Andrew C. Kuchins and Thomas Sanderson, 'Central Asia's northern exposure', *New York Times*, 5 August 2009: 'Uzbek officials are deeply sceptical of Moscow. They believe the Russians see their interests best served by continued instability in Afghanistan'.

27 'Appeal to President of Ukraine Viktor Yushchenko' [*Obrashchenie k prezidenty ukrainiy Viktory Yushchenko*], http://kremlin.ru.

28 *Concept.*

29 Dmitry Medvedev, 'Address to the Federal Assembly of the Russian Federation' [*Poslanie Federal'nomy Sobraniu Rossiyskoy Federatsii*], 5 November 2008, Presidential website and in English in *SWB.*

30 Interview with the television company NTV on 31 August 2008, published on the presidential website the same day.

31 *Concept.*

32 Text of Alexei Miller's address to EU ambassadors, Moscow, 18 April 2006, p. 1. [*Rasshiprovka viystupleniya Predsedatelya Pravleniya OAO 'Gazprom' Alekseya Millera na vstreche s poslami stran Evropeyskogo Soiuza v rezidentsii posla Avstrii*].

33 Vladimir Vorontkov (Director of Department of Pan-European Cooperation, MFA Russia), 'Statement at the Joint Meeting of the OSCE Forum for Security Cooperation and the OSCE Permanent Council', 15 September 2009, FSC-PC, DEL.28/09, www.osce.org.

34 'Statement by Sergei Lavrov at the opening session of the OSCE Annual Security Review Conference', 23 June 2009.

35 For a damning assessment of these prospective accords, see Pyotr Belov, 'Experts Concerned about Russia's Nuclear Deterrence Potential', Interfax, cited in *Johnson's Russia List*, hereafter *JRL*, 30 November 2009. For a more nuanced assessment see Pavel Baev, 'Strategic Countdown and Russia's Escalating Instability', *Eurasia Daily Monitor* (Washington, DC: Jamestown Foundation), 30 November 2009.

36 Vladimir Putin, 'Russia must build missiles to counter US ABM threat', ITAR-TASS, 29 December 2009 (cited in *SWB*).

37 Meeting with Valdai Club, 10 September 2009.

38 A group comprising Armenia, Belarus, Kazakhstan, Kyrgyzstan, Russia, Tajikistan and Turkmenistan.

39 Jacob Kipp, 'More Reboot or a Real Strategic Overload?', *Eurasia Defence Monitor* 6 (229) (14 December 2009), Jamestown Foundation, Washington, DC.

40 Marlène Laruelle, *Beyond the Afghan Trauma: Russia's Return to Afghanistan* (Washington, DC: Jamestown Foundation), August 2009.

41 On the *Arctic Sea* affair, see Yuliya Latynina, 'Recovered ship may have been delivering Russian arms to Syria or Iran', *Novaya Gazeta*, 21 August 2009, cited in *SWB;* and 'Missing channel pirate ship carried Russian arms for Iran', *Sunday Times*, 6 September 2009. On Netanyahu see 'Israeli Prime Minister paid secret visit to Russia – 7 September', *Yediot Aharonot* (cited in *SWB*, 9 September 2009); and 'Israeli President behind US–Russian accord not to deploy missiles', *Ma'ariv*, 21 September (cited in *SWB*).

42 Private interview with the author.

43 *Russia Profile*, Weekly Experts Panel, 'Bad Signs for Russia in the Post-Soviet Space', introduced by Vladimir Frolov, 31 July 2009.

44 Ibid.

45 Deputy Foreign Minister Yevgeniy Gusarov at the November 2000 meeting of the OSCE: 'We have been warning our Western partners that we oppose the use of the OSCE for interference in the internal affairs of the countries situated to the east of Vienna. This time we are sending a clear signal: we won't allow this to happen', *Financial Times*, 23 January 2001.

46 Vladimir Putin, 'Speech at the Munich Conference on Security Policy', Munich, 10 February 2007, cited http://kremlin.ru.

47 Deputy Foreign Minister Alexander Grushko, 'NATO enlargement is a frightful destabilization of security in Europe' [*Rasshirenie NATO chrevato destabilizatsiey situatsii v Evrope*], 2 April 2009, www.rian.ru/politics/20090402/166796711.html.

48 It is laden with provisions that are perilously selective or permissive (Articles 6–11) or encroach on the autonomy of alliances and the confidentiality of their deliberations (Article 3), and it contains provisions that cannot possibly bind because they are intrinsically open to interpretation (e.g. the thrice reiterated obligation in Articles 1 and 2 not to act in ways that affect the 'security of any other Party').

49 See, for example, *The Right Direction for US Policy toward Russia: A Report of the US Commission on Policy toward Russia*, published by the Belfer Center for Science & International Affairs, Harvard Kennedy School and the Nixon Center, March 2009. The Commission, chaired by Senators Chuck Hagel and Gary Hart, and directed by Dmitry Simes, consists of 22 serving and former political figures, officials, diplomats and experts. See also Robert Legvold, testimony to the House Foreign Affairs Committee, US Congress, 25 February 2009; Thomas Graham, *Resurgent Russia and US Purposes* (New York: The Century Foundation, April 2009); and *US–Russia Relations: Facing Reality Pragmatically* (Project Co-Directors: Andrew Kuchins and Thomas Gomart) (Washington, DC: CSIS & IFRI, July 2008), p. 6.

50 Wood, 'Reflections on Russia and the West'.

51 James Sherr in Conflict Studies Research Centre, Advanced Research and Assessment Group, Ministry of Defence, 'Material Offered in Evidence to the House of Commons Foreign Affairs Committee', May 2007; HCDC, Russia: A New Confrontation, Tenth Report of Session 2008-9, Ordered by the House of Commons to be printed 30 June 2009, pp. EV134-40, http://www.publications.parliament.uk/pa/cm 200809/cmselect/cmdfence/276/276.pdf.

52 Samuel Charap (with Laura Conley, Peter Juul, Andrew Light and Julian Wong), *After the 'Reset': A Strategy and New Agenda for US–Russia Policy* (Washington, DC: Center for American Progress, July 2009), pp. 3ff.

10

Europe: transatlantic relations still drifting

Robin Niblett

INTRODUCTION

At the end of the Obama administration's first year, the transition from euphoria to reluctant disappointment was apparent in European capitals. In Washington, there was matching frustration with European reticence to back wholeheartedly some of the US administration's new policy initiatives. Was this a temporary disillusionment, as the hopes for a more intimate US–European relationship clashed with political realities on both sides of the Atlantic (as had been forewarned in the lead-up to the 2008 presidential election)?[1] Or was it an inevitable return to the transatlantic doldrums of 2001–05, reflecting a continuing, structural drifting apart of the policy orbits on either side of the Atlantic?

Although there is truth both in the idea of structural limits to future transatlantic cooperation and in the notion of unrealistically high hopes now being deflated, neither of these two dynamics captures fully the essence of the change that is under way in the relationship between the United States and its European allies. There are two additional important facets to the transatlantic relationship. The first reflects important differences in geopolitical interests and priorities and points to the limits of future transatlantic cooperation in the security realm. The second, however, offers some likely avenues for retaining a meaningful transatlantic relationship and reflects common interests and approaches to dealing with the growing roster of global challenges, from proliferation to international financial stability. Before dealing with these two facets, it is worth reviewing the state of the transatlantic relationship that President Barack Obama inherited in January 2009.

SURVIVING THE COLD WAR

The Atlantic Alliance has been one of the most enduring in recent times. Forged in the wake of the Second World War as a bulwark against the spread of communism into Western Europe, it survived the break-up of the Soviet Union and the fall of communism throughout Central and Eastern Europe in 1989–90. It did so initially by launching a programme of NATO enlargement towards many of its former Warsaw Pact enemies and by engaging in stabilization efforts in those countries in the Balkans where the collapse of communism led to ethnic and sectarian strife. NATO governments also began a series of studies into the feasibility of the organization taking on a larger international role as a defender of transatlantic security interests beyond the geographical boundaries of the North Atlantic area.

At the same time, the end of the Cold War and the reunification of Germany led to the evolution of the European Community into a more integrated European Union, a process that was formalized in the Maastricht Treaty of 1991. Under Maastricht, EU members agreed to coordinate their foreign and security policies more closely through the Common Foreign and Security Policy (CFSP). This resulted in a series of negotiations between the United States, NATO and EU member states on the potential for the EU to share NATO military capabilities for operations of mutual interest in which EU nations might take the lead.

In 1995, the Clinton administration and the EU operating under its Spanish presidency came to an agreement on a New Transatlantic Agenda (NTA), which sought to capture the breadth of the common interests shared by the allies on either side of the Atlantic.[2] The NTA also underscored the significance of the transatlantic economic relationship and set in train a continuous process of consultation between the US Commerce Department, the European Commission and business leaders on both sides of the Atlantic, with the aim of overcoming some of the persistent non-tariff barriers to greater trade and investment between their respective markets.

Overall, the 1990s witnessed the deepening of the EU in a number of important areas of economic and social policy, not least the negotiations leading to the establishment of a single currency at the end of the decade among 11 of its members. At the same time, EU leaders spent much of their time concerned about the impact of the expected eastern enlargement of the Union upon the cohesion and effectiveness of the institution as a whole. As a result, the Maastricht Treaty was followed by the Amsterdam Treaty (signed on 2 October 1997 and entering into force on 1 May 1999)[3] and the Nice Treaty (signed on 26 February 2001 and entering into force on 1 February 2003).[4] These took place in parallel with intense discussions on the governance mechanisms of the single currency area and the European Central Bank. Throughout this period, many continental European economies struggled to maintain strong growth rates and lived with persistently high levels of unemployment. The perception grew of a Europe focused more on its internal problems than on the important changes taking place in its neighbourhood and further afield.

For their part, US policy-makers appeared divided about what they wanted from Europe. On the one hand, there was a clear desire to limit the extent to which EU members would integrate their foreign and security policies lest this diminish the relevance and influence of NATO, in which the United States possessed a structurally secure leadership role. For example, considerable concern was expressed in Washington at British Prime Minister Tony Blair's partnership with French President Jacques Chirac following the Kosovo war in 1999, to start to give shape to a new European Security and Defence Policy (ESDP).[5] Yet US policy-makers also bemoaned the lack of a strong European partner with which to work on the growing list of challenges facing international stability and security from the Balkans to Iran.

The inauguration of President George W. Bush in January 2001 was greeted with some trepidation in European capitals. America's economic productivity and power had increased in the previous decade on the back of the technology boom, while most European economies appeared to be lagging behind. President Bush and his senior advisers were also explicit in their determination to exercise America's unchallenged international power to promote a clear set of national interests on the world stage. Its withdrawal from the Anti-Ballistic Missile Treaty and refusal to sign up to the Kyoto Treaty and the newly conceived International Criminal Court struck many in Europe as an outright rejection of their long-term vision of an international order that would gradually adopt EU-style multilateral negotiation and compromise to arrive at broadly common solutions.

The terrorist attacks of 11 September 2001 promised for a brief moment to reconfirm the enduring value of the Atlantic Alliance, as NATO's European members invoked Article 5 of the treaty to come to America's assistance.[6] The practical experience of the conflict in Afghanistan and the lead-up to the war in Iraq, however, rapidly dispelled those notions. Instead, the debate over the Iraq war led to one of the deepest ruptures in the history of the transatlantic relationship as well as to highly disruptive fissures within the EU itself. It also confirmed a belief among many on either side of the Atlantic that, in the post-Cold War era, Americans and Europeans not only saw the world through different lenses, but would tend towards policy choices that reflected the reality of their differing military capabilities and decision-making processes.[7] The American accusation was that Europeans favoured process over policy decision and implementation.

Transatlantic relations set off on a far more constructive track in 2005 at the start of President Bush's second term. Changes in senior administration personnel were important, but it was also during this period that policy-makers on each side of the Atlantic settled on the idea that the enduring value of the transatlantic partnership rested upon the shared common interests of the United States and its European allies across the entire international agenda – whether in combating international terrorism and proliferation of weapons of mass destruction; dealing with Russia's growing regional assertiveness and China's encroachment in parts of the developing world; challenging Iran over its nuclear programme; rebuilding Afghanistan; or developing coordinated policies on climate change.[8] Building a partnership to deal with these common international challenges would become the essence of the transatlantic relationship, rather than the past focus on a specifically bilateral Atlantic security agenda. Tacit American support from 2005 for the efforts of the 'EU3' (comprising France, Germany and the United Kingdom, plus the EU High Representative for the CFSP) to draw Iran into negotiations over its nuclear enrichment programme was a good example of this new collaboration.

But it soon became apparent that policy-makers on either side of the Atlantic disagreed in most cases on the tactics that should be pursued towards their common international interests. Differences between American and European officials emerged in their respective approaches towards combating international terrorism and on pushing forward with the reconstruction and stabilization mission in Iraq. Europeans became frustrated with the Bush administration's refusal to play a constructive (as opposed to permissive) role in the EU3's negotiations with Iran; with the episodic nature of its engagement in the Arab–Israeli peace process; and its near total disengagement from the UN-sponsored climate negotiations until the waning days of the Bush presidency. Reflecting this frustration, by 2008, five years after the Iraq war, European support for US international leadership had fallen from an average range of 50–70 per cent to a dismal 19 per cent.[9]

ROLE REVERSAL: US PROCESS AND EUROPEAN POLICY

Not surprisingly, the election of President Obama in November 2008 was greeted with great excitement across Europe. The turnaround in the polling numbers was striking, with a jump from 19 per cent supporting President Bush's handling of international affairs to 77 per cent in support of President Obama's approach.[10] Why this remarkable change? At an emotional level, Barack Obama appealed to many Europeans because he appeared to contrast so clearly, both in terms of character and policy, with the individualistic, country-first American stereotype embodied by his predecessor. President Obama's international upbringing and outlook resonated with many Europeans' romantic belief in their own multicultural tolerance. His promise to reconnect America's foreign and security policy with its values on human rights appealed to Europeans' image of their own commitment to universal liberal values. His pragmatic political style and approach contrasted with the absolutist, good-versus-evil tone that was common to the Bush administration but that is relatively rare in European political debate. His political programme to heal social divisions within the United States, most notably on health care, echoed the generally bipartisan support across Europe for effective welfare programmes to support the most disadvantaged. And, perhaps most importantly, President Obama's commitment to engage the United States in a multilateral approach to its foreign policy appeared to align him with the European view of how international order can best be achieved in the world today. The decision of the Nobel Committee to award President Obama the 2009 Peace Prize was emblematic of the hope that his arrival in office had engendered across Europe.

To be sure, there were voices of caution in cabinet rooms, parliaments and the opinion pages of European newspapers, warning that President Obama would not be able to live up to the image that was being constructed and that, at the very least, his political and diplomatic inexperience would hamper his ability to achieve the goals that he had set himself and that others expected of him.[11] But these voices tended to be in the minority and did not dampen the sense of expectation.

One year after his inauguration, how have Europeans perceived President Obama's track record from a practical perspective? Most noticeably, from the start of 2009, European leaders now had a US president who largely agreed with his European counterparts on the tactics for dealing with each of the major international challenges that they faced in common. President Obama banned the use of the term 'global war on terrorism' that had so alienated Europeans and that had appeared to justify the excesses epitomized by the Guantánamo Bay detention facility and Abu Ghraib prison. He rescinded many of the most egregious US methods of dealing with captured and suspected terrorists, which had caused deep rifts not only with European publics and legislators, but even with America's closest government allies from London to Berlin. He reached out to the Muslim world through his Cairo speech, going some way to defusing the radical anti-Americanism that had spilled over into Muslim communities in Europe. He involved American negotiators proactively alongside their EU3 counterparts in negotiating with the Iranian government on the nuclear issue. In appointing a new commanding officer in Afghanistan who placed the emphasis on protecting Afghan civilians rather than on killing the enemy, he offered the prospect for those European countries with forces deployed in the country that a more nuanced and successful strategy would be implemented. He promised to take what many Europeans saw as a more 'even-handed' approach to the Israeli–Palestinian conflict, one of the most potent sources of public and political anxiety in Europe, by making a clear demand that the Israeli government halt the construction of all new settlements. He engaged the United States directly in multilateral negotiations on how to reform the international financial system within a new G20 framework that was not built around implicit US leadership, as had been the case with the G7 and even more so with the Bretton Woods institutions. And his administration made an early effort to push the US Congress towards accepting a cap-and-trade system on carbon emissions that would then engage the United States constructively alongside the EU in negotiating a successor agreement to the Kyoto Protocol.

But something strange has happened to undercut the value of this convergence of approaches across the Atlantic. Just when Americans and Europeans were coming together on the matter of tactics, some fundamental divergences became apparent over what had been assumed to be their shared interests. This dawning realization accounts for much of the mutual disappointment at the start of Barack Obama's second year in office. Four topics illustrate the dilemma.

Afghanistan

Despite the shift in US military tactics, Afghanistan stands out as the most contentious area for the transatlantic relationship. The disproportionate share of the fighting and military death toll that has been shouldered by the United States, along with Canada and only a small number of European states, as the conflict intensified in 2008–09 has generated a sense of deep transatlantic frustration. This frustration pits the United States and its closest allies in Afghanistan on the one side and those European countries that have resisted becoming embroiled in proactive military operations against the Taliban on the other. The problem is not just one of disagreement over appropriate military tactics and priorities for stabilization, or over whether each country is providing the right mix of forces to achieve success. However much American leaders and some of their European counterparts stress the persistent risk that a Taliban victory might mean for the direct security of both American and European citizens, the majority of European politicians and their publics cannot make the connection between stabilization in Afghanistan and a decreased al-Qaeda/terrorist threat to their daily lives. Extremists based in Pakistan's ungoverned territories, in North Africa, Yemen and Somalia, and their connections with extremists who live in Europe are often perceived as a greater and more immediate source of concern.[12]

Russia

Much has been made of the Obama administration's strategy of 'resetting' its relationship with Russia away from the implicitly confrontational posture of the Bush administration and towards the position of a number of West European governments, such as those in France, Germany and Italy. Their approach has been to try to integrate Russia into the broader European economy and to avoid political steps that would antagonize its leadership, such as further NATO enlargement. The US 'reset' has been interpreted as a rejection of the hardline approach towards Russia taken by many Central and East European countries, especially Poland and the Baltic states. This impression was deepened by President Obama's announcement on 17 September 2009 that he would halt the Bush administration's plan to station missiles in Poland and an associated radar station in the Czech Republic to counter Iran's future intercontinental missile threat to the United States, in favour of a more graduated US missile defence system focused on Iran's growing short- and mid-range missile capabilities.[13]

However, the Obama administration's attempt to 'reset' its relations with Russia masks continuity in the US approach to Russia that actually diverges from that of West and Central/East Europeans alike. Whether for the Bush or the Obama administration, Russia is a powerful international actor that affects multiple dimensions of US grand strategy beyond Europe, such as prospects for global nuclear disarmament, the stabilization of Afghanistan, energy relations with China and the future of nuclear proliferation in Iran and North Korea.[14] The question for decision-makers in Washington has been whether these strategic US interests can be better pursued through a more confrontational or accommodating diplomatic approach towards Russia. After taking power in 2009, the Obama administration decided to place a greater emphasis on engagement with Russia than on confrontation.

European governments often disagree fiercely over the best policy towards Russia, but West and Central/East European policy interests are driven by the fact that Russia is a powerful and unpredictable neighbour with which almost all European governments are economically interdependent as a result of their energy needs. This has dictated, to date, a consistent if differentiated approach in the various European capitals, depending on their perception of the level of strategic vulnerability or sense of economic opportunity arising from their interaction with Russia. Following the Obama administration's tactical decision on missile defence, Central and East European governments, in particular, drew the conclusion that their particular interests *vis-à-vis* Russia would come second to the United States' own overriding need to adapt tactical policies in the pursuit of larger strategic interests with Russia. West European officials, for their part, must wonder whether American strategic interests might drive another shift in the US approach towards Russia in President Obama's potential second term. These considerations have injected an element of caution into their welcome for his Russia policy.

The Arab–Israeli conflict

American and European tactical thinking on the Arab–Israeli conflict may have converged since President Obama's election, but they conceal some important differences in strategic interests. American interests in resolving the conflict are clear and well stated. Although not in itself sufficient to promote a more stable and prosperous Middle East, resolution of the conflict is a necessary component of such an outcome. And the stability of the Middle East is of paramount importance for every US administration because it carries enormous repercussions for international security as a whole and for the health of the global economy.

European governments share this long-term goal. However, early resolution of this conflict would address an additional, more immediately pressing strategic interest. Its persistence is an important contributor to the radicalization of minorities among European Muslim populations, not only of those who migrated from the Middle East, but of those from far further afield as well. The Obama administration's engagement from the outset with Israel and the Palestinian Authority on the peace process has been seen, therefore, very positively across all European capitals. But the underlying European fear is that the momentum will slip, as US officials bump up against the entrenched obstacles in the region and the ambivalence in the US Congress about trying to pressure the Israeli government and public to make concessions with which they do not agree. The fears of European governments appeared to have been borne out at the end of 2009, as the initial flurry of US diplomatic activity failed to bridge the Israeli–Palestinian divide. The risk for 2010 is that Europeans may conclude that the Obama approach to the peace process is more focused on the process than on near-term policy outcomes.

China

The fourth area where a transatlantic convergence of tactics obscures a divergence of interests concerns the rise of China. In their visits to China in 2009, President Obama and Secretary of State Hillary Clinton sought to avoid any rhetorical clashes with their hosts, focusing on the extent of their economic and strategic interdependence and downplaying fundamental differences over human rights and political systems. This echoes the tactical approach of most European governments, which have also blended a mix of occasional tough comments about human rights with a policy of engagement at the political and economic levels. Although the enormous risks and opportunities created by China's economic rise appear to be having a similar effect on the tactical approach being taken in both Washington and European capitals, the fact is that China's rise carries different strategic implications for the interests of US and European governments.

For the Obama administration, as for its Republican predecessor, the rise of China risks upsetting the security order that the United States has underwritten across the entire Asia-Pacific region since the end of the Second World War. American bilateral relations, military alliances and basing agreements will all be affected by the shifting political and military weight that China is bringing to bear in the Asia-Pacific region, including upon long-standing US allies such as Japan and South Korea. US–India relations are similarly tainted by their respective manoeuvrings towards China.

In contrast, China's rise carries few if any near-term security implications for European governments. EU–China relations operate, therefore, principally at a functional and non-strategic level, heavily laced with bilateral competition for economic advantage between EU member states. For most Europeans, the centre of gravity for future insecurity is instead linked principally to developments in North and sub-Saharan Africa as well as in Eastern Europe, the Balkans and the Eastern Mediterranean. Insecurity around most of Europe's neighbourhood is coming to dominate the attention of European governments and publics because of the increasingly disruptive social and economic effects of rising levels of organized crime, infiltration by Islamist extremists and an ever-growing flood of illegal migrants.

AVOIDING A SPIRAL OF DISAPPOINTED EXPECTATIONS

The four areas discussed above are important examples of where a more engaged US diplomatic approach that appears to converge with European diplomatic approaches is obscuring fundamental underlying differences in interests across the Atlantic. And the divergence in strategic perspective between an increasingly Pacific-focused United States and a neighbourhood-focused European Union could carry important consequences for the future of the transatlantic relationship under President Obama.[15]

Hints of this underlying divergence were apparent in the second half of 2009. During a visit to Brussels in October, Assistant Secretary of State for European

Affairs Philip Gordon said that the Obama administration would weigh up at the start of 2010 what returns it had gained from its European allies as a result of its new policies of international engagement. He warned that, following the unwillingness of many European countries to increase their support for the stabilization process in Afghanistan and to take on prisoners from the Guantánamo base, for example, the status of the transatlantic relationship had slipped from a green to an amber light.[16] In the meantime, President Obama's support at the Pittsburgh G20 summit in September 2009 for an early reapportioning of voting weights in the IMF towards emerging powers such as China, at the expense of the voting power of established European IMF members such as Britain, France and Germany, reminded European leaders that the United States might be open sometimes to trading European national interests in the context of its own shifting relationship with the other half of the so-called G2 (the United States and China).

For their part, instead of worrying about a missed window of opportunity to reset the transatlantic relationship at the outset of the Obama administration, European governments have taken a hard-nosed view. Although apparently pleased to have President Obama in the White House, they have not demonstrated an overwhelming urge to oblige him. Instead, observing a shift of US policy attention eastwards, Europeans are starting to coalesce around their own agenda of interests and priorities; they are willing to work with the United States on this agenda wherever possible, but without it if necessary. As one senior EU leader recently remarked, 'Europeans cannot always be the junior partner to the United States ... the time to be nephew to Uncle Sam has passed'.[17] The added risk of being seen to be the United States' junior partner is that it undermines the EU's credibility in its own dealings with the world's new rising powers. Rather than being satisfied to advise and follow the United States, therefore, European leaders are increasingly convinced that they must themselves be ready to lead on the world stage.

In this vein, European governments and their publics have spent much of his first year in office waiting to see what policy successes President Obama can deliver that match European interests, whether this be actually closing the prison at Guantánamo Bay; making meaningful concessions and contributions to the climate change negotiations at the December 2009 Copenhagen summit; accepting far-reaching reforms to the regulation of the US financial sector; sustaining pressure on the Israeli government and Palestinian Authority to enter into negotiations; or securing Congressional ratification of the Comprehensive Test Ban Treaty as part of his pledge to move towards a world free of nuclear weapons. In each of these cases, Europeans have acknowledged the positive change in tone and real boost to the diplomatic process under President Obama, but they have been disappointed to see few results, most tellingly at the Copenhagen climate change summit.[18] There is also a palpable worry in European capitals that the Obama administration is proving unwilling to follow a European lead in those cases, such as the climate negotiations, where it was offered and might have served as the basis for a transatlantic position.[19]

Rather than allowing the disappointments of 2009 to deepen in 2010, the Obama administration and European governments may now be forced to pose some fundamental questions about the future of the transatlantic relationship. Accepting the differences in each side's concerns and priorities might be healthy in principle, but it risks undermining the notion that European nations and the United States still constitute a standing alliance. For the two sides of the Atlantic only to support each other on an *à la carte* basis – in other words only when their interests clearly overlap – would undermine the idea that they do indeed form an alliance that can be brought to confront a risk to one as if it were a risk to all. At the same time, balancing the idea of the Atlantic Alliance in the defence sphere with a more formalized 'US-EU relationship' that reflects the EU's growing institutional responsibilities might lead to a process-driven and sterile form of coordination of often differing priorities (much as the US–EU summits have appeared to be, as noted below) rather than generating a new sense of transatlantic shared purpose.

A GENUINE TRANSATLANTIC PARTNERSHIP?

What might the strongest drivers be for the United States and its European allies to retain the same sense of common purpose in 2010 that animated the establishment of the Atlantic Alliance some 60 years ago? How might the two sides craft, at the very least, a new transatlantic partnership that is fit to address some of the principal challenges of the twenty-first century?

One lesson of the last decade, as much as of the first year of the Obama administration, is that efforts to expand the concept of common transatlantic security beyond the borders of the Euro-Atlantic area may be a recipe for weakening rather than strengthening the transatlantic relationship. To be sure, the United States and its European allies have shared interests in the maintenance of global order, given their common values, extensive existing international economic interests, dependence on the smooth functioning of the global economy and desire to see its extension to new regions. Neither side benefits, therefore, from rising insecurity or challenges to the existing order. Nor can governments on either side of the Atlantic sit idly by at the sight of failing states that might spawn instability beyond their borders.

But this shared preoccupation with international stability is not the same as fundamentally shared concerns about the *changing balance* of the international security order. As noted earlier, each side perceives the rise of China and the challenge of Russia through a different geopolitical lens. The same might be said for the difference in focus applied by the United States and most European governments towards India and the changing military balance in Asia. It is also the case that most European governments and publics have an increasingly sceptical view about the morality and utility of military force as a means to project security beyond their borders, especially since the experience of the Iraq and Afghanistan wars.

These divergent security perspectives need not mean the end of the Atlantic

Alliance. At one end of the spectrum, NATO is likely to remain a centrally important institution for coordinating US and European military resources and political-military decision-making on direct threats to their collective security. At the other, NATO enables the efficient deployment of shared assets for low-conflict environments and may offer a forum for planning coordinated responses to new risks and threats, whether to cybersecurity or to energy security. These questions are the focus of the review of the NATO Strategic Concept that started its work in the latter half of 2009 and should conclude in 2010. But it is still not clear that NATO will serve as the vehicle for a standing transatlantic commitment to protecting its members' security beyond the Euro-Atlantic area.

In contrast, what is most likely to animate a shared sense of transatlantic purpose in the future is the acceptance that the United States and Europe can manage better collectively than they can apart the unintentional as well as the intentional impacts of the rise of major new world powers that do not currently share US or European commitments to improved global governance. Simply put, over the past 100 years the United States and European countries have learned the costs of an anarchic world dominated by zero-sum power politics, free-riding and rule avoidance. This does not yet appear to be a lesson that drives the diplomacy of the world's rising powers – such as China, India, Russia, Brazil, South Africa or Indonesia – which are still focused on their economic development and believe (with justification in some cases) that existing rules and norms were designed by Western countries in order to retain their own privileges. The rise of these powers over the coming decade will have direct impacts on everything from international financial stability and patterns of development in the world's poorest countries to climate change and nuclear proliferation. The logical response to this trend would be for the US administration and its European counterparts to ensure that transatlantic analysis, coordination, cooperation and action on these vital global issues becomes a central political priority for officials from both sides.[20]

A more open transatlantic market

For example, the Obama administration, the European Commission and EU member states should intensify the halting efforts of the last 15 or so years to create a more open transatlantic market.[21] The rise of dynamic emerging economies offers many growth opportunities for US and European multinational companies. But it will also pose new competitive challenges to smaller companies as well as to employment and wealth creation domestically within the United States and Europe. A more integrated transatlantic market of some 800 million people, currently accounting for some 50 per cent of world GDP, would offer new economies of scale and new opportunities for companies working and investing within the market. It would increase the leverage for US and European regulators and agencies to design product standards and regulations that might then become or contribute to effective and transparent world standards. And it would increase the leverage of Western countries in negotiations about the terms under which they gain access to the emerging markets and under which companies from these markets gain access to the transatlantic market.

Building a more integrated transatlantic market does not require a bilateral negotiation to lower tariffs across the Atlantic, which are already very low for most products, or even the creation of a Transatlantic Free Trade Agreement. It would not compromise multilateral negotiations in the Doha Round of the World Trade Organization. The focus of an integrated transatlantic market will be a greater approximation or mutual recognition of industrial, agricultural and service standards (potentially including new standards for energy efficiency and renewable energy production), product certification, accounting rules and financial regulatory oversight.[22] Each of these issues currently contains non-tariff barriers to closer transatlantic economic integration and puts both the United States and European states at a potential disadvantage in their ability to cope with the reality of a more multipolar world economic order. Overcoming the different political and cultural approaches to regulatory development and oversight will be a complex and difficult task, but no less vital over the coming years.

Coordination on climate change

Second, the Obama administration and its European counterparts need to use the post-Copenhagen period to improve coordination of their approaches to lowering greenhouse gas (GHG) emissions and to supporting the transitions worldwide to low carbon methods of achieving economic growth. President Obama's first year demonstrated an important shift in the American domestic approach to climate change but a continuing resistance towards instituting binding cuts to emissions in the United States. While EU members have taken the lead in setting binding targets for cuts in emissions, this masks the commonalities in the challenges facing both sides of the Atlantic. The United States and European economies are, by far, the principal contributors to the increased levels of carbon dioxide in the atmosphere caused by human activity. It will inevitably fall on them, therefore, to take the most aggressive near-term steps to reverse this trend. The American and European governments will need to coordinate their positions on funds transfers to countries that urgently need support to adapt to warmer climates and on the terms under which carbon-cutting technologies are shared or transferred to developing economies. Otherwise, emerging economies will take advantage of transatlantic divergences in this area to limit their own commitments to cut GHG emissions or to drive harder bargains on the terms under which 'green' technologies must be transferred in order to secure developing country support for carbon emissions. The Copenhagen summit exposed the limits of US influence on the world's emerging powers in this area as much as the inability of the EU to exert leadership through the force of its own example. A more coordinated transatlantic position might carry greater weight.

Iran and nuclear proliferation

As their leaders agreed at the summit on 3 November 2009, the United States and the EU must retain a strong and united stand on the increasingly dangerous challenge of nuclear proliferation.[23] Confronting Iran's nuclear programme proved to be one of the most active areas of transatlantic diplomacy on this topic in 2009. The rest of the world, including Russia and China, is now watching to see how serious and coordinated the transatlantic approach will continue to be. Fortunately, the Obama administration's willingness in its first year to engage in direct negotiations with the Iranian regime on its nuclear programme has coincided with a hardening of attitudes among each of the EU3 governments about the need to ratchet up sanctions should the Iranians continue to prevaricate on making real concessions to the UN demands.[24] As a result, the tactics of transatlantic diplomacy towards Iran are in far better harmony than ever before. At the start of 2010, the toughening of the EU3's stance on Iran (especially following the heavily disputed Iranian elections of June 2009 and post-election crackdown on dissent) could coalesce with growing American frustration at Iran's intransigence in the face of America's diplomatic openings. Whatever the decisions ultimately taken by Iranian leaders, the fact is that the combination of European economic incentives and US security policy towards the government in Tehran is the only real source of international leverage upon them, given Russian and Chinese ambivalence on the issue. And, even if applied only bilaterally, smart US and European sanctions could have serious implications for the the Iranian leadership.

Development policy

American and European policy-makers are acutely aware that the descent of some of the world's poorest countries into poverty and instability risks dangerous spill-over effects, ranging from a rise in illegal migration to the embedding of radicalized extremists who might take their grievances abroad. One of the lessons of the last couple of decades (which was taken forward by the Bush administration) is that raising standards of living in the poorest countries of the world depends less on the quantities of foreign aid distributed there and more on improvements in the quality of local governance. These improvements are dependent, in turn, on a host of factors where outside powers can play a positive role that will then enable local governments to gain legitimacy. In 2009, the Obama administration announced its interest in better coordinating its diplomacy and official development assistance (ODA).[25] Given that the US and EU combined account for over half the world's ODA, enhanced coordination of their foreign assistance programmes in the fields of food security, health promotion and rule of law could improve levels of local governance in ways that have a better prospect of creating sustainable growth. It was noticeable that the United States and the EU agreed at their November 2009 summit to relaunch their High-Level Consultation Group on Development and to hold annual meetings at ministerial level in order to achieve greater coherence between their respective programmes and policies.[26]

International financial governance

Although many of the excesses that led to the financial crash of 2008 originated in the United States and certain European countries, the fact is that the expertise to design better methods of financial oversight and regulation lies largely within the ranks of US and European officials and bankers. The creation of a new Financial Stability Board to encompass all members of the G20 from 2009 was important in terms of strengthening the legitimacy of international financial reform, but it glossed over this reality. Working to adopt a common approach to building a resilient international financial system should be a priority for both sides.

But there is one issue that might undermine this potential consensus: the call for reform of the Bretton Woods institutions in order to give greater representation and voting weight to the emerging economies. The Obama administration actively championed the reweighting of votes in the IMF towards China and other emerging economies at the Pittsburgh G20 summit in September 2009, at the expense of EU members which currently hold a disproportionate voting share. EU governments will need to get ahead of the curve and come forward with their own proposals for reducing their relative voting weight. In this case, the question of whether the United States should be the only country with the potential to exercise its veto on IMF decisions (by virtue of possessing over 16.7 per cent of the total voting weight) may also have to become part of the transatlantic negotiating process.

CONCLUSION: IMPLEMENTING AN AMBITIOUS TRANSATLANTIC AGENDA

President Obama took office at a time when many European leaders had started to question with increasing confidence the right of the United States to assert a leadership role on issues of mutual concern. However, one of the principal obstacles to creating more balanced forms of transatlantic coordination on what is an increasingly pressing global agenda has been the lack of a modern infrastructure for effective consultation and decision-making. NATO has remained the default organization for transatlantic security coordination, even after the end of the Cold War, given that it is the only institution in which the United States sits alongside its European counterparts as an equal member. But NATO remains focused on a security agenda within which the United States also remains the preponderant power. Moreover, as noted above, this agenda presents as many points of transatlantic divergence as convergence. The annual US–EU summits that were designed to address the comprehensive range of global topics described above have atrophied over the past decade; it was noticeable that, of all the summit meetings that President Obama held during his first visit to

Europe in April 2009, the most disappointing and unproductive was his first US–EU summit.[27] That President Obama should have declined to attend the US–EU summit scheduled in Madrid in late May 2010 confirmed this impression, raising further disquiet in European capitals.[28]

Why has this been the case, given the significant benefits that US–European cooperation could achieve for each side's respective interests? Part of the problem is procedural and not just substantive. Whatever the divisions in US policy decision-making (and these are many, particularly given the divisions of responsibility between the executive and legislative branches of the US government, affecting everything from trade to aid and sanctions policy), they have paled into insignificance in comparison with the Byzantine decision-making arrangements of the EU since the emergence of its foreign policy-making procedures in the 1970s. US administrations have been faced with a highly complex partner, given the rotating six-month presidencies between EU member states and the split responsibilities for aspects of the EU's international relations between the European Commission, the Council of Ministers, the EU as a collective body and its sovereign member states. As each side has sought to expand the remit of the transatlantic relationship to a truly global scale, the EU style of decision-making has been an added drag on what would be an immensely complicated process under even the most benign circumstances.

It is in this context that the entry into force of the Lisbon Treaty on 1 December 2009 may be of consequence in the coming years. The treaty has reduced the central role of the rotating EU presidencies by putting in place a sitting EU president. It has also opened the possibility, through the creation of a more powerful High Representative for Foreign Affairs and Security Policy that the EU can start to coordinate and better integrate its collective 'civilian power' tools (trade measures offering and denying market access, and significant financial assistance programmes) with its common foreign and security policy tools (from diplomatic demarches to the deployment of gendarme forces, police training missions, peace-keeping troops and even military force). One manifestation of this more coordinated EU approach will be the changed remit of EU delegations in capitals around the world. They will now be staffed by a mix of European Commission and European Council staff, all reporting to the High Representative, Catherine Ashton, in her dual capacity in the Council and as Vice President of the European Commission. These steps, if successfully implemented over the coming years, could offer to the United States a European partner better able to enter into negotiation on a comprehensive transatlantic response to international challenges and crises. They could also serve as the basis for US and EU officials to create more effective standing working groups on the sorts of global challenges described above. And these, in turn, could report upwards to US–EU summits in the future.

This would not necessarily represent a return to the levels of transatlantic cooperation that existed for much of the Cold War. We are in a different world, where US and European interests are no longer as aligned as before. However, the gradual transition to better internal EU coordination on external affairs could be the forerunner of a more balanced and effective transatlantic partnership. The United States is likely to continue to lead in some specific areas – particularly on issues of importance to international security, such as dealing with the situation in Afghanistan, mediating on the Israeli–Palestinian conflict or halting the process of nuclear proliferation. But the EU and its member states may also lead on certain issues, such as crafting new international proposals to deal with climate change, international financial reform, and the integration of East European states into Western institutions.

Entering the second decade of the twenty-first century and the second year of the Obama administration, it is noticeable that the United States and EU member states are increasingly aligned on the best approaches to take in confronting the major threats to the world's stability and security. However, they have quite a different hierarchy of security interests, meaning that there are significant divergences in thinking about which are the most important issues to tackle first. It is on the broad global challenges that the Obama administration may find that European governments are its best allies and friends. Not allowing disappointments in the security and geo-political realm to cloud the opportunities to create joint transatlantic positions on major global challenges will be a major test for both sides during the rest of President Obama's administration.

NOTES

1 See, for example, Kori Schake, *The US Elections and Europe: The Coming Crisis of High Expectations* (London: Centre for European Reform, 2007).

2 *The New Transatlantic Agenda* (3 December 1995), retrieved 30 November 2009 from Europa website: http://ec.europa.eu/external_relations/us/docs/new_transatlantic_agenda_en.pdf.

3 EUROPA (European Commission, 2009), retrieved 11 December 2009, http://europa.eu/abc/treaties/index_en.htm.

4 Ibid.

5 Henry Kissinger, 'The end of NATO as we know it?', *Washington Post*, 15 August 1999. Strobe Talbott, 'A New NATO for a New Era' (Royal United Services Institute, 10 March 1999), retrieved 19 January 2010, http://www.state.gov/www/policy_remarks/1999/990310_talbott_nato.html; United States House of Representatives Committee on International Relations, 'European Common Foreign, Security, and Defense Policies – Implications for the United States and the Atlantic Alliance' (10 November 1999), retrieved 19 January 2010, http://www.nixoncenter.org/publications/testimony/11_10_99Europe.htm.

6 NATO, 'NATO and the fight against terrorism' (8 December 2009), retrieved 19 January 2010, http://www.nato.int/cps/en/natolive/topics_48801.htm.

7 Robert Kagan, *Of Paradise and Power: America and Europe in the New World Order* (New York: Knopf, 2003).

8 Robin Niblett, *Test of Wills, Test of Efficacy: The Initiative for a Renewed Transatlantic Partnership* (Washington, DC: Center for Strategic and International Studies, 2005).

9 *Transatlantic Trends 2008* (Washington, DC: German Marshall Fund of the US, 2008).

10 *Transatlantic Trends 2009* (Washington, DC: German Marshall Fund of the US, 2009).

11 James Blitz, 'Europe will find it hard to say "No" to Obama', *Financial Times*, 5

November 2008, retrieved 17 December 2009, http://www.ft.com/cms/s/0/e8e81f92-ab2e-11dd-b9e1-000077b07658.html; 'Great Expectations for Project Obama: Part 2: Wanted: Modesty, Patience and a Dose of Humility', *Spiegel Online* (11 November 2008), retrieved 17 December 2009, http://www.spiegel.de/international/world/0,1518, 589816-2,00.html; Bronwen Maddox, 'To the victor the spoils – a world full of problems', *The Times*, 5 November 2008, retrieved 17 December 2009, http://www.timesonline.co.uk/tol/news/world/us_and_americas/us_elections/article5084585.ece.

12 Sam Coates and Jeremy Page, 'Pakistan "linked to 75% of all UK terror plots", warns Gordon Brown', *The Times*, 15 December 2008, retrieved 17 December 2009, http://www.timesonline.co.uk/tol/news/uk/article5339975.ece; Europol, *EU Terrorism Situation and Trend Report* (The Hague: European Police Office, 2009), retrieved 17 December 2009, http://www.europol.europa.eu/publications/EU_Terrorism_Situation_and_Trend_Report_TE-SAT/TESAT2009.pdf.

13 President Obama's missile defence plan will actually lead to an earlier deployment of anti-ballistic missiles in Europe than the plan of the George W. Bush administration. However, the first missiles are likely to be deployed on ships or in Turkey and Romania, rather than in Poland. Moreover, the timing of the announcement of the change in plan was badly handled, catching Czech and Polish leaders by surprise, and falling on the day marking the 60th anniversary of the Soviet invasion of Poland. Department of Defense, 'DoD News Briefing with Secretary Gates and Gen. Cartwright from the Pentagon', 17 September 2009, http://www.defense.gov/transcripts/transcript.aspx?transcriptid=4479; Philippe Naughton and Tony Halpin, 'Dismay in Europe as Obama ditches missile defence', *Times Online*, 17 September 2009. http://www.timesonline.co.uk/tol/news/world/europe/article6838058.ece

14 See James Sherr's chapter on Russia (Chapter 9) in this volume.

15 Barack Obama, 'Remarks by President Barack Obama at Suntory Hall' (The White House Office of the Press Secretary, 14 November 2009), retrieved 15 December 2009, http://www.whitehouse.gov/the-press-office/remarks-president-barack-obama-suntory-hall.

16 'The Atlantic Gap', *The Economist*, 1 October 2009.

17 Comments at a private meeting in the autumn of 2009 attended by the author.

18 John Broder and James Kanter, 'Despite shift on climate by U.S., Europe is wary', *New York Times*, 7 July 2009.

19 Steven Hill, 'Europe's post-Copenhagen view of Obama', *International Herald Tribune*, 14 January 2010.

20 The need for transatlantic coordination to confront common global challenges was raised by Anne-Marie Slaughter, appointed Head of Policy Planning in the US State Department at the start of the Obama administration, in 'America's Edge: Power in the Networked Century', *Foreign Affairs* 99(1) (2009): 94–113.

21 At the EU–US summit in Washington on 3 November 2009, US and EU leaders declared that they would 'intensify our work under the Framework for Advancing Transatlantic Economic Integration and the Transatlantic Economic Council'. See Council of European Union, EN 15352/09 (Presse 316), Brussels, 3 November 2009.

22 For a description of the high existing levels of transatlantic economic engagement, see Daniel S. Hamilton and Joseph P. Quinlan (eds), *Deep Integration: How Transatlantic Markets are Leading Globalization* (Washington, DC and Brussels: Center for Transatlantic Relations and Centre for European Policy Studies, 2005); for a description of the benefits of deeper US–European economic integration, see 'Building a Transatlantic Innovation Economy: TABD Recommendations', *TransAtlantic Business*

Dialogue, October 2009, retrieved 16 December 2009, http://www.tabd.com/storage/ tabd/documents/tabd_summit_recommendations_2009-2010.pdf; and 'Completing the Transatlantic Market', Transatlantic Policy Network, May 2008, retrieved 16 December 2009, http://www.tpnonline.org/pdf/TPN%20Completing%20the%20 Transatlantic%20Market%20-%20Second%20Annual%20Report.pdf.

23 Council of the European Union, EN 15352/09, Annex 3, Declaration on Non-Proliferation and Disarmament, Brussels, 3 November 2009.

24 'Obama, Sarkozy et Brown menacent l'Iran de sanctions', *Le Figaro*, 25 September 2009, retrieved 17 December 2009, http://www.lefigaro.fr/international/2009/09/25/01003-20090925ARTFIG00465-nucleaire-l-iran-affirme-posseder-une-deuxieme-usine-. php.

25 See Secretary of State Hillary Clinton's remarks on this topic at 'Town Hall Meeting to Announce the Quadrennial Diplomacy and Development Review (QDDR)', US Department of State, 10 July 2009, retrieved 17 December 2009, http://www.state.gov/ secretary/rm/2009a/july/125949.htm.

26 See Council of the European Union, EN 15352/09, Annex 1, Statement on Development Dialogue and Cooperation, Brussels, 3 November 2009. For official figures on Overseas Development Assistance, see OECD, 'Statistical Annex of the 2010 Development Co-operation Report', 8 December 2009, retrieved 17 December 2009, http://www.oecd.org/dataoecd/52/9/41808765.xls.

27 Comments at private meetings attended by the author. See also Andrew Rettman, 'EU–US summit exposes divisions over Turkey', *EUObserver.com*, 6 April 2009, retrieved 17 December 2009, http://euobserver.com/9/27917.

28 See, for example, 'Les Européen ébrantés par l'indifférence d'Obama', *Le Monde*, 4 February 2010, p. 1.

PART III

Global Challenges

11

International law and the United Nations: a new era of engagement

Devika Hovell

From an international perspective, the first year of Barack Obama's presidency has been one in which rebranding America has been a top priority. At the conclusion of the George W. Bush presidency, it appeared that one element of the administration's legacy would be long-lasting harm to the international legal order and to America's reputation within it. From the outset, President Obama has made it clear that he is aware of the costs of disengaging from the legal and institutional structures of international order. In his first speech to the United Nations General Assembly, on 23 September 2009, he stated that 'the world had come to view America with skepticism and distrust', as a result of specific policies undertaken by the previous administration and a widespread belief internationally that America had acted unilaterally on certain critical issues.[1] In response, he promised a 'new era of engagement'. If the recent high-level US commitments to dialogue and diplomacy are anything to go by, the United States has demonstrated a reinvigorated willingness to abide by international law and the rules and norms of international institutions. The award of the Nobel Peace Prize to President Obama in his 'freshman' year for 'extraordinary efforts to strengthen international diplomacy and co-operation between peoples' is emblematic of much of the world's faith in his capacity to re-engage with the international community. However, along with the lofty rhetoric comes the risk of dashed expectations if words cannot be converted into deeds. It has prompted some to hark back to Mr Obama's speech at Washington's Gridiron dinner as a recently elected senator in 2006, at which he remarked, 'this appearance is really the capstone of an incredible 18 months. I've been very blessed. Keynote speaker at the Democratic Convention. The cover of *Newsweek*. My book made the best-seller list. I just won a Grammy for reading it on tape ... Really what else is there to do? Well, I guess ... I could pass a law or something'.

This chapter seeks to analyse the extent to which the first year of the Obama presidency has marked a concrete shift in the United States' approach to international law and the United Nations. The chapter begins with an assessment of the shortcomings of the Bush administration's approach to the international legal order. The assessment is not a complete picture, but describes some of the lowest points of the Bush administration's relationship with the international rule of law while pointing out that these occurred principally within its first term and also masked a series of positive steps towards international legal engagement in a number of specific areas. It then moves to examine the extent to which the Obama administration can truly be said to have acted as a force for positive change in the relationship between the United States, international law and the United Nations during its first year in office. As the chapter explains, despite President Obama's initial steps, much remains to be done for the United States to regain its position as a leader in the design and implementation of norms and rules of international law.

THE BUSH ADMINISTRATION, INTERNATIONAL LAW AND THE UNITED NATIONS

The overarching international criticism of the Bush administration can be crudely summarized as a tendency to seek what it wanted from the international legal system without agreeing to be subjected to it itself.[2] This reputation for double standards or 'exceptionalism' was earned by a series of instances during the Bush presidency when the United States (1) withdrew from standing treaties and declined to participate in important new international legal initiatives, (2) failed to comply with existing international law, and (3) put obstacles in the way of the effective working of international law and institutions. However, these criticisms of the Bush administration need to be set alongside a long tradition of US exceptionalism from international legal commitments and the fact that, in a number of areas, the administration did commit the United States to further binding obligations in the international legal system.

(1) Non-participant: treaty law and multilateral institutions

The first couple of years of the Bush administration were marked by its rejection of a number of multilateral treaties, for example its withdrawal from the Anti-Ballistic Missile Treaty and 'unsigning' of the Statute to the International Criminal Court. It also failed to become a party to the Comprehensive Nuclear Test Ban Treaty, the Ottawa Landmines Convention and the Kyoto Protocol. It opposed efforts to negotiate a verification protocol to the Biological Weapons Convention and a treaty to limit the trade in small arms. It is, of course, the right of every sovereign state to decline to enter into treaties or to refuse to participate in international institutions. President Bush's Legal Advisor to the Secretary of State, John Bellinger, argued that, rather than evidencing indifference or obstructionism, America's non-participation in certain international legal initiatives represented the seriousness with which the United States approaches international law. 'Unlike certain countries, we do not join treaties lightly, as a goodwill gesture, or as a substitute for taking meaningful steps to comply,' he said.[3]

However, in its first term, the Bush administration pitted itself as an 'outsider' against most international institutions, even those to which it is formally a party.

In the lead-up to the Iraq intervention in 2003, for example, President Bush famously threatened that the UN would 'fade into history as an irrelevant and ineffective debating society' if it failed to authorize force,[4] making clear that it was UN compliance with US policy, rather than the converse, that was the key to a successful relationship. The nomination of John Bolton, a career-long detractor of the institution, as US ambassador to the United Nations merely emphasized the administration's approach. The United States was one of only three states that voted against the establishment of the new Human Rights Council. President Bush explained the US decision not to seek a seat on the newly formed Council on the basis that the United States would be a more effective defender of human rights from the outside.[5] His decision reflected scepticism in many US circles that the new Council would be as flawed as its predecessor.[6]

(2) Non-compliance: the Bush Doctrine, human rights and international humanitarian law

The 2003 military intervention in Iraq gained the United States (and the United Kingdom) a worldwide reputation as international lawbreakers. Admittedly, it is particularly difficult for governments to accept legal constraints on the resort to armed force and the Bush administration was no exception. However, following the dramatic terrorist attacks of 9/11 launched by enemies not susceptible to traditional forms of deterrence, the so-called 'Bush doctrine' introduced a concept of pre-emptive self-defence that stretched the concept beyond conventionally respected limits. President Bush warned that, 'if we wait for threats to fully materialize, we will have waited too long'.[7] The US National Security Strategy of 2002 stated that the United States had a right to use force in self-defence before a threat had crystallized 'even if uncertainty remains as to the time and place of the enemy's attack'.[8] The Bush doctrine was widely criticized, and the UN Secretary-General's 2004 High Level Panel on Threats, Challenges and Change expressly refuted it, stating that 'in a world full of perceived potential threats, the risk to the global order and the norm of non-intervention on which it continues to be based is simply too great for the legality of unilateral preventive action, as distinct from collectively-endorsed action, to be accepted'.[9]

Perhaps the chief casualty of the Bush administration was the US reputation as an upholder and enforcer of human rights throughout the world. The detention of prisoners at Guantánamo Bay and Abu Ghraib has been taken as the principal symbol of US non-compliance with long-standing rules of international human rights and humanitarian law. The interrogation techniques in both camps, indefinite detention in Guantánamo Bay of 'enemy combatants', deprivation of fair trial rights, resort to measures constituting torture or inhuman, cruel or degrading treatment and 'extraordinary rendition' to secret detention facilities were the subject of particular scrutiny and criticism, even by allies of the United States. The British Court of Appeal described Guantánamo Bay as a 'legal black hole',[10] with Lord Steyn calling it a 'monstrous failure of justice'.[11] German Chancellor Angela Merkel insisted that '[a]n institution like

Guantánamo Bay in its present form cannot and must not exist in the long-term'.[12] In a confidential report issued in July 2004 and leaked to the *New York Times*, Red Cross inspectors concluded that 'the construction of such a system … cannot be considered other than an intentional system of cruel, unusual and degrading treatment and a form of torture'.[13] Two separate UN reports called upon the United States to shut the facility down without further delay, citing violations of international law.[14] In August 2008, the Inter-American Commission on Human Rights issued precautionary measures requesting the United States to desist from cruel, inhuman or degrading treatment of an individual detained at Guantánamo Bay.[15]

UN bodies also criticized the way in which the United States implemented its obligations under the Torture Convention.[16] The Council of Europe's Parliamentary Assembly adopted a resolution declaring that the US 'disregard' for certain key human rights and humanitarian legal norms following the 9/11 attacks had 'done a disservice to the cause of justice and rule of law and has tarnished its own hard-won reputation as a beacon in defending human rights and in upholding well-established rules of international law'.[17] Former UN Human Rights Commissioner Louise Arbour explained just prior to her retirement how perceptions of human rights abuses committed under the Bush administration had affected her capacity to do her job: 'If I try to call to account any government privately or publicly for their human rights records, the first response is: first go and talk to the Americans.'[18]

(3) Obstacle: International Criminal Court

The Bush administration's reaction to the International Criminal Court (ICC) was illustrative of the way in which it sought to create obstacles to the expansion of international law and institutions. In the 1990s, by promoting the establishment of the UN tribunals for the former Yugoslavia and for Rwanda, the United States had been seen as leading efforts to end impunity for the perpetrators of atrocities. The Bush administration's attitude towards the newly created ICC was, therefore, all the more frustrating. Following its withdrawal of the US signature to the Rome Statute, the administration embarked on an aggressive campaign against any possible impact by the Court on US nationals. The US Congress adopted an enactment nicknamed the 'Hague invasion clause' authorizing the President to take all means necessary, including the use of military force, to bring about the release of any US national detained by the ICC.[19] The administration worked to persuade countries to enter bilateral non-surrender agreements under which states promised not to transfer US nationals to the ICC. In threatening to withdraw aid from any country that refused to sign an agreement, the United States did immense damage to its relationships with the countries concerned, to the extent that many questioned whether the small perceived gain was worth the harm done to US interests in prosecuting the war against terror.[20]

The initial hostility of the United States to the Court was lessened in the later years of the administration. A big step was taken in 2005, when the United

States accepted that the situation in Darfur should be referred to the ICC by the UN Security Council, while the US contented itself with an abstention when resolution 1593(2005) was adopted. The United States subsequently gave support to the Court's investigations in Darfur. By 2007, American representatives were stating that the government 'shares [the ICC's] common goals and respects the decision of other States to become parties to the Statute'.[21] The administration also made it clear that it would not support a Security Council request for the postponement of an arrest warrant for President Omar al-Bashir of Sudan. This put the United States in the position of supporting the ICC against those who proposed that its proceedings be suspended.

(4) A fuller picture

It is also worth noting that the exceptionalist approach of the Bush administration's first term was in itself unexceptional. The United States has been in financial arrears to the United Nations for much of the time since 1979.[22] The Ronald Reagan years were described by Burns H. Weston as 'a pattern of unprecedented lawlessness and unilateralism in the conduct of American foreign policy'.[23] Though President Bill Clinton presented an open face to the international community, his administration ultimately declined to support major international initiatives – disagreement with allies over the International Criminal Court, the Kyoto Protocol, the Comprehensive Nuclear Test Ban Treaty and the Ottawa Land Mines Convention arose during that administration. Military interventions of dubious legality including in Grenada (1983), Libya (1986), Panama (1989) and Sudan (1998); wide reservations to human rights treaties; and perceived non-compliance with international law in areas such as the extraterritorial reach of US trade and economic law were all seen outside the United States as reflecting an expectation of a superpower's dispensation from obligations binding on others.

In addition, any portrayal of the Bush administration as entirely averse to multilateral rules and institutions would be inaccurate. In 2003, the United States rejoined UNESCO, having withdrawn in 1984 in protest at the organization's excessive politicization, long-term lack of budgetary restraint and poor management. The United States remained fully engaged with institutions and multilateral rules governing the global economy and international trade, whether in the World Trade Organization or the newer North American Free Trade Agreement. The administration also supported efforts to conclude new counter-terrorism treaties. In developing the Proliferation Security Initiative to restrict the trafficking of weapons of mass destruction, the United States moved from what began as a unilateral initiative to a coalition of the willing, thence to the promotion of a Security Council resolution and finally to seeking global support by negotiating a new multilateral protocol to the Maritime Navigation Convention. Treaties that the administration put to the Senate for advice and consent, allowing ratification or accession – and which were approved – numbered a 'record ninety' in the last Congress of the administration[24] and included the 1954

Hague Convention for the protection of cultural property in armed conflict, and four other agreements on humanitarian law including protocols on explosive remnants of war and blinding laser weapons.

The administration continued to support the UN ad hoc tribunals, the Sierra Leone Special Court and the Cambodian war crimes trials. Its response to the decision of the International Court of Justice (ICJ) in the *Avena* case indicated that the administration did not adopt a negative approach in principle to international courts. The *Avena* case concerned the rights of Mexican nationals convicted and sentenced to death by US courts to be notified of their right under the Vienna Convention to communicate with their consulate. The Bush administration exhibited due deference in accepting the Court's decision that the rights of 51 imprisoned Mexican nationals be reviewed[25] and, in February 2005, sent a Presidential Directive to the state of Texas to give effect to the Court's decision.[26] Regrettably, the US Supreme Court declared the directive to be invalid.[27] Equally regrettably, the spirit in which the President greeted the ICJ decision was undermined when, the following month, the United States withdrew from the Vienna Convention's Optional Protocol, which had formed the basis of US consent to the ICJ's jurisdiction in the case.

In the later years of the Bush administration, there were changes in the way it approached the principles of human rights and international humanitarian law in the context of the 'war on terror'. Admittedly, it was the US Supreme Court that had the greatest influence in rolling back previous measures, through a series of decisions overruling the administration's interpretation of its domestic and international obligations.[28]

Other steps were taken by Congress. A 2005 statute extended the US application of the Torture Convention so that cruel, inhuman and degrading treatment is prohibited in all facilities within US jurisdiction outside the United States; and the crime of genocide can now be prosecuted even when it occurs outside the United States.[29] Lawyers within the Judge Advocate General's corps upheld the provisions of the Geneva Conventions throughout and argued courageously for the rights of suspects before military commissions. Voices within the administration sought specifically to address international criticisms and to convince the international community of US commitment to international law.[30] Ultimately, however, the international legal diplomacy actively conducted by State Department Legal Advisor John Bellinger during the final period of the Bush administration did not serve to repair the harm to the reputation of the United States, which was inflicted by the measures taken during the early years of the 'war on terror'.

International activity during the Bush years exposed not only the indispensability of the United States in the international legal order, but also its vulnerability. The absence of the United States from mainstream international efforts to tackle problems of global concern not only weakened world capacity to solve problems that *can* only be dealt with internationally; it served also to undermine US leadership and damage its international credibility.[31] Although the United States is a key enabler of the concept of an 'international community', it is also the case that the Bush administration's initial attitude towards that community carried real costs for its international reputation and capacity for leadership later on.

THE OBAMA ADMINISTRATION: A FORCE FOR POSITIVE CHANGE IN THE INTERNATIONAL LEGAL ORDER?

The first year of the Obama presidency was heralded as a sea-change in the US approach to international law and the United Nations. His presidency is already being compared to that of President Franklin D. Roosevelt, who ushered in an era of far-reaching change. Indeed, in justifying America's invigorated multilateralism under his administration, President Obama has relied upon President Roosevelt's recognition that the 'structure of world peace cannot be the work of one man, or one party, or one nation ... It cannot be a peace of large nations – or of small nations. It must be a peace which rests on the cooperative effort of the whole world.' Certainly, the first year of the Obama presidency has included many initiatives demonstrating this philosophy. However, perhaps owing to the degree to which exceptionalism not only was the norm animating the Bush administration's governance but is actually ingrained in the US body politic, the Obama administration has yet fully to live up to its stated ambition to enhance global cooperation under the rule of law.

(1) International legal order

The Obama administration's record will ultimately be measured by its conduct rather than its rhetoric, but already the marked change in tone and attitude, as well as high-level statements about the importance of international law, have in themselves been of immense value in strengthening the international legal order. The President has widely acknowledged past mistakes, that America 'went off course', and 'made decisions based upon fear rather than foresight and all too often trimmed facts and evidence to fit ideological predispositions'.[32] In his speech to the UN General Assembly, President Obama affirmed that the world 'must stand together to demonstrate that international law is not an empty promise, and that treaties will be enforced'.[33]

A number of highly important specific Executive Orders and statements have signalled a departure from the extraordinary analyses of the law on torture and treatment of detainees put forward by the Bush administration. In his first few days in office, President Obama prohibited the use of torture by the United States, and expressly rejected future reliance upon interpretations of the Torture Convention adopted by advisers under the previous administration.[34] In the administration's second month in office, the Department of Justice expressed its intention no longer to employ the term 'enemy combatant', but instead to draw on the international laws of war to inform its authority, and only detain individuals who supported al-Qaeda or the Taliban if that support was 'substantial'.[35]

The Obama administration's reaffirmation of US commitment to international law has provided reassurance to its allies and is depriving violators of international law of the powerful argument of hypocrisy when the United States and other global actors seek to expose and challenge such violations.

(2) Treaties

Since taking office, the Obama administration has taken concrete positive steps in relation to a number of multilateral treaty initiatives. It signed the first new human rights convention of the twenty-first century, the UN Convention on the Rights of Persons with Disabilities. It has vowed to impose mandatory limits on the emission of climate-warming greenhouse gases, and is involved in efforts to produce a new international agreement on global warming. President Obama has vowed to pursue ratification of the Comprehensive Test Ban Treaty 'immediately and aggressively', and has launched efforts to rewrite crucial provisions of the 1968 Nuclear Proliferation Treaty to strengthen inspection provisions and close the loophole that makes it easy for countries to drop out, as North Korea did in 2003.

A further treaty now before Congress that merits swift attention is the Law of the Sea Convention. There is wide support for this treaty among a variety of sectors in the United States, including the military, the shipping, oil and gas industries, and environmental groups – and there has been long-standing support for the Law by previous administrations.[36] One reason for continuing US opposition to accession is that the Convention subjects states to dispute-resolution mechanisms in the event of disagreement under the treaty. This central objection to any type of further supranational enforcement upon US sovereign rights echoes once again the arguments surrounding the ICC.

(3) The war against terror, human rights and international humanitarian law

Perhaps the area in which the transition between the Bush and Obama administrations' approaches to the international rule of law is best reflected is in relation to the so-called war against terror. To begin with, the new administration has dropped the use of the term 'global war on terror' or 'long war' in favour of the term 'overseas contingency operation'.[37] The classification of the different engagements with al-Qaeda and other terrorists in terms of a 'war' was one of the factors that divided the United States and Europe during the Bush era. Although John Bellinger, the then US State Department Legal Advisor, stated that the 'war on terror' was not a legal term, it had legal consequences. In particular, it gave the Bush administration its own justification for applying its version of the laws of armed conflict to what it considered to be a unitary conflict, holding detainees indefinitely, and largely discarding criminal law measures in favour of *ius ad bellum* claims for using military force in the territory of other states. This approach affected international humanitarian law, leading to results that might make fighting real wars more difficult. The change in language is therefore a significant shift, although President Obama's continued use of references to the nation being 'at war against violent extremism' still leaves room for legal ambiguity.[38]

A series of highly important substantive steps has also been taken to sever the Obama administration's approach from the costly legacy of the Bush administration. On his first day in office, President Obama made a commitment to close Guantánamo Bay within a year. Though the Military Commission system will not be disbanded completely, President Obama has committed himself to reforming the system so that it is in line with the rule of law. In another highly symbolic indication of the sea-change in American policy, President Obama signed an executive order banning the use of torture or 'enhanced interrogation techniques' by the United States, and ordered the closure of CIA secret prisons and 'black sites' associated with rendition.

Despite these steps, there are four important respects in which the Obama administration has arguably not gone far enough in dismantling the Bush administration's architecture for the war on terror. The most difficult task is what to do with the 240 detainees who remain in legal limbo at Guantánamo Bay. Though for the most part President Obama has adopted a 'try or release' policy, he has also indicated that certain detainees who cannot be prosecuted but who pose a danger to the American people will continue to be subject to administrative detention. This policy of continued indefinite detention has raised serious concerns outside the United States. Preventive detention is only legally permissible in very narrow circumstances and for a short period of time. President Obama has included an assurance that such detainees will be subject to a 'thorough process of periodic review' so that any prolonged detention is carefully evaluated and justified. Nevertheless, previous experience of preventive detention in Northern Ireland and elsewhere shows that it led to further radicalization and recruitment. As far as possible, alternative measures should be pursued, including other means of surveillance such as control orders.

Another area of concern is the new administration's intention to preserve the CIA's authority to carry out the policy of 'extraordinary rendition'. While torture has been banned, and secret CIA prisons have been shuttered, the administration has indicated that it will continue its predecessor's practice of sending terrorism suspects to third countries for detention and interrogation, although it has pledged to monitor their treatment closely to ensure they are not tortured. The practice of relying on diplomatic assurances that an individual will not be tortured has shown itself not always to be effective in preventing torture. The non-refoulement obligation of Article 3 of the Convention against Torture, making it unlawful to return an individual to a country in which he or she is likely to be tortured, also applies to transfers between third countries. Moreover, even terrorist detainees have minimum due process guarantees such as access to a court to challenge arrest, detention and transfer – rights that are often denied in the case of rendition.

Third, although the United States has taken the important step of affirming that its definition of torture complies with international practice, it is currently

struggling with domestic demands that past allegations of torture be investigated and perpetrators brought to justice. Responsibility for authorizing the
unlawful interrogation techniques was the subject of hearings of Senate and
House Committees in 2008, which found among other things that

> [t]he abuse of detainees in US custody cannot simply be attributed to the ac-
> tions of 'a few bad apples' acting on their own. The fact is that senior officials in
> the US government solicited information on how to use aggressive techniques,
> redefined the law to create the appearance of their legality, and authorized their
> use against detainees.

President Obama has said he wants to focus on the future rather than the past,
and has resisted calls for the establishment of an Independent Commission or
criminal inquiry. However, as Richard Holbrooke has noted, 'Because the Bush
administration limited itself to punishing only those at the very bottom of the
chain of command at Abu Ghraib, the damage to the United States' image has
been immense and continuing – the gift that keeps on giving to the United
States' enemies'.[39]

Failure to launch a domestic investigation or prosecutions is giving the green
light to other states to launch their own criminal investigations against past US
actions, a more damaging and less satisfactory resolution for the United States.
Spanish magistrate Baltasar Garzón, best known for the prosecution of General
Augusto Pinochet of Chile leading to his arrest in Britain in 1998, has already
launched a formal investigation into six Bush administration lawyers for their
roles in advising on interrogation techniques.

In order to ensure that those damaging aspects of the Bush legacy are
hermetically sealed and confined to the past, there is a need to establish internationally agreed guidelines for the treatment of detainees in the future. Not
only does this minimize the precedent value that allows other countries to point
to US practice as cover for their own unacceptable practices, but it also remains
a continuing necessity in relation to Iraq and Afghanistan. Already, a US court
has concluded that detainees in the detention facility at the US Bagram base
in Afghanistan are in a very similar situation to those held at Guantánamo.[40]

Discussions are continuing on the treatment of detainees in armed conflict,
in particular with the International Committee of the Red Cross (ICRC).[41] The
United States should recognize, as it once did, that Article 75 of Protocol 1 to the
Geneva Conventions (setting out the fundamental guarantees owed to individuals captured during armed conflict) reflects customary law and is therefore
applicable even if the United States continues not to be a party to the Protocol.

A further question relates to the application of human rights law. The United
States continues to insist that it is bound by international human rights obligations only in respect of actions taken within its own territory. It has also failed
to acknowledge that human rights are generally applicable in armed conflict,
despite the fact that both the International Court of Justice and the Human
Rights Committee have stated that international humanitarian law and human
rights are complementary. This allows US agents not to apply human rights

standards to detention facilities outside US territory, bringing the United States into conflict with the decisions of intergovernmental human rights bodies to the effect that, with regard to persons under their effective control, troops and other state agents must apply human rights obligations overseas.[42] Especially in non-international armed conflicts, which are regulated in less detail, human rights law may offer additional protection with respect to, *inter alia*, the detention, treatment and trial of persons *hors de combat*. If it is a step too far for the Obama administration to accept that human rights obligations apply to their treatment of detainees overseas as a matter of law, the United States' reputation as a defender of human rights would be greatly enhanced if it were able to announce that it would apply these standards in practice.

(4) Relationship with the United Nations

The Obama administration has already dramatically changed the United States' approach to the United Nations. President Obama's appointment of one of his closest advisers, Susan Rice, to the position of ambassador to the United Nations, and the reinstatement of this position to cabinet-level rank, was indicative of a broader desire to strengthen the US relationship with the United Nations. Furthermore, in May 2009, the United States assumed a seat on the Human Rights Council. It has also cleared its debt to the UN's regular and peacekeeping budget, which had accumulated arrears between 2005 and 2008, and the administration expressed the intention of working with Congress to ensure dues are paid in full and on time in future, thereby ending the practice that started in the 1980s of paying US dues nearly a year late.

The United Nations is a flawed institution. Yet, as President Obama has recognized, its imperfections are 'not a reason to walk away from this institution – they are a call for redoubling our efforts'.[43] By reinvigorating its relationship with the UN, the United States is well placed to be a central actor in pushing for essential reform of the organization, instead of being part of the problem that was eroding its credibility. Under Ambassador Rice's leadership, the new administration has embraced the guiding principle to 'work for change from within rather than criticizing from the sidelines'.[44] There are three practical ways in which the United States could now contribute to the UN's enhancement over the term of the next administration:

(a) *Human Rights Council:* The absence of the United States from the Human Rights Council at its inauguration has had an impact on the formation of a strong bloc of countries that defend human rights. As the Global Advocacy Director of Human Rights Watch stated, 'While the United States has played a relatively active role as an observer at the Council, the absence of the United States from the Council's membership has created a leadership imbalance that the EU has been unable to remedy'.[45] In her final report to the Council before leaving office, former UN Human Rights Commissioner Louise Arbour warned that 'scepticism has not been fully dispelled' and that the 'pursuit of consensus' or use of regional or 'communal' positions often 'eroded the clarity' with which members and the Council as a whole 'could and should speak on critical human rights protection'.[46]

The major review of the Human Rights Council will take place in 2011, and the United States could now commence work in advance to obtain widespread support for workable reform measures. For example, the Universal Periodic Review mechanism, a key mechanism in the Council's artillery, could be strengthened by the contributions of independent experts and the creation of follow-up mechanisms.

(b) Security Council: The United States should review its policy towards Security Council reform. One of the central and perennial questions that the United States and other permanent members of the Security Council need to address is the legitimacy of the Council some 60 years after it was created. Can the victors of the Second World War legitimately continue to be the privileged guardians of international peace and security well into the twenty-first century? The United States under both the Bush and Obama administrations has been ambivalent about Security Council enlargement rather than explicitly opposed, though arguably it can take this approach because other permanent members such as China are fixed in their opposition.

However, the present exclusion from permanent membership of major economic and regional giants such as Brazil or India is indefensible and ultimately counter-productive. For President Obama to gain the confidence and respect of many of the world's rising powers as well as many of its weakest, the United States must once again be a lead protagonist in rethinking the governance structure of the UN and actively promote reform of the Security Council.

The Obama administration could also promote more transparent and consultative working methods for the Security Council. American policy initiatives in the Council would benefit from following procedures that avoid antagonizing from the start the wider UN membership. For example, 'legislative' Council resolutions that bypass the General Assembly and negotiations that involve only the five permanent members should be avoided unless they are genuinely necessary in an emergency. A more committed approach to securing due process rights for individuals and entities placed on the sanctions blacklists would be another valuable initiative.[47]

(c) Secretary-General and the better functioning of the institution: The United States can also be a protagonist in reforming the UN for the twenty-first century by taking a more collaborative approach to promoting structural institutional change. One idea would be for the United States to promote making the 'job search' for the UN Secretary-General more transparent. The UN's future success will depend a great deal upon its capacity to employ the most talented individuals, not least at the pinnacle of the institution.

(5) Implementation of international obligations by American states

As evidenced by the difficulty in implementing the ICJ's *Avena* decision, the federal structure of the United States and the complex system of Congressional oversight for agencies making up the executive branch of a presidential administration can prove an obstacle to effective US participation in treaty-making initiatives and the broader implementation of international law. In the recent request for interpretation of the *Avena* case, the Bush administration declared to the ICJ that it had made all possible efforts within constitutional limits to ensure compliance with the earlier decision of the Court. The US Supreme Court, however, decided that the President's directive to the State of Texas to implement the ICJ's decision was not binding.[48]

This issue is ripe to be addressed by the new administration. As things stand, any administration has a limited ability to ensure US compliance with binding international obligations by the individual American states. The logical, but absurd, consequence could be that countries entering into a bilateral agreement with the United States might need to secure the separate agreement of the 50 American states. Following the Supreme Court's *Medellin* decision, affirming that ICJ decisions are not binding under domestic law in the absence of an act of Congress, a general review of the means of implementing international obligations, including ICJ decisions, would seem to be advisable, and might lead to the introduction of legislation in Congress.

(6) The International Criminal Court

Domestic opposition in the United States to ratification of the Rome Statute to the International Criminal Court preceded even the Bush administration. Though one of President Bill Clinton's final actions was to sign the Rome Statute, he also stated that he would not recommend that the next president submit the treaty to the Senate for its consent 'until our fundamental concerns are satisfied'. Although domestic political opposition to the ICC Statute remains strong, thus making US accession unlikely in the foreseeable future,[49] it should be possible for the United States to take some further positive steps to engage with the Court. It does after all agree with the underlying goal of the Statute, which is to end impunity for the perpetrators of atrocities.

Under the Obama administration, the campaign against the ICC appears to have ceased, following the marked thawing of the US relationship with the Court during the second term of the Bush administration. The United States could now take some further positive steps to cooperate with the ICC. The Ten Year Review Conference of the Rome Statute in Kampala, Uganda, which is scheduled to take place in May 2010 provides the opportunity for President Obama to recalibrate the US relationship with the International Criminal Court. For example, it could increase its assistance to the Court by sharing intelligence and other evidence with the Court's investigators, as it does in relation to the Yugoslav and Rwanda Tribunals. The administration could also agree that the mandates of future peacekeeping missions would include cooperation with the ICC.[50]

In more general terms, the United States should take advantage of the fact that the ICC is only a court of last resort, by ensuring that all US nationals can be tried in US courts for crimes within the ICC Statute, rather than leaving them within the jurisdiction of the ICC. This may require a review of US criminal law, including the Uniform Code of Military Justice, to ensure that the law on crimes against humanity and war crimes is updated. Extra-territorial jurisdiction should be applied (as has been the case with the recent US legislation on genocide[51]) to allow US courts to try these crimes wherever they are committed. If the United States wishes to ensure that US nationals are always tried in US courts, the administration can widen its extradition arrangements.

CONCLUSION

It would be misleading to present the eight years of the George W. Bush administration as an entirely anomalous chapter in the US relationship to international law. The United States has long exhibited exceptionalist tendencies, which it has justified on the basis of its special status as the world's superpower and the burdens that come with this status, including protecting its allies around the world from communist intervention or domination during the Cold War. However, the Bush administration demonstrated that, when exceptionalism turns to unilateralism, and unilateralism is presented as a justifiable rule for the United States, then America's long-term interests and international influence suffer. The election of Barack Obama, a man whose personal and career history reflects a deep appreciation of internationalism, civil liberties and the rule of law, opens the opportunity for the United States to play a central role in the reform of the international legal order that it led in establishing 60 years earlier. Taking on such a role will pose significant domestic challenges. However, as Ambassador Rice has noted, a renewed commitment to multilateralist policies by the Obama administration is neither charity nor a quest for international popularity – 'in an interconnected world, what's good for others is often good for the United States as well … the UN is essential to our efforts to galvanize concerted actions that make Americans safer and more secure'.[52]

The Obama administration's early approach to international law and the UN is consistent with the self-interested internationalism of past US administrations, both Republican and Democrat. Respect for the international rule of law by a state as powerful as the United States actually enhances America's capacity to exert global leadership. Moreover, the legitimacy and predictability that broad adherence to international law can provide helps sustain a more secure world for the pursuit of US international political and economic interests. And as power is spread more evenly across the world over the course of this century, the existence of strong structures and habits of international law will usually offer a more affordable, enduring and productive means to resolve disputes and prevent potential threats from escalating than can reliance on military supremacy and the constant exercise of national power alone. In this respect, the new administration appears to recognize that compliance with international law and commitment to adjudication are merely the 'cost of doing business' with the wider world.

NOTES

1 Barack Obama, 'Remarks by the President to the UN General Assembly', UN Headquarters, New York, 23 September 2009.

2 Michael Byers and Georg Nolte (eds), *United States Hegemony and the Foundations of International Law* (Cambridge University Press, 2003); Harold Koh, 'On American Exceptionalism', 55 *Stanford Law Review* (2003): 1479.

3 Speech by John Bellinger, 'The United States and International Law', The Hague, 6 June 2007.

4 George W. Bush, Speech delivered at the Naval Station Mayport, Florida, 13 February 2003.

5 Sean McCormack, 'Press Statement: The United States will not seek election to the UN Human Rights Council', Washington DC, 6 April 2006.

6 See, for example, Editorial, 'The shame of the United Nations', *New York Times*, 26 February 2006; Ronan Farrow, 'The UN's human rights sham', *Wall Street Journal*, 29 January 2008.

7 White House, 'President Bush delivers speech at West Point', 1 June 2002, http://www.whitehouse.gov/news/releases/2002/06/20020601-3.html.

8 White House, National Security Strategy of the United States of America (September 2002), p. 15.

9 Report of the High Level Panel on Threats, Challenges and Change, *A More Secure World: Our Shared Responsibility* (2004), UN doc A/59/565, 63 (para. 191).

10 *R on application of Abbasi v Secretary of State* [2002] EWCA Civ 1598 (UK Court of Appeal).

11 Lord Steyn, 'Guantánamo Bay: The Legal Black Hole', Twenty-seventh F.A. Mann Lecture, 25 November 2003.

12 'Merkel: Guantánamo mustn't exist in the long term', *Spiegel Online International*, 1 September 2006.

13 'Red Cross finds detainee abuse in Guantánamo', *New York Times*, 30 November 2004.

14 UN Commission on Human Rights, 'Situation of Detainees at Guantánamo Bay', UN doc Future E/CN.4/2006/120, 15 February 2006; Committee Against Torture, 'Conclusions and Recommendations: Consideration of Report submitted by United States under Article 19 of the Convention', UN doc CAT/C/USA/CO/2, 18 May 2006.

15 Inter-American Commission for Human Rights, 'Letter re Request for Precautionary Measures no 211-08', 20 August 2008.

16 A summary of the chief criticisms is contained in a report for the Canadian parliament: Laura Barnett, 'Extraordinary Rendition: International Law and the Prohibition of Torture', Library of Parliament, Canada, 17 July 2008: 'A number of UN bodies have expressed concern over the United States' implementation of the various international law prohibitions on torture. The UN Committee Against Torture has expressed concern over the absence of clear legal provisions in United States law ensuring that the prohibition against torture is non-derogable. The Committee has

also criticized the fact that the United States government does not consider that the non-refoulement obligation in section 3 of CAT applies to those detained outside the United States. Finally, the Committee Against Torture has expressed concern over the United States' use of diplomatic assurances. It has stated that a government should rely on diplomatic assurances only with respect to states that do not systematically violate CAT's provisions, after a thorough examination of the merits of each case. The Committee emphasized that the United States government should establish clear procedures for obtaining such assurances, accompanied by adequate judicial mechanisms for review, and effective post-monitoring arrangements. The UN Human Rights Committee has reiterated many of the Committee Against Torture's concerns, and has also criticized the United States' use of the "more likely than not" standard for refoulement.'

17 Resolution 1539 (2007) adopted on the basis of Report to the Council of Europe Parliamentary Assembly Committee on Legal Affairs and Human Rights, 'The United States of America and International Law', 8 February 2007, Doc 11181, para. 34.

18 Interview with Louise Arbour, UN Human Rights Commissioner, *Democracy Now*, 7 September 2007.

19 The American Servicemembers Protection Act 2002. It has been amended twice – in 2006 (waiving restrictions on funding International Military Education Training) and in 2008 (repealing limitations on military assistance).

20 The Coalition for the International Criminal Court has compiled a 24-page table of quotes from high officials opposing the US campaign for bilateral surrender agreements: http://www.iccnow.org/documents/HighOfficialQuotes_Current.pdf.

21 See the statement of a US representative cited in the Report of the meeting of the Council of Europe Committee of Legal Advisers on Public International Law, 22–23 March 2007, para 27.

22 Sean D. Murphy, 'Payments of US Arrears to the United Nations', 94 *American Journal of International Law* (2009): 348.

23 Burns H. Weston, 'The Reagan Administration versus International Law', 19 *Case Western Reserve Journal of International Law* (1987): 295.

24 Figure given in speech of John Bellinger at International Law Weekend, American Branch of the International Law Association, New York City, 17 October 2008.

25 *Case Concerning Avena and Other Mexican Nationals* (Mexico v. USA), Judgment of 31 March 2004, General List No. 128, www.icj-cij.org.

26 George W. Bush, 'Memorandum for the Attorney General' (28 February 2005), Appendix 2 to Brief for United States as *Amicus Curiae* 9a.

27 *Medellín v Texas*, 552 US _____ (2008) (US Supreme Court).

28 *Rasul v Bush,* 542 US 566 (2004); *Hamdi v Rumsfeld* 543 US 507 (2004); *Hamdan v Rumsfeld*, 548 US 557 (2006); *Boumediene v Bush* 553 US _____ (2008).

29 Detainee Treatment Act of 2005; and the Genocide Accountability Act of 2007.

30 John Bellinger, State Department Legal Advisor, has given many speeches on the subject. See for example his talk at San Remo, Italy, on 9 September 2005, 'United Nations Security Council Resolutions and the Application of International Humanitarian Law, Human Rights and Refugee Law'; Speech to Duke University School of Law on 15 November 2006, 'Reflections on Transatlantic Approaches to International Law'; and talk at the London School of Economics, 'Legal Issues in the War on Terrorism' on 31 October 2006.

31 Pierre Klein, 'The Effects of US Predominance on the Elaboration of Treaty Regimes and on the Evolution of the Law of Treaties', in Byers and Nolte (eds), *United States*

Hegemony and the Foundations of International Law, p. 371.

32 Barack Obama, 'Protecting our Security and Our Values', Speech at National Archives Museum, Washington, DC, 21 May 2009.

33 Barack Obama, 'Remarks by the President to the UN General Assembly', UN Headquarters, New York, 23 September 2009.

34 Barack Obama, Executive Order, 'Ensuring Lawful Interrogations', 22 January 2009.

35 Office of Public Affairs, 'Department of Justice Withdraws "Enemy Combatant" Definition for Guantanamo Detainees', 13 March 2009.

36 For an account of the Bush administration's support for the Convention, see the speech of the then State Department Legal Advisor at University of California, Berkeley School of Law's Law of the Sea Institute on 3 November 2008.

37 Al Kamen, 'The end of the Global War on Terror', *Washington Post*, 24 March 2009.

38 President Barack Obama, 'Inaugural Address', Washington DC, 20 January 2009; Obama, 'Protecting our Security and Our Values'.

39 Richard Holbrooke, 'The Next President: Mastering a Daunting Agenda', *Foreign Affairs* 87(5) (September/October 2008): 2–24.

40 *Al Maqaleh v Gates*, 604 F. Supp. 2d 205 (DDC 2009).

41 In 2007, the ICRC presented its institutional guidelines on internment, which set out 'a series of broad principles and specific safeguards that the ICRC believes should, at a minimum, govern any form of detention without criminal charges'. *International Humanitarian Law and the Challenges of Contemporary Armed Conflicts* 11, 30IC/07/8.4 (October 2007), available at http://www.icrc.org/web/eng/siteengo.nsf/htmlall/30-international-conference-working-documents-101207/$File/30IC_8-4_IHLchal-lenges_Report&Annexes_ENG_FINAL.pdf.

42 See, for example, *Lopez Burgos v Uruguay*, Communication No. R12/52, U.N. doc Supp. No. 40 (A/36/40) (1981), 176; General Comment No. 31(80), UN doc. CCPR/C/21/Rev.1/Add.13 (2004), para 10.

43 Obama, 'Remarks by the President to the UN General Assembly'.

44 Ambassador Susan Rice, 'A New Course in the World, a New Approach at the UN', NYU Center for Global Affairs and Center on International Co-operation, 12 August 2009.

45 Peggy Hicks, 'Don't write it off yet', *International Herald Tribune*, 21 June 2007.

46 Address by Ms Louise Arbour, the UN High Commissioner of Human Rights, on the Occasion of the 8th Session of the Human Rights Council', Geneva, 2 June 2008.

47 See, for example, Bardo Fassbender, *Targeted Sanctions and Due Process* (Berlin: Humboldt University, 2006); T.J. Biersteker and S.E. Eckert, *Strengthening Targeted Sanctions through Fair and Clear Procedures* (Providence, RI: Watson Institute for International Studies, Brown University, 2006). An incentive for further due process rights in this area is provided by the *Kadi* decision in the European Court of Justice.

48 *Medellín v Texas* 552 US ＿＿＿ (2008).

49 This was frequently stated by John Bellinger in his speech of 25 April 2008 to DePaul University College of Law. See also John Murphy, *The United States and the Rule of Law in International Affairs* (Cambridge University Press, 2004) – the United States 'is unlikely to support any international tribunal that it cannot control in large measure' (p. 278).

50 Most of the proposals in this paragraph are similar to those put forward by the Atlantic Council of the United States, 'Law & the Lone Superpower: Rebuilding a Transatlantic Consensus on International Law', William H. Taft IV and Frances G. Burwell, Policy Paper, April 2007.

51 Genocide Accountability Act of 2007.
52 Rice, 'A New Course in the World, a New Approach at the UN'.

12

Arms control tomorrow: the challenge of nuclear weapons in the twenty-first century

Paul Cornish

Turning and turning in the widening gyre
The falcon cannot hear the falconer;
Things fall apart; the centre cannot hold;
Mere anarchy is loosed upon the world,
The blood-dimmed tide is loosed, and everywhere
The ceremony of innocence is drowned;
The best lack all conviction, while the worst
Are full of passionate intensity.
Surely some revelation is at hand;
Surely the second coming is at hand.

– W.B. Yeats, 'The Second Coming'

INTRODUCTION

Yeats published 'The Second Coming' in 1920, at a time when he was preoccupied with the ending of one age and its transformation into the next and when, by some accounts, he believed the world was on the threshold of apocalyptic change. 'The Second Coming' has always impressed its readers with its stark and disturbing images and there are indications (noted below) that some in the administration of President Barack Obama – perhaps even the President himself – have read this striking poem and drawn from it the conclusion that important aspects of the international order are indeed on the verge of 'falling apart'.

From the outset, the Obama administration has offered a less dogmatic (and pessimistic) and more constructive (and optimistic) approach to international security than is widely perceived to have been the substance and style of his predecessor, President George W. Bush. The progressive tone of the new approach was set out in President Obama's inaugural address in January 2009:

> Recall that earlier generations faced down fascism and communism not just with missiles and tanks, but with the sturdy alliances and enduring convictions. They understood that our power alone cannot protect us, nor does it entitle us to do as we please. Instead, they knew that our power grows through its prudent use. Our

security emanates from the justness of our cause; the force of our example; the tempering qualities of humility and restraint.[1]

At the risk of reading too much into a short passage, there is both a gritty realism here regarding the world and its dangers, and a sense that in certain circumstances and at certain moments the military advantages enjoyed by the United States will be irreplaceably vital to national security. But the passage also conveys the conviction that so-called 'kinetic' military force is not the answer to everything. Military power does not entitle the United States to 'do as we please' and does not provide the only, or indeed the most suitable, route to enduring security. More so than military power, national and international security is the province of ideas, values, example and cooperation.

The popular response to the Obama inauguration speech is that it offered a clean break from the Bush administration's narrower focus on US national security, its belief in the decisive role of armed force and its preference for self-help before multilateral cooperation. In its first year the Obama administration has shown an energetic and intelligent engagement with the challenges of national and international security in the early twenty-first century. The administration has also taken an imaginative and encouragingly pragmatic line, showing itself to be prepared to adopt those of its predecessor's approaches and initiatives that are considered to have merit. Nevertheless, the challenges the administration confronts are considerable: managing an international campaign against terrorism and insurgency; the operational deployment of armed forces in Iraq and Afghanistan; diplomatic involvement in regional crises in the Middle East, South Asia and East Asia; confronting the problem of insecurity of energy supply; and contending with the human security implications of climate change and with future demands for humanitarian intervention. And as well as all of these challenges, the Obama administration's energy, imagination and intelligence will also be tested in the field of nuclear weapons control.

The purpose of this chapter is to gauge the scale of the nuclear weapons challenge and to assess the style and substance of the Obama administration's response to it. The chapter begins with a brief summary both of the nuclear challenge and of the administration's response, as set forth in Obama's April 2009 speech in Prague and subsequently. Four aspects of the nuclear challenge are then considered in greater detail: the political/diplomatic, the technological, the strategic and (above all) the intellectual.

The title of this chapter plays on that of *Arms Control Today*, the monthly publication of the US Arms Control Association[2] and a noted and highly valued source of expert research and analysis in the field of arms control (loosely defined). The central argument of this chapter is that, while the arms control, non-proliferation and disarmament challenges of today are daunting enough, a still more pressing challenge lies in developing a coherent rationale for nuclear weapons control that can endure into tomorrow and for the foreseeable future.

THE OBAMA ADMINISTRATION'S VISION OF NUCLEAR
WEAPONS CONTROL

The Obama administration's nuclear weapons agenda is certainly full: negotiations with Russia over further nuclear warhead reductions; the proposed ratification and implementation of the Comprehensive Test Ban Treaty (CTBT); agreement on a Fissile Material (Cut-off) Treaty (FMCT); hosting a Global Summit on Global Nuclear Security in April 2010 and the Review Conference of the Nuclear Non-Proliferation Treaty (NPT) in May 2010. Some analysts argue that the NPT will not survive if the disastrous performance seen in 2005 is repeated at the 2010 conference.

This would be a daunting agenda in the best of times, but these are emphatically not the best of times for international agreements on the control of nuclear weapons. There is continued uncertainty as to whether Russia will prove to be a constructive partner in its negotiations with the United States, or will instead insist upon concessions before allowing any progress to be made (over further NATO expansion, for example). How can the growing demand for nuclear energy be met, while ensuring that nuclear weapons materials and technology are not spread yet more widely around the world? Is the long-standing taboo against nuclear weapon use in a state of terminal decay, with some countries and non-state groups keen to acquire a nuclear capability in order to make use of it militarily? If the nuclear taboo is losing its authority, how can the acquisition and use of nuclear weapons be deterred successfully and durably? The purpose (and therefore credibility) of the major treaty-based initiatives is also open to question. Is the goal to contain hostile relationships along the lines of the Cold War confrontation? Is it to protect the interests of the established nuclear weapon states by maintaining discriminatory agreements? Or is the aim the lasting achievement of a nuclear disarmed world?

It was against this stark and disturbing backdrop that President Obama made his April 2009 speech in Prague on the subject of the international security order.[3] Arguing, as at his inauguration, that 'moral leadership is more powerful than any weapon', he focused his remarks on an issue that he described as 'fundamental to the security of our nations and to the peace of the world – that's the future of nuclear weapons in the 21st century'. Obama described the continued existence of thousands of nuclear weapons as 'the most dangerous legacy of the Cold War' – a conflict that had disappeared while nuclear weapons had not. In a particularly compelling passage, Obama summarized the nuclear weapon challenge in the following terms:

> In a strange turn of history, the threat of nuclear war has gone down, but the risk of a nuclear attack has gone up. More nations have acquired these weapons. Testing has continued. Black market trade in nuclear secrets and nuclear materials abound. The technology to build a bomb has spread. Terrorists are determined to buy, build or steal one. Our efforts to contain these dangers are centered on a global-non-proliferation regime, but as more people and nations break the rules, we could reach the point where *the centre cannot hold*. [Emphasis added]

Dismissing the notion that the spread and use of nuclear weapons are inevitable, President Obama argued that the United States had a 'moral responsibility' to 'seek the peace and security of a world without nuclear weapons'. There then followed a series of 'concrete steps' to be undertaken by the United States towards the goal of a denuclearized world. In the first place, Obama promised to reduce the role of nuclear weapons in US national strategy, while noting cautiously that, for as long as nuclear weapons remained, the United States would retain a nuclear arsenal for the purposes of deterrence and defence. As with other nuclear powers such as the United Kingdom, the juxtaposition of a US commitment to nuclear weapons reduction and a commitment to nuclear weapons retention is likely to remain one of the characteristic features of the international nuclear weapons debate for the foreseeable future. Obama then spoke of the need for a new Strategic Arms Reduction Treaty (START) with Russia and mentioned the possibility that all nuclear weapon states might at some point join the initiative. The ratification of the CTBT would be pursued 'immediately and aggressively', and a 'new' treaty to end the production of fissile material would be sought. The NPT would be strengthened with 'more resources and authority' for international inspections and, in an attempt to deal with the risk of break-out from the NPT, President Obama called for 'real and immediate consequences' for 'countries caught breaking the rules or trying to leave the treaty without cause'. An international fuel bank would be created in order to encourage the spread and use of civil nuclear technology without increasing the risks of nuclear weapons proliferation. A new international initiative would seek to secure all vulnerable nuclear material around the world, not least in order to prevent terrorist access to the means and materials of nuclear weapon construction. Various extant programmes such as the Proliferation Security Initiative and the Global Initiative to Combat Nuclear Terrorism (both of which originated during the Bush presidency) would be turned into 'durable international institutions', and, as a first step towards that goal, Obama called for a Global Summit on Nuclear Security to be held in the United States.

President Obama's Prague speech was at once a stark summary of the many problems associated with nuclear weapons control and an agenda involving a wide range of ambitious responses. The remaining sections of this chapter examine the nature of the nuclear weapons challenge and the prospects for success in four key areas: the political and diplomatic, the technological, the strategic and the intellectual.

THE POLITICAL AND DIPLOMATIC CHALLENGE

The political and diplomatic challenge to the Obama administration's aspirations for nuclear weapons control is manifested on three levels: the international, the allied and the domestic. At the international level, the challenge might best be described as *treaty weariness*. To a significant and rather disturbing extent, the triad of agreements with which the administration is most immediately concerned – the replacement for START with Russia, the ratification of the

CTBT and agreement on a verifiable FMCT – are widely regarded as belonging to the Cold War – an era that has long since passed and a geostrategic US–Russian bilateral framework that is scarcely relevant. These negotiations require a burst of energy and enthusiasm – with identifiable results – if they are not to be regarded as either superannuated or geostrategically constrained, or both. Put another way, if these treaties are not perceived to have long-term and (at least in the case of the latter two) universal validity, then what is their point?

Similar questions could be asked of the Non-Proliferation Treaty, which by many accounts is the most worn out of them all. The possibility that the 2010 NPT Review Conference might end in failure like its 2005 predecessor has prompted a trenchant debate as to the likely effect of such failure on the coherence and effectiveness of the international nuclear non-proliferation regime (including the NPT itself, the International Atomic Energy Agency and a range of other treaties and agreements). Some have argued that the regime would inevitably collapse, while others reject such an apocalyptic vision, pointing out that the NPT is widely respected and is the most subscribed treaty in the international system.

The problem for these weary Cold War-era agreements (and this applies equally to agreements addressing chemical and biological 'weapons of mass destruction') is that they are at best little understood and at worst regarded as self-referential, self-perpetuating bureaucracies. These bureaucracies appear alarmingly unconcerned when their core objectives are not met and simply reconvene for another conference some years hence. As the Obama administration seeks to reinject the 'energy and enthusiasm' referred to earlier into nuclear weapons control, its problem is presentational. Clearly, the weaknesses and shortcomings of the NPT must be identified, addressed and rectified. But if the NPT is too loudly and roundly discredited in the process, the risk is not only that non-nuclear weapon states might become wary of its durability and begin to seek security guarantees by other means (possibly including nuclear weapon acquisition), but also that existing nuclear weapon states might lack confidence in a discredited, obsolescent institution and decline to meet their commitment to the NPT bargain. In this regard, Stephen Blank has written of the 'connection between the major nuclear powers' self-restraint and even downsizing of their arsenals and the viability and durability' of the NPT.[4] Equally, the United States should be wary of injecting too much energy and enthusiasm into the nuclear debate in the form of the argument for a 'Global Zero', for example.[5] A dramatic vision such as this, whatever the immediacy of its popular appeal, might well imply that the tired old treaties of the Cold War really have had their day and no longer merit any serious diplomatic and intellectual effort, a greater prize having finally come into view. The problem is, of course, that most analysts would accept that the Global Zero idea is rather like the Holy Grail: all have heard of it; many are attracted to it; but none are ever likely to see it. The danger, then, is that the best is made the enemy of the good and that the world ends up with neither the Global Zero nor a set of functioning (albeit flawed) treaties.

At the allied level, the political and diplomatic challenge is one of managing expectations. As far as the United States' European allies are concerned these expectations are largely (but not entirely) historical, while in East Asia the pressure from allies has a rather more urgent tone to it.

During the Cold War, the basing of US nuclear weapons in Europe – known as 'nuclear sharing' – symbolized the US strategic commitment to Europe and was considered essential to the West's deterrent posture. The continued presence of US nuclear weapons in Europe, now reduced to a rump – 200 or so 'dumb' US nuclear bombs stored in around 90 weapon vaults in Belgium, Germany, the Netherlands, Italy and Turkey – is of questionable value. Originally a demonstration of the indivisibility of American and West European deterrence of Soviet aggression, the nuclear sharing arrangement no longer clearly provides a credible and convincing deterrent umbrella under which America's non-nuclear European allies could take shelter in times of dire emergency. The rationale for the deployment of US nuclear weapons in Europe could scarcely be thinner, or more tenuous. Even without the deterrent rationale, the nuclear sharing arrangement is regarded as a symbol of NATO cohesion at times of tension and uncertainty in Europe. For the Obama administration, however, continuing to share US nuclear weapons in this way might prove to be counter-productive in the light of its other obligations and aspirations in nuclear weapons control. In blunt terms, where does the greater political and diplomatic benefit lie: in nuclear sharing with European allies or in the pursuit of START, CTBT, FMCT and a re-energized NPT? And, more to the point, is it consistent and coherent to hold both sets of objectives at the same time?[6]

In East Asia, the concern on the part of Japan, South Korea and Taiwan is the continued credibility of US extended nuclear deterrence in the face of posturing by nuclear weapon states in the region. There are now calls for the United States to strengthen and institutionalize the nuclear guarantee it extends to its allies, possibly in the form of a nuclear planning forum along the lines of NATO's Nuclear Planning Group.[7] In both cases – Europe and East Asia – the central point, as Clark Murdock has observed, is that America's 'assurance to its allies and friends that its nuclear deterrent extends to them is a key factor affecting their calculus as to whether to pursue nuclear weapons'.[8]

Finally, the domestic political challenge for the Obama administration is essentially a matter of securing the support of the US Senate. Ratification of international treaties – including arms control and non-proliferation agreements – requires a two-thirds majority of the Senate, i.e. a minimum of 67 votes in favour. With a Democratic caucus of 60 Senators (including two Independents), a further seven votes must be sought among the ranks of Republican Senators. While there is bipartisan support for a verifiable FMCT in the US Congress, there remains persistent opposition to other agreements such as the CTBT and the START replacement. These initiatives are often portrayed by their critics as 'appeasement' and an untimely and imprudent weakening of the military pre-eminence of the United States. Others offer a more prosaic explanation for Senate voting patterns, notably for Senators representing states that have had a long involvement in and dependency upon aspects of the US nuclear weapons programme: 'when it comes to arms control treaties, ideological considerations rarely trump pork-barrel politics.'[9]

While Senate voting patterns must clearly be taken seriously, for the present it seems unlikely that an overt and decisive opposition to the nuclear weapons control agenda will develop. But it might not always be safe to make this assumption. If the Senate continues to be preoccupied with other policy concerns (e.g. healthcare), the nuclear weapons control agenda could be crowded out by other, equally legitimate policy concerns. A more coherent opposition might indeed then develop over the coming months, and largely out of neglect. A Senate which has not been actively engaged in the complex weapons control debate and in informing public opinion could all too soon become a Senate that is actively opposed to agreement even on initiatives such as the FMCT. Arms control and non-proliferation negotiations can take years to complete. But, with the next round of Senate elections taking place in November 2010, it is not inconceivable that President Obama's weapons control programme could be knocked off course by an electorate that has not been kept aware of the need for consistency and continuity in these negotiations and that elects to the Senate more of those who are unconvinced of the case for nuclear weapons control. By one view, if the current Senate does not or cannot contribute to substantial progress in weapons control negotiations by the end of 2010, the 'window of opportunity will slam shut on President Obama's plans to reduce nuclear weapons stockpiles, ban nuclear testing, and secure vulnerable nuclear material worldwide'.[10]

THE TECHNOLOGICAL CHALLENGE

The nuclear weapons control agenda is also challenged by what is known as the 'dual-use' phenomenon: the use of militarily significant materials and technology for legitimate, non-military purposes. Nowhere is this challenge more vivid than in the field of nuclear energy generation. According to the 2009 edition of the IAEA's nuclear energy forecast, by the end of 2008 there were some 438 nuclear power reactors in operation around the world, with a further 44 under construction.[11] Representing the international nuclear energy industry, the World Nuclear Association reported that, by September 2009, the number of reactors under construction had risen to 50 and that the global demand for nuclear energy might increase from the 327.5 gigawatt electric (GWe) capacity available in 2009 to more than double that amount by 2030. From 2015 this surge in demand could mean worldwide the equivalent of one GWe power reactor being brought on-line every five days.[12]

Nuclear power generation uses knowledge, processes and materials that are all directly associated with nuclear weapon programmes. An associated difficulty is that an inevitable by-product of nuclear energy generation is unprocessed plutonium. The fuel required for nuclear power generation is uranium-235 (U-235), which is not sufficiently available in nature and must therefore be manufactured from more readily available uranium-238. Uranium ore must first be mined and then dissolved in sulphuric acid, before being 'recovered' in a solid form as uranium oxide (otherwise known as yellowcake). Uranium oxide must then be 'converted' into the gas uranium hexafluoride, where the proportion of U-235 is about 0.7 per cent. The next step in the process is to produce a sufficient quantity of low-enriched uranium (LEU) containing between 3.5 and 5 per cent U-235. Enrichment is undertaken by a variety of methods (gaseous diffusion, gas centrifuge and laser isotope separation, for example) that are either already available or under development. These are complex processes requiring advanced levels of engineering knowledge and infrastructure. But once acquired, the same processes can be duplicated in a 'cascade' in order to enrich U-235 to far higher levels, even to the 93 per cent widely (albeit not universally) considered to be the threshold for weapons-grade highly enriched uranium (HEU). Reactor-grade plutonium (i.e. plutonium containing 50–60 per cent of the fissile isotope plutonium 239 [Pu-239]) is the inevitable by-product of the irradiation of U-235 in any U-235 reactor. This knowledge is the basis on which weapons-grade plutonium (i.e. containing 90–95 per cent Pu-239) can be 'bred' in a power or research reactor. Using chemical separation processes, a relatively small 100 megawatt thermal (MWt) LEU-powered reactor (equivalent to as little as 33 MWe) could produce 100 grams of Pu-239 each day – enough to construct a weapon in just two months.[13]

The expected growth in nuclear energy generation creates a number of difficulties for the nuclear weapons control agenda. Some states might acquire the capability for nuclear power generation but then divert that knowledge and ability into nuclear weapon production. With worldwide stocks of fissile material increasing steadily, terrorists might seek to acquire quantities of either HEU or Pu-239 sufficient to build either a fully functioning nuclear weapon or an improvised nuclear device. Some groups might steal irradiated and highly toxic nuclear waste in order to construct a radiological dispersal device or 'dirty bomb'.[14] The central point to note is that, while the various arms control and non-proliferation agreements are already facing diplomatic and political pressure, the dual-use nature of nuclear technology suggests that this pressure is likely only to increase over the coming 20 years or so. Inspection regimes, weapons ceilings and deployment agreements, nuclear safety and security measures, and novel ideas such as an international nuclear fuel bank – all of these initiatives are rightly considered essential to effective nuclear weapons control in the first years of the twenty-first century.[15] But in the absence of convincing alternatives, these initiatives must also have the diplomatic and political impetus, and be sufficiently dynamic and flexible to be able to manage a still more pressured environment towards the middle of the century as the huge problems associated with dual use expand and proliferate.

THE STRATEGIC CHALLENGE

It has long been supposed that nuclear weapons control benefits from (and is perhaps made possible by) a so-called 'taboo' against both the acquisition and, even more, the use of nuclear weapons. The taboo embodies a number of disincentives: legal constraints and penalties against breaking international treaties; caution at the massive financial investment required for a successful nuclear weapons programme; prudential assessments that a nuclear weapon programme could disappoint an erstwhile ally and protector or, worse still, invite a pre-emptive attack (nuclear or otherwise) by an opponent; and, of course, moral repugnance against the death and destruction that would follow a nuclear attack. It was assumed that the taboo applied both to relations between states and to the behaviour of terrorist groups; a terrorist group that acquired a nuclear weapon, whether or not it chose to use it, would achieve absolute pariah status and would be excluded from political engagement, reconciliation and indeed any conceivable political process.

But the grip of this decades-long taboo may now be easing. It is known, for example, that al-Qaeda has long been interested in acquiring or developing a functioning nuclear weapon, and that Osama bin Laden has declared it a 'religious duty' for the organization to acquire nuclear weapons.[16] By one account, had the Taliban regime not been ejected from Afghanistan, and had al-Qaeda managed to remain relatively unmolested in that country, they would 'eventually' have acquired nuclear weapons.[17] On these grounds, and in spite of the significant technical and engineering that would have to be overcome, nuclear terrorism might reasonably be described as a 'realistic threat'.[18] Other analysts describe this possibility in even starker terms: 'Terrorist acquisition of nuclear weapons poses the greatest single threat to the United States.'[19]

Among states, the disincentives to nuclear weapon acquisition are increasingly matched by the perceived incentives. For decades, the possession of nuclear weapons conferred very high status in the international community (not least, of course, permanent membership of the United Nations Security Council), and this simple message has not been lost on ambitious governments and rising powers around the world. Another, increasingly common, argument is that nuclear weapon possession might be the only thing that Western interventionist forces (with their acknowledged superiority in conventional forces and technology) would respect.

The fraying of the nuclear taboo might also be attributed to the fact that some nuclear weapon states have openly discussed nuclear use for a variety of purposes. The ethical element of the nuclear taboo is challenged by an argument put forward by the late Sir Michael Quinlan in his most erudite and accessible study, *Thinking about Nuclear Weapons*. In calling for a more careful assessment of the 'moral acceptability of possessing nuclear weapons', Quinlan observes that some limited use of such weapons could 'serve to deny an aggressor the attainment of intolerable aims without entailing unlimited catastrophe, and so could lead to an outcome that might legitimately be termed successful and worth the costs'.[20] As with the other incentives described above, it is conceivable that the leaders of non-nuclear weapon states could draw these conclusions themselves, articulating their own diplomatic, strategic and moral case for the acquisition of nuclear weapons. There is also the possibility, finally, that non-familiarity has bred contempt. The complex but familiar rationales to justify nuclear weapon possession have been fading fast since the end of the Cold War two decades ago. In their place, perhaps the more vivid reference point for nuclear weapons is not their non-use during the Cold War but the only moment when they have been used – and conclusively so – in 1945. The breakdown of the nuclear taboo is a subject to approach with some caution, not least because breakdown might, paradoxically, prove to be a stimulus to more effective weapons control, rather than the moment at which nuclear weapon use finally ceased to be unthinkable. As Mark Fitzpatrick points out,

> There is no compelling logic to assume that nuclear weapons would thereby become re-legitimized as instruments of war. The breaking of the nuclear taboo could actually spur either or both of two opposite reactions: an increased salience of nuclear weapons and a stimulus to disarmament.[21]

Taking a rather less cautious line, Michael Krepon notes that 'there is no shortage of nonproliferation specialists predicting impending nuclear disasters' and judges that 'the threat itself has been greatly exaggerated'.[22] Krepon's argument is essentially a complaint against worst-case analysis and the distorted, inappropriate and costly planning and preparation that can follow from it. Yet there is surely a countervailing danger of complacency bred of hindsight. If there is an increasing possibility of nuclear weapon use (which most reasonable analysts would agree on), then it is surely difficult to apply anything other than worst-case analysis to that possibility. Something about the nuclear danger – the loss of life and the damage that can be caused – suggests that the 'threat inflation' against which Krepon argues might be a prudent response to the possibility of nuclear use. It would certainly seem to be a very human response to that scenario.

Even if the nuclear taboo is not about to be broken, it is certainly fraying at the edges. And the mere possibility that some states and terrorist groups might increasingly see nuclear weapons in terms of military advantage should be cause for very considerable concern. The strategic challenge for advocates of nuclear weapons control is to prevent the erosion of the nuclear taboo by promoting a climate of trust. Trust is maintained through the mechanisms discussed elsewhere in this chapter: careful diplomacy and negotiation; well-written treaties, conventions and agreements; consistency of performance; and verification of that performance. When trust fades or is undermined, the strategic challenge is to be able to shift from an inclusive approach based on persuasion and mutual self-interest to a more adversarial position based on the deterrence and, ultimately, the coercion of recalcitrant governments. Yet the deterrence of a terrorist group is a different matter, arguably requiring a far more subtle and imaginative approach. One such approach might lie in forensic attribution and 'deterrence by association': if states and commercial organizations can be exposed for having supplied a nuclear weapon capability to a terrorist group, they can then be subject to sanctions; and the threat of sanctions might have the effect of cutting off supply in the first place.

THE INTELLECTUAL CHALLENGE

The final challenge to the Obama administration is to develop a more convincing and more contemporary way of explaining its aspirations for nuclear weapons control. Each of the three familiar approaches – arms control, non-proliferation and disarmament – pulls in a different direction, yet all seem to be in play in the administration's approach. How can this be explained? Put more simply, what does each of these actually mean in the context of international security in the early twenty-first century?

It is relatively easy to describe what these ideas meant during their heyday in the Cold War. Arms control was the management of a highly weaponized adversarial relationship. It was an elaborate construction: its advocates even devised the apparent absurdity that countries could improve their security by remaining vulnerable to their adversaries. These were extraordinary ideas, but they may also have been a peculiarity of the middle and later years of the twentieth century. There are lingering shadows of the Cold War model in the relations between the United States and Russia, and to some extent between India and Pakistan, but it is difficult to identify a close analogue to Cold War arms control in scope, intensity or sophistication. In important respects non-proliferation was also a thing of the Cold War, its purpose being to prevent the leakage of nuclear weapon expertise from the tightly controlled central relationship. Disarmament, finally, embodied the grand ideal: the goal of a world in which the most destructive weapons ever invented were disposed of once and for all. Disarmament was never a thing of the Cold War and never fared well in the shadow of arms control, the strategically dominant idea. But it is emerging as a new and re-energized element of the triad – although, as Stephen Cimbala observes, nuclear weapons states 'remain far from agreed on the objective of nuclear abolition, nor the means for getting there'.[23]

Twenty-first-century nuclear weapons control is none of the above and all of them; it is a composite of these long-standing and complex ideas. As such, nuclear weapons control is unlikely to be the easiest idea to describe and implement. Yet it is essential that the intellectual effort be made to explain, as precisely and simply as possible, the problems that nuclear weapons control addresses, what it hopes to achieve, and on whose behalf. Without a robust and communicable intellectual underpinning, nuclear weapons control will lack plausibility, authority and normative strength. Furthermore, if it is seen to be in the service of one vested interest or another it will be too easily challenged, bypassed or ignored.

The goal of nuclear weapons control cannot be to prevent all war and violence for all time, although this would doubtless be good, if achievable. Nor, of course, should nuclear weapons control seek to confer strategic advantage upon one country or another. Instead the goal should be to prevent nuclear war. Such a simple, stark and unequivocal goal will not only provide a persuasive intellectual and moral underpinning but also help to ensure that the various means and ideas available do not become ends in themselves. With a clear and unequivocal goal, nuclear weapons control can become a matter of variable geometry; a loose framework in which various means and devices are available in pursuit of the common goal. By this approach, weapons ceilings, verification, test bans, cut-off conventions, weapon-free zones, counter-proliferation, threat reduction and even the notion of a Global Zero can all be evaluated as instruments rather than venerated as ends in themselves.

CONCLUSION

Nuclear weapons control has for decades been driven by three sets of ideas, none of which is now as convincing as it should be. Arms control agreements are widely perceived to be a thing of the past – a product of the Cold War adversarial relationship between the United States and the Soviet Union. In some respects, the only surprise should be that arms control has survived for so long after the end of the Cold War. Similarly, international non-proliferation regimes – elaborate diplomatic and legal arrangements, often supported by large and complex bureaucracies – are widely perceived to be undergoing a crisis of credibility and utility. The idea of non-proliferation is arguably a legacy of a very different and much simpler time, when technology was more controllable (and the problem of dual-use technology was in its infancy), when the core concern was with the activities of governments and states, and when the Cold War provided an ever-present and compelling case for restraint in weapons development and acquisition. The third main approach to the management of nuclear weapons is of course disarmament. This has never been as persuasive as arms control and non-proliferation and was firmly in their shadow during the Cold War. Even now, and in spite of its resurgence in the form of the Global Zero idea, disarmament continues to be associated with the musings of unworldly idealists.

But all of these ideas need to be taken more seriously than ever before. There is no convincing alternative to them and no convincing argument that any one of them could on its own solve the problems of nuclear weapon control. With Iran and North Korea moving ever closer to having deployable nuclear weapons, the simmering antagonism between India and Pakistan, the growing danger of terrorist acquisition and use of either a nuclear or a radiological device, and the dramatic increase in nuclear energy generation creating even greater challenges for the safety and security of nuclear materials, it is not an exaggeration to say that around the world, nuclear weapon challenges are now more pressing and more complex than since the darkest days of the Cold War.

Responding to these challenges, the administration of President Barack Obama has sought to present a new American approach, marking the end of eight years that are widely regarded as having been dominated by a lack of faith in the merits of non-proliferation and an unwillingness to be constrained by international treaties. A great deal of effort has been devoted to securing the various agreements discussed above – START replacement, CTBT and FMCT. And there are many other initiatives, not discussed at any length in this chapter, where the continued support of the United States will be essential. The administration could, for example, put its energy behind the extension of the G8 Global Partnership Against the Spread of Weapons and Materials of Mass Destruction (an area where the enormous and decisive US contribution often goes unnoticed), broadening the initiative to cover other regions of proliferation concern.

But in the end, the Obama administration will have to concentrate on the most urgent question of them all: what can be done about the NPT, due for its next review in 2010? At the heart of the NPT is the so-called 'bargain' between the nuclear weapon states and the 'nuclear have nots'. For many years the bargain has looked more like blatant fraud perpetrated on the 'have nots', and the task now is to find a way to recalibrate the NPT in such a way that nuclear non-proliferation remains a rational option for sovereign governments around the world. The alternative, of course, is to accept that the NPT has run its course. In that case, the Obama administration will need to inject as much energy as possible, and as quickly as possible, into the goal of a world with no nuclear weapons whatsoever, as proposed in 2007 by George Schultz, William Perry, Henry Kissinger and Sam Nunn.

The United States will need all its diplomatic and intellectual resources not only to meet the challenges of today but also, for the longer term, to breathe life back into an old idea: that multilateral arms control, non-proliferation and disarmament (even if only an article of faith for the foreseeable future) are all essential pillars of the global order. If the United States cannot or will not take up this broader and longer-term challenge, then the increasing availability of the materials, technology and expertise needed to make nuclear weapons will mean a world of weapons proliferation, arms races and, ultimately, nuclear use. Although they have very different ancestries, the time has come to see these three schools of thought as different means to a common end – the prevention of nuclear war – rather than as exclusive rivals, as an end in themselves or as a device to assert national interest. It was, after all, one of Barack Obama's predecessors President Harry S. Truman who once warned against becoming 'so preoccupied with weapons' (and, we might add, political ideologies) 'that we lose sight of the fact that war itself is the real villain'.[24]

NOTES

1 President Barack Obama's Inaugural Address, 20 January 2009: http://www.whitehouse. gov/blog/inaugural-address/.
2 Arms Control Association: http://www.armscontrol.org/act/.
3 President Barack Obama, Remarks, Prague, Czech Republic, 5 April 2009: http:// www.whitehouse.gov/the_press_office/Remarks-By-President-Barack-Obama-In-Prague-As-Delivered/.

4   S.J. Blank, *Russia and Arms Control: Are There Opportunities for the Obama Administration?* (Carlisle, PA: US Army War College, Strategic Studies Institute, March 2009), p. 5: http://www.strategicstudiesinstitute.army.mil/Pubs/Display.Cfm?pubID=908.

5   See I. Daalder and J. Lodal, 'The Logic of Zero: Toward a World Without Nuclear Weapons', *Foreign Affairs* 87(6)(November/December 2008): 80–95.

6   See P. Cornish, 'NATO's New Strategic Concept: Going Nuclear', *World Today* 65(12) (December 2009): 23–4.

7   I am grateful to Professor John Simpson for this observation.

8   C.A. Murdock, 'A World Free of Nuclear Weapons: How Realistic is Obama's Vision?', *National Defense* (June 2009): 39.

9   T. Sharp, 'Local Priorities vs. National Interests in Arms Control', *Bulletin of the Atomic Scientists*, web edition, 28 August 2009: http://www.thebulletin.org/web-edition/features/local-priorities-vs-national-interests-arms-control.

10 T. Sharp, 'Senate Sounds of Silence on Nukes', The Center for Arms Control and Non-Proliferation, 8 October 2009: http://www.armscontrolcenter.org/policy/nucle-arweapons/articles/100809_senate_sounds_silence_nukes/.

11 International Atomic Energy Agency, *Energy, Electricity and Nuclear Power Estimates for the Period up to 2030* (Vienna: IAEA, August 2009), pp. 12–13. See http://www-pub.iaea.org/MTCD/publications/PDF/RDS1-29_web.pdf.

12 'Plans for new reactors worldwide', World Nuclear Association, September 2009: http://www.world-nuclear.org/info/inf17.html.

13 J. Pike, 'Special Weapons Primer: Plutonium Production' (Federation of American Scientists, 20 June 2000): http://www.fas.org/nuke/intro/nuke/plutonium.htm.

14 These scenarios are investigated in P. Cornish, *The CBRN System: Assessing the Threat of Terrorist Use of Chemical, Biological, Radiological and Nuclear Weapons in the United Kingdom* (London: Chatham House, February 2007): http://www.chathamhouse.org.uk/research/security/papers/view/-/id/434/.

15 See K.N. Luongo, 'Securing Vulnerable Nuclear Materials: Meeting the Global Challenge' (The Stanley Foundation, Policy Analysis Brief, November 2009): http://www.stanleyfoundation.org/publications/pab/Luongo_PAB1109.pdf.

16 '"Black Dawn": Scenario-Based Exercise', report by Center for Strategic and International Studies, Washington, DC, August 2004. See also M. Braemer Maerli, 'Nuclear Terrorism: Threats, Challenges and Responses', *Security Policy Library* (Oslo: Norwegian Atlantic Committee, 8–2002), p. 8; and A. Kelle and A. Schaper, 'Terrorism Using Biological and Nuclear Weapons', *PRIF Report*, Peace Research Institute Frankfurt, No. 64 (2003), pp. 28–9.

17 D. Albright quoted in B. Zellen, 'Nuclear Terrorism: Re-thinking the Unthinkable', *Intersec* 15(10) (October 2005): 309. See also 'Taliban and al-Qaeda "targeted Pakistani nuclear arms bases"', *Daily Telegraph*, 12 August 2009.

18 D. Bennett, 'Terrorists and Unconventional Weapons: Is the Threat Real?', *Low Intensity Conflict & Law Enforcement* 12(1)(Spring 2004): 22, 38.

19 Carnegie Endowment for International Peace, *Universal Compliance: A Strategy for Nuclear Security* (Washington, DC: CEIP, June 2004. Draft), p. 25.

20 M. Quinlan, *Thinking about Nuclear Weapons: Principles, Problems, Prospects* (Oxford University Press, 2009), p. 47.

21 M. Fitzpatrick, *The World After: Proliferation, Deterrence and Disarmament if the Nuclear Taboo is Broken* (Paris: IFRI and Atomic Energy Commission (CEA), Spring 2009), p. 10.

22 M. Krepon, 'The Mushroom Cloud That Wasn't: Why Inflating Threats Won't Reduce

Them', *Foreign Affairs* 88(3)(May/June 2009): 3.

23 S. J. Cimbala, 'Nuclear Arms Reductions, Abolition and Nonproliferation: What's Ideal, What's Possible, What's Problematical?', *Journal of Slavic Military Studies* 22 (2009): 329.

24 Quoted in Quinlan, *Thinking about Nuclear Weapons*, p. 157.

13

The United States and climate change: from process to action

Bernice Lee and Michael Grubb
with Felix Preston and Benjamin Zala

INTRODUCTION

'We've asked for your leadership, we seek your leadership. But if for some reason you are not willing to lead, leave it to the rest of us. Please get out of the way.'

> – Kevin Conrad, a delegate from Papua New Guinea,
> speaking at the final negotiating session at the UNFCCC
> Conference of Parties in Bali, December 2007

Kevin Conrad's now iconic statement at the eleventh hour of the UN climate change negotiations in Bali in 2007 epitomized the frustration felt by friends and opponents alike about the United States' reluctance during the Bush administration to throw its weight behind multilateral solutions to tackle environmental challenges. Until the final days of the Bush administration, the US policy on climate change went against the grain of most of its allies in the international community during the previous decade,[1] and the United States was described as the 'rogue state' in global green politics.[2] The conflicting range of domestic interests and fractured agendas that have driven its policies on energy security and climate mitigation are also well documented.[3]

Climate change and all the associated resource challenges (in energy, food, water and land use) highlight the nature of interdependencies among states and peoples. The bulk of climate change impacts may need to be managed domestically. But environmental changes such as land degradation, water reductions, shifting agricultural zones, together with extreme weather events, will produce social stresses with effects far beyond national borders.

The implications of dangerous climate change for security and political stability are increasingly recognized by the foreign policy and defence communities in the United States. A 2007 report by the Center for Naval Analysis stated that climate change can become 'a threat multiplier for instability in some of the most volatile regions of the world, and it presents significant national security challenges for the United States'.[4] In 2008, the National Intelligence Council (NIC) completed a new classified assessment that explores how climate change could threaten US security in the next 20 years by causing political instability, mass movements of refugees, terrorism, or conflicts over water and other resources in specific countries.[5]

Until recently, total US greenhouse gas (GHG) emissions were the highest in the world. In historical terms, the United States is responsible for around 30 per cent of the additional carbon in the atmosphere. Its emissions per capita are also among the highest in the world, more than double those of the European Union, and four times those of China. The US economy is among the most emissions-intensive in the OECD. This reflects fundamental features of the US economy and society, notably the abundance of cheap coal and other fossil fuels, vast distances augmenting the need for transport, and an expansive mode of development based on personal mobility through the motor vehicle.[6]

In the aftermath of the December 2009 Copenhagen Conference on Climate Change, and the political agreement that was reached (the Copenhagen Accord), the next section of this chapter considers afresh the scale of global challenge at hand as a result of rapid global warming. This is followed by a description of the record to date of US engagement with the regime to control global warming, including the recent changes in the domestic political landscape.

It is difficult to overestimate the importance of US action – and the cost of US inaction – to the world's ability to seek solutions to dangerous climate change. The United States has a key role in ensuring effective multilateralism so that negotiations do not deliver the lowest common denominator. This will require dealing with powerful domestic interests at home and tackling some tricky fault lines that lie at the nexus of its trade, climate change and China policies. The chapter goes on to focus on the need for a fresh look at US–China relations in the context of global energy and climate security.

During the past century, the United States has led the world by exporting its own way of life and its ubiquitous economic reach. It is easy to forget in the light of recent history that the United States was the pioneer in global environmental governance, from breakthrough technologies that have transformed our capacity to tackle emissions, to innovative legislative tools and market-based mechanisms including the design of the Kyoto Protocol. Later sections of the chapter specifically consider US leadership in low carbon innovations – and outline issues around the US role in the next phase of global climate governance.

The ability of the United States to accelerate the global transition towards a low carbon future has been hampered by its international isolation on this issue. Global climate security requires immediate action not by the United States and developed countries alone but also by the less developed economies. This means that the traditional style of US leadership – changing the world through the sheer scale of its excellence and weight in the market-place – will not suffice. The central challenge will be to accept, respect and work with the efforts of others that have over the past decade continued to shape the global response in the absence of constructive US engagement. The chapter concludes with a summary of key recommendations for the new administration towards a new strategy of engagement with the world on climate change.

MEETING THE CHALLENGE OF DANGEROUS CLIMATE CHANGE

Global climate security demands global efforts and measures to minimize global temperature rises, a point that has been reaffirmed by new scientific evidence. At the 2009 G8 summit, global leaders agreed that minimizing the probability of a 2°C rise over pre-industrial levels would be a credible goal. To give a 50: 50 chance of staying within the 2°C limit, global CO_2 emissions will need to peak before about 2020 and fall by over 50 per cent by 2050.[7]

What would a 50–80 per cent global reduction by 2050 entail? For developed countries including the United States, it implies sharp reductions, moving close to a zero-carbon economy by 2050, with major developing countries following suit well before the end of the century. It implies average annual global emissions of around 2 tonnes of CO_2 per person – less than half the present Chinese level, a fifth of the level in Europe, and a tenth of that in the US. To achieve this, all major emitting countries will need to begin radical decarbonization in the next 20 years, whatever their level of economic development.

Formal negotiations at the United Nations Framework Convention on Climate Change (UNFCCC), though critical for setting ambitious national targets, are but one component of a global climate response. The key question is whether states and markets can stimulate genuine opportunities in low carbon economic activities and investments towards energy efficiency across the globe, creating incentives to move the additional trillions of dollars in investment needed by 2030 (above the business-as-usual scenarios) into low carbon options.[8] A global agreement on climate change will have to be acceptable to all major polluting countries. But the true measure of its success will hinge on whether it generates a transformational shift in international energy finance flows, achieving:

- rapid global diffusion of existing and near-to-market low carbon and energy-efficiency technologies;
- new generations of solutions from breakthrough technologies from 2030 onwards; and
- equitable international collaboration mechanisms on technological development and transfer in order to lower the cost/risk of technology investment and to encourage national action in developing countries.

This transformation would be no mean feat at a time of volatile energy prices and a global economic downturn, unless, of course, these forces could themselves be harnessed in support of lower carbon investment. On the current trajectory, the world is clearly not yet deviating enough from the dangerous business-as-usual pathway – one that is likely to bring serious outcomes that go beyond deepened climate insecurity, such as 'resource nationalism', political instability and heightened import dependencies. Box 1 indicates likely some security implications for the United States.

Box 1: Security implications of climate change impacts on the US

The threats of dangerous climate change and environmental change to the US way of life are beginning to shape a new generation of response. These vulnerabilities afflict many different regions in the US and would require separate and distinct counter-measures. These potentially include:

- Damage to infrastructure, especially along flooded and eroding coast-lines, home to many of the biggest cities in the US and much of its national product;
- Disruption to critical energy infrastructure, threatening the delivery of domestic oil supplies as pipelines are built on increasingly unstable ground (owing to melting permafrost in Alaska);
- Legislative standstill in a litigious culture (with mounting lawsuits against emitters, and between states over water supplies);
- Shifts in boundaries and territory (from coastal retreats and redrawing of maritime zones);
- Water scarcity and falling agricultural outputs (owing to severe droughts in the western and southern agricultural areas);
- Increasing economic cost with decreasing availability of insurance cover, as well as mass movement of internal refugees (as seen with Hurricane Katrina), floods and droughts.

Sources: Cleo Paskal, *Global Warring: How Environmental, Economic and Political Crises Will Redraw the World Map* (New York: Palgrave Macmillan, 2010), pp. 25–62; and Cleo Paskal, *How Climate Change is Pushing the Boundaries of Security and Foreign Policy*, Chatham House Briefing Paper, June 2007.

US ENGAGEMENT IN CLIMATE NEGOTIATIONS: WHERE WE WERE

'The world expects more from a major economy like the United States.'
– José Manuel Barroso, President, European Commission, on the eve of the 2008 G8 summit[9]

The history of US engagement at the UNFCCC provides an important starting point in understanding the potential challenges and opportunities faced by the Obama administration. This history has contributed to the mistrust between the United States and its traditional allies in Europe, as well as between developed and developing countries.

Almost two decades have passed since the 1992 Rio Convention at which almost all the world's governments, including the United States (which was among the first to ratify), agreed to the UNFCCC, a treaty that established the basic principles and institutional processes on which to take subsequent steps to avoid 'dangerous interference' with the earth's climate. Since then, the Kyoto Protocol (1997) and Marrakech Accords (2001) have been agreed, but in these cases without US participation. These agreements aimed to set caps on carbon emissions for the world's industrialized nations, allowing them to trade emission rights with each other as well as develop emission reduction projects in developing countries.

This shift from US leadership and engagement with international efforts to combat climate change to a position of detachment highlights one of the key challenges for the United States and for the world in combating climate change – the minimal Congressional appetite for new international treaties. In July 1997, the Byrd-Hagel 'Sense of the Senate' Resolution argued that a commitment to cap greenhouse gas emissions could seriously harm the US economy, 'including significant job loss, trade disadvantages, increased energy and consumer costs' in the absence of any similar binding commitments on the developing world.[10] Eileen Claussen, the US's chief climate negotiator who resigned shortly thereafter, pointed out that a strict interpretation of the Senate resolution was incompatible not only with the realities of the global negotiations but also with the legally binding mandate for the Kyoto negotiations, which the United States had agreed to in 1995 in Berlin. The negotiating mandate precluded new commitments for developing countries on the grounds that the industrialized world had yet to meet its own promises in the original UNFCCC Treaty. Fulfilling these promises became the declared purpose of the Kyoto negotiations. Given the Byrd-Hagel Resolution, the Clinton administration never submitted the Kyoto Protocol to the Senate for ratification.

The virtually guaranteed vote against ratification was ironic since the protocol's structure had effectively been designed in Washington. The United States had proposed a legally enforceable set of commitments for industrialized countries in early 1997 – to ensure a 'level playing field' of implementation – along with market-based flexibility for where and how these commitments would be implemented. After securing Europe's support, the US delegation focused on explaining to Russia the possible benefits of international emissions trading, and to the developing world the benefits of international emission offsets – an idea that eventually emerged as the Kyoto Protocol's Clean Development Mechanism (CDM). At the Kyoto conference that December, the United States, led by Vice President Al Gore, ratcheted up its commitments in return for each degree of market-based flexibility that it secured.

The treaty design that eventually emerged was in most essential respects based on the US proposal.[11] But it was marred by a problem of US governance: international overreach compared to domestic support had simultaneously created a credible multilateral solution and destroyed the prospect of US Congressional acceptance.

The Bush administration's withdrawal from the Kyoto Protocol upon taking office in 2001 exposed this fissure for all to see. The administration abruptly announced that the agreement was 'fatally flawed' and declared it dead.[12] This became a focal point around which most of the world (except Australia) rallied. Energized by America's behaviour, and especially the abrupt manner of its withdrawal from Kyoto, the EU responded by asserting leadership to rescue the efforts of ten years of global negotiations among nearly 200 countries. Climate change was firmly placed on the agenda of European heads of state, and the issue came to be seen as a test of the EU's credibility with regard to global responsibilities. Stung by US scepticism about Europe's seriousness, the EU also made a remarkable volte-face to embrace the US-pioneered 'cap-and-trade' approach as the key instrument of implementing emissions reductions.

The near-global effort delivered a political agreement that was transcribed into the Marrakech Accords in November 2001, while the United States looked on. It took another three years' diplomacy, increasingly centred upon Russia, to bring the Kyoto Protocol into force as a legally binding treaty, activating the global carbon market mechanisms that US negotiators had done much to pioneer.

The decade following Byrd-Hagel saw the United States grow increasingly isolated in its recalcitrance on climate change.[13] If the main dividing line over climate change in the 1990s was between businesses and environmental interests, US climate policy under the Bush administration appeared to owe as much to instinct and ideology as to considered strategy. President Bush only ordered a review of US climate change policy after withdrawing support for Kyoto in March 2001.[14] The subsequent Clear Skies and Global Climate Change Initiatives focused on voluntary measures and indices (notably an energy intensity reduction of 18 per cent over ten years, only a little above the historical trend) that were never likely to stem the rise in US emissions. President Bush emphasized that he would not 'commit our nation to an unsound international treaty that will throw millions of our citizens out of work'.[15]

The Kyoto Protocol's entry into force without US participation in February 2005 reinforced the international political divide. US attempts to forge international alternatives to the UNFCCC negotiations, such as the Asia-Pacific Partnership on Clean Development and Climate, and the Major Economies Meetings on Energy and Climate Change (MEM), were greeted with scepticism in many European capitals.[16]

Over this same period, however, US public opinion on the need for urgent climate action strengthened, with increased legislative activity. The 2003 Lieberman-McCain Bill, proposing caps on US emissions, drew 43 votes in the Senate. The trend was reinforced as the popular media extensively explored the links between warming temperatures and natural disasters in the wake of Hurricane Katrina and Al Gore's popular film *An Inconvenient Truth*. *Business Week* magazine declared that 2006 'was the year global warming went from controversial to conventional for much of the corporate world'.[17]

Following the 2007 release of the IPCC's Fourth Assessment Report, doubts about the links between human activity and climate change all but evaporated.[18] US grassroots political momentum generated considerable local, state and regional pressure for federal climate action through a cap-and-trade system coupled with international commitments. 'Mitigation through litigation' has also fast been gaining ground.[19]

The victory of Barack Obama in the presidential elections in November 2008 capped this shift in the US political tide towards treating climate change as a serious challenge to US interests and making significant GHG reductions a central policy objective. President Obama's early appointments of Stephen Chu, Todd Stern, John Holdren, Jane Lubchenco, Carol Browner[20] and others to senior positions in the administration all pointed to a new phase of US engagement and, potentially, leadership on this issue. However, the world to which the Obama administration now turned its attention in terms of climate policy had evolved significantly.

INTERNATIONAL DEVELOPMENTS

The world was not idle during the US absence from the international climate arena. The major developments divided into two clear stages, marked roughly by the first and second term of the Bush presidency. The first stage grappled with fundamental uncertainty about whether the supporters of the system built over the previous decade would succeed in rescuing the fruits of that long diplomatic endeavour. Institutional processes continued to put in place the details of institutional machinery, but they remained largely moribund without resolution. However, with widespread international efforts to persuade Russia to ratify finally succeeding in November 2004, thereby bringing the Kyoto Protocol into force, the framework for setting meaningful targets for carbon emissions by its signatories was largely secured.

Domestic legislation in key countries followed swiftly, and the private sector began to invest on the basis of a legally secure international regulatory regime. In effect, the world moved into a second stage characterized by stalemate between the United States and the rest of the world. The G8 continued to strive for accommodation, but a number of multilateral efforts started to focus beyond the Bush administration. These continued to develop the main international machinery and to lay the foundations for the next round of multilateral negotiations.

In terms of implementation, the cornerstone of the global mechanisms was the EU Emissions Trading Scheme (ETS) and its links with the global Kyoto mechanisms. These gave economic value to emission reductions both within the EU and globally. The first phase of the EU ETS, 2005–07, embodied a good market design, and its first year saw carbon prices higher than expected, fuelling an explosive growth of investment in emission-reducing projects under the Clean Development Mechanism. However, the first EU ETS verification data reports in May 2006 revealed a substantial net surplus of emissions allowances, the combined result of over-allocation and greater than expected emission reductions. The price of carbon collapsed over the rest of that year, but the carbon markets continued to trade on the basis of expectations for the second phase, synchronized with Kyoto's first commitment period of 2008–12.

For Phase II, the EU made a big step towards fixing the problems with the overall level of allocation, such that, during 2008, the EU ETS supported a carbon price above €20 per tonne of CO_2 until 2012, several times the price in the United States' voluntary markets. However, many imperfections remain. In spring 2007, the European Council pledged to cut EU greenhouse gas emissions by 2020, unilaterally by 20 per cent relative to 1990 levels, or by 30 per cent in the event of a global deal. In January 2008, the European Commission presented its proposals for implementing these ambitious goals. These included a radical redesign after 2012, with tougher caps and a wholesale move towards auctioning, which would generate tens of billions of euros annually – some of which, the Commission recommended, could be channelled to support low carbon technology R&D. Despite fierce lobbying to weaken the proposals, the essence of the EU package for 2013–20 – with deeper cutbacks in the EU ETS and much higher levels of auctioning – was adopted by the Council in December 2008. If there is one fundamental lesson from the EU ETS, it is that building into a system the capacity to learn and evolve over time is crucial – and, fortunately, that is one thing that the EU design got right.

The importance of the international carbon markets, largely financed through the EU ETS commitments and Japanese investment, cannot be overestimated. More than 4,000 projects have officially entered the CDM pipeline, through which projected emission savings to 2012 total close to $2,000MtCO_2e$. The UNFCCC estimates that the value of credits under the CDM and Joint Implementation mechanism is US$4.5–8.5 billion annually, and that they leverage roughly ten times this amount towards emission reduction projects from the private sector. A market estimated at a minimum of US$50 billion per annum is not going to disappear; one of the few concrete decisions already taken under the post-2012 Kyoto Protocol negotiations is that the global carbon mechanisms will continue in place beyond this deadline.

Away from the carbon markets, the UNFCCC processes continued to ratchet up the pressure to launch global negotiations. The Heiligendamm G8 summit in June 2007 reached a consensus that the world needed negotiations on future actions under the UNFCCC, leading all eyes to the Bali UNFCCC conference in December that year.

The Bali Action Plan opens with a commitment to establish a 'shared vision for long-term cooperative action' – set immediately in the context of 'common but differentiated responsibility and respective capabilities'.[21] The undertaking by developed countries to establish 'quantified emission commitments' was a major US concession, reversing the Bush administration's rejection of quantified emission caps. It remains unclear whether the Bush administration realized it was signing up to language almost identical to that in the Berlin Mandate that launched the Kyoto negotiations, some 13 years earlier. It begs the obvious question as to why the United States has a separate negotiating track for quantified commitments post-2012 while all other industrialized countries are already negotiating second-period commitments under the Kyoto Protocol. The relationship between these two processes bedevilled negotiations in the run-up to Copenhagen.

The concomitant commitment of developing countries to negotiate 'new and additional actions' (a major concession given their earlier intransigence) was matched by the commitment by developed countries that this concession would be 'supported by technology and enabled by financing and capacity-building'. Which of these two commitments was to be 'measurable, reportable and verifiable' was the stumbling block on which Bali almost collapsed; the final compromise was that both would be. Deforestation, adaptation, technology development and transfer, and financial resources also formally had equal prominence in the Bali Action Plan. However, none of these elements were resolved either in terms of detail or with regard to the exact timeframe. The Pew Center's post-Bali assessment observed that 'delegates remained far apart on fundamental issues but in the end agreed to launch a loosely framed negotiating process'.[22] A review of the outcome noted: 'Complexity hardly captures it: Bali has launched the most complicated and interrelated set of global negotiations in diplomatic history.' The nail-biting negotiations that were officially scheduled for completion in Copenhagen in December 2009, and which led to a political accord, testified to the difficulties around global target-setting as well as agreement on the timeframe.

LESSONS OF 2009: COPENHAGEN AND THE DEBATE ON MULTILATERAL PROCESSES

Despite the crucial importance of national and regional initiatives, the world ultimately cannot solve the climate problem without an effective multilateral approach. Ironically, the election of a more multilateralist US president and the events of 2009 culminating with the Copenhagen Accord have only served to increase debate around the form it might take and how inclusive it needs to be. In reality, any major deal is always built upon smaller coalitions of powerful actors. Many proposals have been made for a core of US leadership, bilateral or trilateral leadership by variants of the US–EU–China/Japan/Asia nexus, the G8, the G8+5, the G20, or the Major Economies Forum (MEF). Doubtless, action by most of these groupings is necessary, though it is also of interest that the MEF process did not reach any specific deal until the relationships fostered during the year were put under the pressure of the Copenhagen summit. Ultimately all such efforts face serious limitations if there is no recognition of the need for a truly multilateral framework. This is for three main reasons: scope, competitiveness and political legitimacy.

First, carbon emissions are so widespread geographically that any subset of countries becomes increasingly unable to solve the problem unless others are involved. The dominance of US, EU and Chinese emissions today would be swamped by 2050 if these countries delivered steep reductions while others did not. And none of these are significant contributors to land-use emissions (such as deforestation), which involve a wholly different group of countries. Moreover, models which centre upon innovative solutions by a 'critical mass' of the private sector diffusing technology and investment globally without government incentives can founder – carbon capture and storage (CCS), which inevitably involves significant extra costs over and above coal plants without CCS, is a case in point.

Second, a partial solution that encompassed the big emitters would not solve the perceived risks of loss of competitiveness in energy-intensive sectors *vis-à-vis* non-participants (to smaller economies such as Singapore, for example).

Third, a deal between the big emitters only is unlikely to secure global legitimacy. In no legal or moral system can a solution be imposed by those inflicting the damage, without at some level engaging those that would most suffer the consequences of inadequate action.

Thus all roads ultimately lead back to the need for a global deal. That was perhaps the most difficult, but ultimately completed, journey for the Bush administration, as it conceded at the G8 Heiligendamm summit in June 2007 the need for solutions to be negotiated under UN auspices.

Notwithstanding the relative success of the Bali negotiations, most of the key difficulties, fault lines and questions that arose in the 1990s remained unresolved. A commentary by David Sandalow[23] argued that the Bali battle over emission targets showed that the EU has learned nothing about realistic engagement with the United States; Japan sat uneasily in its seat as a potential but never actual mediator on the transatlantic divide; and a resurgent Russia remained largely apart.

For its part, the Obama administration, while embracing more seriously the UN negotiations launched under its predecessor, placed equal emphasis upon other efforts – notably high-level bilateral discussions with China and a restructured 'Major Economies Forum', which the United States sought (with limited success) to limit to around 20 countries. During 2009 many smaller countries under the UNFCCC expressed growing anxiety about the extent to which negotiations between key players were being conducted in other forums.

The culmination of this process in Copenhagen in December 2009 has reinforced the discourse about multiple forums and subgroups. The final day's negotiations that led to the Copenhagen Accord were conducted largely between the United States., China, India, Brazil and South Africa, albeit subsequently expanded to a wider group. The European Union was uncharacteristically divided, and played a minor role in brokering and drafting the accord. The final outcome was very convoluted: there is little doubt that President Obama played a critical role in leveraging global pressure to strike a deal with the major developing countries, but his premature announcement of success on CNN infuriated many other heads of state at Copenhagen who had not been involved. Only with difficulty did UN Secretary-General Ban Ki-moon and others persuade the Conference itself to formally accept the *fait accompli* – and then only with an ambiguous 'noting' of the Accord, which invites countries officially to sign up with their agreement and commitments, an unprecedented manoeuvre in a UN setting.

In principle, US leadership could yet transform the politics *vis-à-vis* Russia, and the United States could also use its political muscle to persuade additional countries to accept stronger binding commitments – South Korea has already indicated willingness to accept emission caps, and several others clearly could be drawn in, including Mexico, Turkey, possibly South Africa and some Latin American and Southeast Asian countries. However, the Obama administration would still need to explain to the US public why it is simply not possible, or even desirable, for most developing countries to adopt binding national caps in the next phase.

Yet all this is conditional on US domestic credibility. The crucial undercurrent throughout 2009 was the twists and turns of the Obama administration's struggle to get Congressional support for domestic legislation to curb carbon emissions. The fact that this could not be completed during the year drastically curtailed what it could offer internationally. Many blamed China for the inability to get a stronger deal at Copenhagen. But China did offer an emissions target for the first time in the run-up to the summit, and did finally make important concessions on monitoring and verification. The United States could offer almost nothing. The goodwill and forbearance of the rest of the world towards the new administration is unlikely to last through 2010 if it is unable to deliver serious domestic action.

One enduring spike among many thorny issues the world must now face is how the efforts to get more significant action by the United States and China, and to set them in a multilateral context, will relate to the Kyoto system – America's own offspring that it so vehemently rejected in the past. The negotiations on second Kyoto period commitments were also due to culminate at the Copenhagen COP-15. The efforts by other industrialized countries to abandon this legally binding treaty in favour of a single global agreement including clear commitments for the United States and major developing countries crashed disastrously at Copenhagen. The attempts to merge the negotiations on future commitments under Kyoto with the Bali track of negotiations took up precious time in the first week, which contributed to delaying the potential negotiation outcome. The developing countries bluntly refused to accept a proposition that weakened the legal status of commitments on industrialized countries (albeit excluding the US) while trying to increase their own commitments. The rest of the OECD has yet to escape the process of negotiating commitments for Kyoto's second period.

It remains unclear whether the EU's fundamental need is to have the US in a unified treaty structure – akin to the US insistence that China must be on the same legal footing – or to know that the US is taking broadly equivalent action. Undoubtedly, there is a need for fresh thinking and new ideas. However, an obsessive debate about alternate forums risks obscuring the fundamental fact – endlessly emphasized by developing countries in particular – that if the United States cannot sharply reduce its emissions then there is no basis for a global deal. A country dedicated to market-based responses, whose per capita emissions are among the world's highest, that had already agreed under President Bush to negotiate quantified commitments post-2012, and whose president now has a clear mandate and commitment to cap-and-trade legislation, cannot dodge the core need for a domestic commitment that matches up to its aspirations for global architecture and ongoing negotiations.

That remains a challenging test of US leadership for President Obama. Perhaps more than trying to juggle international architecture, therefore, the most obvious area in which the United States could deliver fresh thinking might be in relation to global collaboration to achieve low carbon technology transitions.

FINDING A WAY OUT OF THE CHINA QUESTION: THE TRADE–COMPETITIVENESS AXIS

In America they call it the China question. In Europe they call it the America question.

– *The Economist*, 19 June 2008

Despite the new political impetus, fears over US industries' loss of international competitiveness and the implications for trade policy stand as politically charged stumbling blocks against ambitious climate measures in the United States.[24] As one analyst observed, 'The politics and the economics of cutting global warming emissions are "out of synch" ... Good economics rarely trumps bad politics.'[25] Only a few industries – metals, paper, chemicals and cement – may be at risk, at just over 3 per cent of US output in 2005 and less than 2 per cent of its jobs.[26] The potential economic boom expected from aggressive investment in clean energy is increasingly being recognized. In 2007, the renewables and energy efficiency industries generated more than 9 million jobs in America and \$1,045 billion in revenue.[27] Despite these projections, deep political anxieties persist, especially on the future of US manufacturing. These concerns play out most explicitly through the discussions on 'carbon leakage' – the relocation of high-emitting industries or investments to developing countries that do not have a cap on carbon. Throughout 2009, many US legislators have championed proposals to impose border tariffs on exports from developing countries not taking 'comparable actions' to limit GHG emissions.[28]

Whatever the reality of the economics, the politics of carbon leakage is significant. Unilateral action to impose border tax adjustments outside any global climate agreement is likely to prompt trade-related retaliatory actions, especially if the first steps are taken by the United States with its high current and historical carbon impact. It will also dampen trust. Within such a politicized context, efforts to construct a low carbon energy future for developing countries can be thwarted by the concerns of special interest groups.

The backlash against global trade overall in US politics is another cause for concern. Ambitious decarbonization targets cannot be met by domestic action alone. Trade and investment in low carbon, energy-efficient goods and services are the best tools in the arsenal for mobilization towards a global low carbon future. Enhancing low carbon trade could create virtuous cycles that stimulate further investment opportunities.

What lies behind much of the US concern about its economic competitiveness is the increasing might of emerging economies. China holds an estimated \$790 billion in US Treasury bonds – or national debt – overtaking Japan as the world's largest holder of US government debt.[29] Any reduction in China's dollar assets could hit the US economy hard by driving up long-term yields on US bonds. This would exacerbate pressure on US interest rates and further weaken the dollar. US discomfort is also aggravated by the widespread belief in Washington that China's currency has been artificially held low against others, thus allowing China to export goods more cheaply and contributing to America's $202 billion trade deficit with that country.

In fact, little of China's carbon-intensive production is actually sold in the United States: less than 1 per cent of its steel, 3 per cent of aluminium and 2 per cent of paper.[30] Border tariffs on energy-intensive products would have little meaningful economic impact in the medium term, especially if the real goal is to stifle competitive exports from China overall rather than tackling carhon leakage.

In addition, as manufacturing supply chains integrate across borders, components are often manufactured in one country and then shipped to China or another country for final assembly. Goods are tagged only at their final assembly point. This means that the gross value of exports is not necessarily indicative of economic benefits for the exporting country. Trade figures, as a result, are increasingly inaccurate guides to reality. While China has a trade surplus of some $200 billion with the United States and €110 billion with the EU, it also runs a significant trade deficit with the rest of Asia. China has effectively absorbed part of the surplus that the rest of Asia had with the developed world. For every US$1,000 of Chinese exports to the United States, only US$386 of value accrued in China in 2002.[31] As a specific example, only 35 cents of a Barbie doll that sells for US$20 go to China.[32] Moreover, the majority of China's trade in high-tech products stems from processing operations, of which 80 per cent are carried out by foreign companies established in China, many of them US companies.[33]

Political economy considerations aside, there is no doubt that choices made in China matter. Its immediate decisions about its infrastructure needs and patterns of consumption will have a decisive impact on global efforts to stabilize greenhouse gas emissions and on the feasible rate of reduction to sustainable levels. It recently overtook the United States as the world's largest emitter, and if it continues on a high carbon path, global efforts to mitigate climate change will be seriously constrained.

In recent historical terms, no major economies have managed to decouple economic growth from heavy emissions at early stages of development. There are no off-the-shelf low carbon developmental models for countries like China and India to emulate. The stark differences in economic circumstances should necessitate a collaborative rather than a confrontational approach.

Much is made of China's opening of one or two major coal power stations every week, and the $3.7 trillion of energy investment it will make by 2030. However, the concurrent closure of power stations in the United States and Europe owing to ageing infrastructure and continuing, if modest, demand increases will require both of them to invest in a similar level of new generating capacity over the same period. China, the US and the EU all need to make decisions today to avoid locking in carbon-intensive investments in the coming decades.

Despite the political difficulties, it is in the United States' strategic interest, therefore, to collaborate with China on large-scale decarbonization. Billions of dollars could be saved for such efforts if the two countries put their capital and manufacturing might behind the production of low carbon goods and technologies, driving down the costs of decarbonization for all. For this approach to be acceptable politically, fears in the United States over its competitiveness will need to be addressed clearly, and the US public will have to be convinced that China is doing its best to address climate change.

What is needed from China are concrete efforts to pilot low carbon development on a scale large enough to catalyse change at the national level. One idea is for the United States to work with China and the EU to create low carbon zones in China.[34] Such collaboration will provide the right signal for investors worldwide to hasten capital flow into cleaner technologies that would first be used in the low carbon zones and then diffused throughout their economies. More focused US–Chinese collaboration around these zones – from joint R&D to common efficiency standards – can also generate the scale effects that strengthen the constituencies in China who are beginning to view low carbon economic transition as consistent with the government's wish to move away from high-emission, low value-added exports in its growth model.

FUELLING INNOVATION FOR LOW CARBON TECHNOLOGIES

The reluctance on the part of the United States to commit to international political agreements on climate change is compounded by its vitally important – but as yet unfulfilled – role in accelerating the global development, dissemination and market establishment of new low carbon technologies and practices. With leading scientists in key positions in the Obama administration, the United States now looks set to regain ground on technological leadership on climate change. This will be welcomed across the world, but past experience suggests that such leadership will be in no country's interest more than that of the United States itself.

History has demonstrated that, when the United States focuses serious and sustained political effort on technological development in a given sphere, its industry rapidly becomes a global leader – and everyone gains. It has played a pivotal role in most transformational technological developments since the 1900s – from automobiles, space technologies and the agricultural green revolution to the personal computer. For over a hundred years before 1980, the energy sector fitted this trend: the United States started the global transition to a petroleum economy after the first commercial oil well was drilled in 1859 and embedded it through mass production of the combustion engine. A pioneer in the nuclear industry, it brought 51 reactors (43GW capacity) into operation in the 1970s alone – a remarkable feat of energy engineering.

But the experience of the energy sector also shows that the United States can fall away from technological leadership if political will is not sustained. In response to the two 1970s oil shocks, the Department of Energy had a budget for energy research as high as $6 billion at the end of the decade. About $1 billion of this total was focused on renewable energy – particularly solar power but also wind, geothermal, hydro and biofuels. For a short time, the country led the way in alternative energy technologies. Then, with low oil prices in the 1980s and President Reagan's emphasis on controlling government spending, total Department of Energy research budgets fell below $2 billion in 1985 and had not exceeded this by 2008.[35] Once a leader in solar power, the United States rapidly lost and never regained market share to Japan and Germany. More importantly, US dependence on conventional energy was left essentially unchanged. Renewables provided 6 per cent of America's energy in 1973 and 7 per cent in 2006.

External frustration with the US position is thus rooted in the convictions that Americans are among the most effective in delivering technological transformation on a global scale – and are also set to be one of the largest beneficiaries, once the country's innovators take on the mantle of low carbon technological leadership. The alternative for the United States is to cede this role to EU and emerging economies eager to grow into the strategic industries of the next few generations. Progress towards a global low carbon economy would inevitably be slowed from such a US abdication, with serious consequences for greenhouse gas emissions.

The same lack of political focus may only rarely have allowed the limited public investment in alternative technologies since the 1970s to provide a good return. US academics have led analysis of the technology 'valley of death' in which publicly funded energy innovations languish for decades without being taken forward as commercial developments, owing to a combination of failures around technology push and demand pull forces in the energy sector.[36] Persistent policy uncertainty has entrenched a pattern of boom and bust in the renewables and energy efficiency industries. This stands in contrast to greater certainty and resources provided to the development of conventional technologies related to oil, gas and coal.

It is thus imperative that the Obama administration send unambiguous signals to the market in the direction of change to encourage large-scale investment in the innovation and deployment of low carbon technologies. Early signs have been promising – the first major boost in investment was announced via the 'green recovery' elements of the February 2009 economic stimulus package, and was soon followed by the substantial provisions for clean energy innovation in the American Clean Energy and Security Act, passed by the House of Representatives in June 2009 (committing around $100 billion out to 2025 for research and demonstration of CCS, electric vehicles and advanced renewable and energy-efficiency technologies). Yet great uncertainty over the passage of climate and energy legislation through the Senate raises doubts about the administration's ability to raise federal support to the levels of funding of the 1970s, and to sustain them. The particular uncertainty over establishing a carbon price in the United States via a trading scheme (or tax) will give pause for thought to those looking to invest in innovation, or those ready to respond to the new and potentially sustainable revenue streams these could provide for research.

US politicians are struggling to establish a narrative that fundamentally repositions the US economy towards a low carbon future, making it clear that this vital technological shift will not be allowed to fail. Yet there are great opportunities for the United States to lead in the technology race towards low carbon options which can underpin such a vision. In a study conducted by Chatham House on six energy technologies and patents, the top ten reported locations of patents assignees are primarily OECD economies, with the United States in the lead.[37]

Analysis in the same study demonstrates that critical innovations in energy technology are spread around the world, with a gradual shift to emerging economies. To speed up innovation in low carbon energy globally, cooperation will therefore be essential. Today, only 2 per cent of patents are co-owned by an OECD-based organization and one based in a developing country. In the light of this, successful implementation of the US–China Summit 2009 agreement to facilitate joint research and development on clean energy could be critical. Teams of scientists and engineers from both countries are set to benefit from public and private funding of at least $150 million over five years, split evenly between the two countries. Priority topics to be addressed include energy efficiency in buildings, clean coal (including CCS) and clean vehicles.

The real lesson of experience with energy and environmental innovation is that it requires not only a supportive cultural environment, but a combination of public R&D, market-based incentives and appropriate regulatory structures. The United States showed that direct regulation of an industry can significantly contribute to improving its environmental impact by providing incentives to innovation. The Electric Power Research Institute (EPRI), which pools the research capacities of US utilities firms, illustrates the value of cooperation in an industry where no one actor has sufficient capacity of its own. Further regulation such as the Clean Air Act prompted rapid technological progress.

On the rising tide of US interest in the use of prizes to spur innovation, the Obama administration could spearhead a Global Climate Technology Prize Fund to reward innovators for their R&D for climate change mitigation and adaptation. The method has proved successful in medical innovation and holds promise for the climate sector. Public money would only be awarded after an innovation achieves the objective of the prize. Another major advantage of prizes is that only the problem needs to be identified. The rest can be left to the creativity of participants to produce solutions. Unlike with grants, there is no need to prescribe the shape and form of the final outcome. The winning technology can also be made available for licensing and diffusion, giving prizes a potential advantage over patents. The prize need not consist only of cash – the US government, for example, has guaranteed public procurement for the winning technologies of an efficient lighting competition. Google has offered to invest in for-profit companies that are successful in its plug-in hybrids competition. Prizes could be used to stimulate innovation on climate technologies, from a global prize to reduce carbon emissions funded by a specific tax or tax credit, to prizes to address issues of particular local concern. Awards could also be offered for non-technological achievements, such as for local governors who implement emission-reduction measures; for financial institutions that develop effective ways of lending for clean technology investment; or for management innovations that enhance the effectiveness of climate-related research institutions.

CONCLUSIONS: CHARTING THE PATH TOWARDS GLOBAL DECARBONIZATION

The historically unprecedented need to change the course of entire industrial sectors – with new infrastructure and investments – offers unique opportunities to take positive steps away from highly polluting paths and towards a sustainable low carbon future. However, unilateral measures cannot deliver global climate security. Unilateral steps that trigger political backlash in the arena of global trade would be damaging, generating further distrust and slowing down the much-needed dissemination of low carbon economic options. For much of the last century global changes ensued when the United States believed in their inevitability. The real test of US leadership is subtly different this time round: it requires using the power and imagination of US inventors and entrepreneurs alongside an enabling legislative, funding and regulatory environment to take the existing global effort to the next stage.

The EU is the first major emitter to accept the inevitability of the required transition and has already started down a path intended to lead to decarbonization. Having raided a US toolbox in terms of emissions trading, the EU has made commitments which have been crucial in forming expectations in global business that action on climate change will happen and will create real markets. But solving the problem requires global commitments to decarbonization that are much more widely and urgently applied, most notably by the United States and China alike. The global transition is only likely if these three powers can find a way to lead together, and address the need not only for clear economic incentives but also for radical innovation.

This perspective underpins the approach outlined in this chapter whereby the United States adopts a trilateral political-economic approach: energizing the multilateral process through strong domestic commitment; injecting new ideas around innovation; and forging strategic low carbon partnerships with China and the EU.

First, even though the Obama administration faces an uphill battle in 2010 to put in place ambitious domestic legislation on climate change, this is the only platform from which it could *re-energize multilateral efforts* including setting ambitious emissions targets through the UNFCCC and other forums. Even though the Copenhagen Accord laid 'the foundation for international action in the years to come', according to President Obama, it remains unclear how the world will act in concert within a linked system of incentives to drive more ambitious target-setting that would limit the global temperature rise to 2°C, not least by developed countries. A more ambitious 2020 or 2030 target by the US would energize the ongoing climate negotiations to reach a global long-term agreement around the key issues of adequate emission reductions, finance for decarbonization and adaptation, sufficient new and additional actions by developing countries, and international frameworks for technology transfer and halting deforestation.

Second, the time has come for the United States to *spearhead a dramatic acceleration in climate-related technological innovation and diffusion*. As the long-recognized leader of innovation and free enterprise, the US government could do much more not only in terms of setting international standards but also in driving innovation.

Third, it remains in the US strategic interest to *forge strategic low carbon partnerships with China and the EU to ensure market creation for a global transition to a low carbon economy*. Such efforts would receive a huge boost if all three regions put their capital and manufacturing might behind the production of low carbon goods and technologies, driving down the costs of decarbonization for all. For this to be politically acceptable, competitiveness fears will need to be directly addressed, and the US public will have to be convinced that China is doing its best to address climate change.

Finally, at home, the Obama administration *must make it a priority to bury the narrow view of action to confront climate change as the foe of US industry and competitiveness*. The cost of carbon emissions must be factored into economic policy, and the market will ultimately benefit from strong government regulation over emissions and consistency of policy and investment towards renewable energies and efficiency. European examples have shown that institutionalized government commitment to reduce emissions can create huge economic and technological incentives and gains. If US policy-makers can embed irrevocable signals to reorientate the US economy towards low carbon development, then the transition to a low carbon future could be faster, and more global, than anyone expects.

NOTES

1 See, for example, Joanna Depledge, 'Against the Grain: The United States and the Global Climate Change Regime', *Global Change, Peace and Security* 17(1)(2005): 11–27.
2 Robert Falkner, 'American Hegemony and the Global Environment', *International Studies Review* 7 (2005): 585–99.
3 See, among others, Depledge, 'Against the Grain' and Falkner, 'American Hegemony and the Global Environment'.
4 *National Security and the Threat of Climate Change*, US Center for Naval Analysis, 4 June 2007.
5 Testimony by Dr Fingar in 'National Intelligence Assessment on the National Security Implications of Global Climate Change to 2030?', 25 June 2008 to the US Congress; and press release, 'Climate change may challenge national security, classified report warns', The Center for International Earth Science Information Network (CIESIN), Columbia University, 26 June 2008.
6 Depledge, 'Against the Grain'.
7 M. Meinshausen and W. Hare, *How Much Warming Are We Committed to and How Much Can Be Avoided?*, PIK Report 93 (2004), Figure 8. According to the Swedish Scientific Council on Climate Issues, in *A Scientific Basis for Climate Policy* (2007), the two-degree target can likely be achieved if greenhouse gas concentration in

the atmosphere is stabilized in the long term at 400ppmv carbon dioxide equivalent (CO_2e). If it is stabilized at 450 ppmv CO_2e there is a significant risk that the two-degree target will not be achieved. Full report available at: www.sweden.gov.se/content/1/c6/08/69/68/f8d98215.pdf.

8 IEA, *Energy Technology Perspectives 2008* (Paris: International Energy Agency, 2008).

9 Reuters, 'U.S. must move on climate change at G8: Barroso', 4 July 2008.

10 Byrd-Hagel Resolution (S Res 98), July 1997.

11 For a detailed history of the negotiations and content of the Kyoto Protocol, see M. Grubb, D. Brack and C. Vrolijk, *The Kyoto Protocol: A Guide and Assessment* (London: RIIA/Earthscan, 1999).

12 M. Grubb and J. Depledge, 'The Seven Myths of Kyoto', *Climate Policy* 1(2)(2001): 269–72.

13 This isolation was dramatically demonstrated at the end of 2007 when at the UNFCCC meeting in Bali the newly elected Australian Prime Minister announced Australia's intention to ratify the Kyoto Protocol. Australia had been the last of the United States' traditional allies supporting its position of rejecting the protocol.

14 While the United States has not ratified the protocol it remains a signatory. The ideological stance was by no means confined to the issues of climate change. The Kyoto Protocol was quickly denounced by the Bush administration alongside the Rome statute (establishing the International Criminal Court), the Comprehensive Test Ban Treaty (outlawing nuclear testing) and the Anti-Ballistic Missile Treaty (preventing the United States and Russia from deploying missile defences). See Depledge, 'Against the Grain'.

15 Speech by President George W. Bush Introducing Clear Skies and Global Climate Change Initiatives, 14 February 2002, http://www.whitehouse.gov/news/releases/2002/02/20020214-5.html.

16 For analysis of the Partnership's relationship with the Kyoto process see Jeffrey Mcgee and Ros Taplin, 'The Asia-Pacific Partnership on Clean Development and Climate: A Complement or Competitor to the Kyoto Protocol?', *Global Change, Peace and Security* 18(3)(2006): 173–92.

17 *Business Week*, 'Best of 2006', http://images.businessweek.com/ss/06/12/1207_bestideas/source/11.htm.

18 Trevor Houser, Rob Bradley, Britt Childs, Jacob Werksman and Robert Heilmayr, *Leveling the Carbon Playing Field: International Competition and US Climate Policy Design* (Washington, DC: Peterson Institute for International Economics/World Resources Institute, May 2008), http://pdf.wri.org/leveling_the_carbon_playing_field.pdf.

19 The US Environmental Protection Agency (EPA) is under orders from the Supreme Court to determine whether CO_2 emissions are endangering public health or welfare. If so, the EPA must regulate them. Another court told the Interior Department to decide whether the polar bear should be brought under the protection of the Endangered Species Act as a result of the impacts of climate change.

20 As, respectively, Secretary of State for Energy; Special Envoy for Climate Change; Executive Director of the White House Office of Science and Technology Policy and the President's science adviser; Head of the National Oceanic and Atmospheric Administration; and Assistant to the President for Energy and Climate Change.

21 This section draws in part on M. Grubb, 'The Bali COP: Plus ça change, plus c'est la même chose?', *Climate Policy* 8(1)(2008): 3–6; see also Meeting Report in the same issue by H. Ott et al. (pp. 91–5).

22 Summary of COP13 and COP/MOP 3 prepared by the Pew Center on Global Climate Change, http://www.pewclimate.org/docUploads/Pew Center_COP13Summary.pdf.

23 D. Sandalow, 'Climate Change – beyond Bali', http://www.brookings.edu/opinions/2007/1217_climate_change_sandalow.aspx.

24 For a recent analysis on competitiveness and climate measures, see Houser et al., *Leveling the Carbon Playing Field*.

25 Bruce Stokes, 'Balance of Payments: Carbon Accommodation', *Congress Daily*, 12 June 2008, http://o-www.nationaljournal.com.libus.csd.mu.edu/congressdaily/bpa_20080612_4856.php.

26 Houser et al., *leveling the Carbon Playing Field*.

27 American Solar Energy Society and Management Information Services Inc., 'Defining, Estimating and Forecasting the Renewable Energy and Energy Efficiency Industries in the US and Colorado', December 2008, http://www.ases.org/images/stories/ASES/pdfs/CO_Jobs_Final_Report_December2008.pdf.

28 See, for example, the letter to President Obama on this issue signed by 28 Congressmen of 9 September 2009, http://www.steel.org/AM/Template.cfm?Section=Climate_Change_Focus&TEMPLATE=/CM/ContentDisplay.cfm&CONTENTID=34342.

29 US Department of the Treasury, 'Major Foreign Holders of Treasury Securities', 17 November 2009, http://www.ustreas.gov/tic/mfh.txt.

30 Houser et al., *Leveling the Carbon Playing Field*.

31 Lawrence J. Lau, Xikang Chen, Leonard K. Cheng, K. C. Fung, Jiansuo Pei, Yun-Wing Sung, Zhipeng Tang, Yanyan Xiong, Cuihong Yang and Kunfu Zhu, *Estimates of U.S.–China Trade Balances in Terms of Domestic Value-Added*, Stanford Center for International Development, Working Paper No. 295, September 2006.

32 The figures were cited in David Barboza, 'Some assembly needed: China as Asia's factory', *New York Times*, 9 February 2006.

33 Guillaume Gaulier, Françoise Lemoine and Deniz Ünal-Kesenci, *China's Integration in East Asia: Production Sharing, FDI and High-Tech Trade*, CEPII Working Paper No. 2005-09, June 2005, www.economieinternationale.fr/anglaisgraph/workpap/pdf/.../wp05-09.pdf.

34 The idea for low carbon economic zones was first suggested as a means to rally EU–China collaboration on energy and climate security. See Bernice Lee, Antony Froggatt, Nick Mabey et al., *Changing Climates: Interdependencies on Energy and Climate Security for China and Europe*, Chatham House Report, November 2007.

35 The budget for 2008 was set at $1.3 billion: www.aaas.org/spp/rd/prelo8p.htm.

36 J.P. Holdren et al. (President's Committee of Advisors on Science and Technology, Panel of Energy Research and Development), *Federal Energy Research and Development for the Challenges of the 21st Century* (Washington, DC: Office of Science and Technology Policy, Executive Office of the President of the United States, November 1997); A. Sagar and J.P. Holdren, 'Assessing the Global Energy Innovation System: Some Key Issues', *Energy Policy* 30 (2002): 465–9.

37 Bernice Lee, Ilian Iliev and Felix Preston, *Who Owns Our Low Carbon Future? Energy Technologies and Intellectual Property*, Chatham House Report, September 2009.

14

The role of the United States
in the post-crisis economic order

Paola Subacchi[*]

The economic and financial crisis of 2007–09 has brought up and crystallized problems that had been bubbling beneath the surface of the global economy for some years. It has exposed the limits of unrestricted globalization, the gaps and insufficiencies in the governance of global markets, the intrinsic tension between global financial markets and sovereign states. It has raised questions about the soundness and sustainability of the model of economic growth that underpinned the rise in international prosperity for the past 50 years. In many countries it has further deepened the gap between the pursuit of a liberal global agenda and the need to protect domestic interests. Finally, the relative resilience of China and other emerging market economies to the crisis, and their more rapid recovery, have served as a powerful demonstration of the shift from West to East and of the emergence of a multipolar world in which economic power is more diffused, but also less effective.[1]

If there is a country that lies at the crux of all these different trends, it is the United States. The crisis not only originated in the United States, but also showed the limits and fallacies of the model of economic growth that it had championed. The effort to contain and eventually resolve the crisis has imposed a huge burden on the already strained US public finances, reinforcing arguments about America's relative decline and loss of economic supremacy. For the American middle class, already concerned about the progressive erosion of their relative economic wealth, US international commitments – from the intervention in Afghanistan to the promotion of open markets – are often seen as a burden that diverts resources from domestic priorities. The hanging question is who will eventually pick up the bill for the crisis. As the recovery seems to be less

* The author is indebted for comments on earlier drafts to Alan Alexandroff, Gregory Chin, Benjamin J. Cohen, Nicholas Dungan, DeAnne Julius, Mui Pong Goh, Robin Niblett and Vanessa Rossi, and to the participants at the conference on 'Leadership and the Global Governance Agenda' held at the China Institute of Contemporary International Relations, Beijing in November 2009, and at the seminar on 'Transatlantic Relations in Times of Change', GMFUS and CIDOB, held in Barcelona in December 2009. Thanks also to Rodrigo Delgado Aguilera and Nicolas Bouchet for research and editorial support.

dynamic in the United States than in many emerging market economies, with a large number of jobs lost and fewer created, the pressure for more domestic-focused economic policies is rising.

Within the context of one of the worst economic crises in decades, pressures to give priority to domestic imperatives over international concerns are present in every country. But this chapter argues that the United States is in the best position to address the dichotomy, and intrinsic tension, between global markets and national interests. This is certainly not the case for European nations that seem stuck in a supranational order where they have as yet surrendered insufficient sovereignty to allow for the smooth and efficient functioning of their supra-national institutions.[2] Nor is it the case for the emerging powers that are still learning to be responsible international actors and for whom the balance is still skewed heavily towards national interests.

The United States will need to overcome the more domestic and inward-looking concerns of its middle class by creating a more equitable system at home while promoting stability as well as opportunity in the global economy. These challenges are embedded in the current debate on US healthcare reform. The inequity of the current system, dividing those who have cover from those without it, has come to symbolize all the contradictions – and even to question the morality – of the US economic system, especially the 'capitalism without rules' of the last couple of decades.

The crisis has highlighted the need for rules in the global economy. But the emergence of new powers is challenging the notion that the United States should automatically take the lead in writing those rules simply because of the sheer size of its economy and the dominance of the dollar in international trade and investment. Instead, the crisis clearly poses the question of how the balance of power and leadership in international economic affairs will be shaped in future years. Who will have the moral authority as well as the economic clout to lead the global economic policy debate?

For many involved in discussing the future of the international economic order, the crisis has dramatically ruptured the credibility of and respect for the American model, questioning the soundness of neo-liberalism, US-led global growth and the related dominance of the dollar. The crisis has also undermined America's presumed 'moral' right to lead, as the model of growth and the neo-liberal doctrine that underpins it have been discredited. In geopolitical terms, the financial meltdown, a potentially protracted recession and mounting US federal debt are seen as catalysts that will end US economic hegemony and lead to a shift in the world political order – and the rise of China seems to epitomize such a shift. Great-nation status and global influence rest largely on economic and financial power, which in turn enable military power. Large empires, from Ancient Rome to Great Britain, declined at least in part as a result of economic weakness. Conversely, China's rapid economic growth and the potential for other emerging market economies to expand substantially over coming decades, owing to their large populations and integration in the world economy, seem to indicate the emergence of a new, more multipolar economic order. A powerful symbol of this shift is the upgrade of the G20 into the economic summit for heads of state at the expense of the G8. But is this an accurate portrait of the short-term and long-term challenges posed by the crisis? Or is the debate being hijacked by those – individuals and countries – too keen to predict the end of US hegemony, or too worried about it?[3] The key question here is what the current financial crisis means for the standing of the United States in the world. Has the United States lost the right, the capacity or even the will to lead in economic affairs? And should it continue to lead?

This chapter points to economic indicators that suggest the continuation of America's global economic leadership – despite the crisis and the erosion of its relative position. Besides the sheer size and inherent dynamism of its economy and the continuing centrality of the dollar in the international monetary system, being a liberal democracy as well as a developed market economy is what makes the United States the best candidate to continue to lead on the international economic stage. However, the persistence of US capacity for global economic leadership could generate tensions at the international level if other states do not recognize this reality. And, at the domestic level, the desire of the Obama administration to retain its international economic leadership could equally cause tensions if US international commitments are perceived to be in competition or conflict with domestic priorities. The United States faces two challenges here. It has to recognize the undergoing shift in the international economic order, and the relative erosion of its position within that order. Then it has to prove itself fit to manage international economic affairs from a position of equality – as *primus inter pares* rather than a hegemon – that better reflects the new configuration of the international economic order.[4] Being able to reconcile the country's international goals and domestic interests would give the United States the 'moral advantage' as well as the practical lead in international economic affairs.

Aspects of past US moral leadership could be regained from the country's ability to lead by example: to show the way forward in dealing simultaneously with national objectives and international goals, to devise and implement a sustainable, balanced and equitable model of growth that reconciles the tension between global markets and national interests, and to use its national example as a basis for offering a new model of governance and new rules for global institutions. Reform of the international financial architecture is the most urgent issue on the international economic agenda and one where the United States should play a key role. The critical question here is how the administration of President Barack Obama can ensure the United States is the driving force of the multilateral dialogue on such reform without losing focus on domestic economic concerns.

The rest of this chapter is organized as follows. The next section examines the fundamentals of American economic power, the extraordinary years for the US economy that overlapped with the administrations of Bill Clinton and George W. Bush, the model of growth and the building of global financial imbalances. This is followed by a discussion of whether the financial crisis of 2007–09 has aggravated the structural weaknesses of the American economy and accelerated the relative decline of the United States. The chapter then considers the role of the United States as *primus inter pares* in a multipolar economic order, and its relations with the emerging economic powers. The chapter concludes by advocating a more active and responsible role for the United States in setting an integrated agenda for the reform of the international financial architecture.

THE FUNDAMENTALS OF AMERICAN ECONOMIC POWER, 1992–2007

Strong growth in the 1990s, and a 'new paradigm'

The 2007–09 financial crisis had a long incubation. Its origins lay in the deregulation of the banking and financial sector that started in the 1980s and continued throughout the 1990s when strong GDP growth saw the building up of bubbles and current account imbalances. The peak for the external imbalance was reached in 2006 when the current account deficit hit $800 billion (or 6 per cent of GDP) while the government budget also remained in deficit (just over 2 per cent of GDP) despite the recovery from the dotcom recession of 2001.

The years between the early 1990s and 2007, however, were a prosperous period for the American economy during which productivity accelerated, unemployment fell and wages rose across the board. This was a big change from the malaise of the 1980s and a big boost to national self-esteem.[5] In 1992, the presidential election was fought against the backdrop of a weak economy, struggling to pick up from the 1991 recession, and an electorate worried about its living standards, its healthcare and the country's ability to compete internationally. Bill Clinton won by focusing on middle-class America's economic concerns and promising an activist government that would deliver healthcare reform, big increases in public investment, tax cuts for middle-class families and higher taxes on the rich.[6]

The decade of strong growth began with the recovery from the 1991 recession. From 1992 to 2000, the US economy enjoyed a 'golden age' in which growth only fell below 3 per cent in two years (1993 and 1995, when it was 2.7 per cent and 2.5 per cent respectively). By the end of 1995, American business was doing exceptionally well – profits at large companies were up 18 per cent and the stock market had had its best growth in 20 years. Fiscal and monetary policy were both working well, with the 1996 deficit projected to shrink to less than $110 billion,[7] and inflation still below 3 per cent.[8] Job creation was strong and the unemployment rate fell from over 6 per cent in 1994 to less than 4 per cent in 2000. In the process, the economy spawned 16 million new jobs. Both the economy and the stock market continued to boom. In spring 1996, GDP growth was over 6 per cent – calling into question the conventional view that 2.5 per cent was the maximum growth the US economy could healthily sustain. As noted by the then Chairman of the US Federal Reserve Alan Greenspan, 'We were doing a lot of rethinking at the Fed. [...] *Something* extraordinary was happening.'[9] Clinton asked Greenspan to stay at the Federal Reserve: 'He was asking for faster growth, higher wages, and new jobs. He wanted to see what this rocket could do.'[10]

Bubbling bubbles

These years of exceptional performance for both the real economy and the financial markets saw the formation of a series of bubbles. There were concerns among
economists that interest rates were too low although their analysis tended to
focus more on the risks of inflation than on bubbles. Inflation concerns were
dismissed by the Clinton administration on the basis of high productivity
growth generated by the technology boom – by then, a symbol of America's
success in reforming and modernizing the economy.[11] Even when the dotcom
bubble burst in early 2001, the Federal Reserve hardly changed its stance on
monetary policy. After 9/11, it lowered the federal funds rate to nearly one per
cent and maintained it near that very low level for three years.

The extraordinary performance of the US economy – especially when
compared to those of the euro area and Japan – generated a good deal of complacency; nobody wanted to spoil the party. In addition, Greenspan's near 'god-like
status'[12] somehow constrained the economic policy debate. Research shows a
change in the character of Federal Open Market Committee (FOMC) deliberations after 1993, when policy-makers became less willing to express disagreement with any proposal brought forward by Greenspan.[13] As a result, from the
late 1990s Greenspan went almost unchallenged and could shape the consensus
within the FOMC towards his preferred outcome: in its 65 meetings from 1998
to the end of Greenspan's mandate in 2006 there were only 15 dissenting votes.[14]
'In 2000, as speculation built to a fever pitch, there was not a single dissent.'[15]

With interest rates remaining at a historically low level during most of
Bush's first term in office,[16] liquidity was growing. This reflected, among other
factors, the enormous financial surplus realized by countries like China and the
oil producers – what the then Fed chairman-to-be Ben Bernanke in 2005 called
'the global savings glut'. Until the mid-1990s, most emerging economies had run
balance-of-payments deficits as they imported capital to finance their growth.
But the Asian financial crisis of 1997–98 changed this pattern. In many emerging
markets, increasingly large trade surpluses, resulting from strong manufacturing
activity and rising oil prices, were consistently recycled back to the West, in
particular to the United States, in the form of portfolio investments. Seeking
higher yields, huge amounts of capital thus flowed into the sub-prime mortgage
sector, which provided higher and allegedly low-risk returns through the securi-
tization of mortgages, and towards risky borrowers of all kind. In 2006, for
example, the annual volume of US sub-prime and other securitized mortgages
rose from a long-term average of approximately $100 billion to over $600 billion.
This flow of mortgage money prompted an unprecedented rise in prices for
commercial and residential properties. Whereas the average US property had
appreciated at 1.4 per cent annually over the 30 years before 2000, the appreciation rate was 7.6 per cent annually from 2000 until mid-2006.[17]

From the sub-prime failure to the financial and banking crisis

When house prices began to fall in mid-2006, this started to undermine the value of the multi-trillion dollar pool of sub-prime mortgages. Moreover, many of those mortgages that were structured to be artificially cheap at the outset began to convert to more expensive terms. An increasing number of borrowers could no longer afford such mortgages and delinquencies became more frequent. Losses on these loans began to emerge in mid-2007 and quickly became bigger and bigger. The rest of the story is well known. The final year of the Bush administration saw the escalation of the financial crisis, that had started in August 2007 in the sub-prime mortgage market, with the banking and financial system on the verge of collapse. The first alarm bells in the summer of 2007 were followed by the nationalization or takeover of Fannie Mae and Freddie Mac, AIG, Bear Stearns, Merrill Lynch, Wachovia and others. Lehman Brothers was famously not rescued.

Over the course of the debt-financed spending spree, the debt/income ratio of US households rose steadily and reached a peak of just over 130 per cent in 2008. And, although at this stage government debt was only around 65 per cent of GDP, it ballooned as the crisis deepened in 2009. The heavily leveraged banking and financial sector risked collapse when the property bubble burst. Only the prompt intervention of the Federal Reserve, on an unprecedented scale, allowing banks to stay in business, avoided a bigger disaster. The Federal Reserve injected liquidity in the imploding financial system by expanding its own balance sheet and the monetary base. At the same time, the government intervened to bail out the financial sector and to provide a public-sector substitute for sharply falling private-sector consumption. The result of these policies was a huge increase in the US deficit and debt position.

The US public debt is now a major cause for concern. An ageing population is already putting strains on the Medicare programme of healthcare for the aged, the cost of which is due to rise rapidly in the years ahead – from 2.8 per cent of GDP now to about 6 per cent of GDP in 2030. Further strain is due to come from 47 million Americans, or 16 per cent of the population, without medical insurance. This figure has been rising gradually by one- or two-tenths of a percentage point for the last 20 years and is due to further increase in the years ahead as the recession causes the number of unemployed to rise. Economic hardship will be reflected in further demand for government-provided health insurance, which currently covers about 27 per cent of the American population (40 million, or 14 per cent, insured by Medicare and 38 million, or 13 per cent, by Medicaid). On top of these actual and projected costs comes the cost of the $700 billion bank bailout (and an additional $100 billion of tax provisions for businesses and the middle class).

As a result, the public debt-to-GDP ratio will trend up faster than otherwise in the coming years, although the exact path will depend on the behaviour of interest rates and on the prevailing growth scenario. The most likely scenario currently is one of low growth and high debt accumulation. The US

Congressional Budget Office estimates that the public debt-to-GDP ratio will rise from 40 per cent to 80 per cent in the next decade, depending on the performance of the economy. If long-term interest rates were to increase to 5 per cent, the resulting increase in the interest rate bill alone would be about $450 billion, or 3 per cent of GDP.

THE CRISIS AND THE US ECONOMY

Coming out of the crisis

The financial crisis of 2007–09 was comparable to the Great Crash of 1929 in which stress in financial markets led to prolonged recession. After several weeks of market turmoil, the world economy took a 'synchronized dive',[18] recovery from which promised to be slow. In the case of the US economy, the financial crisis generated a sharp recession. Because of severe strains in financial institutions, extremely loose monetary policy found it difficult to unclog the credit market. In addition, households suffered from large financial and housing wealth losses, much lower earnings prospects and uncertainty about job security, all of which drove consumer confidence to record lows. These shocks depressed consumption, with the result that the household saving rate, having dropped for two decades, increased sharply to average close to 5 per cent in the second quarter of 2009 – from a low point of around 0.5 per cent in 2005–07.

The policy response to the crisis was timely and massive.[19] In October 2008, the Troubled Asset Relief Program (TARP) provided capital injections to stressed financial institutions and bolstered financial markets. Guarantees were offered on selected bank assets and liabilities and expanded on deposits. In the meantime the Fed lowered interest rates to an all-time low and unambiguously communicated the intention of keeping monetary policy loose until clear signs of economic recovery emerged. In February 2009, the administration unveiled a massive fiscal stimulus of more than 5 per cent of GDP (albeit over the period 2009–11). In the same month stress tests to assess banks' resilience to the economic downturn were launched; they bolstered confidence in financial stability when results were announced in May. In the meantime the G20 summit in London helped stabilize confidence, especially in the United States.

Looking at the financial crisis several months after its peak, it is surprising to see the relative speed of adjustment compared with predictions in late 2008 of a deep recession leading to protracted depression. The US economy returned to growth in the third quarter of 2009 even if, at the time of writing, there are still considerable downside risks – in the labour and export markets, in particular – that could constrain recovery.

Besides the short-term picture and the immediate issue of crisis resolution, it is the medium to longer run that poses some major challenges. These include, for the medium term, formulating exit strategies from interventions to stabilize the financial system, as well as extraordinary monetary policy stimulus. For the longer term, challenges include addressing the weaknesses in financial supervision and regulation, stabilizing the public finances and coping with an environment of rising saving and slower growth as household balance sheets adjust. The key question here – and the one with the most serious long-term implications – is whether these challenges will constrain the future expansion of the US economy, undermining the American position in the world economy while at the same time enhancing the current distress and limiting the scope for future policy action. Is the crisis acting as a catalyst for the erosion of the American economic supremacy, accelerating the process of relative decline, or is it provoking a necessary set of adjustments that will strengthen the US economy in the long term?

The end of US economic and monetary hegemony?

The crisis has certainly exacerbated the economic weaknesses that were ignored over the last decade because of foreign investors' willingness to invest in the United States. The US debt position and its long-term projection, which are unlikely to improve soon, are rightly a cause of concern because of the potential instability and vulnerabilities associated with protracted indebtedness. In addition, large fiscal deficits as a consequence of bailout measures and the financial rescue plan, an ageing society[20] and the resulting higher cost of the Medicare programme of healthcare for the aged are likely to put further strains on the already large debt. Despite a substantial improvement in the national savings rate and in the current account deficit, a decline in the rate of dollar-denominated asset accumulation by foreign investors, especially by countries such as China, remains a reason for concern for long-term interest rates and the value of the dollar. International investors may lose confidence in the dollar, thereby undermining its status as the key international currency. The idea floated by the governor of the Chinese Central Bank of using Special Drawing Rights (SDRs) as the international reserve currency has added further concern to the debate.[21] All these vulnerabilities might constrain policy initiatives by the Obama administration, and even its successors, in a number of areas, from military intervention to discretionary international aid and projects.

The case of the relative decline of the United States is intensified by the relatively strong performance of China and other emerging-market economies through the crisis. China stands out as by far the most successful economic story since the 1990s. It has also braved the current economic turmoil better than any other major economy, to the extent that it may achieve its target growth of 8 per cent at a time when most countries have nosedived into recession. In fact, the growth of China and, to a lesser extent, India was the main positive contributor to world GDP for 2009. But even before this, growth rates were very strong, averaging over 10.4 per cent during the 1992–2008 period, translating to a nearly five-fold increase in real GDP. China's share of the world economy has shot up from barely over 4 per cent in 1992 to over 11 per cent in 2008, and its position in world trade is just as prominent, rising from barely 2 per cent to nearly 12 per cent (excluding intra-EU trade) during the period in question; it is now the largest exporter outside the EU.

Equally important are the huge reserves of capital that have transformed China into the world's largest global creditor. Chinese foreign exchange reserves have surpassed the $2 trillion mark and China is the single largest investor in US Treasury securities, with holdings quoted at more than $800 billion in late 2009 (representing around 8 per cent of the US government bond market). While there is much debate over the sustainability of this savings imbalance, it is one of the reasons why the US–Chinese relationship is arguably the most important in global economic affairs today.

Although none of other BRIC economies[22] has achieved the level of ascendancy that China has, their performance during the past two decades has been remarkable as well. India began a series of liberalization reforms in 1991 after decades of centralized economic planning. These reforms opened the nearly bankrupt country to foreign investment, liberalized capital markets, deregulated domestic business and lowered barriers to trade. As a result, India's economic performance improved, numerous industries took off – particularly IT – and, by 2005–07, its GDP was growing at around 9 per cent per annum – nearly as strongly as China's. Furthermore, the country has weathered the current global malaise quite well. Nevertheless, India faces major disadvantages compared to China, particularly its poor trade performance and persistently high levels of poverty. These will hold back its economy from achieving the same level of dynamism as its Asian neighbour.

From a global perspective, the relative strength of China and other emerging market economies has been a stabilizing force during the recession. It has also further revealed the vulnerability of the US economy in the post-crisis economic and political landscape. For many commentators this is a sign of the inevitable shift of economic power – and political influence – from West to East.

Trend growth and relative position

Deleveraging from the excess debt of the past is likely to be a long and slow process for the American economy, and one that will result in lower growth rates for both the United States and the world. As US consumer demand still plays a key role in global growth, an increase in the savings of American households in order to pay off their debt will have a constraining effect. Whether countries will be able to recover their pre-crisis growth rates is crucial to how they will perform in the world economy. Currently, the US share of the world economy in purchasing power parity (PPP) terms is 20.7 per cent while the EU has an even larger share at 22.1 per cent. This compares with 11.5 per cent for China.[23] Is there a risk that reduced trend growth as a result of the crisis will result in a reduced share of the world economy for the United States in the long term? Post-crisis trend growth seems to be more of a concern for Europe than for the United States. Although a few warning shots have been fired regarding a possible scaling back of future trend growth, the authorities in the United States seem to have faith that its economy will not only climb back to its pre-crisis levels of growth, but recover its crisis-related losses as well (see scenario A in Figure

Figure 1: Post-crisis growth scenarios for the US economy

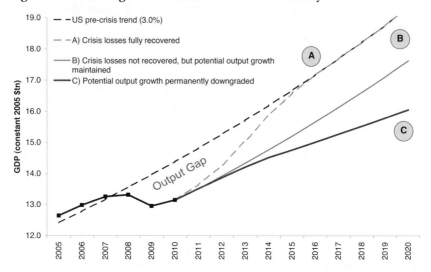

Sources: IMF data and estimates by Chatham House International Economics.

Figure 2: Pre-crisis and post-crisis growth trend for the US and the euro area

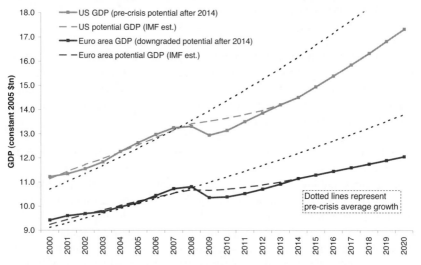

Sources: IMF data and estimates by Chatham House International Economics.

1). Their expectations are based on evidence from previous cycles. American GDP bounced back sharply after the 1991 plunge and even more dramatically after the early 1980s recession, achieving a massive 7.2 per cent growth rate in 1984. Emerging economies have also registered sharp recoveries from even more devastating crises, as happened in most East Asian economies after 1998 and

Latin America after 1995 and 2001–02. Should this be the case again, it will leave the United States not only maintaining a higher rate of growth than the euro area, but widening the GDP gap even more.

Past experience is less reassuring for the euro area, for which the most likely scenario is one where its GDP recovers its pre-crisis growth rates, albeit at a lower level owing to the losses incurred by the crisis, i.e. the output gap is never recovered and the economy grows below potential (Figure 2). A less likely scenario, given recent forecasts for the euro area, is one in which growth surges above trend levels in the next few years because of better than expected GDP growth. In this case the output gap may close, losses may be made up, and the region would return to pre-crisis growth rates, maintaining in any case the GDP gap relative to the United States.[24]

Excessive concern about decline

Claims that American economic hegemony is over are therefore premature, as are predictions of China's imminent takeover. Despite being badly hit by the credit crisis, the United States will still show great resilience. What factors account for the more optimistic prospects for future US output? Labour flexibility and innovation are arguably the most important. The US economy has shed jobs far more rapidly than have European economies, where governments have taken concrete steps to protect employment and where structural characteristics – such as large public sectors – have also prevented dramatic rises in unemployment. But the massive job losses in the United States had a positive effect on productivity, which rebounded in the second quarter of 2009.[25] Job losses have also helped the US economy 'thin out' its less productive sectors. In so far as innovation also feeds into increased productivity, the US economy is likely to be far better poised than Europe to return to 'business as usual' once the effects of the crisis have receded.

Another factor likely to help the United States to recover its pre-crisis growth rates is the ability to attract foreign investors. Over the short term, the attractiveness of the US market may be hindered by concerns about continuing economic risk and low returns due to the US debt position and the weakness of its domestic economy. Empirical evidence, however, seems to support the view that foreign investors will choose to purchase US portfolio investments in order to benefit from what are, compared to many other countries, a highly developed, liquid, and efficient financial market, good standards of corporate governance and strong political and regulatory institutions.[26] Again, evidence from the crisis and the rally first in the dollar and later in the US stock market suggests a relative preference among many foreign investors for the US market.[27] The catch, of course, is that anything that undermines the liquidity and efficiency of US financial markets – and the financial crisis might be such a factor – could also seriously undermine the sustainability of capital inflows. Good policy choices by the Obama administration in managing the next phase of economic recovery will be critical, therefore, in fostering investors' confidence.

The United States is also the country best endowed with the economic flexibility and natural and human resources needed to get past present difficulties: it is highly attractive and open to migration; it hosts the world's leading institutions of higher learning; and, as Anne-Marie Slaughter and others have noted, it possesses the most networked society and economy in the world.[28] Moreover, despite China's call for a 'multipolar reserve currency system', inertia and the lack of serious alternatives will ensure that the dollar will continue to lead the international monetary system for years to come. The euro is far from having a global role and, hence, is still unable to challenge seriously the greenback's dominance, while no other currency is emerging as an international alternative.[29]

As the global monetary hegemon, therefore, the United States will continue issuing its debt in its own currency, and as a result enjoy great flexibility in servicing its dollar-denominated foreign debts.[30] Unlike other countries, the United States can continue to go deeply into debt with the rest of the world in its own currency while facing little foreign exchange risk. However, there are now more potential threats than in the past when the United States could expect all other countries to adjust to its policies. Today surplus countries might decide to stop covering US debt, revalue their currencies, and reduce their dollar reserve holdings. Although this scenario is more likely now, as a result of the US debt position, its probability remains low, given the implied capital losses for dollar-holding countries.

Finally, in spite of all the talk about 'decoupling', the United States remains the engine of the world's economic growth. Following years of high growth, emerging market economies are surely more 'self-reliant' than before and so far better insulated from the effects of the financial crisis, partly because their financial sectors are still relatively small and disconnected from the global economy. However, they still rely on demand from advanced economies for their exports.

PRIMUS INTER PARES AND THE POST-CRISIS ECONOMIC ORDER

Despite the devastating economic and financial crisis, the United States is set to remain the largest economy in the world – and the engine of its growth – at least for some years to come. However, the financial straitjacket it must live within and the loss of its 'moral authority' – not direct consequences of, but exacerbated by, the crisis – now throw into question the United States' 'right to lead' in international economic affairs. The rise of new powers – especially China – challenges the leading role played so far by the United States and its dominant influence in multilateral economic institutions such as the IMF and World Bank. As a result, the United States has to accept that other players have come to the fore; it must take their preferences into account and put up with the resulting constraints to its own policies – something it has never experienced in the post-Second World War international economic order.

Reflecting this shift, during the G20 summit in Pittsburgh in September 2009 President Obama recognized the G20 as the new permanent forum for international economic cooperation – and its transformation from crisis committee in the face of the crisis. President Obama also gave his blessing to the reform of the IMF board. These two issues are implicitly related, as they both acknowledge that the balance of power needs to be tilted towards the new rising powers. Streamlining the 'G' process – something which President Obama hinted at during the July 2009 G8 summit in Italy – and shifting responsibilities from the G8 to the G20 would imply a dilution of influence for some of the G8 countries, in particular Italy and Canada, and to some extent Japan at the regional level. Shifting – by a five percentage point margin – the ownership of the IMF from industrialized to developing countries and cutting the number of directors from 24 to 20 would hit the main European countries – Germany, France and the United Kingdom, each of which has a director on the IMF board. In both cases, then, these European countries would suffer a diminution in power. In the view of the US administration, adjusting the global balance of power involves a shift – in a zero-sum game – from Europe to the developing world.

As in the post-war and Cold War years, when US leadership was closely linked to the creation and extension of international institutions that at once limited and legitimized American power,[31] the post-crisis economic order will be shaped by international institutions where national interests will be tamed and economic policies will be coordinated. Within this context the United States will have the duty to share power with other countries and to engage developed and developing countries alike in the governance of the world economy. It should be able to accept some redistribution of power in order to achieve this. But how much hegemony is the United States likely to give up as it attempts to re-engage in multilateralism? Assuming that the Obama administration is successful in these attempts at re-engagement, and the current crisis does not halt the process of global economic integration, then the most plausible scenario for the years ahead is a world in which economic power is more diffuse,[32] and in which the governance of the world economy is increasingly a matter of multilateral coordination. In this scenario the United States will cease to be a superpower and become *primus inter pares*.

As in the post-war period, the United States should recognize its responsibilities in this position of first among equals by, for instance, initiating a debate on the international monetary system. This debate needs to focus on the still unresolved imbalance, in some economies, between the ability to generate surplus and the capacity to absorb it, and on how to use their surpluses to support the global economy rather than destabilize it. Countries with balance-of-payments surpluses – mainly Asian countries and oil exporters – use the dollar as their key intervention currency while keeping their own currencies anchored to the greenback in order to gain stability from the volatility of international capital flows. The over-accumulation of foreign exchange reserves in Asian countries[33] is a prominent aspect of this system. Even if there is a clear asymmetric advantage for the United States, the lack of any viable alternative means that this system is unlikely to change in the foreseeable future. The crisis, however, has shown the limitations of the dollar-based system and prompted a lively, but so far fruitless, debate on the reform of the international monetary system.[34] This is exemplified by the concerns expressed by China's central bank governor Zhou Xiaochuan on the eve of the G20 London summit in April 2009, as noted above

The coordinated response to the crisis through the work of the G20 has highlighted China's willingness to be engaged in a broad discussion of policy lessons to be learnt from it and of the principles upon which a new financial architecture should be based. Rethinking principles and norms is possibly one of the best contributions that these countries can offer while working to develop a new consensus on rules.[35]

There is no doubt that the current arrangements need some rethinking and the United States should be playing an active role in fostering and leading such debate while supporting the principles – multilateralism, democracy and market economy – on which the economic order is based.[36] Otherwise, the discussion about the reform of the global economic governance risks remaining an intellectually stimulating exercise devoid of any ambitions and practical outcomes.

The United States' international standing has taken a tumble during the current financial crisis. If it wants to maintain its position as international leader, it needs to rethink how it approaches that position and accept the emerging reordering in the world economy. This implies accepting fairer arrangements that reflect the changing distribution of economic power and a more balanced governance of the world economy – especially with regard to the international financial institutions. It also means sharing the burden of the adjustment necessary to rebalance and stabilize the international monetary system. In this new context, the challenge for the Obama administration is to reconcile its domestic agenda with its international economic priorities. This means overcoming domestic opposition to the United States playing an increased multilateral role and persuading Americans to continue paying for global 'public goods'. It is reasonable to expect the United States to remain more effective in implementing international policy than domestic policy. However, the Obama administration should continue in its effort to reconcile domestic interests and international responsibilities. Only if the Obama administration is unable or unwilling to do so will there truly be an American crisis.

NOTES

1 Benjamin J. Cohen, 'The International Monetary System: Diffusion and Ambiguity', *International Affairs* 84(3)(May 2008): 455–70.
2 For Robert Kagan Europe is stuck in a post-modern order that is ill-suited to the 'return of great power nationalism'. Robert Kagan, *The Return of History and the End of Dreams* (London: Atlantic Books 2008), pp. 10–25.
3 For Peer Steinbrück, a former German finance minister, the end of US hegemony is not even a matter of time: 'The United States is no longer a financial superpower', he said in an interview in September 2008. Bertrand Benoit, 'Germany sees an end to US hegemony', *Financial Times*, 26 September 2008, http://www.ft.com/cms/s/0/a8ab34ea-8b63-11dd-b634-0000779fd18c.html. For Fareed Zakaria the rise of new

powers inevitably implies the decline of American power: Fareed Zakaria, *The Post-American World* (New York and London: W.W. Norton, 2008).

4 There is a sense of having been here before. People have been phrasing the question in very much these terms since the 1960s. See Robert O. Keohane, *After Hegemony: Cooperation and Discord in the World Political Economy* (Princeton, NJ: Princeton University Press, 1989).

5 Alan Greenspan, *The Age of Turbulence: Adventures in a New World* (London: Penguin, 2007). 'The economic growth boosted the national psyche, changing the way we saw ourselves in the world. Throughout the 1980s and well into the early 1990s, Americans had gone through a period of being fearful and depressed. People worried we were losing ground to Germany, the newly unifying Europe, and Japan' (p. 183).

6 In practice, however, the Clinton management of the economy was more centrist and less ambitious than he promised. Taxes did go up for the rich, but large public investment plans were quickly ditched in favour of deficit reduction and the healthcare reform collapsed.

7 In fact it moved into surplus in 1998.

8 Greenspan, *Age of Turbulence*, p. 162.

9 Ibid., p. 171.

10 Ibid., p. 163.

11 Ibid., 'While both Europe and Japan slid into economic doldrums, America was on the rise' (p. 183).

12 'After Alan', *The Economist*, print edition, 13 October 2005. '[His] record helps explain his near god-like status. At the Jackson Hole gathering of central bankers in August, two academics gushed that "he has a legitimate claim to being the greatest central banker who ever lived." Politicians seek his benediction on issues as diverse as pensions reform and China's currency policy. A fawning biography by Bob Woodward is simply called *Maestro* (2000). In the 2000 presidential campaign, Sen. John McCain quipped that were Mr Greenspan to die, he would "prop him up and put a pair of dark glasses on him and keep him as long as we could".'

13 After 1993, when FOMC participants knew that their deliberations would be made public, they were less likely to challenge then Federal Reserve chairman Alan Greenspan. Similarly before 1993 FOMC discussions had frequent 'off the cuff' remarks and interruptions; since 1993 there has been an increase in prepared statements. See 'The dangers of increased transparency in monetary policymaking', blog entry by Ellen E. Meade and David Stasavage, 26 June 2008, VoxEU, http://www.voxeu.org/index.php?q=node/1271.

14 'After Alan'.

15 Daniel Gross, 'It Is Unwise to Say "No" to Chairman Al', *Slate*, 30 January 2006, http://www.slate.com/id/2135102/.

16 John Taylor argues that in 2001–06 monetary policy was far looser than historical experience would have suggested. John B. Taylor, 'The financial crisis and the policy responses: an empirical analysis of what went wrong', National Bureau of Economic Research, Cambridge, MA, Working Paper 14631, January 2009, pp. 2–3. Also 'Fast and loose', *The Economist*, print edition, 18 October 2007.

17 Roger C. Altman, 'The Great Crash, 2008', *Foreign Affairs* 88 (1)(January/February 2009): 4.

18 Vanessa Rossi, *Synchronized Dive into Recession: Focus on Damage Limitation*, Chatham House, IEP Briefing Paper 2008/04, October 2008.

19 But the Chinese overwhelmingly believe their own country is doing the best job of

dealing with the crisis – 60 per cent say China, far more than either the United States (20 per cent) or the EU (8 per cent). The Pew Global Attitudes Project, *Confidence in Obama Lifts US Image around the World. 25-Nation Pew Global Attitudes Survey*, Pew Research Center, Washington, DC, July 2009, http://pewglobal.org/reports/pdf/264.pdf.

20 Ageing, however, is not yet as critical an issue in the United States as it is in Japan and Europe.

21 Governor Zhou suggested that the status of the dollar as the key reserve currency should be halted, as the costs of the current system may have exceeded its benefits: 'The price is becoming increasingly higher, not only for the users, but also for the issuers of the reserve currencies. Zhou Xiaochuan, 'Reform the International Monetary System', speech on 23 March 2009, http://www.pbc.gov.cn/english.

22 Brazil, Russia, India and China. The acronym first appeared in a paper published by the US bank Goldman Sachs: Dominic Wilson and Roopa Purushothaman, 'Dreaming with BRICs: The Path to 2050', Goldman Sachs Global Economic Paper No. 99 (2003), reprinted in *The World and the BRICs Dream* (New York: Goldman Sachs Group, 2006), pp. 21–35.

23 Arguably the share of total GDP is an imperfect indicator of a country's economic influence. The 'new powers' are emerging as the new poles in the global economic order not just because of the size of their economies. They have a wide range of military and political resources; some capacity to shape the international order, regionally or globally; some degree of internal cohesion and capacity for state action; a belief in their entitlement to a more influential role in world affairs; the ability to differentiate themselves from other second-tier states. On this point, see Andrew Hurrell, 'Hegemony, Liberalism and Global Order: What Space for Would-be Great Powers?', *International Affairs* 82 (1)(January 2006): 1–3.

24 One risk to this scenario is the reaction of European authorities that are highly cautious of incurring inflationary growth and might therefore resort to policy tightening if recovery speeds up more than anticipated.

25 The latest available figures (for Q4 2009) show productivity growth up by 6.2% (annualized) on a quarter-on-quarter basis, and up by 5.1 % compared to the previous year: see United States Department of Labor, Bureau of Labor Statistics, www.bls.gov.

26 A key theme in recent theoretical and empirical literature is that lower levels of financial market development in other countries will continue to encourage capital flows into the United States. Such flows are likely to decrease as emerging market economies continue to develop and strengthen their own financial markets. For a recent survey of existing literature and empirical analysis, see Kristin J. Forbes, 'Why Do Foreigners Invest in the United States?', National Bureau of Economic Research, Cambridge, MA, Working Paper 13908, April 2008, pp. 1–54.

27 According to data from the World Federation of Exchanges, the US stock market (NYSE and Nasdaq) grew by 49% from March 2009 in terms of market capitalization. This growth, however, was not as strong as that of European markets such as Euronext (58%) and London (67%), or of many Asian markets including Korea (65%), Taiwan (68%) and Hong Kong (76%).

28 Anne-Marie Slaughter relates the United States' advantage over other countries to its being part of several networks – from defence and military networks to technology and business. Anne-Marie Slaughter, 'America's Edge: Power in the Networked Century', *Foreign Affairs* 88(1)(January/February 2009): 94–113.

29 Benjamin Cohen and Paola Subacchi, 'A One-and-a-Half Currency System', *Journal*

of International Affairs 62(1)(2008): 151–63; Eric Helleiner and Jonathan Kirshner (eds), *The Future of the Dollar* (Ithaca, NY: Cornell University Press, 2009); Paola Subacchi, 'From Bretton Woods Onwards: The Birth and Rebirth of the World's Hegemon', *Cambridge Review of International Affairs* 21(3)(2008): 347–65.

30 It is worth stressing here that the 2007–09 financial and banking crisis was not a currency crisis.

31 G. John Ikenberry, *After Victory: Institutions, Strategic Restraint and the Rebuilding of Order After Major Wars* (Princeton, NJ: Princeton University Press, 2001).

32 Benjamin J. Cohen, 'The International Monetary System: Diffusion and Ambiguity', *International Affairs* 84(3)(May 2008): 455–70.

33 By order of magnitude the most significant case is China, with more than $2 trillion in FX reserves, an amount that is well beyond the buffer that is deemed necessary for precautionary reasons.

34 Paola Subacchi and John Driffill (eds), *The International Monetary System: Recommendations for Reform* (London: Chatham House, forthcoming 2010).

35 For an assessment of the G20 London summit in April 2009, see Paola Subacchi and Eric Helleiner, *From London to L'Aquila: Building a Bridge Between the G20 and the G8*, Chatham House IE/CIGI Briefing Paper 2009/01, June 2009.

36 And, by being involved, the United States has the potential to gain from the shift to a multipolar economic order. On this point, see G. John Ikenberry, 'The Rise of China and the Future of the West: Can the Liberal System Survive?', *Foreign Affairs* 87(1) (January/February 2008): 23–37.

Index

Index

Biden, Joe 66, 132, 173
bin Laden, Osama 111, 231
Biological Weapons Convention 206
Bolivia 17
Bosnia 165
Brazil 6, 17, 20, 21, 22, 24, 25–6
Broader Middle East and North Africa
  (BMENA) 34
Bush, George W. 1, 35, 187; and China 148,
  152; and climate change 238, 242, 243;
  and East Asia 72; and Europe 187; and
  Georgia 127, 137; and India 90, 97, 98;
  and international law/United Nations
  206–11, 218; and Iraq war 207; and
  Latin America 16, 17; and Pakistan
  89–90, 93, 105; South Caucasus policy
  134–5; and sub-Saharan Africa 52–4,
  64–5, 66
Byrd-Hagel resolution (1997) 242

carbon/carbon dioxide emissions 4, 81,
  189, 196, 239, 240
'carbon leakage' 249
Carson, Johnnie 55, 60, 61
Castro, Fidel 15
Castro, Raúl 26
Central Asia 109–21; capacity of US to
  exert influence in 116–19; decline of
  US in influence 109–10; democracy
  promotion in 116–17, 120; linking to
  South Asia plan 114–15; problems of
  opposing perceptions 114–15; recommendations for future US engagement 119–21; role of in fight against
  terrorism in Afghanistan 109, 110–11,
  114, 115, 118–20; US energy interests
  113–14, 115, 120–1; US policy in 110–15;
  see also Kazakhstan; Turkmenistan;
  Uzbekistan
Central Intelligence Agency (CIA) 213
Chávez, Hugo 16, 20, 21, 22
Chiang Mai initiative 80
Chile 15, 16, 20
China 3, 5, 10, 73, 110, 145–60; and Africa
  51, 64, 152; bilateral trade imbalance
  issue 156, 158; bombing of Chinese
  embassy in Belgrade by NATO (1999)
  148; challenges to future US relations
  with 159–60; and climate change 81,

146, 248, 249–51, 255; Clinton's visit to
(2009) 75, 76; competition with US
over energy security 150–1; constraints
limiting scope of economic confrontation 158; economic growth and reforms
79, 155, 259, 265–6; economic tensions
between US and 155–8; energy interests in Central Asia 114; and EU–US
relations 192; factors impeding government efficiency 147; fragmented nature
of political and economic landscape
159; history of US relations with 148–9;
internal dynamics 146–8; managing
transition to Obama presidency 149–51;
military spending and expansion 71, 155;
and North Korea 150; political transitions 152–4; and post-crisis economic
order 271; relations with India 91, 97–8,
101; relations with Middle East 39;
relations with Pakistan 97; rise of international importance 151–2, 159; Special
Economic Dialogue 147, 151, 156; and
Sudan 150; Taiwan issue 147, 154–5
Chirac, Jacques 186
Clean Air Act 253
Clean Energy and Security Act (2009)
252
climate change 4, 8–9, 24, 238–55; and
Bali Action Plan 245–6; and Bush
238, 242, 243; and 'carbon leakage' 249;
and China 81, 146, 248, 249–51, 255;
climate measures in US and obstacles
to 248, 249; and Copenhagen Accord
239, 246, 247, 254; debate on multilateral processes 246–9; and East Asia
80–1; and EU 196, 242–3, 247, 254;
and EU Emissions Trading Scheme
(ETS) 244–5; and EU–US relations
196; history of US engagement in
negotiations over 241–4; international
developments 244–6; low carbon
technologies 251–4; meeting the
challenge of dangerous 240–1; path
towards global decarbonization 254–5;
security implications for US 241
Clinton, Bill 15–16, 25, 63, 127, 152, 186, 209,
217, 261
Clinton, Hillary 2, 33; and Africa 55, 57,
58–9, 60, 61–2, 63–4, 65; and China 146,

Index